CASES IN FINANCIAL REPORTING

CHARLES T. HORNGREN SERIES IN ACCOUNTING

Auditing: An Integrated Approach, 7/E Revised • ARENS/LOEBBECKE

Kohler's Dictionary for Accountants, 6/E • COOPER/IJIRI

Financial Statement Analysis, 2/E • FOSTER

Governmental and Nonprofit Accounting: Theory and Practice, 5/E • FREEMAN/SHOULDERS

Financial Accounting, 3/E • HARRISON/HORNGREN

Cost Accounting: A Managerial Emphasis, 9/E • HORNGREN/FOSTER/DATAR

Accounting, 3/E • HORNGREN/HARRISON/ROBINSON

Cases in Financial Reporting, 2/E • HIRST/MCANALLY

Principles of Financial and Management Accounting:
A Sole Proprietorship Approach • HORNGREN/HARRISON/ROBINSON

Principles of Financial and Management Accounting:
A Corporate Approach • HORNGREN/HARRISON/ROBINSON

Introduction to Financial Accounting, 6/E • HORNGREN/SUNDEM/ELLIOTT

Introduction to Management Accounting, 10/E • HORNGREN/SUNDEM/STRATTON

Budgeting, 5/E • WELSCH/HILTON/GORDON

CASES IN FINANCIAL REPORTING

AN INTEGRATED APPROACH
WITH AN EMPHASIS ON EARNINGS QUALITY AND PERSISTENCE

SECOND EDITION

D. Eric Hirst
Mary Lea McAnally

UNIVERSITY OF TEXAS AT AUSTIN

 PRENTICE HALL, Upper Saddle River, NJ 07458

Senior Acquisitions Editor: *Annie Todd*
Assistant Editor: *Natacha St. Hill*
Editorial Assistant: *Elaine Oyzon-Mast*
Production Editor: *Lynda Paolucci*
Managing Editor: *Katherine Evancie*
Senior Manufacturing Supervisor: *Paul Smolenski*
Production Coordinator: *Cindy Spreder*
Cover Designer: *Suzanne Behnke*

 © 1998, 1996 by Prentice Hall, Inc.
A Simon & Schuster Company
Upper Saddle River, NJ 07458

Printed in the United States of America

10 9 8 7 6 5 4

ISBN 0-13-748997-8

Prentice-Hall International (UK) Limited, *London*
Prentice-Hall of Australia Pty. Limited, *Sydney*
Prentice-Hall Canada Inc., *Toronto*
Prentice-Hall Hispanoamericana, S.A., *Mexico*
Prentice-Hall of India Private Limited, *New Delhi*
Prentice-Hall of Japan, Inc., *Tokyo*
Simon & Schuster Asia Pte. Ltd., *Singapore*
Editora Prentice-Hall do Brasil, Ltda., *Rio de Janiero*

Cases in Financial Reporting

An Integrated Approach
with an Emphasis on Earnings Quality and Persistence

CONTENTS

BECOMING FAMILIAR WITH FINANCIAL REPORTING—
Basics, Tools, and the Persistence of Earnings

Basics—Interpretation and Preparation of Financial Statements

Maytag Corp.—Understanding Financial Statements 1
Nike—Basic Ratio Analysis 15
Yokohama Rubber & Goodyear Tire—Comparing Ratios...19
Fuji Photo Film & Eastman Kodak—Inferring Transactions 23
Club Méditerranée S. A.—International GAAP 29
Food Lion, Inc.—Preparation of Financial Statements..34
Black & Decker—Adjusting Journal Entries...38
Liz Claiborne Inc.—Transactions & Financial Statements 43

Tools—Discounted Cash Flow

Maya, Inc.—Return on Investment 47
Hydron Technologies Corporation—Lease or Buy..48
Cadillac DeVille—Implicit Interest Rate 49

Tools—Basic Valuation and the Persistence of Earnings

Maple Leaf Gardens—Valuation 50
GTE—Persistence of Earnings 60
Curragh Inc.—Going Concern..65

Tools—Cash Basis versus Accrual Basis Reporting

Mattel, Inc.—Analyzing the Cash Flow Statement 72
Frederick's of Hollywood—Statement of Cash Flows 76
Weis Markets, Inc.—Statement of Cash Flows 84
Jan Bell Marketing Inc.—Statement of Cash Flows 90

EVALUATING FINANCIAL REPORTING DISCLOSURES—
Balance Sheet Components and Issues in the Quality of Earnings

Assets

L.A. Gear, Inc.—Cash and Balance Sheet Issues 95
Kendall Square Research Corp.—Revenue Recognition 97
The Warnaco Group Inc.—Accounts Receivable 104
Imasco Limited—Financial Services Assets 113
Clearly Canadian Beverage Corporation—Inventory 117
Lands' End, Inc.—Inventory 122
Callaway Golf Company—Manufacturing Inventory 129
Frederick's of Hollywood—Property & Equipment 137
Hilton Hotels Corporation—Capitalized Costs 143
Chambers Development Co. Inc.—Capitalizing Costs 148
Merck & Co., Inc.—Research & Development 155
CIS Technologies, Inc.—Software Development 162
America Online, Inc.—Deferred Costs 165

Liabilities

E.I. du Pont de Nemours—Environmental Matters 174
Maytag Corporation—Warranties & Deferred Taxes 180
Eastman Kodak and Polaroid—Contingencies 183
Exxon—Tiger in Your Tank *vs.* Tony the Tiger 193
Bally Entertainment Corporation—Long-Term Debt 194
The Home Depot—Long Term Debt 196
American Airlines, Inc.—Leases 203
The Robert Mondavi Corporation—Deferred Taxes 211
Dell Computer Corporation—Income Taxes 216
Enron Corp.—Pension Obligations 221
Black Clawson—Other Post–Employment Benefits 224

Owners' Equity

Gannett Company, Inc.—Treasury Stock 226
L.A. Gear, Inc.—Mandatorily Redeemable Preferred Stock 231

Intercorporate Investments

Deere & Company—Marketable Securities 235
J.P. Morgan & Co. Inc.—Marketable Securities 240
BCE Inc.—Investments in Other Companies 248
Abitibi-Price Inc.—Joint Ventures 257
The Seagram Company—Investments in Common Stock 264
General Electric Company—Consolidations 274
Ford Motor Co.—Accounting for Investment in Jaguar 281

Financial Statement Analysis

Boston Beer & Lion Brewery—Financial Statement Analysis 282

Cases in Financial Reporting
An Integrated Approach
with an Emphasis on Earnings Quality and Persistence

PREFACE

This book is a collection of financial accounting cases designed to help you become a financial statement user. Learning accounting is very much like learning a new language. The best way to learn any language is to immerse yourself in the language and to converse with many people. Conversations speed up language acquisition and teach the nuances of the language. Conversations strengthen language skills and build breadth. We have created, with this collection of cases, a set of conversational opportunities for you in accounting. You will learn accounting by reading financial statements and by responding to topical questions about those financials. By reading and using many different companies' financial statements, you will speed-up your acquisition of accounting concepts and skills. By observing the nuances of financial reporting, you will quickly learn to speak "accounting," the language of business.

These materials bridge a void in introductory financial statement materials at both the undergraduate and the graduate level. Typically, students are required to read a textbook chapter and do some exercises to ensure concept comprehension. Assigned end of chapter material, however, is often not sufficiently challenging to students with stronger analytical abilities. Questions often focus on financial statement preparation rather than, as appropriate for many students, financial statement use. At the other extreme, unstructured discussion cases can leave students with a weak grasp of the mechanics and nuances of financial accounting. The cases presented here fill the void.

Each case deals with a specific financial accounting topic framed within the context of one corporation's financial statements. Usually, a case contains financial statement information (a balance sheet, income statement, statement of cash flows, and footnotes) and a set of specific questions pertaining to one financial accounting issue. You will use the financial statement information to infer and interpret the economic events underlying the numbers. Some cases are accompanied by a related article taken from the business press. In those instances, information from the article is incorporated into the questions in the case. Some cases involve two companies within an industry and the case questions focus on intercompany comparisons of financial information.

Why These Materials are Unique

These materials have a proven track record. The book was developed from the course materials used since 1991 at the University of Texas at Austin. The course (a semester-long, compulsory, first-year introductory class) has been extremely well-received by students each semester it is taught. The course consistently receives among the highest student evaluations in the UT M.B.A. core. We have both received teaching awards for delivery of the course.

Several unique features distinguish this casebook:

Financial Statement Diversity—This book comprises 52 cases covering 50 reporting entities. We believe that you will appreciate the exposure to many different companies and quickly learn that, while financial statements do not all look the same, they *can* all be understood and used.

Current Financial Statements—The cases are very current; primarily dated 1994 through 1997. This affords you the opportunity to read and use pertinent and timely financial information. Some older cases have been included because they explicate a concept particularly well or because they demonstrate an uncommon trend.

International Financial Statements—Cases cover companies from France, Japan, and Canada as well as from the U.S. Many of the U.S. companies are major multinationals. Increased globalization of business necessitates your facility with financial statements other than those prepared in accordance with U.S. GAAP. Some international cases require you to recast the financials to U.S. GAAP. Thus, you will become a sophisticated user of financial information.

Internet Format of Corporate Reports—Many of the financial statements, MD&A, Forms 10-K and 10-Q, and other corporate information in the casebook have been retrieved from the Securities and Exchange Commission's EDGAR database. The presentation of the material has been deliberately left consistent with the on-line presentation. If you are already accessing this type of information on-line, the presentation in these cases will be familiar to you.

Learning Objectives—Cases are prefaced with a set of learning objectives. These become your learning goals as you work through the cases. The focus of each case is made clear through these objectives.

Corporate Descriptions—Each case focuses on one or two sets of financial statements. A brief description of the companies in the case is designed to remind you that accounting information is used in specific business contexts. Reported financial accounting numbers are the result of a series of complex, professional estimates and judgments. Many of these are influenced by industry practice. Correctly reading and interpreting financial information is predicated on your awareness of a company's business and industry.

New in the Second Edition

While the second edition retains many of the same companies from the first edition, we have updated their financials to include more recent statements. The second edition has more breadth and depth of coverage. New companies and several new topics are included; for example, pensions (Enron) and finance receivables (Imasco). As well, several topics are now dealt with in more than one case; marketable securities (JPMorgan and Deere), deferred taxes (Maytag, Robert Mondavi, and Dell), and long-term debt (Home Depot and Bally).

In this second edition the questions are organized in "C.P.A." order.

Concepts   The typical case begins with a set of conceptual questions. As we introduce each topic area, we want to ensure that you are familiar with the vocabulary and the broader concepts before moving into the specific application to the case-corporation. These general questions focus each case on its topic area. For example, the Maytag case on warranties begins with the conceptual questions "from the consumer's standpoint, what is a warranty?" and "from Maytag's standpoint, what is a warranty?" Here too, you will be required to retrieve specific information from the financial statements but not to manipulate it. For example, the Deere case on marketable securities asks "what balance did the company report on its balance sheet for trading securities?" These concept questions call for factual responses that you are likely to easily provide.

Process   Before you become a sophisticated consumer of accounting information you need an understanding of the accounting process and the basics of financial statement preparation. Thus, the second set of questions in each case focuses on the process. Process questions require you to manipulate financial statement information via calculations, journal entries, and T-accounts. It is at this point that many textbook exercises end. However, we believe that the accounting process is not the end but the means by which you will build a firm understanding of how financial accounting works the way it does.

Analysis   With a strong understanding of the concepts and a solid knowledge of the accounting cycle, you are ready for higher level analytical questions. These questions have you synthesize, analyze, interpret information and formulate and defend your opinion. Thus, higher-order thinking skills are required in the analysis questions.

By grouping the case questions into the C.P.A. categories, the text has broad audience. Taken alone, the Concept and Process questions are perfectly aimed at undergraduate introductory financial accounting classes. Because many M.B.A. students have taken some accounting and most have had some business experience, they are better prepared to handle the Analysis questions even at the introductory level. Several topics (e.g. pensions, OPEB, marketable securities, financing receivables, deferred taxes) included in this second edition are not typically covered in an introductory course. These can be used at the intermediate level for undergraduate and M.B.A. classes. For intermediate and financial statement analysis courses, the Concept questions might be used by your instructor to start class discussion. Taking up these questions first ensures that you are on firm ground before you go on to tackle the more challenging Analysis questions. The full set of financial statements included with each case affords you and your class instructor the opportunity to explore issues the Analysis questions do not touch upon.

How to Use These Materials

These cases are designed to be used in conjunction with an introductory, intermediate, or financial statement analysis textbook. The cases are presented in the order we use them at the University of Texas at Austin. The order in which material is presented by your instructor does not affect the relevance of the cases. Each case stands alone and while some cases naturally precede others, there is no prescribed order.

As you use these materials, notice two main themes—earnings persistence and the quality of earnings. The first third of the cases in the book relate to the framework of financial reporting. In these cases you are acquiring skills in basic financial statement preparation, and in understanding how financial statements aid in the investment decision process. In achieving the latter, we emphasize how financial statements classify items and how such classifications are important in the prediction of the nature, uncertainty, and timing of future cash flows. Thus, we introduce the notion of earnings *persistence* and how it affects firm valuation. The remainder of the cases explore the accounting issues for the major financial statement line items. We place particular emphasis on the latitude and judgment management has in arriving at the reported numbers and the economic consequences of their choices. This introduces the notion of the *quality* of earnings. The cases are designed to help you acquire the skills necessary to identify quality of earnings issues and learn how to deal with them (for example, by restating the financials under different assumptions or accounting methods).

Acknowledgments

A number of people need to be thanked. First, the University of Texas at Austin students who have used prior versions of the cases have provided tremendous feedback. Second, our teaching assistants have helped craft some of the best questions in the book. Special thanks are due to Pat Hopkins, Paul Simko, Fred Phillips, Mike Goldman, Bryce Birdsong and Kris Weinman. Bob May provided invaluable help in organizing and structuring the package as a whole. We received many helpful suggestions from Lauren Kelly who taught from the materials at UT. Feedback from several reviewers, including Joan Luft (Michigan State) and Charles Horngren (Stanford) was also appreciated. Patty Webb diligently proofread the text and provided many suggestions. Finally, Annie Todd and her crew at Prentice Hall kept the project going and saw it to completion. Thanks to all!

Although we have made every effort to avoid errors, any that remain are solely our responsibility. Should you have any suggestions for improving this product, we would love to hear from you. We can be reached by telephone, fax, or e-mail as follows:

	Telephone	Fax	E-mail
Eric Hirst	512-471-5565	512-471-3904	ehirst@mail.utexas.edu
Mary Lea McAnally	512-471-2163	512-471-3904	mcanally@utxvms.cc.utexas.edu

About the Authors

D. Eric Hirst, Ph.D., CA is an associate professor and KPMG Peat Marwick Faculty Fellow at the University of Texas at Austin. Professor Hirst received his Ph.D. in accounting from the University of Minnesota and his M.Acc. and B.A. from the University of Waterloo. Professor Hirst is a Canadian Chartered Accountant with experience in public practice. His research has been published in *The Journal of Accounting Research, Contemporary Accounting Research, The Journal of Financial Statement Analysis, Auditing: A Journal of Practice & Theory, The International Tax Journal, CA Magazine,* and *Organizational Behavior and Human Decision Processes.* At the University of Texas, Professor Hirst teaches financial accounting and financial statement analysis in the regular and executive M.B.A. programs. In 1995, he was awarded the Joe D. Beasley award for teaching excellence in the M.B.A. core

Mary Lea McAnally, Ph.D., CA is an assistant professor of accounting at the University of Texas at Austin. Professor McAnally obtained her Ph.D. from Stanford University and her B.Comm. from the University of Alberta. Professor McAnally is a Canadian Chartered Accountant with experience in public practice and industry. She is also a Certified Internal Auditor. Professor McAnally's research interests include capital markets, accounting and disclosure in regulated environments, and accounting for risk. She has published articles in *The Journal of Accounting and Economics* and *The Journal of Accounting, Auditing, and Finance.* At the University of Texas, Professor McAnally teaches financial accounting in the M.B.A. and undergraduate programs. In 1994, she received the Teaching Excellence Award for Outstanding Professor in an M.B.A. Core Class and in 1997 she was awarded the Joe D. Beasley award for teaching excellence in the M.B.A. core.

CASES IN FINANCIAL REPORTING

Maytag Corp.—Understanding Financial Statements

Maytag Corporation is a leading appliance enterprise headquartered in Newton, Iowa. The company is focused on five principal areas of home management: laundry, cooking, dishwashing, refrigeration and floor care. Vending equipment is an additional corporate business. Maytag's appliance brands include Maytag, Hoover, Jenn-Air, Magic Chef, Dixie-Narco, Admiral, and RSD.

Learning Objectives
- Become familiar with a set of financial statements and the notes thereto.
- Perform a basic analysis and interpretation of the financial statements.
- Recognize the role of estimation in the preparation of financial statements.

Refer to the 1995 Maytag Corporation financial statements.

Concepts

a. What financial statements are commonly prepared for external reporting purposes? What titles does Maytag give these statements? What does "consolidated" mean?

b. How often do publicly traded corporations (including Maytag) prepare financial statements for external reporting purposes?

c. Speculate on who uses the financial statements Maytag prepares.

d. What is the nature of Maytag's business? That is, based on what you know about the company and on the accompanying financial statements, how does Maytag make money?

e. Who are Maytag's external auditors? What sort of audit opinion did Maytag receive in 1995? In your own words, what does the opinion mean? Why is the audit report dated one month after Maytag's year end?

Analysis

f. Construct common-size balance sheets for 1994 and 1995. To do this, recast each line of the balance sheet as a percentage of that year's total assets.

g. Construct common-size income statements for 1993, 1994, and 1995. To do this, recast each line of the income statement as a percentage of that year's net sales.

h. Refer to the common-size balance sheet to answer the following questions.

   i. What are Maytag's major investments? That is, what are its major assets?

   ii. How has Maytag financed (i.e. paid for) these investments? That is, what are Maytag's major liabilities and equities?

i. Refer to the common-size income statement to answer the following questions.

   i. What are Maytag's major sources of revenues? That is, what products generate the bulk of its sales?

   ii. What are Maytag's major expenses?

   iii. Was Maytag profitable during 1995? Why or why not?

j. Refer to the statement of cash flows. Did Maytag generate cash from operations during 1995? What were some significant uses of Maytag's cash during the year?

k. Refer to the notes to the Consolidated Financial Statements.

   i. Briefly explain the following expenses which appear on the income statement: "Loss on business dispositions," "Settlement of lawsuit," and "Loss on guarantee of indebtedness."

Are these income statement expenses you expect to recur, or be persistent, in future years? That is, are these expenses likely to appear on the 1996 income statement?

ii.   Several notes refer to "significant amounts." What does Maytag mean by this term?

iii.   The first note discusses the use of estimates in Maytag's financial statements. List as many of the estimates underlying the financial statements as you can. Are any accounts "estimate-free?"

REPORT OF INDEPENDENT AUDITORS

Shareowners and Board of Directors
Maytag Corporation

We have audited the accompanying statements of consolidated financial condition of Maytag Corporation and subsidiaries as of December 31, 1995 and 1994, and the related consolidated statements of income (loss), shareowners' equity and cash flows for each of three years in the period ended December 31, 1995. Our audits also included the financial statement schedule listed in the Index at Item 14(a). These financial statements and related schedule are the responsibility of the Company's management. Our responsibility is to express an opinion on these financial statements and related schedule based on our audits.

We conducted our audits in accordance with generally accepted auditing standards. Those standards require that we plan and perform the audit to obtain reasonable assurance about whether the financial statements are free of material misstatement. An audit includes examining, on a test basis, evidence supporting the amounts and disclosures in the financial statements. An audit also includes assessing the accounting principles used and significant estimates made by management, as well as evaluating the overall financial statement presentation. We believe that our audits provide a reasonable basis for our opinion.

In our opinion, the financial statements referred to above present fairly, in all material respects, the consolidated financial position of Maytag Corporation and subsidiaries at December 31, 1995 and 1994, and the consolidated results of their operations and their cash flows for each of the three years in the period ended December 31, 1995, in conformity with generally accepted accounting principles. Also, in our opinion, the related financial statement schedule, when considered in relation to the basic financial statement taken as a whole, presents fairly in all material respects the information set forth therein.

Ernst & Young LLP
Chicago, Illinois
January 30, 1996

MAYTAG CORPORATION

STATEMENTS OF CONSOLIDATED INCOME (LOSS)

In thousands except per share data	Year Ended December 31		
	1995	1994	1993
Net sales	$ 3,039,524	$ 3,372,515	$ 2,987,054
Cost of sales	2,250,616	2,496,065	2,262,942
Gross profit	788,908	876,450	724,112
Selling, general and administrative expenses	500,674	553,682	515,234
Special charge	—	—	50,000
Operating income	288,234	322,768	158,878
Interest expense	(52,087)	(74,077)	(75,364)
Loss on business dispositions	(146,785)	(13,088)	—
Settlement of lawsuit	(16,500)	—	—
Loss on guarantee of indebtedness	(18,000)	—	—
Other—net	4,942	5,734	6,356
Income before income taxes, extraordinary item and cumulative effect of accounting change	59,804	241,337	89,870
Income taxes	74,800	90,200	38,600
Income (loss) before extraordinary item and cumulative effect of accounting change	(14,996)	151,137	51,270
Extraordinary item—loss on early retirement of debt	(5,480)	—	—
Cumulative effect of accounting change	—	(3,190)	—
Net income (loss)	$ (20,476)	$ 147,947	$ 51,270

Income (loss) per average share of Common stock:

	1995	1994	1993
Income (loss) before extraordinary item and cumulative effect of accounting change	$ (0.14)	$ 1.42	$ 0.48
Extraordinary item —loss on early retirement of debt	$ (0.05)	—	—
Cumulative effect of accounting change	—	$ (0.03)	—
Net income (loss) per Common share	$ (0.19)	$ 1.39	$ 0.48

See notes to consolidated financial statements.

MAYTAG CORPORATION

STATEMENTS OF CONSOLIDATED FINANCIAL CONDITION

In thousands except share data	December 31 1995	1994
Assets		
Current assets		
Cash and cash equivalents	$ 141,214	$ 110,403
Accounts receivable, less allowance—		
(1995—$12,540; 1994—$20,037)	417,457	567,531
Inventories	265,119	387,269
Deferred income taxes	42,785	45,589
Other current assets	43,559	19,345
Total current assets	910,134	1,130,137
Noncurrent assets		
Deferred income taxes	91,610	72,394
Pension investments	1,489	112,522
Intangible pension asset	91,291	84,653
Other intangibles, less allowance for		
amortization—(1995—$65,039; 1994—$56,250)	300,086	310,343
Other noncurrent assets	29,321	44,979
Total noncurrent assets	513,797	624,891
Property, plant and equipment		
Land	24,246	32,600
Buildings and improvements	260,394	284,439
Machinery and equipment	1,030,233	1,109,411
Construction in progress	97,053	30,305
	1,411,926	1,456,755
Less allowance for depreciation	710,791	707,456
Total property, plant and equipment	701,135	749,299
Total assets	$ 2,125,066	$ 2,504,327

MAYTAG CORPORATION

STATEMENTS OF CONSOLIDATED FINANCIAL CONDITION

In thousands except share data	1995	1994
Liabilities and Shareowners' Equity		
Current liabilities		
Notes payable	$ —	$ 45,148
Accounts payable	142,676	212,441
Compensation to employees	61,644	61,311
Accrued liabilities	156,041	146,086
Income taxes payable	3,141	26,037
Current maturities of long-term debt	3,201	43,411
Total current liabilities	366,703	534,434
Noncurrent liabilities		
Deferred income taxes	14,367	38,375
Long-term debt	536,579	663,205
Postretirement benefits other than pensions	428,478	412,832
Pension liability	88,883	59,363
Other noncurrent liabilities	52,705	64,406
Total noncurrent liabilities	1,121,012	1,238,181
Shareowners' equity		
Common stock:		
Authorized—200,000,000 shares (par value $1.25)		
Issued—117,150,593 shares, including shares in treasury	146,438	146,438
Additional paid-in capital	472,602	477,153
Retained earnings	344,346	420,174
Cost of Common stock in treasury (1995—11,745,395 shares; 1994—9,813,893 shares)	(255,663)	(218,745)
Employee stock plans	(57,319)	(60,816)
Minimum pension liability adjustment	(5,656)	
Foreign currency translation	(7,397)	(32,492)
Total shareowners' equity	637,351	731,712
Total liabilities and shareowners' equity	$ 2,125,066	$ 2,504,327

See notes to consolidated financial statements.

MAYTAG CORPORATION

STATEMENTS OF CONSOLIDATED CASH FLOWS

In thousands	Year Ended December 31		
	1995	1994	1993
Operating activities			
Net income (loss)	$ (20,476)	$ 147,947	$ 51,270
Adjustments to reconcile net income (loss) to net cash provided by operating activities:			
Loss on business dispositions	146,785	13,088	—
Cumulative effect of accounting change	—	3,190	—
Depreciation and amortization	111,861	119,358	111,781
Deferred income taxes	(42,036)	(10,058)	(35,833)
Reorganization expenses	—	(5,000)	(5,000)
"Free flights" promotion expenses	—	700	60,379
Changes in selected working capital items exclusive of business dispositions:			
Inventories	13,248	24,503	(29,323)
Receivables	60,156	(53,074)	(59,745)
Other current assets	5,548	(2,537)	11,136
Other current liabilities	4,624	43,387	(17,383)
Reorganization reserve	(903)	(26,686)	(39,671)
"Free flights" promotion reserve	(388)	(26,709)	(42,981)
Pension assets and liabilities	17,735	14,089	43,513
Postretirement benefits	15,702	21,197	11,259
Other—net	2,643	5,967	11,913
Net cash provided by operating activities	314,499	269,362	71,315
Investing activities			
Capital expenditures—net	(148,349)	(79,024)	(95,990)
Proceeds from business dispositions (net of cash in businesses sold of $15,783 in 1995 and $2,650 in 1994)	148,497	79,428	—
Total investing activities	148	404	(95,990)
Financing activities			
Proceeds from credit agreements and long-term borrowings	—	—	5,500
(Decrease) increase in notes payable	(29,808)	(118,134)	138,951
Reduction in long-term debt	(163,609)	(36,001)	(94,449)
Stock repurchases	(54,775)	—	—
Stock options exercised and other Common stock transactions	16,801	12,377	5,903
Dividends	(55,352)	(53,596)	(53,569)
Total financing activities	(286,743)	(195,354)	2,336
Effect of exchange rates on cash	2,907	4,261	(2,963)
Increase (decrease) in cash and cash equivalents	30,811	78,673	(25,302)
Cash and cash equivalents at beginning of year	110,403	31,730	57,032
Cash and cash equivalents at end of year	$ 141,214	$ 110,403	$ 31,730

See notes to consolidated financial statements.

MAYTAG CORPORATION

NOTES TO CONSOLIDATED FINANCIAL STATEMENTS

Summary of Significant Accounting Policies:

Principles of Consolidation: The consolidated financial statements include the accounts and transactions of the Company and its wholly-owned subsidiaries. Intercompany accounts and transactions are eliminated in consolidation.

Prior to the quarter ended December 31, 1994, the Company's European subsidiaries were consolidated as of a date one month earlier than subsidiaries in the United States. In the fourth quarter of 1994, this one month reporting lag was eliminated and European results for the quarter ended December 31, 1994 included activity for four months. The effect of this change increased net sales by $25.2 million in the fourth quarter of 1994, and the impact on net income was not significant.

Exchange rate fluctuations from translating the financial statements of subsidiaries located outside the United States into U.S. dollars and exchange gains and losses from designated intercompany foreign currency transactions are recorded in a separate component of shareowners' equity. All other foreign exchange gains and losses are included in income.

Certain previously reported amounts have been reclassified to conform with the current period presentation.

Use of Estimates: The preparation of financial statements in conformity with generally accepted accounting principles requires management to make estimates and assumptions that affect the amounts reported in the financial statements and accompanying notes. Actual results could differ from these estimates.

Cash Equivalents: Highly liquid investments with a maturity of 90 days or less when purchased are considered by the Company to be cash equivalents.

Inventories: Inventories are stated at the lower of cost or market. Inventory costs are determined by the last-in, first-out (LIFO) method for approximately 96 percent and 80 percent of the Company's inventories at December 31, 1995 and 1994. Costs for other inventories have been determined principally by the first-in, first-out (FIFO) method.

Intangibles: Intangibles principally represent goodwill, which is the cost of business acquisitions in excess of the fair value of identifiable net tangible assets of businesses acquired. Goodwill is amortized over 40 years on the straight-line basis and the carrying value is reviewed annually. If this review indicates that goodwill will not be recoverable as determined based on the undiscounted cash flows of the entity acquired over the remaining amortization period, the Company's carrying value of the goodwill will be reduced by the estimated shortfall of cash flows.

Income Taxes: Certain expenses (principally related to accelerated tax depreciation, employee benefits and various other accruals) are recognized in different periods for financial reporting and income tax purposes.

Property, Plant and Equipment: Property, plant and equipment is stated on the basis of cost. Depreciation expense is calculated principally on the straight-line method to amortize the cost of the assets over their estimated useful lives.

Short and Long-Term Debt: The carrying amounts of the Company's borrowings under its short-term revolving credit agreements approximate their fair value. The fair values of the Company's long-term debt are estimated based on quoted market prices of comparable instruments.

Forward Foreign Exchange Contracts: The Company enters into forward foreign exchange contracts to hedge exposures related to foreign currency transactions. Losses on hedges of firm identifiable commitments are recognized in the same period in which the underlying transaction is recorded. Gains and losses on other contracts are marked to market each period and the gains and losses are included in income.

Business Dispositions
In the second quarter of 1995, the Company sold its home appliance operations in Europe for $164.3 million in cash, subject to a post closing adjustment to the price. The pretax loss from the sale was $140.8 million and resulted in an after-tax loss of $135.4 million. In the fourth quarter of 1995, the Company sold the business and assets of a Dixie-Narco manufacturing operation in Eastlake, Ohio. The pretax loss from the sale was $6 million and resulted in an after-tax loss of $3.6 million. In the fourth quarter of 1994, the Company sold its home appliance operations in Australia and New Zealand for $82.1 million in cash. The pretax loss on the sale was $13.1 million and resulted in an after-tax loss of $16.4 million. See industry segment and geographic information for financial information related to these businesses.

Other Expenses
In the third quarter of 1995, the Company recorded a $16.5 million charge to settle a lawsuit relating to the 1991 closing of a former Dixie-Narco plant in Ranson, West Virginia. The after-tax charge was $9.9 million.

The Company is contingently liable under guarantees for indebtedness owed by a third party ("borrower") of $23 million relating to the sale in 1992 of one of the Company's manufacturing facilities. The borrower is presently in default under the terms of the loan agreement. Although the indebtedness is collateralized by the assets of the borrower, the net realizable value of these assets is substantially less than the amount of indebtedness. The borrower also has another outstanding debt of $2.5 million to the Company. In the fourth quarter of 1995, the Company recorded an $18 million charge to establish a reserve for the loan guarantees and other debt. The after-tax charge was $10.8 million.

Inventories

	December 31	
In thousands	1995	1994
Finished products	$ 163,968	$ 254,345
Work in process, raw materials and supplies	101,151	132,924
	$ 265,119	$ 387,269

If the FIFO method of inventory accounting, which approximates current cost, had been used for all inventories, they would have been $82.1 million and $77.1 million higher than reported at December 31, 1995 and 1994.

Pension Benefits (excerpts)
The Company and its subsidiaries have noncontributory defined benefit pension plans covering most employees. Plans covering salaried and management employees generally provide pension benefits that are based on an average of the employee's earnings and credited service. Plans covering hourly employees generally provide benefits of stated amounts for each year of service. The Company's funding policy is to contribute amounts to the plans sufficient to meet minimum funding requirements.

For the valuation of pension obligations at the end of 1995 set forth in the table below, and for determining pension expense in 1996, the discount rate and rate of compensation increase have been decreased to 7.5 percent and 5.0 percent, respectively. The majority of the increase in the projected benefit obligation between 1994 and 1995 is due to the decrease in the discount rate. Assumptions for defined benefit plans outside the United States are comparable to the above in all periods.

As of December 31, 1995, approximately 96 percent of the plan assets are invested in listed stocks and bonds. The balance is invested in real estate and short term investments.

In 1995 and 1994, the Company recorded $96.9 million and $84.7 million, respectively, to recognize the minimum pension liability required by the provisions of Financial Accounting Standards Board Statement No. 87 (FAS 87), "Employers' Accounting for Pensions." The transaction, which had no effect on income, was offset by recording an intangible asset of $91.2 million in 1995 and $84.7 million in 1994. The intangible asset represents a future economic benefit arising from the granting of retroactive pension benefits over many years and will be amortized to expense over the remaining average working lifetime of the affected employees. The intangible asset is required to be recognized in accordance with FAS 87 due to an increase in the accumulated benefit obligation resulting from the decrease in the discount rate. In addition, because the intangible asset recognized may not exceed the amount of unrecognized prior service cost and transition obligation on an individual plan basis, the balance in 1995 of $5.7 million, net of income tax benefits is recorded as a separate reduction of shareowners' equity at December 31, 1995.

Postretirement Benefits Other Than Pensions (excerpts)
In addition to providing pension benefits, the Company provides postretirement health care and life insurance benefits for its employees in the United States. Most of the postretirement plans are contributory and contain certain other cost sharing features such as deductibles and coinsurance. The plans are unfunded. Employees do not vest, and these benefits are subject to change. Death benefits for certain retired employees are funded as part of, and paid out of, pension plans.

Employee Stock Ownership Plan and Other Employee Benefits (excerpts)
The Company has established a trust to administer a leveraged employee stock ownership plan (ESOP) within an existing employee savings plan. The Company has guaranteed the debt of the trust and will service the repayment of the debt, including interest, through the Company's employee savings plan contribution and from the quarterly dividends paid on stock held by the ESOP. Dividends paid by the Company on stock held by the ESOP totaled $1.5 million, $1.4 million and $1.4 million in 1995, 1994 and 1993.

In the first quarter of 1994, the Company adopted Financial Accounting Standards Board Statement No. 112 (FAS 112), "Employers' Accounting for Postemployment Benefits." The new rules require recognition of a liability for certain disability and severance benefits to former or inactive employees. The cumulative effect of the accounting change was $3.2 million. The ongoing expenses associated with the adoption of this standard are not significant.

Income Taxes (excerpts)
Deferred income taxes reflect the net tax effects of temporary differences between the carrying amount of assets and liabilities for financial reporting purposes and the amounts used for income tax purposes.

At December 31, 1995, the Company has available for tax purposes approximately $13 million of net operating loss carryforwards outside the United States which expire in various years through 2005. The Company also has a capital loss carryforward available in the United States of $108 million which expires in the year 2000.

Income (loss) before income taxes, extraordinary item and cumulative effect of accounting change consists of the following:

	Year Ended December 31		
In thousands	1995	1994	1993
United States	$ 65,041	$ 230,320	$ 162,554
Non-United States	(5,237)	11,017	(72,684)
	$ 59,804	$ 241,337	$ 89,870

Significant components of the provision for income taxes are as follows:

Year Ended December 31 In thousands	1995	1994	1993
Current provision:			
Federal	$ 81,200	$ 78,200	$ 51,700
State	16,400	16,400	9,100
Non-United States	1,100	12,900	20,000
	98,700	107,500	80,800
Deferred provision:			
Federal	(19,900)	(9,400)	400
State	(5,200)	(2,500)	700
Non-United States	1,200	(5,400)	(43,300)
	(23,900)	(17,300)	(42,200)
Provision for income taxes	$ 74,800	$ 90,200	$ 38,600

Since the Company plans to continue to finance expansion and operating requirements of subsidiaries outside the United States through reinvestment of the undistributed earnings of these subsidiaries (approximately $21 million at December 31, 1995), taxes which would result from distribution have not been provided on such earnings. If such earnings were distributed, additional taxes payable would be significantly reduced by available tax credits arising from taxes paid outside the United States.

Income taxes paid, net of refunds received, during 1995, 1994 and 1993 were $123 million, $103 million, and $68.3 million, respectively.

Notes Payable

Notes payable at December 31, 1994 consisted of notes payable to banks of $29 million, in addition to $16 million in commercial paper borrowings. The Company's commercial paper program is supported by a credit agreement totaling $400 million which expires on July 27, 2000. Subject to certain exceptions, the credit agreement requires the Company to be within certain quarterly levels of maximum leverage and minimum interest coverage. At December 31, 1995, the Company was in compliance with all covenants. The weighted average interest rate on all notes payable and commercial paper borrowings was 6.5 percent at December 31, 1994. There were no notes payable and commercial paper borrowings at December 31, 1995.

Long-Term Debt

Long-term debt consisted of the following:

In thousands	December 31 1995	1994
Notes payable with interest payable semiannually:		
Due May 15, 2002 at 9.75%	$ 177,425	$ 200,000
Due July 15, 1999 at 8.875%	148,550	175,000
Due July 1, 1997 at 8.875%	53,741	100,000
Medium-term notes, maturing from 2001 to 2010, from 7.69% to 9.03% with interest payable semiannually	101,500	162,750
Employee stock ownership plan notes payable semiannually through July 2, 2004 at 9.35%	55,373	57,504
Other	3,191	11,362
	539,780	706,616
Less current maturities of long-term debt	3,201	43,411
Long-term debt	$ 536,579	$ 663,205

The 9.75 percent notes, the 8.875 percent notes due in 1999 and the medium-term notes grant the holders the right to require the Company to repurchase all or any portion of their notes at 100 percent of the principal amount thereof, together with accrued interest, following the occurrence of both a change in Company control and a credit rating decline.

The fair value of the Company's long-term debt, based on public quotes if available, exceeded the amount recorded in the statements of consolidated financial condition at December 31, 1995 and 1994 by $68.1 million and $17.3 million, respectively.

Interest paid during 1995, 1994 and 1993 was $60.2 million, $75.2 million, and $76.2 million. The aggregate maturities of long-term debt in each of the next five years is as follows (in thousands): 1996—$3,201; 1997—$57,489; 1998—$4,378; 1999—$153,696; 2000—$6,119.

In 1995, the Company retired $116.5 million of long-term debt. Included in this amount was $22.6 million of the 9.75 percent notes due May 15, 2002, $26.4 million of the 8.875 percent notes due July 15, 1999, $46.3 million of the 8.875 percent notes due July 1, 1997 and $21.2 million of medium term notes ranging in maturities from November 15, 2001 to February 23, 2010. As a result of these early retirements, the Company recorded an after-tax charge of $5.5 million (net of income tax benefit of $3.6 million), which has been reflected in the consolidated statement of income (loss) as an extraordinary item.

Leases

The Company leases buildings, machinery, equipment and automobiles under operating leases. Rental expense for operating leases amounted to $20.6 million, $24.4 million, and $22.8 million for 1995, 1994 and 1993.

Minimum lease payments under leases expiring subsequent to December 31, 1995 are:

Year Ending In thousands	
1996	$ 14,441
1997	8,625
1998	6,249
1999	5,293
2000	4,100
Thereafter	8,745
Total minimum lease payments	$ 47,453

Forward Foreign Exchange Contracts (this note has been omitted)

Stock Options (excerpts)

In 1992, the shareowners approved the 1992 stock option plan for executives and key employees. The plan provides that options could be granted to key employees for not more than 3.6 million shares of the Common stock of the Company. The option price under the plan is the fair market value at the date of the grant. Options may not be exercised until one year after the date granted. In the event of a change of Company control, all options become immediately exercisable.

Stock Awards (excerpts)

In 1991, the shareowners approved the 1991 Stock Incentive Award Plan For Key Executives. This plan authorizes the issuance of up to 2.5 million shares of Common stock to certain key employees of the Company, of which 1,700,250 shares are available for future grants as of December 31, 1995. Under the terms of the plan, the granted stock vests three years after the award date and is contingent upon pre-established performance objectives. In the event of a change of Company control, all incentive stock awards become fully vested. No incentive stock awards may be granted under this plan on or after May 1, 1996.

Shareowners' Equity (excerpts)

The Company has 24 million authorized shares of Preferred stock, par value $1 per share, none of which is issued.

Pursuant to a Shareholder Rights Plan approved by the Company in 1988, each share of Common stock carries with it one Right. Until exercisable, the Rights will not be transferable apart from the Company's Common stock. When exercisable, each Right will entitle its holder to purchase one one-hundredth of a share of Preferred stock of the Company at a price of $75.

Industry Segment and Geographic Information

Principal financial data by industry segment is as follows:

In thousands	1995	1994	1993
Net sales			
Home appliances	$2,844,811	$3,180,766	$2,830,457
Vending equipment	194,713	191,749	156,597
Total	$3,039,524	$3,372,515	$2,987,054
Income before income taxes, extraordinary item and cumulative effect of accounting change			
Home appliances	$ 295,806	$ 334,027	$ 163,177
Vending equipment	23,466	21,866	17,944
General corporate	(31,038)	(33,125)	(22,243)
Operating income	288,234	322,768	158,878
Interest expense	(52,087)	(74,077)	(75,364)
Other (see statements of consolidated income/loss)	(176,343)	(7,354)	6,356
Total	$ 59,804	$ 241,337	$ 89,870
Capital expenditures-net			
Home appliances	$ 140,549	$ 75,017	$ 92,194
Vending equipment	3,998	1,902	1,028
General corporate	3,802	2,105	2,768
Total	$ 148,349	$ 79,024	$ 95,990
Depreciation and amortization			
Home appliances	$ 105,271	$ 113,160	$ 105,916
Vending equipment	4,307	4,434	4,377
General corporate	2,283	1,764	1,488
Total	$ 111,861	$ 119,358	$ 111,781
Identifiable assets			
Home appliances	$1,593,538	$2,053,175	$2,147,174
Vending equipment	94,299	98,109	103,765
General corporate	437,229	353,043	218,559
Total	$2,125,066	$2,504,327	$2,469,498

Information about the Company's operations in different geographic locations is as follows:

In thousands	1995	1994	1993
Net sales			
North America	$ 2,858,347	$ 2,831,583	$ 2,468,374
Europe	181,177	398,966	390,761
Australia and New Zealand	—	141,966	127,919
Total	$ 3,039,524	$ 3,372,515	$ 2,987,054
Income before income taxes, extraordinary item and cumulative effect of accounting change			
North America	$ 326,451	$ 342,887	$ 251,328
Europe	(7,179)	420	(73,581)
Australia and New Zealand	—	12,586	3,374
General corporate	(31,038)	(33,125)	(22,243)
Operating income	288,234	322,768	158,878
Interest expense	(52,087)	(74,077)	(75,364)
Other (see statements of consolidated income/loss)	(176,343)	(7,354)	6,356
Total	$ 59,804	$ 241,337	$ 89,870

Identifiable assets			
North America	$ 1,687,837	$ 1,768,629	$ 1,794,271
Europe	–	382,655	359,323
Australia and New Zealand	–	–	97,345
General corporate	437,229	353,043	218,559
Total	$ 2,125,066	$ 2,504,327	$ 2,469,498

Sales between affiliates of different geographic regions are not significant. The amount of exchange gain or loss included in operations in any of the years presented was not significant.

In June 1995, the Company sold its home appliance operations in Europe and in December 1994, the Company sold its home appliance operations in Australia and New Zealand.

The general Corporate asset category includes items such as cash, deferred tax assets, pension investments and other assets.

Prior to the quarter ended December 31, 1994, the Company's European subsidiaries were consolidated as of a date one month earlier than subsidiaries in the United States. In the fourth quarter of 1994, this one month reporting lag was eliminated and European results for the quarter ended December 31, 1994 include activity for four months. The effect of this change increased net sales by $25.2 million in the fourth quarter and the impact on income before income taxes and cumulative effect of accounting change was not significant.

Supplementary Expense Information

	Year Ended December 31		
In thousands	1995	1994	1993
Advertising costs	$ 134,411	$ 153,233	$ 136,452
Research and development expenses	47,013	45,926	42,717

The Company expenses the production costs of advertising as incurred.

Contingencies and Disclosure of Certain Risks and Uncertainties (excerpts)

In connection with the sale of the Company's home appliance operations in Europe, the terms of the contract provide for a post closing adjustment to the price under which the company has asserted an additional amount of approximately $15 million is owed by the buyer. The post closing adjustment is in dispute and may ultimately depend on the decision of an independent third party. Also in connection with the sale, the Company has made various warranties to the buyer, including the accuracy of tax net operating losses in the United Kingdom, and has agreed to indemnify the buyer for liability resulting from customer claims under the "free flights" promotions in excess of the reserve balance at the time of sale. There are limitations on the Company's liability in the event the buyer incurs a loss as a result of breach of the warranties. The Company does not expect the resolution of these items to have a material adverse effect on its financial condition.

The Company recently announced that it will conduct an in-home inspection program to eliminate a potential problem with a small electrical component in Maytag brand dishwashers. Although the ultimate cost of the repair will not be known until the inspection program is complete, it is not expected to have a material impact on the Company's results. The Company will seek reimbursement from the supplier of the component.

Other contingent liabilities arising in the normal course of business, including guarantees, repurchase agreements, pending litigation, environmental issues, taxes and other claims are not considered to be significant in relation to the Company's consolidated financial position.

Nike—Basic Ratio Analysis

Nike, Inc. designs, develops, and markets, both domestically and internationally, a wide variety of athletic and leisure footwear and apparel for competitive and recreational uses. Nike is based in Beaverton, Oregon.

Learning Objectives
- Compute basic solvency and profitability ratios.
- Interpret basic solvency and profitability ratios.

Refer to the 1995 Consolidated Financial Statements of Nike, Inc.

Concepts

a. In general, what do measures of solvency and profitability represent? Why might users of Nike's financial statements calculate such measures?

Analysis

b. Using the information in Nike's 1995 financial statements, compute the following (note that at May 31, 1993, total shareholders' equity was $1,642,819 and total assets were $2,186,269):

   i. Current ratio at May 31, 1995 and 1994. The current ratio is defined as: $\dfrac{Current\ Assets}{Current\ Liabilities}$.

   ii. Working capital at May 31, 1995 and 1994. Working capital is defined as: *current assets less current liabilities.*

   iii. Gross margin percent for 1995 and 1994. Gross margin percent is defined as: $\dfrac{Sales\ \text{-}\ Cost\ of\ Goods\ Sold}{Sales} \times 100$.

   iv. Return on equity for fiscal 1995 and 1994. Return on equity is defined as: $\dfrac{Net\ Income\ \text{-}\ Preferred\ Dividends}{Average\ Common\ Shareholders'\ Equity}$. Note: the exact amount of preferred dividends is not provided. Assume that there were no preferred dividends in 1995 and 1994.

   v. Return on assets for fiscal 1995 and 1994. Return on assets is defined as: $\dfrac{Net\ Income\ +\ Interest\ Expense\ (1\ \text{-}\ tax\ rate)}{Average\ Total\ Assets}$.

c. Did Nike earn more or less money in 1995 than 1994? Use the financial statements to determine the major reasons for the change.

d. Was Nike more or less profitable in 1995 than 1994? (*Hint*: Simply comparing net income year to year ignores the changing level of assets or shareholders' equity used to generate the income. To determine whether Nike's profitability changed, determine whether Nike's return on assets increased or decreased and whether return on equity increased or decreased.)

e. How much cash did Nike have at May 31, 1995?

f. Was Nike in a position to pay its short-term obligations at May 31, 1995? (*Hint*: what was Nike's current ratio at May 31, 1995?) Did Nike have positive working capital?

g. Were Nike's operations a source or a use of cash in fiscal 1995?

h. What were Nike's major sources and uses of cash in fiscal 1995?

NIKE, INC.
CONSOLIDATED BALANCE SHEET

(In Thousands)

May 31

Assets	1995	1994
Current Assets:		
Cash and equivalents	$ 216,071	$ 518,816
Accounts receivable, less allowance for doubtful accounts of $ 32,663 and $ 28,291	1,053,237	703,682
Inventories (Note 2)	629,742	470,023
Deferred income taxes (Note 6)	72,657	37,603
Prepaid expenses	74,221	40,307
Total current assets	2,045,928	1,770,431
Property, plant and equipment, net (Notes 3 and 5)	554,879	405,845
Goodwill (Note 1)	495,907	163,036
Other assets	46,031	34,503
	$3,142,745	$2,373,815

Liabilities and Shareholders' Equity	1995	1994
Current Liabilities:		
Current portion of long-term debt (Note 5)	$ 31,943	$ 3,857
Notes payable (Note 4)	397,100	127,378
Accounts payable (Note 4)	297,656	210,576
Accrued liabilities	345,224	181,889
Income taxes payable	35,612	38,287
Total current liabilities	1,107,535	561,987
Long-term debt (Notes 5 and 13)	10,565	12,364
Non-current deferred income taxes (Note 6)	17,789	18,228
Other non-current liabilities (Note 1)	41,867	39,987
Commitments and contingencies (Notes 11 an 14)	—	—
Redeemable Preferred Stock (Note 7)	300	300
Shareholders' equity (Note 8):		
Common Stock at stated value:		
Class A convertible—25,895 and 26,679 shares outstanding	155	159
Class B—45,550 and 46,521 shares outstanding	2,698	2,704
Capital in excess of stated value	122,436	108,284
Foreign currency translation adjustment	1,585	(15,123)
Retained earnings	1,837,815	1,644,925
	1,964,689	1,740,949
	$3,142,745	$2,373,815

The accompanying notes to consolidated financial statements are an integral part of this statement.

NIKE, INC.

CONSOLIDATED STATEMENT OF INCOME

Year Ended May 31

(In Thousands, Except Per Share Data)

	1995	1994	1993
Revenues	$4,760,834	$3,789,668	$3,930,984
Costs and expenses:			
Cost of sales	2,865,280	2,301,423	2,386,993
Selling and administrative	1,209,760	974,099	922,261
Interest (Notes 3, 4 and 5)	24,208	15,282	25,739
Other (income)/expense, net (Notes 1, 9 and 10)	11,722	8,270	1,475
	4,110,970	3,299,074	3,336,468
Income before income taxes	649,864	490,594	594,516
Income taxes (Note 6)	250,200	191,800	229,500
Net income	$ 399,664	$ 298,794	$ 365,016
Net income per common share (Note 1)	$ 5.44	$ 3.96	$ 4.74
Average number of common and common equivalent shares (Note 1)	73,503	75,456	77,063

The accompanying notes to consolidated financial statements are an integral part of this statement.

NIKE, INC.

CONSOLIDATED STATEMENT OF CASH FLOWS

Year Ended May 31 (In Thousands)	1995	1994	1993
Cash Provided (Used) by Operations:			
Net income	$ 399,664	$ 298,794	$ 365,016
Income charges (credits) not affecting cash:			
Depreciation	71,113	64,531	60,393
Deferred income taxes and purchased tax benefits	(24,668)	(23,876)	4,310
Other non-current liabilities	(1,359)	(3,588)	19,847
Other, including amortization	19,125	8,067	12,951
Changes in certain working capital components:			
(Increase) decrease in inventory	(69,676)	160,823	(97,471)
(Increase) decrease in accounts receivable	(301,648)	23,979	(62,538)
(Increase) decrease in other current assets	(10,276)	6,888	(5,133)
Increase (decrease) in accounts payable, accrued liabilities and income taxes payable	172,638	40,845	(32,083)
Cash provided by operations	254,913	576,463	265,292
Cash Provided (Used) by Investing Activities:			
Additions to property, plant and equipment	(154,125)	(95,266)	(97,041)
Disposals of property, plant and equipment	9,011	12,650	5,006
Acquisition of subsidiaries:			
Identifiable intangible assets & Goodwill	(345,901)	(2,185)	(52,003)
Net assets acquired	(84,119)	(1,367)	(25,858)
Additions to other non-current assets	(6,260)	(5,450)	(3,036)
Cash used by investing activities	(581,394)	(91,618)	(172,932)
Cash Provided (Used) by Financing Activities:			
Additions to long-term debt	2,971	6,044	1,536
Reductions in long-term debt including current portion	(39,804)	(56,986)	(5,817)
Increase (Decrease) in notes payable	263,874	(2,939)	(2,017)
Proceeds from exercise of options	6,154	4,288	7,055
Repurchase of stock	(142,919)	(140,104)	—
Dividends—common and preferred	(65,418)	(60,282)	(53,017)
Cash provided/(used) by financing activities	24,858	(249,979)	(52,260)
Effect of exchange rate changes on cash	(1,122)	(7,334)	8,866
Net increase in cash and equivalents	(302,745)	227,532	31,234
Cash and equivalents, beginning of year	518,816	291,284	260,050
Cash and equivalents, end of year	$ 216,071	$ 518,816	$ 291,284

Yokohama Rubber & Goodyear Tire—Comparing Ratios

The Yokohama Rubber Company is a world leader in the design and manufacture of high-performance tires. Yokohama also manufactures golf-related products, fertilizers, and surfacing materials for waterproofing the running surfaces in track and field stadiums. The company is headquartered in Tokyo, Japan.

The Goodyear Tire & Rubber Company's principal business is the development, manufacture, distribution and sale of tires throughout the world. Goodyear also manufactures and sells a broad spectrum of rubber, chemical and plastic products for the transportation industry and various industrial and consumer markets.

Learning Objectives
- Prepare common-size balance sheets for a U.S. and a Japanese company that operate in the same industry.
- Compare and contrast the investment and financing decisions of different companies.
- Explain why cultural differences can lead to substantially different balance sheet relationships.

Refer to the Consolidated balance sheets of The Yokohama Rubber Co. Ltd. and The Goodyear Tire & Rubber Company for 1990.

Analysis

a. Prepare a common-size 1990 balance sheet for each company. That is, recast each balance sheet line as a percentage of total assets. Compare the two companies based on their 1990 balance sheets. What similarities and differences do you note in relationships between accounts?

b. Calculate each company's total debt to equity ratio. Compare the two. What might explain the difference?

THE YOKOHAMA RUBBER CO., LTD. AND CONSOLIDATED SUBSIDIARIES

CONSOLIDATED BALANCE SHEETS
As of December 31, 1990 and 1989

Assets

	Millions of yen		Thousands of U.S. dollars (Note 1)
	1990	1989	1990
Current Assets:			
Cash and time deposits	¥ 30,688	¥ 42,203	$ 227,994
Marketable securities (Notes 2 and 4)	21,486	36,044	159,629
Trade receivables:			
Notes and accounts (Notes 4 and 6)	115,355	105,366	857,021
Unconsolidated subsidiaries and associated companies	10,074	8,852	74,844
Allowance for doubtful receivables	(2,121)	(2,095)	(15,759)
Inventories (Notes 2 and 3)	57,884	50,520	430,045
Deferred income taxes (Notes 2)	3,215	3,511	23,886
Other current assets	14,257	7,472	105,921
Total current assets	250,838	251,873	1,863,581
Property, Plant and Equipment—at Cost (Notes 2,4, and 5):			
Land	22,082	20,884	164,056
Buildings and structures	58,456	52,673	434,294
Machinery and equipment	195,990	171,861	1,456,092
Construction in progress	16,020	7,137	119,019
	292,548	252,555	2,173,461
Less accumulated depreciation	(168,428)	(153,508)	(1,251,322)
Total property, plant and equipment	124,120	99,047	922,139
Investments and Other Assets:			
Investment securities (Note 2)			
Unconsolidated subsidiaries and associated companies	5,370	16,525	39,896
Other	4,177	3,971	31,033
Long-term loans receivable	3,802	8,662	28,247
Other investments and other assets	17,796	6,998	132,214
Allowance for doubtful receivables	(181)	(185)	(1,345)
Total investments and other assets	30,964	35,971	230,045
Total	¥405,922	¥386,891	$3,015,765

See accompanying notes to The Consolidated Financial Statements.

THE YOKOHAMA RUBBER CO., LTD. AND CONSOLIDATED SUBSIDIARIES

CONSOLIDATED BALANCE SHEETS
As of December 31, 1990 and 1989

Liabilities and Shareholders' Equity

	Millions of yen 1990	Millions of yen 1989	Thousands of U.S. dollars (Note 1) 1990
Current Liabilities:			
Bank loans	¥ 99,149	¥ 93,855	$ 736,620
Current maturities of long-term debt	12,872	17,808	95,631
Trade notes and accounts payable	84,926	86,069	630,951
Accrued income taxes (Note 2)	5,620	7,376	41,753
Accrued expenses	14,247	12,866	105,847
Other current liabilities	22,208	19,033	164,993
Total current liabilities	239,022	237,007	1,775,795
Long-term Debt (Note 4)	80,897	73,764	601,018
Other Long-term Liabilities	4,627	4,208	34,376
Liabilities for Severance Payments (Note 2)	11,918	11,186	88,544
Deferred Income Taxes (Note 2)	2,057	450	15,282
Minority Interests	4,053	3,817	30,111
Contingent Liabilities (Note 6)			
Shareholders' Equity:			
Common Stock			
Authorized 480,000,000 shares			
Issued—1990—244,062,693 shares			
1989—243,745,575 shares	18,089	17,967	134,391
Capital surplus	11,072	10,951	82,258
Legal reserve (Note 7)	4,713	4,619	35,015
Retained earnings (Note 8)	31,387	23,572	233,187
Foreign currency translation adjustments	(1,913)	(650)	(14,212)
Total shareholders' equity	63,348	56,459	470,639
Total	¥405,922	¥386,891	$3,015,765

THE GOODYEAR TIRE & RUBBER COMPANY AND SUBSIDIARIES

CONSOLIDATED BALANCE SHEET

(Dollars in millions)	December 31, 1990	1989
Assets		
Current Assets:		
Cash and cash equivalents	$ 220.3	$ 122.5
Short-term securities	56.4	92.1
Accounts and notes receivable	1,495.2	1,244.6
Inventories	1,346.0	1,642.0
Prepaid expenses	206.3	170.7
Total Current Assets	3,324.2	3,271.9
Other Assets:		
Investments in affiliates, at equity	127.6	125.9
Long-term accounts and notes receivable	292.5	189.2
Deferred charges and other miscellaneous assets	410.9	258.0
	831.0	573.1
Properties and Plants	4,808.4	4,615.3
	$8,963.6	$8,460.3
Liabilities and Shareholders' Equity		
Current Liabilities:		
Accounts payable—trade	$986.8	$924.0
Accrued payrolls and other compensation	442.7	395.6
Other current liabilities	282.5	278.9
United States and foreign taxes	248.6	219.3
Notes payable to banks and overdrafts	247.6	316.0
Long-term debt due within one year	85.4	66.4
Total Current Liabilities	2,293.6	2,200.2
Long-term Debt and Capital Leases	3,286.4	2,963.4
Other Long-term Liabilities	550.0	364.7
Deferred Income Taxes	622.9	681.8
Minority Equity in Subsidiaries	112.8	106.4
Shareholders' Equity:		
Preferred stock, no par value:		
Authorized, 50,000,000 shares, unissued	—	—
Common stock, no par value:		
Authorized, 150,000,000 shares;		
Outstanding shares, 58,477,890		
(57,806,869 in 1989)	58.5	57.8
Capital surplus	65.1	46.5
Retained earnings	2,135.4	2,278.4
	2,259.0	2,382.7
Foreign currency translation adjustment	(161.1)	(238.9)
Total Shareholders' Equity	2,097.9	2,143.8
	$8,963.6	$8,460.3

The accompanying accounting policies and notes are an integral part of this financial statement.

Fuji Photo Film & Eastman Kodak—Inferring Transactions

Fuji Photo Film Co. is Japan's largest maker of photographic film and paper and ranks second worldwide behind Eastman Kodak. Fuji also produces photo equipment, movie films, electronic imaging, magnetic tapes and disks with manufacturing plants in Japan and throughout Europe and the U.S.

Eastman Kodak is an international conglomerate based in Rochester, New York. It is the world's largest producer of photographic products, specializing in amateur, professional and commercial imaging equipment and supplies. In 1992, Kodak also produced synthetic textile fibers, plastics, chemicals and health related products. Recent restructurings have eliminated some of these product lines.

Learning Objectives
- Infer transactions from account balances.
- Reconstruct the activity that took place in an account.
- Compare and contrast the operating results of a U.S. and a Japanese company that operate in common industries.
- Explain how cultural differences and business decisions can lead to different balance sheet relationships.

Refer to the 1992 financial statements of Fuji Photo Film Co. Ltd. and Eastman Kodak Company.

Process

a. Set up a T-account for Fuji Photo Film's trade accounts receivable account. Fill in the opening and closing balances. Provide the journal entry to record each of the following economic events. For each event, assume that the company booked a single journal entry. Use the journal entries to fill in the activity in the T-account.

   i. Fuji's net sales for 1992. Assume that all sales were made on account.

   ii. Fuji's 1992 collections of amounts due from customers. Assume that no receivables were written-off in 1992. Ignore information about the allowance for doubtful accounts.

b. Provide the journal entry to record Fuji's 1992 interest expense. Assume the company booked interest expense in a single journal entry.

c. Set up T-accounts for Eastman Kodak's inventory and payables accounts. Assume that all activity in the payables account relates to inventory. Fill in the opening and closing balances for each account. Provide the journal entry to record each of the following economic events. For each event, assume that the company booked a single journal entry. Use the journal entries to fill in the activity in the T-accounts.

   i. Kodak's 1992 cost of goods sold.

   ii. Kodak's 1992 purchases of inventory. Assume all purchases were made on account.

   iii. Kodak's 1992 payments for inventory. Assume that payables represents only purchases of inventory on account.

d. Provide the journal entry to record Kodak's 1992 research and development costs. Assume the company booked a single journal entry.

Analysis

e. Common-size income statements express each revenue and expense line item as percentage of net sales. Prepare common-size income statements for Fuji Photo Film for 1991 and 1992. Use the statements to 'explain' why earnings are down in 1992.

f. Calculate and compare each company's debt to equity ratio. What might explain the difference?

FUJI PHOTO FILM CO., LTD. AND CONSOLIDATED SUBSIDIARIES

CONSOLIDATED BALANCE SHEET

October 20

	Yen (millions)		U.S. dollars (Thousands) (Note 2)
Assets	1992	1991	1992
Current assets:			
Cash and cash equivalents (Note 3)	¥ 457,713	¥ 441,409	$ 3,782,752
Marketable securities (Note 4)	51,706	8,170	427,322
Notes and accounts receivable (Note 5)			
Trade	181,044	179,974	1,496,232
Affiliated companies	41,098	39,514	339,653
Allowance for doubtful receivables	(4,759)	(5,214)	(39,331)
Inventories (Note 6)	192,460	192,884	1,590,579
Income tax prepayments	26,378	24,873	218,000
Prepaid expenses and other	13,110	18,399	108,347
Total current assets	958,750	900,009	7,923,554
Investments and long-term receivables:			
Investments in and advances to affiliated companies (Note 7)	144,661	141,970	1,195,546
Marketable securities (Note 4)	73,645	118,483	608,636
Long-term receivables	8,431	6,278	69,678
	226,737	266,731	1,873,860
Property, plant and equipment (Notes 8 and 13)			
Land	21,977	19,189	181,628
Buildings	234,469	191,734	1,937,760
Machinery and equipment	751,847	658,525	6,213,612
Construction in progress	46,967	64,100	388,157
	1,055,260	933,548	8,721,157
Less-Accumulated depreciation	(575,385)	(501,230)	(4,755,248)
	479,875	432,318	3,965,909
Other assets:			
Accumulated income tax prepayments	12,376	14,114	102,281
Other	20,341	19,286	168,107
	32,717	33,400	270,388
	¥1,698,079	¥1,632,458	$14,033,711

FUJI PHOTO FILM CO., LTD. AND CONSOLIDATED SUBSIDIARIES
CONSOLIDATED BALANCE SHEET
October 20

	Yen (Millions)		U.S. dollars (Thousands) (Note 2)
Liabilities and Shareholders' Equity	1992	1991	1992
Current liabilities:			
Short-term debt (Note 8)	¥ 181,925	¥ 184,890	$ 1,503,512
Notes and accounts payable—			
Trade	109,571	118,003	905,546
Construction	42,749	50,787	353,298
Accrued taxes on income (Note 11)	40,758	46,199	336,843
Accrued liabilities	75,513	75,672	624,074
Other current liabilities	10,510	4,825	86,859
Total current liabilities	461,026	480,376	3,810,132
Long-term liabilities:			
Long-term debt (Note 8)	54,656	44,831	451,703
Accrued pension and severance costs (Note 9)	60,621	58,959	501,000
Customers' guarantee deposits and other (Note 10)	50,152	49,238	414,479
	165,429	153,028	1,367,182
Minority interest in consolidated subsidiaries	4,557	3,542	37,661
Shareholders' equity (Note 12):			
Common stock, ¥50 par value—			
Authorized—800,000,000 shares			
Issued: 1992—514,385,571 shares	40,147	37,555	331,794
1991—512,561,249 shares			
Additional paid-in capital	67,919	65,327	561,314
Legal reserve	10,617	9,957	87,744
Retained earnings	952,328	886,279	7,870,479
Cumulative translation adjustment	(3,944)	(3,606)	(32,595)
	1,067,067	995,512	8,818,736
Commitments and contingent liabilities (Note 13)			
	¥1,698,079	¥1,632,458	$14,033,711

The accompanying notes are an integral part of this statement.

FUJI PHOTO FILM CO., LTD. AND CONSOLIDATED SUBSIDIARIES

CONSOLIDATED STATEMENT OF INCOME
Year ended October 20

	Yen (Millions)			U.S. dollars (Thousands) (Note 2)
	1992	1991	1990	1992
Net sales	¥1,142,303	¥1,117,429	¥1,064,919	$9,440,520
Cost of sales	610,106	592,753	560,078	5,042,198
Gross profit	532,197	524,676	504,841	4,398,322
Operating expenses:				
Selling, general and administrative	290,693	278,870	267,640	2,402,421
Research and development	75,027	68,202	59,531	620,058
Operating income	166,477	177,604	177,670	1,375,843
Other income and (expenses):				
Interest and dividend income	33,319	43,187	38,921	275,363
Interest expense	(22,144)	(23,024)	(19,854)	(183,008)
Exchange losses, net	(4,021)	(4,367)	(964)	(33,231)
Loss on disposition of property and equipment, net	(3,510)	(4,772)	(2,438)	(29,008)
Miscellaneous	(3,146)	1,942	2,595	(26,000)
	498	12,966	18,260	4,116
Income before income taxes	166,975	190,570	195,930	1,379,959
Income taxes (note 11):				
Current	93,050	99,635	107,375	769,008
Deferred	(18)	(32)	2,115	(149)
	93,032	99,603	109,490	768,859
Income from consolidated companies	73,943	90,967	86,440	611,100
Equity in net earnings of affiliated companies	1,752	3,811	3,838	14,479
Net income	¥ 75,695	¥ 94,778	¥ 90,278	$ 625,579

	Yen			U.S. dollars
	1992	1991	1990	1992
Net income per share of common stock:				
Primary	¥147.46	¥184.95	¥176.20	$1.22
Fully diluted	¥147.08	¥184.86	¥176.08	$1.22
Cash dividends declared per share of common stock	¥17.50	¥14.09	¥12.40	$0.14

FUJI PHOTO FILM CO., LTD. AND CONSOLIDATED SUBSIDIARIES

CONSOLIDATED STATEMENT OF RETAINED EARNINGS
Year ended October 20

	Yen (Millions)			U.S. dollars (Thousands) (Note 2)
	1992	1991	1990	1992
Balance at beginning of year	¥886,279	¥798,777	¥714,937	$7,324,620
Net income for the year	75,695	94,778	90,278	625,579
Deduct:				
Cash dividends applicable to earnings of the year	(8,986)	(7,221)	(6,352)	(74,265)
Transfer to legal reserve	(660)	(55)	(86)	(5,455)
Balance at end of year	¥952,328	¥886,279	¥798,777	$7,870,479

The accompanying notes are an integral part of this statement.

EASTMAN KODAK COMPANY AND SUBSIDIARY COMPANIES
CONSOLIDATED STATEMENT OF FINANCIAL POSITION

December 31,	1992	1991
	(In Millions)	

Assets

	1992	1991
Current Assets		
Cash and cash equivalents	$ 374	$ 783
Marketable securities	186	141
Receivables (net of allowances of $ 198 and $ 200)	3,984	4,348
Inventories	2,379	2,311
Deferred income tax charges	244	421
Other	238	254
Total current assets	7,405	8,258
Properties		
Land, buildings and equipment at cost	19,840	19,034
Less: Accumulated depreciation	10,005	9,432
Net properties	9,835	9,602
Other Assets		
Unamortized goodwill (net of accumulated amortization of $ 697 and $ 551)	4,273	4,349
Long-term receivables and other noncurrent assets	1,625	1,961
Total assets	$ 23,138	$ 24,170

Liabilities and Shareowners' Equity

	1992	1991
Current Liabilities		
Payables	$ 3,594	$ 3,835
Short-term borrowings	1,736	2,610
Taxes-income and other	505	292
Dividends payable	163	162
Total current liabilities	5,998	6,899
Other Liabilities		
Long-term borrowings	7,202	7,597
Other long-term liabilities	2,312	2,080
Deferred income tax credits	1,069	1,490
Total liabilities	16,581	18,066
Shareowners' Equity		
Common stock, par value $ 2.50 per share	936	934
950,000,000 shares authorized; issued 374,479,114 in 1992, 373,785,298 in 1991 and 373,638,981 in 1990		
Additional capital paid in or transferred from retained earnings	26	9
Retained earnings	7,721	7,225
Accumulated translation adjustment	(85)	(12)
	8,598	8,156
Less: Treasury stock shares at cost	2,041	2,052
48,562,835 shares in 1992, 48,852,102 shares in 1991 and 49,001,140 shares in 1990		
Total shareowners' equity	6,557	6,104
Total liabilities and shareowners' equity	$ 23,138	$ 24,170

EASTMAN KODAK COMPANY AND SUBSIDIARY COMPANIES

CONSOLIDATED STATEMENT OF EARNINGS

(in millions, except per share data)	1992	1991	1990
Revenues			
Sales	$ 20,183	$ 19,419	$ 18,908
Earnings from equity interests and other revenues	394	255	289
Total Revenues	20,577	19,674	19,197
Costs			
Cost of goods sold	10,392	9,985	9,637
Marketing and administrative expenses	5,869	5,565	5,098
Research and development costs	1,587	1,494	1,329
Interest expense	813	844	855
Restructuring costs/Litigation judgment	220	1,605	888
Other charges	95	170	133
Total costs	18,976	19,663	17,940
Earnings before income taxes	1,601	11	1,257
Provision (benefit) for income taxes	607	(6)	554
Earnings before cumulative effect of change in accounting principle	994	17	703
Cumulative effect of change in accounting principle	152	—	—
Net earnings	$ 1,146	$ 17	$ 703
Primary earnings per share before cumulative effect of change in accounting principle	$ 3.06	$ .05	$ 2.17
Cumulative effect of change in accounting principle	.47	—	—
Primary earnings per share	$ 3.53	$ .05	$ 2.17
Fully diluted earnings per share before cumulative effect of change in accounting principle	$ 2.98	$ .05	$ 2.16
Cumulative effect of change in accounting principle	.43	—	—
Fully diluted earnings per share	$ 3.41	$ .05	$ 2.16

Club Méditerranée S. A.—International GAAP

Club Méditerranée S. A. is a French business corporation established in 1957. It fully develops and manages holiday centers and the centers' activities. More generally, this consists of all industrial, commercial, and financial operations involving both stocks in the centers and shares of real estate.

Learning Objectives
- Read a set of foreign financial statements.
- Observe the differences between French and U.S. GAAP.
- Restate foreign financial statements to U.S. presentation format.
- Evaluate liquidity and solvency using simple ratios.

Refer to the 1992 financial statements of Club Méditerranée S. A. (Club Med).

Concepts

a. The balance sheet of Club Med is presented in a format that differs from that of U.S. companies.

    i.   What notable differences exist with respect to the ordering of the assets and liabilities?

    ii.   What differences are there with respect to the columns of data presented?

    iii.   What other differences do you note?

    iv.   Prepare the 1992 balance sheet for Club Med in accordance with U.S. GAAP presentation. Leave the amounts in French francs. (*Hint*: Note 11 provides useful information.)

b. The income statement for Club Med also differs from U.S. GAAP income statements.

    i.   List some of the notable differences.

    ii.   Which of Club Med's accounting principles would you be interested in reading about before you relied on their income statement?

Analysis

c. Based on your answer to part *a*, calculate the October 31, 1992 working capital balance and the current ratio for Club Med. Was the company in a position to pay its short-term obligations at October 31, 1992? Explain.

CLUB MÉDITERRANÉE S.A.

CONSOLIDATED BALANCE SHEET
in thousands of FRF

Assets	Gross	Depreciation or provisions	31/10/1992 Net	31/10/1991 Net	31/10/1990 Net
Intangible assets	1,024,276	122,558	901,718	748,572	203,931
Property and equipment	8,632,878	2,909,405	5,723,473	5,002,709	4,216,705
Financial assets:					
Investments in and advances to unconsolidated subsidiaries and affiliates	531,413	60,144	471,269	401,726	386,575
Loans and advances	196,264	–	196,264	191,077	183,497
Debenture receivables and deposits	169,898	–	169,898	184,681	134,567
Total fixed assets	10,554,729	3,092,107	7,462,622	6,528,765	5,125,275
Inventories and work in progress	169,446	141	169,305	159,959	154,845
Equipment and real estate	72,007	4,209	67,798	75,793	69,600
Trade accounts receivable	340,319	29,103	311,216	301,711	291,252
Other accounts receivable	859,504	5,587	853,917	739,798	739,766
Cash	665,930	–	665,930	873,230	824,874
Total current assets	2,107,206	39,040	2,068,166	2,150,491	2,080,337
Foreign currency translation adjustment	58,260	–	58,260	14,552	18,065
Total assets	12,720,195	3,131,147	9,589,048	8,693,808	7,223,677

Liabilities	31/10/1992 Net	31/10/1991 Net	31/10/1990 Net
Common stock	272,120	269,744	245,218
Additional paid-in capital	1,385,247	1,344,051	956,546
Retained earnings of parent company	1,128,616	1,366,191	1,194,916
Retained earnings of subsidiaries and affiliates	640,737	647,119	420,322
Minority interests	506,766	490,398	370,174
Group net income excluding minority int.	161,261	(17,326)	395,463
Total shareholders' equity and minority interests	4,094,747	4,100,177	3,582,639
Provisions and allowances	177,264	118,825	158,188
Bonds, banks and other loans	3,594,859	2,809,590	1,940,007
Trade accounts payable	379,398	483,922	379,128
Amounts received for future vacations	312,322	332,933	347,487
Other accounts payable	1,010,961	838,610	806,714
Total debt	5,297,540	4,465,055	3,473,336
Foreign currency translation adjustment	19,497	9,751	9,514
Total liabilities	9,589,048	8,693,808	7,223,677

CLUB MÉDITERRANÉE S.A.

CONSOLIDATED INCOME STATEMENT
in thousands of FRF

	31/10/1992	31/10/1991	31/10/1990
Revenues	8,251,049	7,841,939	8,181,608
Other income	103,916	87,285	45,417
	8,354,965	7,929,224	8,227,025
Operating expenses			
Purchases	3,243,892	2,877,094	3,366,664
External services	2,327,328	2,345,764	2,050,655
Taxes other than income	148,755	161,296	130,943
Salaries other than fringe benefits	1,890,730	1,810,951	1,749,260
Other operating expenses	45,544	26,581	17,006
Depreciation	444,543	391,987	355,063
Amortization, net	(19,415)	36,789	2,502
	8,081,377	7,650,462	7,672,093
Operating income	273,588	278,762	554,932
Financial income	94,661	131,776	148,579
Financial expenses	246,403	371,027	212,248
Foreign currency translation gains (losses)	(57,083)	24,183	24,668
Net financial charge	(208,825)	(215,068)	(39,001)
Income before extraordinary items, minority interests and income tax	64,763	63,694	515,931
Extraordinary gains			
Asset disposals	213,980	32,161	37,801
Other	59,553	68,435	16,504
	273,533	100,596	54,305
Extraordinary losses			
Net book value of assets sold	101,751	22,536	36,305
Other	38,381	37,776	6,522
	140,132	60,312	42,827
Net extraordinary gains	133,401	40,284	11,478
Income before tax	198,164	103,978	527,409
Provision for income tax	23,265	20,066	47,458
Net income of fully-integrated companies	174,899	83,912	479,951
Net income from equity companies	34,414	(22,898)	(33,308)
Consolidated net income	209,313	61,014	446,643
Minority interests	36,065	66,912	51,119
Group net income (ex. minority interests) before depreciation of goodwill	173,248	(5,898)	395,524
Net depreciation of goodwill	11,987	11,428	61
Group net income	161,261	(17,326)	395,463

CLUB MÉDITERRANÉE S.A.

CONSOLIDATED STATEMENT OF CASH FLOW
in thousands of FRF

	31/10/1992	31/10/1991	31/10/1990
Cash Flow from Operating Activities			
Net income (including minority interests)	197,326	49,586	446,582
Depreciation	456,529	403,415	355,124
Provisions	(16,273)	142,383	(22,630)
Gain (loss) on sale of fixed assets	(122,229)	(9,625)	(1,496)
Other	276	22,517	42,342
Funds generated by operations	515,629	608,276	819,922
(Increase) decrease in inventories	4,486	(9,951)	(19,624)
Decrease (increase) in trade and other receivables	(117,562)	(83,744)	20,092
Increase in accounts payable and advances	42,199	110,150	43,341
Changes in working capital requirements	(70,877)	16,455	43,809
Net cash provided by operating activities	444,752	624,731	863,731
Cash Flows from Investing Activities			
Acquisition of intangible assets	(133,841)	(92,133)	(35,643)
Acquisition of property and equipment	(1,010,191)	(638,969)	(774,447)
Acquisition of financial assets			
—Investments in affiliated companies*	(453,289)	(288,370)	(309,562)
—Other financial assets	(32,814)	(40,160)	(3,311)
Prepaid expenses	(45,452)	(866)	(710)
	(1,675,587)	(1,060,498)	(1,123,673)
Proceeds of fixed assets disposals	223,450	36,549	56,553
Investment subsidies received	2,194	3,455	3,531
Net cash provided (used) by investing activities	(1,449,943)	(1,020,494)	(1,063,589)
Cash Flows from Financing Activities			
Capital increases	62,065	424,613	11,694
Dividends paid	(104,434)	(138,138)	(153,242)
Proceeds from issuance of long-term debt	1,680,830	507,097	352,021
Repayment of long-term debt	(742,277)	(174,023)	(343,921)
Proceeds of long-term loans	5,251	62,959	23,689
Increases in long-term loans	(31,062)	(31,188)	(67,468)
Net cash provided (used) by financing activities	870,373	651,320	(177,227)
Total cash flow	(134,818)	255,557	(377,085)
Impact of foreign exchange fluctuations	(18,393)	46,829	(83,770)
Effect of changes in list of integrated companies	9,706	(326,570)	(44,049)
Net cash flow	(143,505)	(24,184)	(504,904)
Cash at beginning of year	460,116	484,300	989,204
Cash at end of year	316,611	460,116	484,300
Net change in cash	(143,505)	(24,184)	(504,904)

* Mainly including acquisition of village landlords (Dieulefit, Pompadour, Kos, Tignes) and acquisition of a minority stake by the Club in Situr and Forum Voyages.

CLUB MÉDITERRANÉE S.A.

NOTES TO THE CONSOLIDATED FINANCIAL STATEMENTS

Note 11. Bonds, Banks and Other Loans

	Opening amounts	Closing amounts
Long-term debts	2,396,477	3,245,541
Due to banks	413,113	349,318
	2,809,590	3,594,859

Leasing operations account for FRF 810,959,000 of aggregate long-term debt at year-end, against FRF 765,172,000 at the start of the year.

Long-term debts consist of the following:

By repayment currency:		By maturity date:	
French franc (inc. franc zone)	2,214,152	1992/1993	414,498
US dollar	355,603	1993/1994	128,780
Swiss Franc	256,212	1994/1995	174,108
Australian dollar	156,072	1995/1996	131,653
Tunisian dinar	44,351	1996/1997	113,274
Japanese yen	42,327	1997/1998 and beyond	2,283,228
Austrian schilling	39,592		
Italian lira	33,205		
Moroccan dirham	28,486		
Spanish peseta	26,257		
Malaysian Ringgit	21,086		
ECU	11,719		
Portuguese escudo	11,069		
Greek drachma	2,273		
Turkish pound	2,135		
Egyptian pound	979		
Others	23		
Total	3,245,541	Total	3,245,541

* The floating rate portion of debt represented 27% of total debt at year-end, against 53% at the start of the year.

* FRF 817,951 of long-term debt was secured by collateral and mortgages at year-end, against FRF 730,103,000 at the start of the year.

During the year, the parent company issued convertible bonds with a redemption premium amounting to FRF 1,001,000,000 (made up of 1,820,000 bonds with a par value of FRF 550) with an annual coupon of 6.5%, for a maximum of 7 years and 3 months. These bonds are convertible at all times without restriction or obligation, on the basis of one share for one bond.

This loan is recorded under debts in the balance sheet, with the exception of bonds already converted (25 at October 31, 1992) recorded under capital and additional paid-in capital.

Food Lion, Inc.—Preparation of Financial Statements

Food Lion, Inc. operates a chain of retail food supermarkets in fourteen states, principally located in the Southeast. The Company competes with national, regional, and local supermarket chains, supercenters, discount food stores, single unit stores, convenience stores and warehouse clubs. The Company's stores sell a wide variety of groceries, produce, meats, dairy products, seafood, frozen food, deli/bakery and non-food items such as health and beauty aids and other household and personal products. Warehousing and distribution facilities, including a transportation fleet, are also owned and operated by the Company. On December 28, 1996, 1,112 Food Lion stores were in operation employing 27,924 full-time and 45,246 part-time workers.

Learning Objectives
- Determine how economic events affect a company's financial statements.
- Record economic events and prepare a simple set of financial statements.
- Understand the concepts of accrual, deferral, and reclassification.

Note: to complete this case you will need to develop a simple computerized spreadsheet. The structure of the two-page spreadsheet follows immediately after the case questions. Be sure to enter the opening (i.e., December 30, 1995) and closing (i.e., December 28, 1996) balances into the balance sheet accounts on the first page of your spreadsheet. The income statement accounts on the second page should have opening balances of $0. All figures are in thousands of dollars. You should incorporate the following logic into the spreadsheet:

- The row labeled "subtotal" should be set up so that each cell equals the sum of the opening balance and the transactions in that column. If you enter the data for transactions 18 and 20, your subtotals should equal the ones on the sample spreadsheet.
- The row labeled "difference" should be set up so that each cell equals the sum of the opening balance, the transactions, the adjustments and reclassifications less the ending balance in that column. If you enter the data for transactions 18 and 20, your differences should equal the ones on the sample spreadsheet.
- The column labeled "Retained Earnings" should be set up so that each cell equals that row's *net* value from the income statement accounts on the second page. That is, every income statement item will simultaneously have an effect on retained earnings: sales will increase retained earnings and expenses will decrease retained earnings. See transaction 20—which has already been entered—for an example.

A necessary, but not sufficient, condition for completing this assignment is to have "zero" differences between the beginning balances plus journal entry activity and the ending balances.

Concepts

a. Prior to examining the opening balance sheet, think about what a grocery chain does. What accounts do you expect to see on the balance sheet? Which are the major assets? Liabilities?

Process

b. Prepare journal entries, if necessary, for each of the following fiscal 1996 "transactions." All figures are in thousands of dollars.

   1. The company purchased $7,222,670 of groceries on account.

   2. The company made $8,476,918 of cash sales to customers.

   3. The company made $529,014 of credit sales to large institutional customers.

   4. The cost of the groceries sold was $7,071,925.

   5. The company paid $7,115,247 of accounts payable.

   6. The company paid cash for wages to employees and other operating expenses totaling $1,252,553.

   7. The company purchased property and equipment for $283,564 in cash.

8. A consulting firm issued a report stating that the "Food Lion" brand name is worth $500,000.

9. The company collected $505,846 of accounts receivable.

10. The company received $250,010 when it issued a short-term note payable.

11. The company repaid $83,420 of its long-term debt.

12. The company acquired the Kash N Karry food chain for $121,578 in cash. The purchase included inventory of $49,229, property, plant and equipment of $103,078, goodwill (an intangible asset) of $269,348. As well, Food Lion assumed Kash N Karry's noncurrent liabilities of $300,077.

13. Food Lion disposed of property with a book value of $27,930 for cash proceeds of $27,464. The difference is considered an operating loss on the income statement.

14. During fiscal 1996, the company paid bondholders $76,631 of interest.

15. Food Lion management signed a new labor agreement with its employees. The two-year agreement takes effect on January 1, 1997 and calls for total wage increases of $150,000 per year.

16. The company paid $12,258 to settle certain noncurrent liabilities.

17. The company issued additional shares of Class A common stock and received $3,086 in cash.

18. During the year the company had several other transactions. In particular, the company repurchased $44,345 worth of its own stock, converted $927 worth of debt to stock, signed additional long-term leases. These transactions have already been entered into the spreadsheet in aggregate. Only the stock repurchase transaction affected cash.

19. The company declared and paid $52,310 of dividends.

20. The company paid income tax and recorded deferred tax assets and liabilities. These transactions have already been entered into the spreadsheet.

21. On December 28, 1996, the company paid $33,660 for a one year casualty and property insurance policy that covers calendar 1997.

c. Post the journal entries for the transactions to the spreadsheet. Note that some of the spreadsheet headings for liability and shareholders' equity accounts are in summary form.

d. Prepare an unadjusted trial balance from the subtotal line on the first page of the spreadsheet.

e. Based on the transactions you recorded in parts *b* and *c*, list at least three adjustments or reclassifications that need to be made prior to preparing the final financial statements.

f. Prepare journal entries for the following "adjustments and reclassifications."

22. Food Lion employees took a physical count of inventory on December 28, 1996. The cost of goods in the company's possession on that date was $1,065,743.

23. The last payday for the company was December 22, 1996. Employees had earned, but the company had not yet paid, $49,229 of additional wages and profit sharing through December 28, 1996.

24. On December 30, 1995, the casualty and property insurance premium of $23,344 (covering fiscal 1996) was paid and recorded as "prepaid expense" (on the balance sheet) by Food Lion. Adjust for this expired insurance premium at December 28, 1996.

25. Depreciation and amortization expense was $165,286 for the fiscal year.

26. $7,911 of the long-term debt and long-term leases are due on or before December 31, 1997.

27. A review of the company's long-term debt indicated that $3,889 of interest had accrued but had not yet been paid.

28. In December, 1996, an independent appraiser determined that the value of certain of the company's assets (recorded as property, plant and equipment) were overstated by $9,587 and that this impairment of value is permanent.

g. Post the journal entries for the adjustments and reclassifications to the spreadsheet.

h. Prepare the December 28, 1996 balance sheet. Use the headings from page one of your spreadsheet as the account titles.

i. Construct an income statement for the year ended December 28, 1996. Use the headings from page two of your spreadsheet as the account titles.

j. For each of the transactions that involve cash, indicate whether the transaction would appear in the "operating," "investing," or "financing" section of the statement of cash flows.

FOOD LION, INC.
Balance Sheet accounts (Figures in $000's)

	Cash & Cash Equivalents	Receivables	Inventories	Prepaid Expenses & Other	Property, at Cost, Less Depreciation	Goodwill & Noncurrent Assets	Current Liabilities	Noncurrent Liabilities	Contributed Capital	Retained Earnings
December 30, 1995 Balances	70,035	127,995	881,021	73,362	1,491,069	1,783	698,695	844,060	237,568	864,942
Transactions:										
1.										
2.										
3.										
4.										
5.										
6.										
7.										
8.										
9.										
10.										
11.										
12.										
13.										
14.										
15.										
16.										
17.										
18. Leases, debt, and stock	-44,345				97,595	12,703	31,500	77,871	-4,412	-39,006
19.										
20. Income tax expense	-155,422			25,789		3,511	5,578			-131,700
21.										
Subtotal	-129,732	127,995	881,021	99,151	1,588,664	17,997	735,773	921,931	233,156	694,236
Adjustments:										
22.										
23.										
24.										
25.										
26.										
27.										
28.										
December 28, 1996 Balances	102,371	151,163	1,065,743	109,467	1,772,503	287,345	1,154,235	1,118,419	236,242	979,696
Difference	-232,463	-23,168	-184,722	-10,316	-183,839	-269,348	-418,462	-196,488	-3,086	-285,460

FOOD LION, INC. Income Statement accounts (Figures in $000's)	Net Sales	Cost of Goods Sold	Selling & Admin. Expenses	Depreciation & Amortization	Asset Impairment	Interest expense	Income Tax Provision (expense)
December 30, 1995 Balances	0	0	0	0	0	0	0
Transactions:							
1.							
2.							
3.							
4.							
5.							
6.							
7.							
8.							
9.							
10.							
11.							
12.							
13.							
14.							
15.							
16.							
17.							
18. Leases, debt, and stock							
19.							131,700
20. Income tax expense							
21.							
Subtotal	0	0	0	0	0	0	131,700
Adjustments:							
22.							
23.							
24.							
25.							
26.							
27.							
28							
December 28, 1996 Balances	9,005,932	7,087,177	1,325,592	165,286	9,587	80,520	131,700
Difference	-9,005,932	-7,087,177	-1,325,592	-165,286	-9,587	-80,520	0

Black & Decker—Adjusting Journal Entries

The Black & Decker Corporation is a large, international manufacturer and marketer of home and commercial products. These products include power tools, household appliances, security hardware, lawn and garden equipment, plumbing accessories, and information systems and services.

Learning Objectives
- Use financial statement information to infer underlying transactions.
- Analyze the year over year change in balance sheet accounts and explain what transactions and events caused the account to increase and to decrease.
- Understand which balance sheet and income statement accounts are commonly linked together in transactions.
- Understand the difference between transaction and adjusting journal entries.
- Discover the economic significance of the three types of adjusting journal entries.
- Prepare common types of transaction and adjusting journal entries.

Refer to the 1993 financial statements of the Black & Decker Corporation. Each part of this case is independent. Restrict the account titles used in your answers to those used in the Black & Decker financial statements.

Concepts

a. To prepare accrual-based financial statements, adjustments must be made to a company's accounts. This is accomplished with adjusting journal entries.

    i.   What types of transactions or events necessitate year-end adjustments to the inventory account?

    ii.   What types of transactions or events necessitate year-end adjustments to the accounts receivable account?

    iii.   What types of transactions or events necessitate year-end adjustments to the other accrued liabilities account?

    iv.   Aside from those mentioned in parts *a. i.* to *a. iii.*, which of Black and Decker's balance sheet accounts are most likely to require adjusting journal entries? Explain.

Process

b. For each financial statement account in quotations, provide the account balance disclosed in Black & Decker's 1993 financial statements. Provide a journal entry that reflects the activity in the account in 1993. Except as noted, for each part, assume that the company recorded a single (summary) journal entry.

    i.   "Revenues—Product sales." Assume that all sales were on account.

    ii.   "Revenues—Information systems and services." Assume that all this revenue was on account.

    iii.   "Cost of revenues—Information systems and services." State any assumptions you make.

    iv.   "Interest expense." The net "Interest expense" line item is actually the result of two different journal entries: one for interest income and one for interest expense. Record these two journal entries separately. Assume the transactions were cash-based.

    v.   "Common stock" and "Capital in excess of par value." The entry was made when the company issued 417,088 new shares of stock for cash on December 15, 1993.

    vi.   "Property, plant and equipment." You will need to make two journal entries. Assume that the company did not dispose of any "Property, plant and equipment" during 1993.

Footnote 6 to the Black and Decker financial statements indicates that accumulated depreciation was $821.4 and $814.3 at December 31, 1993 and 1992, respectively. Assume that all fixed asset purchases were made with cash.

c. Provide the adjusting journal entries required to obtain the final account balances disclosed in the 1993 financial statements if the following balances appeared in the December 31, 1993 unadjusted trial balance.

   i. The unadjusted trial balance had a balance of $1,400 for "Inventories."

   ii. The unadjusted trial balance had a balance of $600 for "Other accrued liabilities." Provide some examples of the type of expenses that might give rise to this type of year-end adjusting journal entry.

   iii. The unadjusted trial balance had a balance of $297.8 for "Postemployment Benefits."

   iv. The unadjusted trial balance had a balance of $0 for "Amortization of goodwill" ("Amortization of goodwill" is an income statement account included among the various "Cost of revenues" accounts). Assume that the company did not purchase or dispose of any Goodwill ("Goodwill" is a balance sheet account) during the year.

   v. The unadjusted trial balance had a balance of $0 for "Restructuring costs (credits)"—an income statement account. More than one journal entry is required. To simplify this part, assume that when the company records restructuring expense, the corresponding credit is to the "Other accrued liabilities" account. (*Hint*: refer to the accompanying note to the financial statements entitled, Restructuring.)

Analysis

d. Set up a T-account for the "Inventories" information presented in the Black and Decker financial statements. (*Hint*: the 1993 opening balance for inventory comes from the 1992 balance sheet.) Assume that the "Inventories" amount on the balance sheet only refers to items sold through "Product sales." Using only information from the income statement and balance sheet, determine the total debits to the inventory account made during 1993. What do these debits represent?

THE BLACK & DECKER CORPORATION AND SUBSIDIARIES

CONSOLIDATED STATEMENT OF EARNINGS (EXCERPTS)
(Millions Of Dollars Except Per Share Data)

	Year Ended	
	Dec. 31, 1993	Dec. 31, 1992
Revenues		
Product sales	$4,121.5	$4,045.7
Information systems and services	760.7	733.9
Total Revenues	4,882.2	4,779.6
Cost of revenues		
Products	2,657.4	2,577.2
Information systems and services	575.1	550.3
Marketing and Administrative expenses	1,320.7	1,310.5
Restructuring costs (credits)	(6.3)	142.4
Operating Income	335.3	199.2
Interest expense (net of interest income of $8.3 for 1993, $10.8 for 1992, and $19.4 for 1991)	171.7	216.8
Other expense	7.7	11.4
Earnings (Loss) Before Income Taxes, Extraordinary Item, and Cumulative Effects of Changes in Accounting Principles	155.9	(29.0)
Income taxes	60.7	44.3
Net Earnings (Loss) Before Extraordinary Item and Cumulative Effects of Changes in Accounting Principles	95.2	(73.3)
Extraordinary loss from early extinguishment of debt	—	(22.7)
Cumulative effect to January 1, 1993, of change in accounting principle for postemployment benefits	(29.2)	—
Cumulative effect to January 1, 1992, of change in accounting principle for postretirement benefits	—	(249.8)
Cumulative effect to January 1, 1992, of change in accounting principle for income taxes	—	12.2
Net Earnings (Loss)	$ 66.0	$ (333.6)
Net Earnings (Loss) Applicable to Common Shares	$ 54.4	$ (345.2)

THE BLACK & DECKER CORPORATION AND SUBSIDIARIES

CONSOLIDATED BALANCE SHEET
(Millions Of Dollars)

	Dec. 31, 1993	Dec. 31, 1992
Assets		
Cash and cash equivalents	$ 82.0	$ 66.3
Trade receivables, less allowances of $38.5 ($49.9 for 1992)	832.1	815.0
Inventories	728.9	746.8
Other current assets	121.1	155.0
Total Current Assets	1,764.1	1,783.1
Property, Plant and Equipment	796.2	755.7
Goodwill	2,333.6	2,492.1
Other Assets	416.7	361.0
	$5,310.6	$5,391.9
Liabilities and Stockholders' Equity		
Short-term borrowings	$ 332.3	$ 350.7
Current maturity of long-term debt	163.1	104.6
Trade accounts payable	369.3	320.9
Other accrued liabilities	643.8	713.9
Total Current Liabilities	1,508.5	1,490.1
Long-Term Debt	2,069.2	2,108.5
Deferred Income Taxes	47.9	42.3
Postemployment Benefits	319.3	297.8
Other Long-Term Liabilities	316.8	379.2
Stockholders' Equity		
Convertible preferred stock (outstanding: Dec. 31, 1993, and Dec. 31, 1992—150,000 shares)	150.0	150.0
Common stock (outstanding: Dec. 31, 1993—83,845,194 shares, Dec. 31, 1992—83,428,106 shares)	41.9	41.7
Capital in excess of par value	1,034.8	1,028.6
Retained earnings (deficit)	(57.5)	(78.4)
Equity adjustment from translation	(120.3)	(67.9)
Total Stockholders' Equity	1,048.9	1,074.0
	$5,310.6	$5,391.9

See Notes to Consolidated Financial Statements

THE BLACK & DECKER CORPORATION AND SUBSIDIARIES

NOTE 2: RESTRUCTURING

During 1992, the Corporation commenced a restructuring of certain of its operations and accrued costs of $142.4 million. Of this amount, $98.9 million related to the Corporation's decision to reorganize Dynapert, the Corporation's printed circuit board assembly equipment business, including the withdrawal from the manufacturing of surface-mount machinery in Europe. Costs associated with the Dynapert restructuring included the write-off of goodwill, write-down of property, plant and equipment, termination of leases, employee severance, and anticipated losses during the withdrawal period. The remainder of the restructuring plan included a reduction of manufacturing capacity of other businesses at a cost of $43.5 million. These costs related predominantly to operations in Europe and included the write-down of property, plant and equipment to net realizable value, relocation and transfer costs, and employee severance and related costs.

During 1993, the Corporation substantially completed its restructuring plan related to Dynapert by withdrawing from the manufacture of surface-mount machinery. In addition, during the fourth quarter of 1993, the Corporation sold the Dynapert through-hole business at a gain of $19.4 million, which has been reflected as a credit to restructuring costs in 1993. Also during 1993, the Corporation sold its Corbin Russwin commercial hardware business at a gain of $15.9 million, which has been reflected as a credit to restructuring costs. The combined 1993 revenues and operating income of the two businesses, including the surface-mount machinery business that was liquidated, amounted to $112.5 million and $9.0 million, respectively, compared to revenues and operating loss of $138.1 million and $(3.3) million, respectively, in 1992. In 1993, the Corporation realized cash proceeds of approximately $108 million from the sale of Dynapert and Corbin Russwin, which were used to reduce debt.

Restructuring costs for 1993 also included a charge of $29.0 million for the closure and reorganization of certain manufacturing sites. These costs primarily included the write-down of property, plant and equipment to net realizable value and employee severance and related costs. Of the total amount, approximately $10 million represents cash spending. These plant actions are part of the Corporation's continuing effort to identify opportunities to improve its manufacturing cost structure. These actions will be substantially completed during 1994.

Liz Claiborne Inc.—Transactions & Financial Statements

> *Liz Claiborne, Inc. is a designer and marketer of women's apparel and related items, with collections designed for the work and leisure-time needs of the career woman. The Company also designs sportswear and furnishings for men and markets fragrances and cosmetic items. Products are manufactured to the Company's specifications in the United States and abroad and are marketed through leading department and specialty stores and other channels in the United States, Canada, the United Kingdom and a number of other international markets. Liz Claiborne's principal lines are generally considered designer fashion, but at a price which offers consumers unusually high quality and value.*

Learning Objectives
- Record basic transactions, adjusting journal entries, and closing entries.
- Prepare a balance sheet and income statement.

Refer to the 1995 financial statements of Liz Claiborne, Inc.

Process

a. Open T-accounts for each balance sheet and income statement line item (i.e., for the permanent accounts: 8 asset T-accounts and 10 liability and owners' equity T-accounts; for the temporary accounts: 6 T-accounts). Enter the December 31, 1994 balance sheet amounts as the opening balance for fiscal 1995 and post the following 1995 transactions (figures in thousands of dollars):

1. Inventory costing $1,261,289 was purchased on account during the year.

2. During the year, sales of $2,081,630 were made, all on account.

3. The cost of merchandise sold during 1995 was $1,250,000.

4. The company collected cash of $2,115,343 from its customers for sales previously recorded as accounts receivable.

5. Cash of $1,298,561 was used to pay suppliers for goods previously received on account.

6. Cash of $112 was used to repay principal on the long-term debt.

7. Property and equipment were acquired on account (accounts payable) for $37,491.

8. Dividends declared and paid in cash were $33,627.

9. The company purchased $200,000 of marketable securities for cash and sold $75,804 of marketable securities for cash. There was no gain or loss on these transactions.

10. The company paid $63,975 for 3,312,234 shares of its own common stock. This is known as treasury stock. It is recorded at cost as a debit in the owners' equity section of the balance sheet.

11. The following represents a *single* composite journal entry for all remaining transactions during the year. Record the entry in the appropriate accounts:

(Dr.)	Other Current Assets	20,000	
(Dr.)	Selling, General and Admin. Exp.	546,733	
(Dr.)	Provision for Income Taxes (Exp.)	76,200	
(Dr.)	Accrued Expenses	1,475	
(Dr.)	Capital in Excess of Par Value	21,639	
(Dr.)	Retained earnings	2,812	
(Cr.)	Cash		611,569
(Cr.)	Other Assets		6,006
(Cr.)	Income Taxes Payable		4,754
(Cr.)	Deferred Income Taxes		5,670
(Cr.)	Investment and Other Income		12,884
(Cr.)	Put Warrants		25,283
(Cr.)	Deferred Income Tax Benefits		2,312
(Cr.)	Cumulative Translation Adjustment		381
	TOTAL	668,859	668,859

Explanation: to record all other activity for fiscal 1995

b. Prepare an unadjusted trial balance as at December 30, 1995 using the ending balances in the T-accounts obtained in part *a*.

c. Prepare 1995 adjusting journal entries for the following items and post them to the T-accounts prepared in part *a*.

   12a. Liz Claiborne employees counted the company's merchandise inventory on December 30, 1995. The cost of inventory in stock on that day was $393,363.

   12b. Assume that all of the activity in the "other current assets" account is related to the company's insurance policies. The unadjusted amount in "other current assets" (*Hint*: $96,864) represents the beginning balance for prepaid insurance premiums plus all cash payments for insurance during the year. At December 30, 1995, the amount of insurance that had not expired was $77,710.

   12c. The company recorded $34,584 of depreciation—part of selling, general, and administration expenses—on the property and equipment.

d. Prepare an adjusted trial balance as at December 30, 1995 using the ending balances in the T-accounts obtained after recording the adjustments listed in part *c*.

e. Prepare the 1995 income statement.

f. Close the temporary accounts and provide the 1995 closing entry.

g. Prepare the December 30, 1995 balance sheet.

Analysis

h. Calculate the year-over-year percentage change in Net Sales for 1994 and 1995. Comment on this trend.

i. Comment on the level of inventory in 1995 compared to 1994 and 1993. (Inventory in 1993 was $436,593 and total assets were $1,238,341.) What conclusions do you draw from this trend?

j. The following excerpts are from an article entitled "It was a Tough Year for Sales" by Susan Hasty for the June 1996 edition of *Apparel Industry Magazine* (AIM). In light of these excerpts, how would you interpret the sales and inventory trends identified in parts *h* and *i*, above?

> The 1996 AIM Top 100 sewn products companies listing reflects more the tough year that 1995 was than the brighter reality currently unfolding. A revenue ranking based largely on 1995 sales, the 1996 AIM 100 does not reflect the resurgence in apparel sales that has occurred in the first two quarters of this year.
>
> It does, however, reflect an industry caught in turmoil, as manufacturers scrambled to cut inventories and bring production in line with diminishing demand. Eight major retail chains filed for bankruptcy in 1995, and the after-effects ripped through the wholesale softgoods market like a twister. By year's end, 99,400 apparel workers were jobless, the largest contraction in 14 years.
>
> The tailored clothing segment, already made vulnerable by high costs and changing consumer preferences, was especially hard-hit.
>
> Those manufacturers that were heavily domestic in production also were hit hard as they struggled to compete with cheaper imports for a disinterested consumer's dollar.
>
> Who prospered? The litany of industry woes continues through every segment, but there were bright spots. Despite the abysmal retail environment, there were companies that excelled.
>
> Children's wear maker OshKosh B'Gosh posted its best year since 1993. Sales were up 19% to $432 million, while profits rose 55% to $11 million. Women's sportswear leader Liz Claiborne posted slightly lower sales for the year at $2 billion, but profits were up 49% to $127 million.
>
> What do these ... companies have in common? All are well into major re-engineering programs to slash cycle times and eliminate nonvalue-added events in the production pipeline.
>
> The re-engineering efforts are clearly paying off at OshKosh and Claiborne. Both have been plagued in recent years by staleness in their designs and failure to supply retailers' orders on a timely basis. Now Claiborne is working on its fifth consecutive quarter of improved profits, and OshKosh is well on its way to returning to the record levels of profitability it experienced in the early years of this decade.

k. What additional information might an investor in Liz Claiborne seek in order to evaluate the company's future level of profitability?

Reprinted courtesy of Apparel Industry Magazine.

LIZ CLAIBORNE, INC. AND SUBSIDIARIES
CONSOLIDATED BALANCE SHEETS

All amounts in thousands except share data

	December 30, 1995	December 31, 1994
Assets		
Current Assets:		
Cash and cash equivalents		$ 71,419
Marketable securities		258,932
Accounts receivable—trade		159,766
Inventories		423,003
Deferred income tax benefits		32,547
Other current assets		76,864
Total current assets		1,022,531
Property and Equipment—net		236,560
Other Assets		30,571
		$1,289,662

?

	December 30, 1995	December 31, 1994
Liabilities and Stockholders' Equity		
Current Liabilities:		
Accounts payable		$ 138,581
Accrued expenses		156,924
Income taxes payable		7,894
Total current liabilities		303,399
Long-Term Debt		1,227
Deferred Income Taxes		2,052
Commitments and Contingencies		
Put Warrants		—
Stockholders' Equity:		
Preferred stock, $ .01 par value, authorized shares—50,000,000, issued shares—none		—
Common stock, $1 par value, authorized shares—250,000,000, issued shares—88,218,617		88,219
Capital in excess of par value		56,714
Retained earnings		1,164,850
Cumulative translation adjustment		(1,637)
		1,308,146
Common stock in treasury, at cost—14,526,922 shares in 1995 and 11,214,688 shares in 1994		(325,162)
Total stockholders' equity		982,984
		$1,289,662

The accompanying notes to consolidated financial statements are an integral part of these statements.

LIZ CLAIBORNE, INC. AND SUBSIDIARIES

CONSOLIDATED STATEMENTS OF INCOME

All dollar amounts in thousands except per common share data

Fiscal Years Ended

	December 30, 1995	December 31, 1994	December 25, 1993
Net Sales		$2,162,901	$2,204,297
Cost of goods sold		1,407,694	1,453,381
Gross Profit		755,207	750,916
Selling, general and administrative expenses		604,421	568,286
Restructuring charge		30,000	
Operating income		120,786	182,630
Investment and other income—net		10,663	16,151
Income before provision for income taxes and cumulative effect of a change in accounting principle	?	131,449	198,781
Provision for income taxes		48,600	73,500
Income before cumulative effect of a change in accounting principle		82,849	125,281
Cumulative effect of a change in the method of accounting for income taxes		–	1,643
Net Income		$ 82,849	$ 126,924
Earnings per Common Share: income before cumulative effect of a change in accounting principle		$ 1.06	$ 1.54
Cumulative effect of a change in the method of accounting for income taxes		–	.02
Net Income per Common Share		$ 1.06	$ 1.56
Dividends Paid per Common Share		$ .45	$ .44

The accompanying notes to consolidated financial statements are an integral part of these statements.

Maya, Inc.—Return on Investment

Evaluating investment alternatives involves the use of time-value-of-money concepts. In this case, the cash flows associated with Maya, Inc.—a hypothetical company—are evaluated.

Learning Objectives
- Calculate the present value and the future value of a single payment.
- Calculate the present value of a stream of payments.
- Understand the effect of compounding on present and future values.
- Determine the effective interest rate underlying a series of cash flows.

Concepts

a. The following questions test your understanding of time-value-of-money concepts.

    i.   Would you rather receive $100 today or $100 in exactly one year? Explain your choice.

    ii.   What is a lump sum payment?

    iii.   What is an annuity? What is an ordinary annuity (annuity in arrears)? What is an annuity due?

    iv.   How does compound interest differ from simple interest?

    v.   Define the "return" on a share of stock.

Process

b. On September 1, 1990, you bought 100 shares of Maya, Inc. for $45/share. Assume that you expect to earn a 12% return compounded annually on this investment.

    i.   What minimum share price would achieve this return by August 31, 1991?

    ii.   What minimum share price would achieve this return by August 31, 1992?

    iii.   What minimum share price would achieve this return by August 31, 1995?

c. On August 31, 1995, you decide to sell these shares. After commissions and fees, you received $5,000. What compound annual rate of return did you earn on your investment?

d. You would like to earn a 12% return, compounded annually, on your investments.

    i.   How much would you be willing to pay per share for 100 shares of Maya that you expect to be able to sell for a total of $5,000 in one year?

    ii.   How much would you be willing to pay per share for 100 shares of Maya that you expect to be able to sell for a total of $5,000 in two years?

    iii.   How much would you be willing to pay per share for 100 shares of Maya that you expect to be able to sell for a total of $5,000 in five years?

    iv.   How much would you be willing to pay per share for 100 shares of Maya that you expect to sell for $5,000 in one year and that pay an annual dividend of $4.50 per share? (Assume that you receive the dividend one year from the date of purchase.)

    v.   How much would you be willing to pay per share for 100 shares of Maya that you expect to sell for $5,000 in five years and that pay an annual dividend of $4.50 per share? (Assume that you receive the dividends each year on the anniversary of the date of purchase.)

(Note: This problem is easier to solve if you use a financial calculator or spreadsheet.)

Hydron Technologies Corporation—Lease or Buy

The decision to invest in fixed assets includes a decision about how to finance the investment. A popular alternative to outright purchase is a leasing arrangement. Making the lease or buy decision involves consideration of both qualitative factors and quantitative factors including the time-value-of-money.

Learning Objectives
- Use present value and discounted cash flow techniques to make a lease or buy decision.
- Calculate the effective periodic discount rate for use in a net present value analysis.
- Determine the qualitative factors that must be considered in such a decision.

Hydron Technologies Corporation is in the process of replacing the computer system it uses for sales and marketing. The area vice president has decided on the system to be installed; however, she can't decide whether to lease or buy the system. The company plans to use the system for six years. However, leasing can only be arranged for three years. The monthly lease payments are $305 and the company must pay the first and last of the 36 installments at the inception of the contract. The contract includes a $8,500 "purchase option" at the expiration of the lease (i.e., at the end of the 36th month). Because the company plans to use the system for six years, it would purchase the system after three years. Alternatively, the company could purchase the equipment for $15,000.

Concepts

a. What is a lease?

b. What types of equipment are typically leased by companies?

Analysis

c. If Hydron's annual discount rate is 8.5%, compounded monthly, which option is most cost effective? Ignore any potential income tax effects.

d. In addition to the quantitative analysis performed in part *c*, what qualitative issues need to be considered in deciding whether to lease or buy the computer?

(Note: This problem is easier to solve if you use a financial calculator or spreadsheet.)

Cadillac DeVille—Implicit Interest Rate

Automobile advertisements often tout special lease arrangements or low interest rates. General Motors' Cadillac division is no exception. Savvy consumers are able to evaluate the savings using discounted cash flow techniques.

Learning Objectives
- Use present value and discounted cash flow techniques to make an investment decision.
- Compare financing alternatives for the investment.
- Critically evaluate the claims made in an advertisement.

Refer to the accompanying Cadillac DeVille advertisement which appeared in a recent issue of The *Wall Street Journal*.

Analysis

a. Explain how the company arrived at the $1,521 savings figure. Does a single up-front payment of $10,875 really "save" $1,521 on a new DeVille?

b. What is the implicit interest rate of the lease? That is, what monthly discount rate is required to make the two leasing options equivalent? How would you choose between the options?

c. Assume that you can borrow money from your bank at 10% per year, compounded monthly. How much would you save by using the up-front payment plan instead of the SmartLease?

(Note: This problem is easier to solve if you use a financial calculator or spreadsheet.)

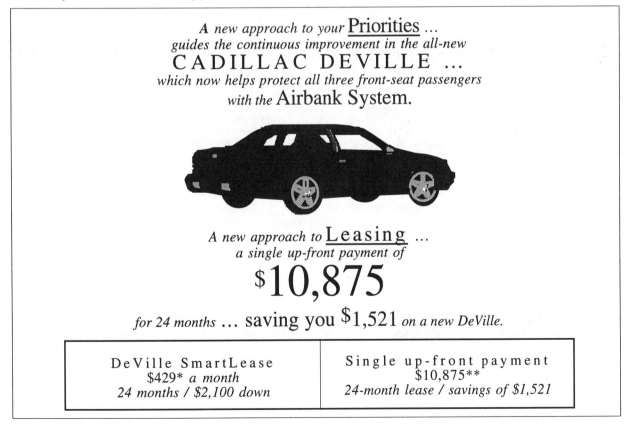

A new approach to your <u>Priorities</u> ...
guides the continuous improvement in the all-new
CADILLAC DEVILLE ...
which now helps protect all three front-seat passengers
with the Airbank System.

A new approach to <u>Leasing</u> ...
a single up-front payment of

$10,875

for 24 months ... saving you $1,521 *on a new DeVille.*

DeVille SmartLease	Single up-front payment
$429* a month	$10,875**
24 months / $2,100 down	24-month lease / savings of $1,521

Maple Leaf Gardens—Valuation

Maple Leaf Gardens, Ltd. is in the entertainment business in Canada through its ownership and operation of the Toronto Maple Leaf Hockey Club and the arena facilities at 60 Carlton Street, Toronto, Ontario. It derives all of its operating income from these assets. Its revenues are derived from four sources: (1) admission fees from Maple Leaf games, (2) broadcast, promotional and advertising rights, (3) building use fees from other than Maple Leaf games and (4) merchandising and concession sales.

Learning Objectives
- Explain how important assumptions underlying GAAP are reflected in the financial statements.
- Understand the difference between net book value and fair market value.
- Perform and interpret basic balance sheet and income statement-based valuation analyses.

Refer to the 1992 financial statements of Maple Leaf Gardens, Ltd.

Concepts

a. A number of important assumptions and principles underlie financial statements prepared using generally accepted accounting principles. Draw on these assumptions as you answer the following questions.

   i. At May 31, 1992 a large portion of the shares of Maple Leaf Gardens were owned by the Molson Companies (owners of North America's oldest brewery). Are Molson's brewing assets and operations included in the Maple Leaf Gardens financial statements? Why or why not?

   ii. Speculate as to why Maple Leaf Gardens has a May 31 year end.

   iii. What is accrual-basis accounting? How does it differ from cash-basis accounting? Does Maple Leaf Gardens use accrual-basis or cash-basis accounting?

   iv. Financial statements are normally prepared under the assumption that the entity is a going concern. Explain what is meant by a "going concern" and how that assumption affects figures on the Maple Leaf Gardens financial statements.

   v. According to International Accounting Standards, the matching concept states:

      "Expenses are recognised in the income statement on the basis of a direct association between the costs incurred and the earning of specific items of income. This process involves simultaneous or combined recognition of revenues and expenses that result directly and jointly from the same transactions or other events. However, the application of the matching concept does not allow the recognition of items in the balance sheet which do not meet the definition of assets or liabilities."

      Provide examples of how the matching concept has been applied to the Maple Leaf Gardens financial statements.

   vi. What is meant by the term "revenue recognition"? When does Maple Leaf Gardens recognize revenue?

Analysis

b. For this question, refer only to the May 31, 1992 financial statements of Maple Leaf Gardens.

   i. What is the net book value of Maple Leaf Gardens, Ltd. (the company, not the individual assets or liabilities) at May 31, 1992? What does this amount represent?

   ii. Which individual accounts will most likely have fair market values that differ significantly from the book values recorded on the balance sheet? What accounting principles give rise to these differences?

iii. Assume that the fair market value of the company's National Hockey League (NHL) franchise is equal to the amount charged new teams entering the League (see Note 3—assume that $1 Cdn = $.75 U.S.). In addition, as the land owned by the company is a prime parcel of real estate located in downtown Toronto, assume that the book value of the land is only 15% of its fair market value. Finally, assume that all other amounts recorded on the balance sheet approximate their fair market values. Based on your restated balance sheet, what is the net fair market value of Maple Leaf Gardens, Ltd. at December 31, 1992?

iv. Compare your responses to parts *b i.* (net book value) and *b iii.* (fair market value of net assets) of this question. Why are these amounts so different? What do the differences represent?

c. One way that financial analysts approximate the value of a company is by applying a "multiple" to the company's net income. This multiple is commonly known as the Price-Earnings (or PE) multiple. It is a crude, but easy to apply valuation method. For example, if a company had net income per share of $5 and analysts considered the appropriate PE multiple to be 12, then the share would be valued at $60. The fair market value of the company would be $60 times the number of outstanding shares.

Conceptually, a PE multiple is akin to a present value of an annuity factor. When an annuity payment is constant and is expected to be perpetual (i.e., an infinite number of equal payments), the present value of an annuity factor converges to $(1 / r)$. Thus, a PE multiple of 12 is equivalent to $1 / .08333$. Applying the multiple to a given level of earnings is equivalent to valuing the company as though it would provide an annuity of "earnings" every year, for an infinite number of years, using 8.333% as the discount rate.

i. If Maple Leaf Gardens' shares are trading at a PE multiple (based on 1992 net income) of 15.38, what is the implied discount rate? (Assume, as above, an annuity paying a constant amount for an infinite number of years.) Does this discount rate seem reasonable? Explain.

ii. Based on a PE multiple of 15.38, use Net Income from Continuing Operations to estimate the fair market value of Maple Leaf Gardens' equity. In using Net Income from Continuing Operations, what assumption are you implicitly making?

iii. PE multiples can also accommodate growing series of earnings. If earnings are predicted to grow at a constant rate, *g*, then the PE multiple can be written as $(1 + g) / (r - g)$. Assume that Maple Leaf Gardens' shares have a PE multiple of 15.38 and that you believe that 15% is an appropriate discount rate for the company given its risk level. What is the implied growth rate embedded in the PE multiple of 15.38? Explain how you would assess whether the growth rate was reasonable.

iv. Compare your responses to parts *b iii.* (fair market value of net assets) and *c ii.* (fair market value of the equity). Why are these amounts so different? What do the differences represent?

d. Refer to the *Wall Street Journal* article ("Ontario Pension Fund..." April 5, 1994) that appears after Maple Leaf Gardens, Ltd.'s financial statements. Compute the fair market value of the company based on information provided in the article. Why is this value different than the value computed in part *c ii.* above?

MAPLE LEAF GARDENS, LIMITED

(Incorporated under the laws of Ontario)
BALANCE SHEETS
May 31, 1992 and 1991

	1992	1991
Assets		
Current assets:		
Cash and interest-bearing deposits	$ 4,622,115	$ 4,657,808
Accounts Receivable (note 7)	1,597,442	1,402,951
Prepaid expenses and other assets	456,254	232,877
	6,675,811	6,293,636
Fixed assets (note 2):		
Land, building and equipment	22,310,285	18,524,076
Less accumulated depreciation	(9,325,069)	(8,538,294)
	12,985,216	9,985,782
Deferred charges	1,400,428	363,052
Deferred income taxes	468,980	647,980
Franchises:		
National Hockey League	100,001	100,001
	$21,630,436	$17,390,451

AUDITORS' REPORT TO THE SHAREHOLDERS

We have audited the balance sheets of Maple Leaf Gardens, Limited as at May 31, 1992 and 1991 and the statements of income, retained earnings and changes in cash flow for the years then ended. These financial statements are the responsibility of the Corporation's management. Our responsibility is to express an opinion on these financial statements based on our audits.

We conducted our audits in accordance with generally accepted auditing standards. Those standards require that we plan and perform an audit to obtain reasonable assurance whether the financial statements are free of material misstatements. An audit includes examining, on a test basis, evidence supporting the amounts and disclosures in the financial statements. An audit also includes assessing the accounting principles used and significant estimates made by management, as well as evaluating the overall financial statement presentation.

In our opinion, these financial statements present fairly, in all material respects, the financial position of the Corporation as at May 31, 1992 and 1991 and the results of its operations and the changes in its financial position for the years then ended in accordance with generally accepted accounting principles.

Toronto, Canada
July 3, 1992

PEAT MARWICK THORNE
Chartered Accountants

MAPLE LEAF GARDENS, LIMITED

BALANCE SHEETS

May 31, 1992 and 1991

	1992	1991
Liabilities and Shareholders' Equity		
Current liabilities:		
Accounts payable and accrued liabilities	$ 3,766,694	$ 3,068,605
Income and other taxes payable	1,349,313	2,010,252
Deferred income	1,379,629	1,211,184
	6,495,636	6,290,041
Net liabilities of discontinued operations (note 4)	—	191,575
Shareholders' equity:		
Capital stock:		
Authorized: 5,000,000 common shares		
Issued: 3,677,900 common shares	36,779	36,779
Retained earnings	15,098,021	10,872,056
	15,134,800	10,908,835
Commitments and contingencies (note 5)		
	$21,630,436	$17,390,451

See accompanying notes to financial statements.

MAPLE LEAF GARDENS, LIMITED

STATEMENTS OF INCOME
Years ended May 31, 1992 and 1991

	1992	1991
Revenue from operations	$41,191,271	$36,263,051
Investment and other income	947,356	1,195,984
	42,138,627	37,459,035
Operating expenses other than the undernoted	32,901,247	26,417,459
Operating income before the following	9,237,380	11,041,576
Depreciation	786,774	603,297
Amortization	1,243,892	969,804
	7,206,714	9,468,475
N.H.L. expansion fees (note 3)	4,958,571	3,276,927
Income before income taxes	12,165,285	12,745,402
Income taxes (note 6)		
Current	4,818,000	5,263,000
Deferred	179,000	150,000
	4,997,000	5,413,000
Income before gain from discontinued operations	7,168,285	7,332,402
Gain from discontinued operations (note 4)	—	167,000
Net income	$ 7,168,285	$ 7,499,402
Earnings per share:		
Before discontinued operations	$1.95	$1.99
Net income	$1.95	$2.04

See accompanying notes to financial statements.

STATEMENTS OF RETAINED EARNINGS

	1992	1991
Years ended May 31, 1992 and 1991		
Retained earnings, beginning of year	$10,872,056	$15,693,619
Net income	7,168,285	7,499,402
	18,040,341	23,193,021
Dividends—$0.80 per share in 1992 and $3.35 per share in 1991, including a special dividend of $2.75 per share	2,942,320	12,320,965
Retained earnings, end of year	$15,098,021	$10,872,056

See accompanying notes to financial statements.

MAPLE LEAF GARDENS, LIMITED

STATEMENTS OF CHANGES IN CASH FLOW
Years ended May 31, 1992 and 1991

	1992	1991
Cash provided by (used for):		
(a) Operations	$ 8,974,103	$10,335,168
(b) Investments	(6,067,476)	(2,886,185)
Dividends	(2,942,320)	(12,320,965)
Decrease during the year	(35,693)	(4,871,982)
Cash and interest-bearing deposits, beginning of year	4,657,808	9,529,790
Cash and interest-bearing deposits, end of year	$ 4,622,115	$ 4,657,808
(a) Operating Activities:		
Net income	$ 7,168,285	$ 7,499,402
Items not involving cash from operations:		
Depreciation and amortization	2,030,666	1,573,101
Deferred income taxes	179,000	150,000
Gain from discontinued operations	—	(167,000)
	9,377,951	9,055,503
Other non-cash working capital items	(403,848)	1,279,665
	$ 8,974,103	$10,335,168
(b) Investment activities:		
Purchase of fixed assets	$(3,786,208)	$(2,005,197)
Increase in deferred charges	(2,281,268)	(720,608)
Advances to fund discontinued operations	—	(160,380)
	$(6,067,476)	$(2,886,185)
Other non-cash working capital items:		
Increase in accounts receivable	$(194,491)	$(65,176)
Decrease (increase) in prepaid expenses and other assets	(223,377)	40,185
Increase (decrease) in accounts payable and accrued liabilities	506,514	(593,114)
Increase (decrease) in income and other taxes payable	(660,939)	1,675,134
Increase in deferred income	168,445	222,636
	$ (403,848)	$ 1,279,665

See accompanying notes to financial statements.

MAPLE LEAF GARDENS, LIMITED

1. Significant Accounting Policies:

(a) Segmented reporting:

The Corporation's directors have determined that the dominant industry segment of the Corporation is its operations in the entertainment industry in Canada.

(b) Fixed assets:

Land, building and equipment are stated at cost. Depreciation is provided on a diminishing balance basis using rates of 5% per annum for buildings and 20% and 30% per annum for equipment.

(c) Deferred charges:

The Corporation has entered into employment contracts with certain of its employees which provide for substantial initial cash payments. These cash payments are reflected on the balance sheet as deferred charges and are being amortized over the life of the employment contracts. Any unamortized balance relating to a terminated contract is written off in the year of termination.

(d) Franchises:

The National Hockey League ("N.H.L.") franchise represents the costs of purchase of the predecessor hockey club which upon reorganization eventually became the Toronto Maple Leaf Hockey Club and a member of the N.H.L. The franchise rights are recorded as an intangible asset.

(e) Deferred income:

Deferred income represents payments received in advance for events and services which have not yet been performed. These amounts will be recorded in income as earned.

(f) Revenue:

Included in revenue from operations are:

(i)   the gross revenues for those attractions for which the Corporation is the promoter;

(ii)   the Corporation's share of the gross revenues for those attractions for which the Corporation is a co-promoter; and

(iii) a minimum rent or percentage of the gate (whichever is greater) in those cases where the Corporation offers its facility as a landlord.

2. Fixed Assets:

	Cost	1992 Accumulated depreciation	Net book value	1991 Net book value
Land	$ 358,811	$ —	$ 358,811	$ 358,811
Building	16,618,730	5,583,670	11,035,060	7,842,780
Equipment	5,297,874	3,741,399	1,556,475	1,008,142
Construction-in-progress	34,870	—	34,870	776,049
	$22,310,285	$9,325,069	$12,985,216	$9,985,782

3. N.H.L. Expansion Fees:

In 1991, the N.H.L. granted expansion franchises to groups representing the cities of San Jose, California, Tampa Bay, Florida, and Ottawa, Ontario. These franchises were granted on a conditional basis as both the N.H.L. and the owners of the expansion franchises were obligated to meet certain conditions. Accordingly, the Corporation chose to record the fees as income only when both the cash was received and the conditions which the N.H.L. was obligated to meet had been met. The fee charged for these individual franchises was $50,000,000 (U.S.), including a deposit (non-refundable) of $5,000,000 (U.S.) upon the granting of the franchise, and the fee was allocated equally to the then existing 21 N.H.L. member clubs. The initial expansion fees from the Tampa Bay and Ottawa franchises and the entire expansion fee of the San Jose franchise were received by the N.H.L. in 1991 and were distributed to its member clubs. The Corporation's share of these fees amounted to $3,276,927 (Cdn.) which was recorded as income in 1991.

In 1992, the Corporation received its share of the remaining expansion fees due from the groups representing the cities of Tampa Bay and Ottawa, aggregating $4,958,571 (Cdn.) which has been recorded as income.

4. Loss (Gain) from Discontinued Operations:

Effective May 31, 1990, the Board of Directors approved formal plans to sell or otherwise dispose of the Davis Printing Division. The operations were closed on October 15, 1990 and its assets, excluding accounts receivable were sold to a third party on October 27, 1990 for cash proceeds in the amount of $470,000. The gain from discontinued operations represented the result of recording a provision for loss in excess of the required amount which excess, net of income tax, was recorded as income in 1991. The net liabilities of discontinued operations was principally a provision for future rental payments, the net liability for which has been included in accounts payable in 1992.

5. Commitments and Contingencies:

(a)   There are a number of actions in Canada against the Corporation for unpaid amounts and breach of contract, among other things. While these actions are being defended, it is not possible, in the opinion of the Corporation's solicitors, to predict the outcome or the extent of any liability should any of the actions ultimately be successful.

There are a number of actions in the United States against the N.H.L. and its member clubs for damages and costs allegedly sustained by plaintiff by reason of, amongst other items, alleged violations of United States anti-trust laws.

In addition to the above described litigation, certain retired N.H.L. players have commenced actions, both in the United States and Canada, seeking to set aside an amendment to the N.H.L. Club Pension Plan and Trust Agreement. The players are seeking the reallocation of approximately $32 million plus interest to the Pension Plan. Should this application be successful in whole or in part, individual N.H.L. member clubs will have to pay into the Pension Society those amounts which would otherwise have been payable. The total exposure is not shared equally by all N.H.L. member clubs because of their respective date of entry into the league. The Corporation is not able to determine its share of any potential liability in this matter at this time.

While the actions described in the preceding two paragraphs are being defended, it is not possible, in the opinion of the N.H.L's solicitors, to predict the outcome or the extent of any liability should any of the actions ultimately be successful.

No provision has been made in the accounts for any legal awards which may be incurred as a result of the above described actions. Any amounts awarded against the Corporation as a result of the actions will be recorded as a prior period adjustment in the year of such award.

(b) \In discussions with another N.H.L. member club, Revenue Canada has indicated they intend to challenge the tax filing position adopted by the corporation and fellow Canadian member clubs on expansion receipts received in 1991 and 1992. The Corporation intends to oppose this proposed reassessment and believes they have very strong defenses on this matter. Should Revenue Canada reassess in the manner they are proposing and should this reassessment be upheld, the exposure to the Corporation at present, including interest, would be approximately $750,000. Any amounts awarded against the Corporation as a result of this proposed reassessment will be recorded as a prior period adjustment in the year of such award.

(c) At May 31, 1992, the Corporation has planned capital expenditures for the 1993 fiscal year of approximately $2,000,000.

(d) The Corporation has an employment contract with its chief operating officer. This agreement has a remaining term of four years and provides for salary continuation of $625,000 on expiration which is being amortized over the initial five-year term of the employment contract. This agreement provides the employee with the right to terminate this contract if a change in control as defined occurs and his responsibilities are altered in a meaningful fashion. The agreement also provides for severance arrangements if the employee is terminated without cause. The compensation payable to this executive, should the contract be terminated as described above, is approximately $1.5 million.

6. Income Taxes:

Income tax expense differs from the amount which would be obtained by applying the combined Federal/Provincial statutory income tax rate to the respective year's income before income taxes. The difference results from the following items:

	1992	1991
Statutory income tax rate	44.3%	44.3%
Increase (decrease) in tax rate resulting from:		
Non-taxable portion of N.H.L. expansion fees	(3.3)	(2.2)
Non-deductible expenses	0.1	0.4
Effective income tax rate	41.1%	42.5%

7. Related Party Transactions:

(a) The Corporation earned revenue on the sale of television and radio rights to N.H.L. hockey, promotional and other advertising activities in the amount of approximately $8,108,000 (1991 $7,100,000) from the Molson Companies Limited which beneficially owns approximately 19.9% of the common shares of the Corporation. These shares were acquired under an option agreement, are held in trust and are subject to cross-ownership rules of the N.H.L. These cross-ownership rules may require the Molson Companies Limited to dispose of these shares.

Included in accounts receivable is an amount of $458,061 (1991—$499,544) due from this party.

(b) During 1992, the Corporation licensed arena space for a number of entertainment events to BCL Entertainment Corp., a corporation partially owned by a related party. This party owned a significant interest in a holding corporation until November, 1991. This holding corporation in turn owns a majority interest in the Corporation. Subsequent to November, 1991, BCL Entertainment Corp. is no longer considered to be a related party. Total license revenue from this corporation amounted to approximately $116,000 in 1992 (1991—$220,000).

Ontario Pension Fund To Buy 49% of Owner Of NHL Maple Leafs

By a WALL STREET JOURNAL *Staff Reporter*

TORONTO—An Ontario teachers pension fund agreed to pay about 61 million Canadian dollars (US $44 million) for a 49% stake in **Maple Leaf Gardens** Ltd., the owner of the Toronto Maple Leafs hockey team.

The purchase will be made under a takeover offer, valued at about C$125 million, for Maple Leaf Gardens by its chairman and chief executive officer, Steve Stavro. Mr. Stavro agreed to acquire the 19.9% stake in Maple Leaf Gardens held by Molson Cos., and the 60.3% stake held by the estate of former Maple leaf Gardens owner Harold Ballard. Mr. Stavro also plans to bid for the remaining public shares of Maple Leaf Gardens. All shareholders will receive C$34 per share.

After the acquisition, Mr. Stavro will sell the 49% stake to the **Ontario Teachers Pension Plan Board**, which invests the C$34 billion of pension funds held by Ontario's 200,000 teachers. Toronto Dominion Bank also will purchase a small stake, but control of Maple Leaf Gardens will rest with Mr. Stavro.

Several pension fund managers and consultants to professional sports teams said they didn't know of any pension funds owning stakes in a pro team.

"We didn't really look at it as a pro team," said George Engman, vice president of investment research and development for the pension fund. Maple Leaf Gardens is a well-run business with good cash flow, he said. Two fund officials will be named to the board of Maple Leaf Gardens, but the fund isn't interested in influencing the day-to-day operations of the hockey club, Mr. Engman said.

Maple Leaf Gardens jumped C$4, or 14%, to C$32.50 in light trading on the Toronto Stock Exchange yesterday.

The deal is subject to regulatory and National Hockey League approval.

GTE—Persistence of Earnings

GTE Corporation is a large, international telecommunications company. GTE provides local telephone service to over 20 million customers in 40 states, Canada, the Dominican Republic, and Venezuela. In addition, the company provides mobile-cellular telecommunications products and services throughout the United States.

Learning Objectives
- Explain why income statements are "classified."
- Understand the concept of earnings persistence.
- Perform a basic income statement-based valuation for a company reporting losses.

Refer to the 1992 financial statements of GTE Corporation.

Concepts

a. What are the major classifications on an income statement?

b. Explain why, under generally accepted accounting principles, companies are required to provide financial statements with "classified" income statements. Consider in particular whether items on the income statement are equally persistent. That is, are all the elements on GTE's 1992 income statement expected to recur in future years?

Analysis

c. Net income from continuing operations can be used to approximate the average annual cash flow from an entity over an extended period of time. As GTE Corporation incurred a $754 million net loss during 1992, how would you use the income statement to value the company? Keep your answers to parts *a* and *b* in mind as you answer this question.

d. Using a 6.5% annual discount rate, a 40-year time horizon, and information in the 1992 income statement, estimate the current value of GTE.

e. Estimate the market value of the company by multiplying the number of common shares outstanding by the closing common stock market price at December 31, 1992 ($34.63). Compare this estimate to your answer to part *d*. What factors might cause these two estimates to differ? (*Note*: the number of *outstanding* shares equals the number of issued shares less the number of shares in treasury.)

GTE CORPORATION AND SUBSIDIARIES

CONSOLIDATED BALANCE SHEETS

	December 31	
	1992	1991
	(Millions of Dollars)	
Assets		
Current Assets:		
Cash and temporary cash investments	$ 354	$ 517
Receivables, less allowances of $ 154 and $ 115	3,565	3,663
Inventories	814	910
Deferred income tax benefits	111	206
Net assets of discontinued operations	1,114	1,299
Other	338	971
Total current assets	6,296	7,566
Property, Plant and Equipment, at cost:		
Telephone subsidiaries	43,354	41,846
Accumulated depreciation	(16,054)	(14,877)
	27,300	26,969
Other subsidiaries	4,075	3,766
Accumulated depreciation	(1,555)	(1,412)
	2,520	2,354
Total property, plant and equipment, net	29,820	29,323
Investments and Other Assets:		
Franchises, goodwill and other intangibles	2,167	2,180
Investments in unconsolidated companies	1,361	1,374
Deferred charges	1,683	1,114
Long-term receivables and other assets	817	880
Total investments and other assets	6,028	5,548
Total assets	$42,144	$42,437

GTE CORPORATION AND SUBSIDIARIES
CONSOLIDATED BALANCE SHEETS

	December 31	
	1992	1991
	(Millions of Dollars)	
Liabilities and Shareholders' Equity		
Current Liabilities:		
Short-term obligations, including		
current maturities	$ 2,692	$ 2,291
Accounts and payrolls payable	1,609	1,895
Accrued taxes	754	612
Dividends payable	447	407
Accrued interest	297	332
Advance billings	399	384
Other	1,313	1,305
Total current liabilities	7,511	7,226
Long-Term Debt	14,182	16,049
Reserves and Deferred Credits:		
Deferred income taxes	3,071	4,612
Deferred investment tax credits	414	507
Employee benefit obligations	4,436	524
Other	1,203	880
Total reserves and deferred credits	9,124	6,523
Minority interests in equity of subsidiaries	1,077	1,123
Preferred Stock, subject to mandatory redemption	174	203
Shareholders' Equity:		
Preferred stock	112	459
Common stock - shares issued 945,147,187		
and 911,311,077	47	46
Amounts paid in, in excess of par value	7,134	6,232
Reinvested earnings	3,621	5,977
Guaranteed ESOP obligation	(657)	(673)
Common stock held in treasury - 5,616,851		
and 22,403,669, at cost	(181)	(728)
Total shareholders' equity	10,076	11,313
Total liabilities and shareholders' equity	$42,114	$42,437

See accompanying summary on page 30 for details of preferred stock and long-term debt.

See Notes to Financial Statements.

GTE CORPORATION AND SUBSIDIARIES

CONSOLIDATED STATEMENTS OF INCOME

| | Years Ended December 31 | | |
	1992	1991	1990
	(Millions of Dollars)		
Revenues and Sales:			
Telephone operations	$15,862	$15,652	$15,393
Telecommunications products and services	4,122	3,969	3,764
Total revenues and sales	19,984	19,621	19,157
Costs and Expenses:			
Telephone operations	11,828	11,695	11,622
Telecommunications products and services (*)	3,940	3,842	3,748
Merger consummation and integration costs	—	342	—
Total costs and expenses	15,768	15,879	15,370
Operating income	4,216	3,742	3,787
Other Deductions:			
Interest expense—net	1,332	1,384	1,296
Other - net	130	167	170
Total	1,462	1,551	1,466
Income before income taxes	2,754	2,191	2,321
Income tax provision	967	662	698
Income from continuing operations	1,787	1,529	1,623
Discontinued operations	(48)	51	92
Extraordinary charge—early retirement of debt	(52)	—	—
Cumulative effect of accounting changes	(2,441)	—	—
Net income (loss)	(754)	1,580	1,715
Preferred stock dividends of parent	26	37	44
Net income (loss) applicable to common stock	$ (780)	$ 1,543	$ 1,671
Earnings (loss) per common share			
Continuing operations	$ 1.95	$ 1.69	$ 1.82
Discontinued operations	(.05)	.06	.11
Extraordinary charge - early retirement of debt	(.06)	—	—
Cumulative effect of accounting changes	(2.70)	—	—
Consolidated	$ (.86)	$ 1.75	$ 1.93
Average common shares (in millions)	905	882	867

(*) Includes cost of sales of $ 3,143, $ 3,160 and $ 3,082 for the years 1992-1990, respectively.

See Notes to Financial Statements.

GTE CORPORATION AND SUBSIDIARIES

CONSOLIDATED STATEMENTS OF CASH FLOWS

	Years Ended December 31		
	1992	1991	1990
	(Millions of Dollars)		
Cash Flows from Operations:			
Income from continuing operations	$1,787	$1,529	$1,623
Adjustments to reconcile net income to net cash from continuing operations:			
Depreciation and amortization	3,289	3,254	3,189
Deferred taxes and investment tax credits	37	37	(3)
Change in current assets and current liabilities, excluding the effects of acquisitions and dispositions	(268)	(732)	(716)
Other-net	(13)	555	214
Net cash from continuing operations	4,832	4,643	4,307
Net cash from discontinued operations	–	141	83
Net cash from operations	4,832	4,784	4,390
Cash Flows from Investing:			
Capital expenditures	(3,909)	(3,965)	(4,158)
Acquisitions and investments	(84)	(1,132)	(2,122)
Proceeds from sales of businesses	662	177	36
Other-net	55	(104)	86
Net cash used in investing	(3,276)	(5,024)	(6,158)
Cash Flows from Financing:			
GTE common stock issued	1,513	412	452
Stock of subsidiaries issued	31	38	42
Long-term debt issued	590	3,958	2,046
Long-term debt and preferred stock retirements	(2,002)	(1,539)	(782)
Dividends to shareholders of parent	(1,572)	(1,447)	(1,229)
Preferred dividends of subsidiaries	(22)	(25)	(28)
Purchase of treasury shares	–	–	(241)
Increase (decrease) in short-term obligations, excluding current maturities	(254)	(1,094)	1,523
Other-net	(3)	(8)	41
Net cash provided from/(used in) financing	(1,719)	295	1,824
Increase (decrease) in cash and temporary cash investments	(163)	55	56
Cash and temporary cash investments:			
Beginning of year	517	462	406
End of year	$ 354	$ 517	$ 462

See Note 15 for supplemental cash flow disclosures.

See Notes to Financial Statements.

Curragh Inc.—Going Concern

Curragh Inc. is a Canadian resource company and a major producer of zinc and lead concentrates. Its shares are traded on the New York, Toronto and Montreal exchanges. In 1992, the Company suffered a mining disaster in which 26 lives were lost. The Company's ability to continue operations is in question.

Learning Objectives
* Read and understand going concern footnote disclosure.
* Identify evidence that financial statements are prepared under the going concern assumption.
* Critically evaluate disparate needs of financial statement users.

Refer to the 1992 Financial Statements, Auditors' Report, and Notes for Curragh, Inc.

Concepts

a. The company's ability to continue as a going-concern seems to be in question.

    i.   What evidence is there that Curragh's financial statements have been prepared under the assumption that the company *is* a going concern? Describe the problems with using "standard" generally accepted accounting principles (i.e., historical cost-based accounting) when the going-concern assumption is violated.

    ii.   What facts would lead the reader of Curragh's financial statements to conclude that the company may not be able to maintain operations?

    iii.   Identify the main users of these financial statements. For each user, comment on what their interests are and whether they are concerned about the Company's future operations.

b. The Auditors' Report, which was prepared in accordance with auditing standards generally accepted in Canada, makes reference to differences with U.S. standards. What are these differences and why might the Canadian auditors have included the reference in the audit report?

Analysis

c. Refer to the balance sheet included in Note 2.

    i.   What information is provided in this note? How does this information differ from the Consolidated balance sheet for Curragh?

    ii.   Why was this information presented in the financials?

    iii.   Prepare a proforma balance sheet for the Westray Mine at December 31, 1992. Comment on the financial position of the Westray Mine at December 31, 1992.

AUDITORS' REPORT

To the Shareholders of Curragh Inc.

We have audited the consolidated balance sheets of Curragh Inc. as at December 31, 1992 and 1991 and the consolidated statements of earnings, shareholders' equity and cash flows for each of the two years then ended and the year ended December 31, 1990. These financial statements are the responsibility of the Company's management. Our responsibility is to express an opinion on these financial statements based on our audit.

We conducted our audit in accordance with generally accepted auditing standards. Those standards require that we plan and perform an audit to obtain reasonable assurance whether the financial statements are free of material misstatement. An audit includes examining, on a test basis, evidence supporting the amounts and disclosures in the financial statements. An audit also includes assessing the accounting principles used and significant estimates made by management, as well as evaluating the overall financial statement presentation.

In our opinion, these consolidated financial statements present fairly, in all material respects, the financial position of the Company as at December 31, 1992 and 1991 and the results of its operations and its cash flows for each of the two years then ended and the year ended December 31, 1990 in accordance with generally accepted accounting principles which differ in certain respects from accounting principles generally accepted in the United States (see Note 17).

PRICE WATERHOUSE
Chartered Accountants
Toronto, Ontario
January 22, 1993

Comments by Auditor for U.S. Readers on Canada—U.S. Reporting Conflict

In the United States, reporting standards for auditors require the addition of an explanatory paragraph when the financial statements are affected by significant uncertainties such as that referred to in the attached balance sheets as at December 31, 1992 and 1991 and as described in Note 2 of the financial statements. Our report to the shareholders dated January 22, 1993 is expressed accordance with Canadian reporting standards which do not permit a reference to such an uncertainty in the auditors' report when the uncertainty is adequately disclosed in the financial statements.

PRICE WATERHOUSE
Chartered Accountants
Toronto, Ontario
January 22, 1993

CURRAGH INC.
CONSOLIDATED BALANCE SHEET

	December 31	
With comparative figures (in thousands of Canadian dollars)	1992	1991
Assets		
Current:		
Current Cash and temporary investments (Notes 2 and 4)	$12,558	$20,715
Accounts receivable and concentrates in transit (Note 2)	35,977	43,828
Materials and supplies (Note 2)	14,484	14,002
Other (Notes 2 and 8)	30,240	21,039
	93,259	99,584
Property, plant and equipment (Note 2 and 5)	394,141	408,351
Investments (Notes 2 and 7)	—	100,679
Other non-current assets (Notes 2 and 10 (a),(c))	7,842	13,891
	$495,242	$622,505
Liabilities and Shareholders' Equity		
Current		
Operating loans (Notes 2 and 9)	$ 24,334	$16,033
Accounts payable and accrued liabilities (Note 2)	44,702	34,210
Income and resource taxes payable (Note 2)	711	733
Current portion of long-term debt (Note 2)	16,070	27,807
	85,817	78,783
Westray limited recourse loans (Notes 2 and 10)	92,750	—
	178,567	78,783
Long-term debt (Notes 2 and 10)		
Senior notes, loan and leases	167,471	155,970
Other limited recourse project financing	11,367	133,258
Deferred income taxes (Notes 2 and 12)	4,659	38,012
Minority interest	—	9,774
Shareholders' equity:		
Share capital (Notes 2 and 13)	115,515	115,515
Retained earnings	17,663	71,934
Cumulative translation adjustment	—	19,259
Total shareholders' equity	133,178	206,708
	$495,242	$622,505

Financial position and future operations (Note 2)
Contingencies and commitments (Note 16)

CURRAGH INC.

CONSOLIDATED STATEMENT OF EARNINGS

With comparative figures (in thousands of Canadian dollars except share and per share amounts)	Year ended December 31,		
	1992	1991	1990
Sales of concentrate	$352,660	$ 225,245	$ 352,792
Treatment charges	(147,151)	(84,433)	(118,023)
Net Sales	205,509	140,812	234,769
Cost of Sales:			
Cost of products	151,330	106,514	116,902
Depletion, depreciation and amortization	51,349	30,348	26,367
General and administrative	26,510	20,571	22,720
Marketing and delivery	21,855	13,042	19,826
	251,044	170,475	185,815
Profit (loss) before other items	(45,535)	(29,663)	48,954
Other earnings and expenses:			
Interest expense	16,993	16,805	18,059
Interest income	(2,876)	(3,578)	(5,576)
Dividend income	—	—	(318)
Other expense (income) (Note 18)	4,297	(412)	(7,781)
	18,414	12,815	4,384
Earnings (loss) before taxes, equity earnings, loss on investments and extraordinary item	(63,949)	(42,478)	44,570
Income and resource taxes (Note 12)	26,307	14,080	(12,214)
Earnings (loss) before equity earnings, loss on investments and extraordinary item	(37,642)	(28,398)	32,356
Equity earnings (loss) in Asturiana (Notes 3 and 7)	—	(19,253)	(342)
Loss on write-down of investment in Asturiana (Notes 3 and 7)	—	(31,398)	—
Loss on sale of investment (Note 7)	—	(19,233)	—
Earnings (loss) before extraordinary item	(37,642)	(98,282)	32,014
Extraordinary item:			
Loss on write-down of Westray assets (net of deferred taxes of $5,500) (Note 6)	(16,629)	—	—
Net earnings (loss) for the year	$(54,271)	$(98,282)	$32,014
Average number of shares outstanding (Note 13)	32,126	32,126	28,518
Earnings (loss) per share before extraordinary item	$ (1.17)	$ (3.06)	$ 1.12
Net earnings (loss) per share (Note 13)	$ (1.69)	$ (3.06)	$ 1.12

CURRAGH INC.

CONSOLIDATED STATEMENT OF CASH FLOWS

With comparative figures (in thousands of Canadian dollars)

	Year ended December 31,		
	1992	1991	1990
Operating Activities:			
Earnings (loss) before extraordinary item	$(37,642)	$(98,282)	$32,014
Adjustments to reconcile earnings to net cash provided by operating activities			
Depletion, depreciation and amortization	51,349	30,348	26,367
Deferred income taxes	(27,853)	(15,853)	13,999
Dividends received from Asturiana	—	2,169	4,201
Equity loss in Asturiana	—	19,253	342
Loss on write-down of investment in Asturiana	—	31,398	—
Gain on dilution of shares in subsidiary	—	—	(2,852)
Loss on sale of investment	11	19,233	—
Unrealized exchange gains and losses	1,807	582	214
Changes in certain assets and liabilities —			
Accounts receivable and concentrates in transit	7,851	(19,522)	9,743
Materials and supplies	(482)	270	(6,043)
Other current assets	(9,201)	(8,780)	(2,614)
Accounts payable and accrued liabilities	10,492	(8,263)	13,710
Income and resource taxes payable	(22)	(88)	(928)
Net cash provided by (used in) operating activities	(3,690)	(47,535)	88,153
Investing Activities:			
Investments (Note 7)	63,877	17,429	76
Resource properties	(1,266)	(1,137)	(5,911)
Mill and equipment	(10,753)	(103,639)	(37,350)
Capitalized development costs	(54,065)	(42,676)	(47,277)
Westray insurance proceeds (Note 6)	16,000	—	—
Other assets	1,451	(3,463)	(5,790)
Net cash provided by (used in) investing activities	15,244	(133,486)	(96,252)
Financing Activities:			
Recourse debt financing —			
Bank borrowings	—	—	(164,806)
Notes and amounts due to related companies	1,492	—	(30,264)
Note payable to Cyprus Anvil Mining Corporation	(4,747)	(4,225)	(6,493)
Silver loan	—	(10,226)	(6,548)
Senior notes	—	(85)	149,633
Equipment lease financing	(524)	(981)	6,013
Proceeds for new marketing agreement	11,604	—	—
Other	(25)	(336)	(1,263)
Limited recourse debt financing —			
Province of Nova Scotia loan	—	—	3,850
Westray term loan	(9,650)	78,020	12,380
SA Dena Hes term and silver loans.	(30,090)	45,214	7,655
Net proceeds from share issues	—	—	90,912
Subsidiary share issue for cash	—	—	10,000
Net cash provided by (used in) financing activities	(31,940)	107,381	71,069
Net increase (decrease) in cash during the year	(20,386)	(73,640)	62,970
Cash and cash equivalents at beginning of year	8,610	82,250	19,280
Cash and cash equivalents at end of year	$(11,776)	$8,610	$82,250
Cash and cash equivalents defined:			
Cash and temporary investments	$ 12,558	$20,715	$74,725
Operating loans	(24,334)	(16,033)	—
Cash included with other assets (Note 10 (d))	—	3,928	7,525
Net cash and cash equivalents	$(11,776)	$8,610	$82,250

CURRAGH INC.

NOTES TO CONSOLIDATED FINANCIAL STATEMENTS
DECEMBER 31, 1992, 1991, 1990

1.   Business and Incorporation

Curragh Inc., (the Company), a Canadian resource company and one of Canada's significant exporters, is a major producer of zinc and lead concentrates. The Company was incorporated under the Business Corporations Act (Ontario), and in May, 1992 changed its name from Curragh Resources Inc, to Curragh Inc. Its shares are traded on the New York, Toronto and Montreal exchanges.

2.   Financial Position and Future Operations

In early 1992, it became apparent that the SA Dena Hes Joint Venture would comply with all the required physical completion tests but not the Protection Ratio (a test which determines the amount of debt the project can support by assessing metal prices, reserves, mining costs, capital costs and future cash flows) contained in the loan agreement with The Bank of Nova Scotia (the Bank). In addition, Hillsborough Resources Limited, the other Joint Venture partner, was unwilling to make further cash contributions. Consequently, the Company was required to make unplanned repayments of the term loan of $21,885,000 (U.S. $18,165,000) in addition to the scheduled $8,500,000 repayment in 1992.

On June 9, 1992, as a result of the Westray mine accident in May 1992, the Bank demanded repayment of the related limited recourse project loan. The Company consequently was required to repay its full obligation of $15,590,000 under the Company's loan indemnity to the Bank and, in December 1992, the federal government of Canada (Federal Government) paid the Bank the remaining $80,750,000 under the terms of the federal loan insurance program (see Note 10 (c)).

During the fourth quarter of 1992, prices for zinc and lead metal fell sharply and resulted in a significant reduction in cash flow from operations. As a result, the Company temporarily suspended mining operations at its zinc and lead mines in the Yukon in December 1992.

As a consequence of the aforementioned events, the Company used virtually all of its liquidity which had been reestablished in the first quarter of 1992 by realizing on its investment in Asturiana de Zinc, S.A. (Asturiana).

In order to meet ongoing obligations, the Company is continuing to process ore from stockpile and has, subsequent to year end, obtained a temporary bridge loan facility for $10,000,000 from the Bank (see Note 20).

The future of the Company is dependent on its ability to obtain additional financing in the near future in order to enable it to continue operations until the prices of zinc and lead return to normal levels. Although a number of initiatives to increase capital and restore liquidity were started in 1992, these had not been completed at December 31, 1992 and are ongoing. They include negotiations for a new partner in the Stronsay project, attempts to realize cash from the sale of unused assets and steps to raise additional equity.

The Company also continues to negotiate for $29,000,000 of financial support from the current Yukon government to fund the balance of the capital spending program needed to develop its new Grum ore body which is scheduled to commence production in 1993. This support, in the form of a loan guarantee, was originally approved in principle by the Federal Government and the previous Yukon government in April 1992. Final negotiations were suspended until the outcome of the Westray mine accident could be assessed and the new Yukon government had the opportunity to review the merits of the proposal.

The consolidated financial statements of the Company are presented on the basis of accounting policies applicable to a going concern which contemplates that the Company will continue in operations for the foreseeable future and will be able to realize its asset values and discharge its liabilities in the normal course of its operations. If additional capital or short-term financing cannot be obtained, the assumption that the Company will be able to continue as a going concern, at present market lead and zinc prices, may not be valid. It is expected however, that the Company's financing alternatives currently being pursued will resolve the Company's immediate financial difficulties.

Due to the Westray mine accident (see Note 6), the Company's underground mining permits in Nova Scotia have been suspended resulting in a standstill situation at the Westray mine. As a result of the Company's inability to control Westray coal division assets and the need to undertake a financial restructuring before operations recommence, the following information is presented to illustrate the base metal assets and liabilities of the Company and its net investments in Westray:

With comparative figures (in thousands of Canadian dollars)

	December 31, 1992	1991
Assets		
Current:		
Cash and temporary investments	$ 12,558	$ 12,465
Accounts receivable and concentrates in transit	35,977	43,571
Materials and supplies	11,393	11,682
Other	12,686	18,019
	72,614	85,737
Property, plant and equipment	296,226	293,513
Investment in Westray (net)	22,264	16,120
Other investments	—	100,679
Other non-current assets	7,842	13,891
	$398,946	$509,940
Liabilities and Shareholders' equity		
Current:		
Operating loans	$24,334	$11,033
Accounts payable and accrued liabilities	41,156	29,045
Income and resource taxes payable	711	733
Current portion of long-term debt	16,070	22,807
	82,271	63,618
Long-term debt		
Senior notes, loans and leases	167,471	155,970
Limited recourse project financing	11,367	35,858
Deferred income taxes	4,659	38,012
Minority interest	—	9,774
Shareholders' equity:		
Share capital	115,515	115,515
Retained earnings	17,663	71,934
Cumulative translation adjustment	—	19,259
Total shareholders' equity	133,178	206,708
	$398,946	$509,940

6. Westray Coal Mine

On May 9, 1992 there was an underground explosion which resulted in 26 fatalities and the suspension of mining operations at the Company's Westray coal mine ("Westray") in the Province of Nova Scotia, before commercial production was achieved.

Since the accident, the Company has incurred total costs of $14,797,000 in connection with the rescue effort, redevelopment planning, ongoing care and maintenance costs and legal fees. In addition, the Company lost $14,425,000 of underground production equipment and $8,907,000 of mine development expenditures. On December 31, 1992 the Company settled the insurance claim for $16,000,000 and has provided for a loss from the accident of $22,129,000 before deferred income taxes of $5,500,000. The Company is negotiating with the Federal Government as to the final recipient of the insurance proceeds.

The Company is in the process of taking several steps to reestablish operations at the Westray underground coal mine. These efforts will continue in 1993 and may be funded from the $16,000,000 insurance proceeds and cash flow from a small open-pit to be operated after required environmental approvals are obtained. As the Company is also a debtor in possession, a restructuring of the relationship between the various participants will be required. Reestablishment of underground mining requires the approval of the Nova Scotia Department of Labour.

Mattel, Inc.—Analyzing the Cash Flow Statement

> *Mattel designs, develops, manufactures, markets and distributes a broad variety of toy products on a worldwide basis. The Company's four strongest principal product lines are Barbie fashion dolls and doll clothing and accessories, Fisher-Price toys and juvenile products, the Company's Disney-licensed toys and die-cast Hot Wheels vehicles, each of which has broad worldwide appeal. Additional current principal product lines consist of Power Wheels battery-powered ride-on vehicles; large dolls; preschool toys, including See'N Say talking toys; and the Uno and Skip-Bo games.*

Learning Objectives
- Contrast and compare the information contained in the Statement of Cash Flows to the Income Statement.
- Identify the three components of the Statement of Cash Flows.
- Explain the reconciling current asset and liability items in the cash flows from operations section.
- Analyze the effects of errors and omissions on the cash flow statement.

Refer to the 1996 consolidated financial statements of Mattel, Inc.

Concepts

a. What information is provided by the statement of cash flows? How is this different from the information contained in the income statement?

b. How do each of the three sections of the statement of cash flows relate to the balance sheet?

Analysis

c. Note that the statement of cash flows includes a $62,152 increase in receivables during 1996. Explain why an *increase* in receivables is *subtracted* from net income to arrive at operating cash flows.

d. Note that the statement of cash flows includes a $50,007 increase in payables, other accrued liabilities and income taxes payable during 1996. Explain why an *increase* in accrued liabilities is *added* to net income to arrive at operating cash flows.

e. Assume that the controller of Mattel, Inc. forgot to record $50 million of dividends payable (due on February 1, 1997) which were declared on December 29, 1996.

    i. Provide the journal entry required to record this dividend.

    ii. How does not recording this transaction affect the operating, investing, and financing sections of the statement of cash flows?

f. Disregard the instructions and your answer to part *e*. Instead, assume that the controller forgot to record $40 million of sales on account during 1996.

    i. Provide the journal entry required to record this revenue.

    ii. What is the impact on pre-tax income of forgetting to record this journal entry?

    iii. What is the impact on net cash flows from operating activities? Investing activities?

MATTEL, INC. AND SUBSIDIARIES
CONSOLIDATED BALANCE SHEETS

(In thousands)	December 31, 1996	December 31, 1995
Assets		
Current Assets		
Cash	$ 500,625	$ 466,082
Marketable securities	—	17,375
Accounts receivable, less allowances of $14,354 at December 31, 1996 and $10,788 at December 31, 1995	732,307	679,283
Inventories	372,686	350,841
Prepaid expenses and other current assets	165,223	177,238
Total current assets	1,770,841	1,690,819
Property, Plant and Equipment		
Land	30,864	25,724
Buildings	207,382	192,323
Machinery and equipment	409,675	354,469
Capitalized leases	24,271	24,271
Leasehold improvements	59,908	51,629
	732,100	648,416
Less: accumulated depreciation	293,160	265,885
	438,940	382,531
Tools, dies and molds, net	140,673	116,783
Property, plant and equipment, net	579,613	499,314
Other Noncurrent Assets		
Intangible assets, net	407,444	422,796
Sundry assets	135,624	82,580
	$2,893,522	$2,695,509
Liabilities and Shareholders' Equity		
Current Liabilities		
Short-term borrowings	$ 20,485	$ 15,520
Current portion of long-term liabilities	106,069	33,215
Accounts payable	259,721	250,401
Accrued liabilities	406,344	410,362
Income taxes payable	167,749	138,183
Total current liabilities	960,368	847,681
Long-Term Liabilities		
6-7/8% Senior Notes	—	99,752
6-3/4% Senior Notes	100,000	100,000
Medium-Term Notes	220,000	220,000
Mortgage note	44,086	44,585
Other	121,281	108,322
Total long-term liabilities	485,367	572,659
Shareholders' Equity		
Common stock $1.00 par value, 600.0 million and 300.0 million shares authorized in 1996 and 1995, respectively; 279.1 million shares issued (a)	279,058	279,058
Additional paid-in capital	95,965	103,512
Treasury stock at cost; 8.1 million shares for 1996 and 3.6 million shares for 1995 (a)	(215,999)	(75,574)
Retained earnings (b)	1,353,551	1,041,735
Currency translation and other adjustments (b)	(64,788)	(73,562)
Total shareholders' equity	1,447,787	1,275,169
	$2,893,522	$2,695,509

Commitments and Contingencies (See accompanying notes.)
(a) Share data for 1995 has been restated for the effects of the five-for-four stock split distributed in March 1996.
(b) Since December 26, 1987 (Note 1).

MATTEL, INC. AND SUBSIDIARIES
CONSOLIDATED STATEMENTS OF INCOME

(In thousands, except per share amounts)	For the Year 1996	1995	1994
Net Sales	$3,785,958	$3,638,812	$3,205,025
Cost of sales	1,877,335	1,849,650	1,603,522
Gross Profit	1,908,623	1,789,162	1,601,503
Advertising and promotion expenses	614,433	584,497	516,485
Other selling and administrative expenses	647,112	603,061	536,443
Restructuring and integration charges	—	—	72,000
Interest expense	75,529	73,589	55,449
Other expense (income), net	25,808	(4,887)	27,494
Income Before Income Taxes	545,741	532,902	393,632
Provision for income taxes	168,100	175,100	137,800
Net Income	377,641	357,802	255,832
Preference stock dividend requirements	—	3,342	4,689
Net Income Applicable to Common Shares	$ 377,641	$ 354,460	$ 251,143
Primary Income Per Common and Common Equivalent Share			
Net income	$ 1.36	$ 1.26	$ 0.90
Average number of common and common equivalent shares	278,385	281,015	279,923
Dividends Declared Per Common Share	$ 0.24	$ 0.19	$ 0.15

The accompanying notes are an integral part of these statements.

MATTEL, INC. AND SUBSIDIARIES
CONSOLIDATED STATEMENTS OF CASH FLOWS

(In thousands)	1996	1995	1994
Cash Flows From Operating Activities:			
Net income	$ 377,641	$ 357,802	$ 255,832
Adjustments to reconcile net income to net cash flows from operating activities:			
Gain on sale of business	—	(9,142)	—
Depreciation	122,537	105,943	105,687
Amortization of intangibles	26,520	27,041	18,585
Increase (decrease) from changes in assets and liabilities:			
Accounts receivable	(62,152)	70,509	(155,265)
Inventories	(24,220)	(15,279)	(74,148)
Prepaid expenses and other current assets	13,464	3,400	(38,626)
Accounts payable, accrued liabilities and income taxes payable	50,007	(126,290)	215,403
Deferred compensation and other retirement plans	8,364	9,516	13,533
Deferred income taxes	1,411	(5,365)	6,966
Other, net	1,644	(12,643)	(1,415)
Net cash flows from operating activities	515,216	405,492	346,552
Cash Flows From Investing Activities:			
Purchases of tools, dies and molds	(88,677)	(89,730)	(75,285)
Purchases of other property, plant and equipment	(120,333)	(117,155)	(88,097)
Purchases of marketable securities	(8,000)	(29,154)	(29,032)
Purchase of other long-term investment	(25,114)	—	—
Proceeds from sales of other property, plant and equipment	6,007	10,903	12,221
Proceeds from sales of marketable securities	25,315	32,237	25,637
Proceeds from sale of business	—	21,129	—
Contingent consideration and investment in acquired businesses	(8,625)	(8,625)	(374,965)
Other, net	317	318	(89)
Net cash flows used for investing activities	(219,110)	(180,077)	(529,610)
Cash Flows From Financing Activities:			
Short-term borrowing, net	6,829	18,637	(5,966)
Issuance of Medium-Term Notes	—	139,500	110,500
Payment of Medium-Term Notes	(30,000)	—	—
Long-term foreign borrowing	(3,717)	(2,572)	(4,337)
Redemption of Fisher-Price term loan	—	—	(120,629)
Tax benefit of employee stock options exercised	26,300	8,500	23,923
Exercise of stock options and warrants	73,188	24,353	39,209
Purchase of treasury stock	(269,771)	(64,284)	(80,885)
Repurchase of Series F Preference Stock	—	(73,866)	—
Dividends paid on common and preference stock	(62,747)	(50,963)	(47,840)
Payment for tendered Fisher-Price warrants	—	—	(4,891)
Other, net	(1,012)	578	4,863
Net cash flows used for financing activities	(260,930)	(117)	(86,053)
Effect of Exchange Rate Changes on Cash	(633)	1,684	2,098
Net Increase (Decrease) in Cash	34,543	226,982	(267,013)
Cash at Beginning of Year	466,082	239,100	506,113
Cash at End of Year	$ 500,625	$ 466,082	$ 239,100

The accompanying notes are an integral part of these statements.

Frederick's of Hollywood—Statement of Cash Flows

Frederick's of Hollywood, Inc. is a specialty retailer, operating a chain of 206 women's intimate apparel stores throughout the United States. The Company also has a national mail order apparel business selling lingerie, bras, foundations, dresses, sportswear, leisurewear, swimwear, hosiery, specialty menswear and accessories. Frederick's of Hollywood purchases its merchandise from a variety of manufacturers.

Learning Objectives
- Understand the operations section of the statement of cash flows and how it ties into line items on the balance sheet and the income statement.
- Analyze year over year changes in balance sheet accounts.
- Infer non-cash transactions from balance sheet accounts and footnote disclosures.
- Provide journal entries associated with non-cash transactions.
- Recreate the "cash flow from operations" section of a statement of cash flows.

Refer to the 1996 financial statements of Frederick's of Hollywood.

Concepts

a. What are the two different methods for preparing the statement of cash flows. Which method does Frederick's use?

b. What are the three sections of the statement of cash flows?

c. What are "Cash equivalents?"

d. Net income is determined on an accrual basis. Yet, net income is the first item on the statement of cash flows. Explain this apparent inconsistency.

Process

e. Using information from the balance sheet, the income statement, and the footnotes only, determine the following components of Frederick's cash flow statement:

   i.   Net income.

   ii.   Depreciation and amortization. Provide the journal entry that Frederick's made to record this depreciation.

   iii. Capital expenditures. Provide the journal entry that Frederick's made to record these purchases.

   iv.   Loss on disposals of fixed assets. Assume that proceeds on the disposals and write-downs were $7,000. (*Hint*: Use one T-account for total gross property and equipment (i.e., at cost), another for accumulated depreciation, and the information from parts *ii* and *iii*, above.) Provide the journal entry that Frederick's made to record these disposals.

   v.   Deferred tax expense (provision). Provide the journal entry that Frederick's made to record this provision. (*Hint*: total tax expense as reported on the income statement consists of two components. Current tax expense (benefit) is the amount due to (from) the relevant tax authorities. Deferred tax expense is derived as the net change in deferred tax assets and liabilities (it is a non-cash expense). Note that in 1996, Frederick's reported a negative tax expense (an income tax benefit).)

f. Current asset and liability account balances changed over the year. Which of these amounts would be included in the operating activities section of Frederick's statement of cash flows?

g. Using only the balance sheet, income statement, footnotes and your answers to parts *e* and *f*, create the operating activities section of Frederick's 1996 statement of cash flows on an indirect basis. Assume "Deferred catalog costs" are considered operating assets and "Deferred rent" is considered an operating liability. Also, during the year, Frederick's charged $257,000 to earnings for non-cash ESOP expense. This amount must be added back to net income in the operations section of the statement of cash flows. Do not try to reconcile this item to either the "ESOP Loan Guarantee" liability or to the "Reduction for ESOP Loan Guarantee" shareholders' equity contra-account. While possible, such a reconciliation is beyond the scope of this case.

✦ Analysis ✦

h. Using the statement of cash flows provided by Frederick's, compare net cash provided by operating activities to net income for the past three years. What pattern do you notice? Explain the long-run relationship between cash flow from operations and net income.

FREDERICK'S OF HOLLYWOOD, INC.
CONSOLIDATED STATEMENTS OF OPERATIONS

For the fiscal year ended	August 31 1996	September 3 1995	August 28 1994
Net sales	$148,090	$142,931	$132,153
Costs and expenses:			
Cost of goods sold, buying and occupancy costs	88,059	84,203	77,409
Selling, general and administrative expenses	60,871	54,957	52,530
Provision for store closing	—	(790)	3,442
	148,930	138,370	133,381
Operating profit(loss)	(840)	4,561	(1,228)
Other income (expense):			
Interest expense	(107)	(118)	(150)
Miscellaneous	283	(31)	(327)
	176	(149)	(477)
Earnings(loss) before income taxes	(664)	4,412	(1,705)
Income taxes (benefit)	(226)	1,760	(682)
Earnings (loss) before cumulative effect of a change in accounting principle	(438)	2,652	(1,023)
Cumulative effect of a change in accounting principle	—	—	120
Net earnings(loss)	$ (438)	$ 2,652	$ (903)
Earnings(loss) per share			
Primary - Classes A & B	$ (.05)	$ .31	$ (.10)
Fully diluted - Classes A & B	$ (.05)	$ .30	$ (.10)
Weighted average shares outstanding			
Primary - Classes A & B	8 745	8,693	8,876
Fully diluted - Classes A & B	8,745	8,702	8,875

See accompanying notes to consolidated financial statements.

FREDERICK'S OF HOLLYWOOD, INC.

CONSOLIDATED BALANCE SHEETS

	August 31 1996	September 2 1995
Assets		
Current assets:		
Cash and cash equivalents	$ 8,379	$11,441
Short term investment	480	—
Accounts receivable	499	658
Income tax receivable	945	213
Merchandise inventories	19,553	19,862
Deferred income taxes	843	765
Prepaid expenses	2,215	2,615
Total current assets	32,914	35,554
Property and equipment, at cost:		
Land	128	128
Buildings and improvements	881	698
Fixtures and equipment	14,687	13,473
Leasehold improvements	20,130	18,878
Property under capital leases	1,686	1,686
	37,512	34,863
Less accumulated depreciation and amortization	(19,479)	(16,638)
Net property and equipment	18,033	18,225
Deferred catalog costs	1,723	2,107
Other assets	39	39
	$ 52,709	$ 55,925
Liabilities and Stockholders' Equity		
Current liabilities:		
Accounts payable	$ 10,298	$11,617
Dividends payable	221	221
Current portion of:		
Capital lease obligations	212	200
ESOP loan guarantee	240	240
Accrued payroll	430	526
Accrued insurance	828	1,018
Other accrued expenses	238	469
Total current liabilities	12,467	14,291
Capital lease obligations	672	884
ESOP loan guarantee	240	480
Deferred rent	811	669
Deferred income taxes	2,994	3,002
Stockholders' equity:		
Capital stock of $1 par value		
Authorized 15,000,000 Class A shares, 35,000,000 Class B shares; issued 2,955,000 Class A shares, 5,903,000 Class B shares in 1996 and 1995	8,858	8,858
Additional paid-in capital	732	738
Reduction for ESOP loan guarantee	(456)	(701)
Treasury stock	(6)	(5)
Retained earnings	26,397	27,709
Total stockholders' equity	35,525	36,599
	$ 52,709	$ 55,925

See accompanying notes to consolidated financial statements.

FREDERICK'S OF HOLLYWOOD, INC.

CONSOLIDATED STATEMENTS OF CASH FLOWS

For the fiscal year ended	August 31 1996	Sept. 2 1995	Sept. 3 1994
Cash Flows from Operating Activities:			
Net income (loss)	$ (438)	$ 2,652	$ (903)
Adjustments to reconcile net income (loss) to net cash provided by operating activities:			
Provision for store closing	—	(1,852)	3,290
Depreciation and amortization	4,174	4,105	4,206
ESOP compensation	257	224	—
Loss on sale of fixed assets	84	431	358
Changes in assets and liabilities:			
Accounts receivable	159	(130)	(54)
Income tax receivable	(732)	668	(881)
Merchandise inventories	309	(1,948)	(753)
Prepaid expenses	400	(403)	(746)
Deferred catalog costs	384	(524)	183
Other assets	—	(1)	5
Accounts payable and accrued expenses	(1,836)	677	3,011
Deferred rent	142	158	215
Deferred income taxes	(86)	779	(1,062)
Income taxes payable	—	—	(258)
Net cash provided by operating activities	2,817	4,836	6,611
Cash Flows from Investing Activities:			
Proceeds from sale of fixed assets	7	205	2
Purchase of short term investments	(480)	—	—
Capital expenditures	(4,073)	(3,082)	(2,348)
Net cash used for investing activities	(4,546)	(2,877)	(2,346)
Cash Flows from Financing Activities:			
Payment of capital lease obligations	(200)	(365)	(506)
Payment of dividends	(869)	(431)	(443)
Payment of dividends on unearned ESOP shares	(17)	(11)	—
Purchase of treasury stock	(7)	(26)	—
Proceeds from exercise of stock options	—	—	108
Net increase (decrease) in ESOP loan guarantee (liability)	(240)	(240)	960
Reduction for ESOP loan guarantee (equity)	—	—	(960)
Stock split	—	(1)	(4)
Net cash used for financing activities	(1,333)	(1,074)	(845)
Net increase (decrease) in cash and cash equivalents	(3,062)	885	3,420
Cash and cash equivalents at beginning of year	11,441	10,556	7,136
Cash and cash equivalents at end of year	$ 8,379	$11,441	$10,556

Supplemental disclosure to consolidated statements of cash flows:

Cash flow information:			
Interest paid	$ 111	$ 118	$ 150
Income taxes paid	601	802	1,386
Non-cash investing and financing transactions:			
Leases capitalized	—	747	—
Dividends declared	221	221	—
Provision for store closing			
Fixed asset disposal	—	756	475
Inventory disposal	—	183	24

FREDERICK'S OF HOLLYWOOD, INC.

NOTES TO CONSOLIDATED FINANCIAL STATEMENTS

(excerpts)

One. Summary of Significant Accounting Policies

The Company and Basis of Presentation. The consolidated financial statements include the account of Frederick's of Hollywood, Inc. and its subsidiaries (collectively referred to as the Company). All significant intercompany balances and transactions have been eliminated in consolidation.

Fiscal Year. The Company's fiscal year ends on the Saturday closest to August 31. Fiscal years 1996, 1995, and 1994 ended on August 31, September 2, and September 3 respectively. Fiscal years 1996 and 1995 consisted of 52 weeks, while fiscal year 1994 consisted of 53 weeks.

Cash Equivalents and Short Term Investments. The Company considers highly liquid investments with an initial maturity of three months or less to be cash equivalents. Cash equivalents and short term investments are carried at cost, which approximates fair value. Short term investments consist solely of a certificate of deposit with a maturity at date of purchase of 12 months.

Use of Estimates. The preparation of financial statements in conformity with generally accepted accounting principles requires management to make estimates and assumptions that affect the reported amounts of assets and liabilities at the date of the financial statements and the reported amounts of revenues and expenses during the reporting period. Actual results may differ from those estimates.

Merchandise Inventories. Merchandise inventories are valued at the lower of cost or market on the first-in, first-out basis.

Depreciation and Amortization. Properties and equipment are depreciated on the straight-line method based upon useful lives which range from 10 to 25 years for buildings and improvements and four to ten years for equipment. Leasehold improvements are amortized over the remaining term of the lease or their useful lives, whichever is shorter.

Income Taxes. Income taxes are accounted for under the asset and liability method. Under the asset and liability method, deferred tax assets and liabilities are recognized for the future tax consequences attributable to differences between the financial statement carrying amounts of existing assets and liabilities and their respective tax bases. Deferred tax assets and liabilities are measured using enacted tax rates expected to apply to taxable income in the years in which those temporary differences are expected to be recovered or settled. The effect on deferred tax assets and liabilities of a change in tax rates is recognized in income in the period that includes the enactment date.

Adoption of Accounting Standards. In October 1995 the Financial Accounting Standards Board issued Statement of Financial Accounting Standards No. 123, "Accounting for Stock-based Compensation" (FAS 123). The Company has elected to adopt FAS 123 in fiscal 1997 through disclosure only.

Deferred Catalog Costs. The Company expenses the costs of advertising for magazines, radio, and other media the first time the advertising takes place, except for direct-response advertising, which is capitalized and amortized over its expected period of future benefits.

Direct-response advertising consists primarily of catalog production and mailing costs that have not yet been fully amortized over the expected revenue stream, and are classified as non-current assets. Prior to mailing, catalog costs are classified as prepaid expenses.

Catalog costs reported as prepaid expenses were $829,000 and $1,351,000 for 1996 and 1995, respectively. Advertising expense (excluding postage) was $18,742,000, $15,168,000 and $13,766,000 for 1996, 1995, and 1994, respectively.

Impairment of Long-Lived Assets. In the event that facts and circumstances indicate that the cost of long-lived assets or other assets may be impaired, an evaluation of recoverability would be performed. If an evaluation is required, the estimated future undiscounted cash flows associated with the asset would be compared to the asset's carrying amount to determine if a write-down to market value or discounted cash flow value is required.

Reclassifications. Certain reclassifications have been made to the prior years' consolidated financial statements to conform to the 1996 presentation.

Five. Employee Stock Option and Benefit Plans (excerpts)

During fiscal 1993, the Company established a trust to administer a leveraged Employee Stock Ownership Plan (ESOP). In January 1994, the ESOP purchased 357,143 shares of the Company's Class A Capital Stock, financed by the proceeds from a $1,200,000 note issued by the ESOP and an initial contribution of $318,968 from the Company. The Company guaranteed the loan and is obligated to make annual contributions sufficient to enable the ESOP to repay the loan principal and interest. The loan guarantee is secured by a certificate of deposit in an amount equal to the outstanding principal balance. The terms of the ESOP loan guarantee include various covenants, all of which the Company was in full compliance. Charges to operations for this plan were $288,000, $303,000, and $288,000 for 1996, 1995, and 1994, respectively. The shares of stock held by the ESOP have been placed with the ESOP trustee and are allocated to eligible employees annually. These shares are allocated in the same proportion that the current year's principal and interest payments bear to the total principal and interest paid over the life of the borrowing.

The ESOP shares, as of the end of 1996 and 1995 were as follows:

	1996	1995
Allocated shares	185,584	129,700
Shares released for allocation	58,418	61,617
Unreleased shares	107,165	165,583
Shares distributed	(2,505)	(5,733)
ESOP shares	348,662	351,167

Earnings per share includes 241,497 and 185,584 ESOP shares for 1996 and 1995 respectively.

The ESOP plan provides that, upon a change in control (see Note 1), the Company will provide for the full payment of any outstanding loan, allocate all shares and that all participant's accounts shall be fully vested.

Seven. Segment Information

The Company, through its wholly owned subsidiaries, operates a catalog mail order business and a retail chain of women's specialty boutique stores. Financial information for each of these two business segments follows (000's Omitted):

	Retail Stores	Catalog Mail Order	Corporate	Consol. Total
1996				
Net sales	$77,780	$70,310	—	$148,090
Operating profit(loss)	(1,762)	922	—	(840)
Depreciation and amortization				
of property and equipment	3,758	416	—	4,174
Capital expenditures	3,832	241	—	4,073
Identifiable assets	26,430	15,632	$10,647	52,709
1995:				
Net sales	$76,117	$66,814	—	$142,931
Operating profit	866	3,695	—	4,561
Depreciation and amortization				
of property and equipment	3,691	414	—	4,105
Capital expenditures	3,281	548	—	3,829
Identifiable assets	26,124	17,382	$12,419	55,925
1994:				
Net sales	$72,386	$59,767	—	$132,153
Operating profit (loss)	(3,641)	2,413	—	(1,228)
Depreciation and amortization				
of property and equipment	3,804	402	—	4,206
Capital expenditures	2,148	200	—	2,348
Identifiable assets	27,361	14,989	$13,067	55,417

In determining operating profit, various expenses are allocated to segments on the basis of sales, payroll and estimated assets employed. Identifiable assets are those directly employed by each segment and allocated on the basis of estimated usage. Corporate assets are principally cash and cash equivalents.

Weis Markets, Inc.—Statement of Cash Flows

Weis Markets, Inc. is a Pennsylvania business corporation formed in 1924. The Company is engaged principally in the retail sale of food. The business of the Company is highly competitive and the Company competes based on price and service with national retail food chains, local chains and independent food stores. Weis Markets continues to expand operations in its primary marketing areas: Pennsylvania and Maryland. The Company operates 151 supermarkets under the names Weis Markets, Mr. Z's, Scot's, and King's, and 35 SuperPetz pet supply stores.

Learning Objectives
* Analyze the changes in balance sheet accounts by inferring transactions.
* Construct a complete statement of cash flows on the indirect basis.

Refer to the 1995 financial statements of Weis Markets, Inc.

Process

Given the following additional information, construct the 1995 statement of cash flows using the indirect method. All figures are in thousands.

1. Note 4 to the 1995 financial statements follows:

(4) Property and Equipment

Property and equipment, as of December 30, 1995 and December 31, 1994, consisted of:

(dollars in thousands)	Useful Life (in years)	1995	1994
Land		$42,940	$32,557
Buildings & Improvements	10-60	197,277	177,025
Equipment	3-12	326,689	293,043
Leasehold Improvements	5-20	46,195	39,811
Total, at cost		613,101	542,436
Less accumulated depreciation and amortization		327,108	297,173
Property and equipment, net		$285,993	$245,263

2. The company purchased $72,759 of new property, plant, and equipment in 1995.

3. In 1995, depreciation on property and equipment was $31,504; amortization of intangible assets was $1,664.

4. Property and equipment which cost $2,094 was sold for $1,107 in 1995. No other property and equipment was sold in 1995.

5. The company purchased $3,284 of new intangible assets in 1995.

6. Weis Markets records its Marketable Securities at market value. Unrealized gains and losses are added to or subtracted from a separate component of owners' equity. At the end of fiscal 1995, the company recorded the following journal entry to reflect the unrealized gain on marketable securities for 1995:

Dr.	Marketable Securities (B/S)	16,585	
Cr.	Net Unrealized Gain on Marketable Securities (B/S)		9,815
Cr.	Deferred Income Taxes (B/S)		6,770

7. The company sold $37,428 of marketable securities in 1995. There was no gain or loss recorded on the sale. No additional marketable securities were purchased.

8. According to Note 2—Income Taxes, a deferred income tax benefit of $136 was recorded in 1995. The company recorded the following journal entry to reflect the benefit:

Dr.	Deferred Income Taxes (B/S)	136	
Cr.	Provision for Income Taxes (I/S)		136

(*Hint*: Group all three Deferred Income Tax accounts on the balance sheet for purposes of your analysis.)

WEIS MARKETS, INC. AND SUBSIDIARIES
CONSOLIDATED BALANCE SHEETS

(dollars in thousands)
December 30, 1995
and December 31, 1994

	1995	1994
Assets		
Current:		
Cash	$ 3,285	$ 4,011
Marketable securities	432,174	453,017
Accounts receivable, net	31,517	24,132
Inventories	131,727	130,019
Prepaid expenses	7,764	4,229
Deferred income taxes	—	2,344
Total current assets	606,467	617,752
Property and equipment, net	285,993	245,263
Intangible and other assets, net	30,698	29,078
	$923,158	$892,093
Liabilities		
Current:		
Accounts payable	$ 72,262	$ 82,529
Accrued expenses	12,997	8,266
Accrued self-insurance	13,285	10,462
Payable to employee benefit plans	7,453	7,957
Income taxes payable	4,077	3,089
Deferred income taxes	5,258	—
Total current liabilities	115,332	112,303
Deferred income taxes	16,527	17,495
Minority Interest	(263)	(85)
Shareholders' equity:		
Common stock, no par value,		
100,800,000 shares authorized, 47,445,929 and		
47,445,929 shares issued, respectively	7,380	7,380
Retained earnings	879,916	834,995
Net unrealized gain on marketable securities	14,748	4,933
	902,044	847,308
Treasury stock at costÑ4,912,312 and 3,962,388		
shares, respectively	(110,482)	(84,928)
Total shareholders' equity	791,562	762,380
	$923,158	$892,093

See accompanying notes to consolidated financial statements

WEIS MARKETS, INC. AND SUBSIDIARIES
CONSOLIDATED STATEMENTS OF INCOME

(dollars in thousands, except per share amounts)
For the Fiscal Years Ended December 30, 1995,
December 31, 1994, and December 25, 1993

	1995	1994	1993
Net sales	$1,646,435	$1,556,663	$1,441,090
Cost of sales, including warehousing and distribution expenses	1,224,339	1,162,068	1,073,140
Gross profit on sales	422,096	394,595	367,950
Operating, general and administrative expenses	335,899	314,593	288,280
Income from operations	86,197	80,002	79,670
Interest and dividend income	21,383	21,607	21,528
Other income	13,959	15,499	12,456
Minority Interest	178	85	—
Income before income taxes	121,717	117,193	113,654
Provision for income taxes	42,297	40,944	40,701
Net income	$ 79,420	$ 76,249	$ 72,953
Per share of common stock:			
Net income	$ 1.84	$ 1.75	$ 1.66
Cash dividends	$ .80	$ .74	$ .70
Weighted average shares outstanding	43,083,449	43,662,031	43,827,168

See accompanying notes to consolidated financial statements

WEIS MARKETS, INC. AND SUBSIDIARIES

STATEMENTS OF CONSOLIDATED STOCKHOLDERS' EQUITY
For the Fiscal Years Ended December 30, 1995
December 31, 1994 and December 25, 1993

	Common Stock	Retained Earnings	Net Unrealized Gain (Loss) on Marketable Securities	Minimum Pension Liability	Treasury Stock	Total Shareholders' Equity
Balance-December 26, 1992	$7,147	$748,796	$ —	$ —	$ (75,678)	$680,265
Shares issued for options	108	—	—	—	—	108
Treasury stock purchased (41,790 shares)	—	—	—	—	(1,149)	(1,149)
Dividends paid	—	(30,677)	—	—	—	(30,677)
Change in accounting for marketable securities	—	—	16,740	—	—	16,740
Minimum pension liability	—	—	—	(125)	—	(125)
Net income	—	72,953	—	—	—	72,953
Balance-December 25, 1993	7,255	791,072	16,740	(125)	(76,827)	738,115
Shares issued for options	125	—	—	—	—	125
Treasury stock purchased (320,542 shares)	—	—	—	—	(8,101)	(8,101)
Dividends paid	—	(32,326)	—	—	—	(32,326)
Net unrealized loss on marketable securities	—	—	(11,807)	—	—	(11,807)
Minimum pension liability	—	—	—	125	—	125
Net income	—	76,249	—	—	—	76,249
Balance-December 31, 1994	7,380	834,995	4,933	—	(84,928)	762,380
Treasury stock purchased (949,924 shares)	—	—	—	—	(25,554)	(25,554)
Dividends paid	—	(34,499)	—	—	—	(34,499)
Net unrealized gain on marketable securities	—	—	9,815	—	—	9,815
Net income	—	79,420	—	—	—	79,420
Balance-December 30, 1995	$7,380	$879,916	$14,748	$ —	$(110,482)	$791,562

See accompanying notes to consolidated financial statements.

WEIS MARKETS, INC. AND SUBSIDIARIES

CONSOLIDATED STATEMENTS OF CASH FLOWS

(dollars in thousands)

For the Fiscal Years Ended December 30, 1995,
December 31, 1994, and December 25, 1993

	1995	1994	1993
Cash flows from operating activities:			
Net income		$76,249	$72,953
Adjustments to reconcile net income to			
net cash provided by operating activities:			
Depreciation and amortization		30,607	28,959
Gain on sale of fixed assets		(298)	(798)
Changes in operating assets and liabilities:			
Increase in inventories		(18,172)	(14,188)
(Increase) decrease in accounts			
receivable and prepaid expenses		(1,603)	3,302
Decrease in prepaid income taxes		—	419
Increase (decrease) in accounts			
payable, other liabilities and			
minority interest		28,669	11,652
Increase in income taxes payable		1,151	1,938
Increase (decrease) in deferred income taxes		2,769	(134)
	?		
Net cash provided by operating activities		119,372	104,103
Cash flows from investing activities:			
Purchase of property and equipment		(49,421)	(49,188)
Proceeds from the sale of property			
and equipment		985	1,928
(Increase) decrease in marketable securities		(15,631)	(9,448)
(Increase) in intangible and other assets		(20,058)	(7,909)
Net cash used by investing activities		(84,125)	(64,617)
Cash flows from financing activities:			
Proceeds from issuance of common stock		125	108
Dividends paid		(32,326)	(30,677)
Purchase of treasury stock		(8,101)	(1,149)
Net cash used by financing activities		(40,302)	(31,718)
Net increase (decrease) in cash		(5,055)	7,768
Cash at beginning of year		9,066	1,298
Cash at end of year	$	$ 4,011	$ 9,066

See accompanying notes to consolidated financial statements.

Jan Bell Marketing Inc.—Statement of Cash Flows

Jan Bell Marketing Inc. provides fine jewelry, watches and certain other select non-jewelry consumer products to the value-conscious fashion consumer. The Company markets its products principally through Sam's Club, a division of Wal-Mart, Inc. ("Sam's"), pursuant to an arrangement whereby the Company operates an exclusive leased department at all of Sam's existing and future domestic and Puerto Rican locations through February 1, 2001. In the Company's fiscal year ended February 3, 1996, sales through Sam's accounted for approximately 91% of the Company's net sales.

Learning Objectives
- Compare and contrast the direct and indirect methods of preparing the statement of cash flows.
- Understand how to recast operating cash flows from the indirect method to the direct method.
- Understand why most companies choose to use the indirect method.

Refer to the 1996 financial statements of Jan Bell Marketing Inc.

Concepts

a. Which method—the direct method or the indirect method—does the Jan Bell use to prepare its statement of cash flows? How do you know? Describe the differences between the method used by the company and the other, more commonly used, method.

b. Why do most companies prepare their statement of cash flows on an indirect basis?

c. A reconciliation of net loss to net cash provided by operating activities is provided immediately after the statement of cash flows. The reconciliation includes the following:

    Depreciation and amortization $ 8,704

    i.   Provide the journal entry made by Jan Bell to record Depreciation and amortization for the year ended February 3, 1996.

    ii. Explain why depreciation is added to the net loss to arrive at cash flow from operations. If Jan Bell depreciated its assets more quickly, would the company generate more cash?

Analysis

d. Where does the cash-based equivalent of "Net sales" appear on Jan Bell's statement of cash flows? Where does it appear in the reconciliation of Net loss to operating cash flows? Show numerically how the net income adjustment works at Jan Bell for the year ended February 3, 1996. (*Hint*: your analysis will be off by $1 due to rounding.)

e. Where does the cash-based equivalent of "Cost of sales" appear on Jan Bell's statement of cash flows? Where does it appear in the reconciliation of Net loss to operating cash flows? (*Note*: Jan Bell manufactures some of the jewelry it sells.)

JAN BELL MARKETING, INC.

CONSOLIDATED BALANCE SHEETS

(Amounts shown in thousands except share and per share data)

	February 3, 1996	January 28, 1995
Assets		
Current Assets:		
Cash and cash equivalents	$ 14,955	$ 28,212
Accounts receivable (net of allowance for doubtful accounts and sales returns of $702 and $5,630, respectively)	5,855	12,156
Inventories	95,486	106,053
Other current assets	914	1,738
Total current assets	117,210	148,159
Property, net	25,943	29,639
Excess of cost over fair value of net assets acquired	2,685	2,869
Other assets	7,335	6,085
	$153,173	$186,752
Liabilities and Stockholders' Equity		
Current Liabilities:		
Accounts payable	$ 6,043	$ 14,249
Accrued expenses	4,405	10,168
Senior notes payable classified as current	10,000	35,000
Total current liabilities	20,448	59,417
Long-term debt	7,500	—
Commitments and Contingencies (Notes B and H)		
Stockholders' Equity:		
Common stock, $.0001 par value, 50,000,000 shares authorized, 25,833,541 and 25,741,991 shares issued and outstanding, respectively	3	3
Additional paid-in capital	180,716	178,896
Accumulated deficit	(54,099)	(50,657)
Foreign currency translation adjustment	(1,395)	(907)
	125,225	127,335
	$153,173	$186,752

See notes to consolidated financial statements.

JAN BELL MARKETING, INC.

CONSOLIDATED STATEMENTS OF OPERATIONS

(Amounts shown in thousands except share and per share data)

	Fifty-three Weeks Ended February 3, 1996	Fifty-two Weeks Ended January 28, 1995	Year Ended December 31, 1993
Net sales	$ 254,004	$ 305,685	$ 275,177
Less:			
Effect of Sam's agreement (Note B)	—	—	99,718
	254,004	305,685	175,459
Cost of sales	199,579	255,725	243,350
Less:			
Effect of Sam's agreement (Note B)	—	—	79,687
	199,579	255,725	163,663
Gross profit	54,425	49,960	11,796
Store and warehouse operating and selling expenses	36,598	44,131	16,400
General and administrative expenses	17,694	21,744	27,871
Other charges (Note J)	—	47,773	10,217
Amortization expense	1,129	2,427	2,181
Currency exchange loss	597	5,474	—
Operating loss	(1,593)	(71,589)	(44,873)
Interest expense	(3,196)	(3,534)	(3,195)
Interest and other income	1,477	419	635
Loss before income taxes	(3,312)	(74,704)	(47,433)
Income tax provision (benefit)	130	353	(11,709)
Net loss	$ (3,442)	$ (75,057)	$ (35,724)
Net loss per common share	$ (.13)	$ (2.92)	$ (1.40)
Weighted average number of common shares	25,774,018	25,688,592	25,484,544

See notes to consolidated financial statements.

JAN BELL MARKETING, INC.

CONSOLIDATED STATEMENTS OF CASH FLOWS

(Amounts shown in thousands)

	Fifty-three Weeks Ended February 3, 1996	Fifty-two Weeks Ended January 28, 1995	Year Ended December 31, 1993
Cash flows from operating activities:			
Cash received from customers	$ 260,304	$ 313,163	$ 319,907
Cash paid to suppliers and employees	(253,058)	(292,249)	(324,893)
Interest and other income received	1,477	419	635
Interest paid	(3,196)	(3,534)	(3,195)
Income taxes received	506	14,348	499
Net cash provided by (used in) operating activities	6,033	32,147	(7,047)
Cash flows used in investing activities:			
Capital expenditures	(1,826)	(6,316)	(12,611)
Cash flows from financing activities:			
Debt repayment	(17,500)	—	—
Proceeds from exercise of options	—	—	323
Proceeds from issuance of common stock	—	—	25
Stock purchase plan	71	78	112
Purchase and retirement of common stock	(35)	—	(258)
Net cash (used in) provided by financing activities	(17,464)	78	202
Net (decrease) increase in cash and cash equivalents	(13,257)	25,909	(19,456)
Cash and cash equivalents at beginning of year	28,212	2,303	49,634
Cash and cash equivalents at end of year	$ 14,955	$ 28,212	$ 30,178

JAN BELL MARKETING, INC.

CONSOLIDATED STATEMENTS OF CASH FLOWS
(Amounts shown in thousands)
(continued)

	Fifty-three Weeks Ended February 3, 1996	Fifty-two Weeks Ended January 28, 1995	Year Ended December 31, 1993
Reconciliation of net loss to net cash provided by (used in) operating activities:			
Net loss	$ (3,442)	$(75,057)	$(35,724)
Adjustments to reconcile net loss to net cash provided by (used in) operating activities:			
Depreciation and amortization	8,704	9,147	7,210
Goodwill write-off	—	23,795	—
Foreign currency translation adjustment	(488)	(907)	—
Stock compensation expense	350	404	5,929
(Increase) decrease in assets:			
Accounts receivable (net)	6,301	7,478	44,730
Inventories	10,567	79,306	(70,799)
Other assets	(1,990)	15,470	2,168
Increase (decrease) in liabilities:			
Accounts payable	(8,206)	(10,430)	3,488
Accrued expenses	(5,763)	1,107	4,607
Liability for inventory repurchased	—	(18,166)	33,426
Deferred income taxes	—	—	(2,082)
Net cash provided by (used in) operating activities	$ 6,033	$ 32,147	$ (7,047)

See notes to consolidated financial statements.

L.A. Gear, Inc.—Cash and Balance Sheet Issues

L.A. Gear designs, develops, and markets fashionable, high-quality athletic and leisure footwear and apparel. Products are typically sold through retail department and sporting goods stores. The company manufacturers its shoe related products in South Korea and Taiwan and its apparel in the U.S. Distributions are made to approximately 10 different countries.

Learning Objectives
- Calculate liquidity ratios.
- Understand collateralization of cash, and lines and letters of credit.
- Calculate pro-forma ratios based on footnote disclosures.

Refer to the 1992 consolidated balance sheets of L.A. Gear, Inc.

Concepts

a. The following excerpt was taken from the 1992 Notes to the Consolidated Financial Statements for L.A. Gear.

"On December 1, 1992, the Company replaced its revolving bank credit facility with a new $50 million letter of credit facility with Bank of America, under which outstanding letters of credit (approximately $28.8 million at November 30, 1992) are required to be cash collateralized, generally on a dollar for dollar basis."

  i.   What is collateralized cash?

  ii. The balance sheet for 1991 shows "Borrowings under line of credit" as a liability. What distinguishes the 1992 letter of credit from the 1991 revolving bank credit facility?

  iii. The collateralized cash under the letter of credit facility is less than the amount listed as collateralized cash on the balance sheet. Why?

Analysis

b. What are L.A. Gear's current assets and liabilities at the end of the reporting period? Calculate L.A. Gear's working capital as of November 30, 1992.

c. Calculate L.A. Gear's current and quick ratios as of November 30, 1992.

d. Based on the figures derived in *b* and *c*, is L.A. Gear is a position to meet its current obligations as they come due?

e. Should the working capital and the quick ratios be adjusted for the effects of the letter of credit facility with Bank of America? For the collateralized cash?

L.A. GEAR, INC. AND SUBSIDIARIES
CONSOLIDATED BALANCE SHEETS

(in thousands)	November 30, 1992	1991
Assets		
Current assets:		
Cash and cash equivalents	$ 55,027	$ 1,422
Collateralized cash	28,955	—
Accounts receivable, net	56,369	111,470
Inventories	61,923	141,115
Prepaid expenses and other current assets	2,557	8,506
Refundable income taxes	25,269	22,795
Deferred income taxes	—	11,763
Total current assets	230,100	297,071
Property and equipment, net	17,667	26,869
Other assets	1,735	1,631
	$ 249,502	$ 325,571

Liabilities, Mandatorily Redeemable Preferred Stock and Shareholders' Equity

	1992	1991
Current liabilities:		
Borrowings under line of credit	$ —	$ 20,000
Accounts payable and accrued liabilities	49,753	55,856
Dividends payable on mandatorily redeemable preferred stock	7,746	—
Costs related to discontinued operations	4,552	18,000
Total current liabilities	62,051	93,856
Mandatorily redeemable preferred stock:		
7.5% series a cumulative convertible preferred stock, $100 stated value; 1,000,000 shares authorized, issued and outstanding; redemption value of $100 per share	100,000	100,000
Shareholders' equity:		
Common stock, no par value; 80,000,000 shares authorized; 22,898,182 shares issued and outstanding at November 30, 1992 (19,542,513 shares issued and outstanding at November 30, 1991)	127,714	92,331
Preferred stock, no stated value; 9,000,000 shares authorized; no shares issued	—	—
Retained earnings (accumulated deficit)	(40,263)	39,384
Total shareholders' equity	87,451	131,715
Commitments and contingencies	—	—
	$ 249,502	$ 325,571

Kendall Square Research Corp.—Revenue Recognition

Kendall Square Research Corporation develops, manufactures, markets, and supports a family of high performance, general purpose parallel computing systems for a broad range of mainstream applications, including numerically intensive computation, on-line transaction processing, and database management and inquiry.

Learning Objectives
- Define revenues and gains. Explain the difference between the two.
- Explain when revenues are recognized by different companies.
- Critically assess the revenue recognition policies of a particular company.
- Explain how financial statement users can evaluate the quality of a company's reported revenue.

Refer to the 1992 financial statements of Kendall Square Research Corporation.

Concepts

a. In your own words, define "revenues." Explain how revenues are different from "gains."

b. Describe what it means for a business to "recognize" revenues. What specific accounts and financial statements are usually affected by the process of revenue recognition?

Process

c. When would a movie theater normally recognize its revenues? (For example, when the theater signs a contract to show the movie? When the film is delivered? When the film is known to be a "hit"? When movie-goers pay to see the film?) Why?

d. When would a recorded-music store recognize revenues? (For example, when it orders new CDs? When it receives the new CDs? When customers pay for the new CDs?) Why?

e. When would a publishing company, like Prentice Hall, recognize revenues? (For example, when the books are printed? When the books are shipped to bookstores? When the books are sold by bookstores? When the bookstores pay Prentice Hall for the books?) Why?

f. How would your answer to part *e* change if bookstores could return books at any time? Has a sale really occurred? What if Prentice Hall could not estimate whether a bookstore would ultimately pay for its books?

g. When would a company, like Kendall Square, that manufactures, markets, and supports various supercomputers recognize revenues?

h. Refer to the revenue-recognition policy described in Note 1 to Kendall Square's financial statements for the year ended December 26, 1992. Describe and critique Kendall Square's policy.

i. Assume that all of Kendall Square's revenues listed in the financial statements were "on account." Prepare a journal entry that summarizes the sales activity for fiscal 1992.

Analysis

j. Read the accompanying October 28, 1994, *Wall Street Journal* article, "Missing the Boat…" The article reports three cases where Kendall Square recorded revenue in a suspect manner—a sale with an indefinite return period, a sale contingent on a scientist receiving a research grant, and a sale with a processing capacity "buyback" clause. Critique Kendall Square's revenue recognition policy for each of these cases. Was Kendall Square correct in recognizing revenues in each of these instances?

k. When the practices described in part *j* were discovered by outside auditors and the Board of Directors, Kendall Square corrected its 1992 financial statements and filed an amended Form 10-K with the Securities and Exchange Commission on May 4, 1994. A number of adjustments were made to the previously reported numbers, including a reduction in revenue of $10,663,000 and an increase in inventory of $3,081,000.

    i. Provide the journal entries required to correct Kendall Square's 1992 financial statements for these misstatements.

    ii. Based on the original financial statements and the adjustments in k(i), calculate the original and restated current ratio. Is the difference significant?

    iii. How can an astute investor or other user of the financial statements recognize when a company is engaged in aggressive revenue recognition accounting? That is, how can financial statement users assess the quality of a company's earnings?

KENDALL SQUARE RESEARCH CORPORATION

CONSOLIDATED BALANCE SHEET
(In thousands, except share and per share data)

	December 28, 1991	December 26, 1992
Assets		
Current assets:		
Cash and cash equivalents	$ 4,035	$ 7,392
Short-term investments	—	10,372
Accounts receivable	804	13,328
Inventories	4,316	8,939
Prepaid expenses and other current assets	1,137	1,149
Total current assets	10,292	41,180
Fixed assets, net	2,635	3,108
Software development costs, net	—	3,451
Other assets, net	202	994
	$13,129	$48,733
Liabilities and Stockholders' Equity		
Current liabilities:		
Accounts payable	$ 2,885	$ 3,001
Accrued payroll costs	1,019	1,575
Other accrued expenses	612	2,047
Deferred revenue	428	196
Current portion of long-term capital lease obligations	885	888
Total current liabilities	5,829	7,707
Long-term capital lease obligations	892	599
Stockholders' equity:		
Convertible preferred stock	50,098	—
Convertible subordinated notes, converted into common stock upon the closing of the initial public offering	13,029	—
Common stock, $ .01 par value; 35,000,000 shares authorized; 375,578 and 11,356,517 shares issued at December 28, 1991 and December 26, 1992, respectively	4	114
Additional paid-in capital	215	109,987
Accumulated deficit	(56,938)	(69,660)
	6,408	40,441
Less—1,263 shares of common stock held in treasury, at cost	—	(14)
Total stockholders' equity	6,408	40,427
Commitments (Note 7)	—	—
	$13,129	$48,733

The accompanying notes are an integral part of the financial statements.

KENDALL SQUARE RESEARCH CORPORATION

CONSOLIDATED STATEMENT OF OPERATIONS
(In thousands, except per share data)

	Year ended		
	December 29, 1990	December 28, 1991	December 26, 1992
Revenue	—	$ 904	$ 20,729
Cost of revenue	—	332	9,189
Gross profit	—	572	11,540
Costs and expenses:			
Research and development	$ 10,575	15,786	14,113
Selling, general and administrative	3,099	6,441	10,475
Other operating costs and expenses	363	850	—
	14,037	23,077	24,588
Loss from operations	(14,037)	(22,505)	(13,048)
Other income (expense):			
Interest income	755	380	775
Interest expense	(68)	(382)	(449)
	687	(2)	326
Net loss	$(13,350)	$(22,507)	$(12,722)
Unaudited pro forma net loss per share assuming conversion of convertible preferred stock and convertible subordinated notes (Note 1)	$ (2.77)	$ (3.90)	$ (1.22)
Weighted average shares outstanding	4,814	5,712	10,171

The accompanying notes are an integral part of the financial statements.

KENDALL SQUARE RESEARCH CORPORATION
NOTES TO CONSOLIDATED FINANCIAL STATEMENTS

NOTE 1—NATURE OF BUSINESS AND SUMMARY OF SIGNIFICANT ACCOUNTING POLICIES

Kendall Square Research Corporation (the "Company") was incorporated on February 4, 1986. The Company develops, manufactures, markets and supports a family of high performance, general purpose parallel computer systems for a broad range of mainstream applications, including numerically intensive computation, on-line transaction processing and database management and inquiry.

Principles of Consolidation
The consolidated financial statements include the accounts of the Company and its wholly-owned subsidiaries. All significant intercompany transactions are eliminated in consolidation.

Fiscal Year
The Company's fiscal year ends on the last Saturday of December.

Cash Equivalents and Short-Term Investments
The Company considers all highly liquid debt instruments purchased with original maturities of three months or less to be cash equivalents. Short-term investments, which include treasury bills with original maturities of greater than three months, are recorded at cost which approximates market.

Revenue Recognition
The Company recognizes revenue from product sales upon written customer acceptance. Warranty costs are accrued as product sales revenue is recognized.

Inventories
Inventories are stated at the lower of cost or market. Cost is determined by the first-in, first-out (FIFO) method.

Fixed Assets
Fixed assets are recorded at cost and depreciated by use of the straight-line method over their estimated useful lives. Repair and maintenance costs are expensed as incurred.

Software Development Costs
Certain software development costs incurred subsequent to the establishment of technological feasibility are capitalized and amortized under straight-line and units-shipped methods over the lesser of the estimated economic life of the products or three years commencing when the products are available for general release. Amortization of software development costs is included in cost of revenue and in 1992 totaled $55,000.

Missing the Boat

Yachtsman Bill Koch Lost His Golden Touch With Kendall Square

Venture in Supercomputers Ran Aground on Practice Of Inflating Revenue

Making 'Gong-Show Deals'

By WILLIAM M. BULKELEY
Staff Reporter of THE WALL STREET JOURNAL

In a life graced by wealth and good luck, William Koch has been many things: oil man, yachtsman, philanthropist and collector of rarities, from precious coins to fine wines.

At nearly everything he has tried he has succeeded, parlaying family wealth into a personal fortune of more than $600 million. Perhaps his most audacious feat came in 1992, when, as an upstart sailor rated by Las Vegas as a 100-to-1 shot, he won the America's Cup.

But at Kendall Square Research Corp., Mr. Koch's winning ways have ended. As the Waltham, Mass., company's main bankroller, he dreamed of building a high-tech colossus based on innovative supercomputers. This year, taking over as Kendall Square's chief executive, Mr. Koch tried to extricate the company from an accounting mess that had inflated reported revenue. But it was too late, and last month he laid off all but a skeleton crew and shut down computer-making operations.

Kendall Square has been dogged by an accounting scandal, which resulted in a Securities and Exchange Commission investigation and at least a dozen shareholder suits accusing management of making misleading statements. Mr. Koch has already been involved in one expensive settlement, in which he had to invest another $25 million in the company, atop the $40 million he had previously put in. Kendall Square, valued at $360 million by the stock market only 14 months ago when its shares sold for over $25 apiece, now trades at less than five cents a share.

Seduced or Overreached?

How could a man who had once succeeded so conspicuously stumble so badly? Mr. Koch contends he was, in essence, seduced by Henry Burkhardt III, a computer whiz who founded Kendall Square and who was ousted as chief executive last December after auditors uncovered a pattern of booking questionable revenue. "We got sucked in because of Henry's brilliance, Henry's vision and the desire to make a lot of money in a short amount of time," Mr. Koch says.

But Mr. Burkhardt says Mr. Koch knew what he was doing as an investor. "Bill saw

the big changes in the industry and saw an opportunity to create an interesting business," Mr. Burkhardt asserts. He and some other current and former Kendall Square employees contend Mr. Koch overreached—that he assumed his business skills could apply to high technology.

They also say Mr. Koch spread himself too thin: Even while trying to fix Kendall Square this year, Mr. Koch has been managing his Oxbow Group, a $500 million energy and trading firm in West Palm Beach, Fla. He also has been fighting over foreign claims to his coin collection; starting an all-woman team to vie in the next America's Cup qualifying races; battling Massachusetts over taxes; and heading the Koch Crime Commission, a Kansas crime-fighting initiative.

Mr. Burkhardt says: "Bill made a big mistake by thinking he could run the business by bringing in a few of the slogans he'd used to win a sailboat race. It's a very complex business."

Koch Industries

Mr. Koch (pronounced "coke"), who is 54 years old, followed his brothers to Massachusetts Institute of Technology, where he studied chemistry. He later joined them at Koch Industries in Wichita, Kan., a privately held energy company started by his father. After launching and losing a proxy fight for control in 1980, he was fired. A bitter court fight still continues over how much Mr. Koch is entitled to for the 21% stake he held, even though his brothers in 1983 bought out his interest for $470 million.

Mr. Koch used that money to start Oxbow, and then began to dabble in venture capital. He had met Mr. Burkhardt, now 49, a co-founder of Data General Corp. in Westboro, Mass. "I was restructuring my life," recalls Mr. Koch, who says he was charmed by Mr. Burkhardt's brilliance. "We became very good buddies."

In 1986, he backed Mr. Burkhardt's effort to start a company to create a new kind of supercomputer that would use many small processors working together. A few others were already making these "massively parallel processing" computers, but they were hard to program. Mr. Burkhardt had a design called "shared memory" that he said could make them as easy to program as a mainframe.

Mr. Koch claims Mr. Burkhardt predicted a product in two years and "had a goal of a $1 billion company in five or six years." Mr. Burkhardt replies that while he thought it was possible to build a $1 billion company, "there wasn't any timetable."

Two years later, the company sought funds from experienced venture capitalists. One who came aboard was Arthur J. Marks of New Enterprise

Associates in Baltimore. "It was a wonderful idea," says Mr. Marks, who became a director. "They had a real good idea of how to solve the programming nightmare of massively parallel computers. They were the first."

In 1991, Kendall Square finally shipped its first computer. The buzz in the supercomputer business was that the brash newcomer had something special. In March 1992, still with no earnings, Kendall Square raised $40 million in an initial public offering.

Business surged. Users said Kendall's KSR1 was simpler to use and crashed less than similar supercomputers. But Mr. Koch says the board was frustrated as early as 1992 by Mr. Burkhardt's refusal to provide cash-flow analyses or detailed marketing plans. Mr. Burkhardt intimidated them, Mr. Koch and some other directors claim.

Riding the Fat Pig

Louis Cabot, former chairman of the Brookings Institution, who recently resigned as a Kendall director, says, "Burkhardt didn't really want anyone looking closely over his shoulder. When Bill got people like me on the board, we also were asking tough questions. Burkhardt didn't always answer as fully as it turns out he should have."

As business improved and the stock rose, directors swallowed their misgivings. "We were riding the fat pig," says Mr. Koch. Kendall sold $43 million more in stock in April 1993, at $16 a share. But short sellers started betting against the stock because of its widening receivables—often a sign that customers aren't paying.

Mr. Koch says that Mr. Burkhardt insisted that the company's auditors, Price Waterhouse & Co., stay out of the building until just before the end of each quarter—ostensibly because they might interfere with crucial deal closings—and then would push them to work round the clock to bless the financials. Mr. Burkhardt replies that auditors worked on a schedule and never complained of their access to information.

But last year, Mr. Koch says that a new Price Waterhouse auditor discovered a side-letter about a sale to a Greek company that indicated the customer could return the computer at any time. That proviso led the auditors to reject the sale and start looking for "more snakes in the woodpile," Mr. Koch says. When they gave directors details of some other deals, the board was astounded. One insider says people referred to them as "Gong-show deals."

Mr. Koch says that unknown to him, Kendall Square, starting in late 1992, made astonishingly generous arrangements with customers, some of whom never paid. When William Goddard, a chemist at California

Institute of Technology, was pleased with his first supercomputer, Kendall asked him if he would buy another; Dr. Goddard says he replied that he would have to apply for a grant to afford it. But, he says, Kendall Square shipped it immediately in March 1993. The grant still hasn't come through, Dr. Goddard says. But Kendall booked a $1.4 million sale.

In 1992, according to company documents, Kendall Square received $1 million for a computer sold to the University of Houston and booked it all as revenue without subtracting the $420,000 in "grants" it promised to pay the school.

In another case, internal documents show, Kendall converted the loan of a computer to the University of Manchester in the U.K. to a sale at the end of 1992. Letters between Kendall salespeople and the university show that the university agreed to acquire the computer at the end of 1992 for about $450,000 payable the next year, with the proviso that it would rent back to Kendall Square half the time on the machine for a price "that will exactly cancel out our obligation to pay them." In effect, Kendall Square gave the university the computer and called it a sale.

Mr. Burkhardt "was paying customers to give us sales and not disclosing it," Mr. Koch asserts. "My personal opinion is that some of this activity was basically fraudulent."

Mr. Marks of New Enterprise says, "There were definitely problems with management revealing the information the board wanted." William H. Congleton, another venture capitalist and director, tells of Mr. Burkhardt's avoiding direct questions from directors: "Henry dances around; he's very persuasive."

Mr. Burkhardt says he produced the reports directors wanted and says the notion that he wouldn't answer their questions is "ridiculous." He denies knowing about questionable accounting practices. He says that he made many decisions "that in retrospect were wrong" because he believed the sales were valid. "As soon as I found out what was wrong, I immediately made the directors aware," he says, adding that he lost $1.5 million himself in Kendall. He says he is sorry Mr. Koch "feels I intentionally misled him. I'm not surprised he's bitter."

Mr. Burkhardt says that if the company hadn't fired him last December, he could have rebuilt its reputation. "If I'd been there, the outcome would have been different. There's no way to argue that point," he says.

A Dual Role

As the auditors' questions piled up, the board turned to Chief Financial Officer Karl Wassmann III with questions of its own. Mr. Wassmann served a dual role, which directors now say was a conflict of interest: He had to approve the terms of Kendall's sales, and he also was the designated "closer," taking over from the salesperson to clinch sales. "Karl was a very effective deal maker. He enjoyed doing that," says James B. Rothnie, executive vice president, development. "It's very clear in retrospect that the guy who has responsibility to keep score shouldn't be a deal maker." Mr. Wassmann didn't return calls seeking comment.

At the end of October 1993, Kendall said it was delaying its third-quarter financial report because of revenue-recognition questions. The shares lost a third of their value, falling to just over $16. A few days later, a shareholder suit was filed citing SEC insider-seller filings by Mr. Burkhardt covering the sale of more than $1 million of stock in August, mostly at around $20 a share.

Later suits also mentioned stock sales by Mr. Wassmann and Peter Appleton Jones, Kendall's top sales executive. When Price Waterhouse removed its certification from the 1992 results, which had been cited in the second stock offering, more shareholder suits were filed. The stock sales by insiders also set the SEC investigation in motion.

The directors eventually forced Messrs. Wassmann and Jones to resign, before dismissing Mr. Burkhardt. Mr. Koch says he made the shareholder suits the first priority after he took over as CEO. The company needed funds, but Mr. Koch says he and other investors wouldn't pour in money only to watch it go for legal expenses. The company's increasingly public problems fed the reluctance of customers, who already were questioning Kendall's long-term viability. Mr. Koch, with his deep pockets, was a highly visible target for lawsuits.

Mr. Koch says he could have settled the shareholder suits for $10 million and liquidated the company in January. But he says he felt a responsibility to customers and share-holders, including his family and crew members on his winning America's Cup team, to whom he had given stock. Moreover, some customers raved about the KSR1's capabilities.

Mr. Koch reassured existing customers and sought payments for shipped computers. He personally collected $3 million from Canon Inc., Kendall's Japanese distributor, after a quick trip to Tokyo. But other customers drifted away, and when auditors were finished, they halved the 1992 revenue and said 1993 revenue was only $18.1 million—far from the $60 million once forecast by Mr. Burkhardt.

In March, Mr. Koch reached a tentative agreement with shareholders under which they would take about $5 million in cash and considerable stock and warrants on the condition that he would inject $25 million into the company. He provided a loan, but the litigation talks dragged on. Mr. Marks says the raft of troubles made it nearly impossible to recruit an experienced high-tech CEO.

Still, by late summer, things were looking up. Lawrence Reeder, a venture capitalist and board member, agreed to become CEO. Kendall announced two computer sales. Philip Morris Cos., whose executives Mr. Koch treated to a yacht race off Newport, R.I., decided to buy a machine to run the company's vast database of smokers, he says.

Brownian Motion

But experts hired by the directors concluded the company's newly announced second computer, the KSR2, was too slow and inherently unreliable. Steve Frank, Kendall's vice president for architecture, says that after Mr. Koch decided to try to revive the company in January, "no one felt a sense of responsibility or urgency. There was a lot of Brownian random motion. Nobody wanted to tell the boss the bad news."

Mr. Koch discovered that developing a third computer would take at least two years and $30 million, and by then rivals would be ahead. Kendall tried to find a partner that would inject cash to license the technology. Individuals close to Kendall say Compaq Computer Corp. was interested, but it hasn't acted so far. Compaq won't comment.

On Sept. 16, Mr. Koch provided the $25 million he had promised under the suits, settling them. A week later, he ended computer manufacturing and sales and laid off all but 50 of the company's 170 workers. The stock collapsed from over $2 a share to less than 10 cents on the Nasdaq Stock Market. Glenn DeValerio, an attorney for the suing shareholders, says he was surprised by the decision to end computer sales, but he believes Mr. Koch acted in good faith.

Mr. Koch says he still hopes Kendall can create a business licensing technology, although he concedes there aren't any immediate prospects.

Once supremely confident, Mr. Koch now says he is chastened. Last year, when Kendall Square was still booming, Mr. Koch startled Hollywood by declaring an interest in buying troubled Metro-Goldwyn-Mayer Inc. from Credit Lyonnais SA. Today he says, "I'll put that under wishful thinking. It's an industry I don't know about."

The Warnaco Group Inc.—Accounts Receivable

The Warnaco Group, Inc. designs, manufactures, and markets a broad line of women's intimate apparel, such as bras, panties, and sleepwear, and men's dress and sport shirts, neckwear, sweaters and accessories, including jewelry, and small leather goods. These goods are sold under a variety of internationally recognized brand names, including Fruit of the Loom, Christian Dior, Chaps by Ralph Lauren, and Hathaway.

Learning Objectives
- Understand accounts receivable terminology.
- Read a Form 10-Q and compare information therein to that in a Form 10-K and an annual report.
- See the effects of business seasonality on financial reports.
- Calculate annual and quarterly ratios for accounts receivable and consider the validity of assumptions incorporated into those calculations.
- Compare information contained in a press article to similar information and ratios you calculate yourself and explore the differences.
- Learn about short-selling of stock and understand the role financial information plays in such decisions.

Refer to Warnaco's Form 10-Q for the quarter ended April 3, 1993. All figures are in thousands of dollars.

Concepts

a. What is an account receivable? What other names does this asset go by?

b. How do accounts receivable differ from notes receivable?

c. Warnaco's balance sheet reports a balance for accounts receivable, net. What are the accounts receivable net of?

d. If Warnaco anticipates that some accounts are uncollectible, why did the company extend credit to those customers in the first place?

e. What is a Form 10-Q? How do the financial statements included in a Form 10-Q differ from the financial statements included in a Form 10-K filing?

f. Why don't Warnaco's financial reporting periods end on the same date each quarter or year?

Process

g. Assume that the balance in Warnaco's allowance for doubtful accounts was $2,508 at January 2, $2,838 at April 3, 1993, and that $1,000 of accounts receivable were written off as uncollectible during the first quarter of 1993. Provide the journal entries for all events that reconcile the gross accounts receivable and allowance for doubtful accounts balances between January 2 and April 3, 1993. Four entries are required: one to record sales, one to record the collection of receivables, one to record bad debt expense, and one to record the write-off of accounts receivable. (*Hint*: set up T-accounts with the beginning and ending balances for each account and post each of the journal entries thereto.)

Analysis

h. What percentage of total assets does Warnaco hold as accounts receivable at the end of the quarter? How does this compare to the year ended January 2, 1993? Interpret this difference in light of the seasonality of Warnaco's operations.

i. Based on the results of the first quarter, what is the accounts receivable turnover ratio for the year? Remember, you are using quarterly data to compute this ratio. What assumption do you need to make in calculating this ratio? Comment on the reasonableness of that assumption. What is the average number of days receivables are held before they are collected?

j. In its January 2, 1993 annual report, Warnaco reported that accounts receivable were $122,894 and $87,180 at January 2, 1993 and January 4, 1992, respectively. Net revenues for the year ended January 2, 1993 were $625,064. What was the company's accounts receivable turnover ratio for the year ended January 2, 1993? Average number of days receivables held before collection? Assume that receivables were collected, on average, in about 50 days during the year ended January 4, 1991. What does this trend suggest?

k. Refer to the accompanying *Wall Street Journal* article (Warnaco Short-Sellers Cite Receivables, Debt, Paltry Cash Level Despite Analysts' Support). What could account for the difference between the analysts' and Warnaco's calculations of the average collection period?

l. How much cash does the company have as of April 3, 1993? Compare this to the amount at January 2, 1993. Discuss the difference in these balances. What factors would contribute to the reduction in cash from January 2 to April 3?

m. Refer again to the accompanying *Wall Street Journal* article. Is the comparison of Warnaco's cash balance to the cash balance at Jones Apparel Group, Crystal Brands, and Phillips-Van Heusen a fair one? Why or why not?

n. Refer again to the accompanying *Wall Street Journal* article. What is a "short" seller? What factors would support a short position in Warnaco's stock?

THE WARNACO GROUP INC.

90 PARK AVENUE
NEW YORK, NY 10016
212-661-1300

FORM 10Q

PART I - FINANCIAL INFORMATION
ITEM 1. FINANCIAL STATEMENTS

CONSOLIDATED CONDENSED BALANCE SHEETS
(in thousands of dollars)

	April 3, 1993	January 2, 1993
(unaudited)		
Assets		
Current assets:		
Cash (restricted none and $1,266, respectively)	$ 35	$ 3,763
Accounts receivable - net	139,072	122,894
Inventories:		
Finished goods	121,702	104,973
Work in process	51,784	57,217
Raw materials	42,932	47,107
Total inventories	216,418	209,297
Other current assets	25,694	20,029
Total current assets	381,219	355,983
Property, plant and equipment, (net of accumulated depreciation of $58,863 and $56,166, respectively)	75,245	73,985
Other assets:		
Intangibles and other assets - net	202,098	199,678
	$658,562	$629,646
Liabilities and Stockholders' Equity		
Current liabilities:		
Accounts payable	$ 6,035	$ 4,290
Borrowing under revolving credit facility	83,121	61,944
Current portion of long-term debt	44,883	44,533
Accounts payable and accrued liabilities	97,267	102,853
Federal and other income taxes	1,476	910
Total current liabilities	232,782	214,530
Long-term debt	278,217	277,601
Other long-term liabilities	12,137	1,673
Stockholders' equity:		
Common Stock; $ .01 par value	202	202
Capital in excess of par value	315,379	315,411
Cumulative translation adjustment	1,191	1,960
Accumulated deficit	(171,089)	(171,341)
Receivable for common stock issued	(10,257)	(10,390)
Total stockholders' equity	135,426	135,842
	$658,562	$629,646

This statement should be read in conjunction with the accompanying Notes to Consolidated Condensed Financial Statements.

THE WARNACO GROUP INC.

CONSOLIDATED CONDENSED STATEMENTS OF OPERATIONS (UNAUDITED)
(in thousands of dollars except share data)

	Quarter ended	
	April 3, 1993	April 4, 1992
Net revenues	$156,750	$130,518
Cost of goods sold	101,953	81,256
Gross profit	54,797	49,262
Selling, administrative and general expenses	32,790	28,601
Income before interest and income taxes	22,007	20,661
Interest expense	9,905	15,737
Provision for income taxes	1,350	509
Income from continuing operations	10,752	4,415
Cumulative effect of change in method of accounting for postretirement benefits	(10,500)	—
Extraordinary items	—	(46,454)
Net income (loss)	$ 252	$ (42,039)
Net income (loss) applicable to common stockholders	$ 252	$ (43,414)
Income (loss) per common share:		
Income from continuing operations	$0.54	$0.20
Cumulative effect of change in method of accounting for postretirement benefits	(0.53)	—
Extraordinary items	—	(3.04)
Net income (loss) per common share	$0.01	$ (2.84)
Weighted average number of common shares outstanding	19,881,729	15,284,251

This statement should be read in conjunction with the accompanying Notes to Consolidated Condensed Financial Statements.

THE WARNACO GROUP INC.

CONSOLIDATED CONDENSED STATEMENTS OF CASH FLOW (UNAUDITED)
INCREASE (DECREASE) IN CASH
(in thousands of dollars)

	Quarter ended	
	April 3, 1993	April 4, 1992
Cash Flow from Operations:		
Net income (loss)	$ 252	$(42,039)
Non cash items included in net income (loss):		
Depreciation and amortization	5,303	4,862
Interest	976	1,909
Cumulative effect of change in method of accounting for postretirement benefits	10,500	—
Extraordinary items	—	46,454
Income taxes paid	(784)	(1,596)
Other changes in operating accounts	(33,200)	(45,489)
Change in the net assets of discontinued operations	—	(557)
Other	(6,503)	(1,705)
Cash used in operations	(23,456)	(38,161)
Cash Flow from Investing Activities:		
Purchase of property, plant & equipment	(4,261)	(3,598)
Cash used in investing activities	(4,261)	(3,598)
Cash Flow from Financing Activities:		
Borrowings (repayments) under revolving credit facilities	21,524	(53,906)
Net proceeds from the sale of Class A common stock and repayment of notes receivable from employees	101	161,524
Repayments of debt	(223)	(77,275)
Proceeds from other financings	2,587	97,392
Preferred stock dividends paid	—	(1,375)
Increase in deferred financing costs	—	(11,399)
Cash provided from financing activities	23,989	114,961
Increase (decrease) in cash	(3,728)	73,202
Cash at beginning of period	3,763	3,719
Cash at end of period	$ 35	$ 76,921
Other changes in operating accounts:		
Accounts receivable	$(16,178)	$(15,735)
Inventories	(7,121)	(19,348)
Other current assets	(5,665)	(6,638)
Accounts payable and accrued liabilities	(5,586)	(4,277)
Income taxes payable	1,350	509
	$(33,200)	$(45,489)

This statement should be read in conjunction with the accompanying Notes to Consolidated Condensed Financial Statements.

THE WARNACO GROUP INC.
NOTES TO CONSOLIDATED CONDENSED FINANCIAL STATEMENTS

1. In the opinion of the Company, the accompanying consolidated condensed financial statements contain all the adjustments (all of which were of a normal recurring nature) necessary to present fairly the financial position of the Company as of April 3, 1993 as well as its results of operations and cash flows for the periods ended April 3, 1993 and April 4, 1992. Operating results for interim periods may not be indicative of results for the full fiscal year.

2. Certain amounts for prior periods have been reclassified to be comparable with the current period presentation.

3. Effective with the 1993 fiscal year the Company adopted Statement on Financial Accounting Standards No. 106, Employers' Accounting for Postretirement Benefits Other Than Pensions ("FAS No. 106"), and, as a result, recorded an expense for the cumulative effect of a change in the method of accounting for postretirement benefits of $10,500,000 (without income tax benefit), of which $2,814,000 pertains to benefits related to active employees.

The Company has defined benefit health care, life insurance and other plans that provide postretirement benefits to retired employees. The plans are contributory, with retiree contributions adjusted annually, and contain cost sharing features including deductibles and co-insurance. Postretirement benefit cost for the first quarter of 1993 was approximately $200,000, of which $150,000 represents interest cost. Postretirement benefit cost for the first quarter of 1992 of approximately $175,000 was recorded on an as incurred basis and has not been restated. The Company does not fund postretirement benefits.

The weighted average annual assumed rate of increase in the per capita cost of covered benefits (health care cost trend rate) is 10% for years 1-4, 7% for years 5-9, and 5% thereafter. A 1% increase in the trend rate assumption in each year would increase the cumulative effect adjustment by approximately $300,000 and the first quarter expense by approximately $30,000. The weighted average discount rate used in determining the accumulated postretirement benefit obligation is 8.75%, which is consistent with the discount rate used in valuing the Company's pension plans.

ITEM 2. MANAGEMENT'S DISCUSSION AND ANALYSIS OF FINANCIAL CONDITION AND RESULTS OF OPERATIONS

Results of Operations

STATEMENT OF OPERATIONS (SELECTED DATA)
(amounts in millions of dollars)

	First Quarter 1993	First Quarter 1992
Net revenues	$156.8	$130.5
Cost of goods sold	102.0	81.3
Gross profit	54.8	49.2
% to net revenues	35.0%	37.7%
Selling, administrative and general	32.8	28.6
Income before interest and income taxes	22.0	20.6
% to net revenues	14.0%	15.8%
Interest expense	9.9	15.7
Provision for income taxes	1.3	0.5
Income from continuing operations	$ 10.8	$ 4.4

Net revenues increased 20.1% from $130.5 million in the first quarter of 1992 to $156.8 million in the first quarter of 1993. Intimate apparel division net revenues increased 16.6% in the first quarter of 1993 to $96.0 million from $82.3 million in the first quarter of 1992. Fruit of the Loom generated approximately $8.0 million of incremental revenues continuing its successful launch into the mass merchandise market and domestic intimate apparel revenues increased 10.5%. Menswear division net revenues increased 31.8% from $40.2 million in the first quarter of 1992 to $53.0 million in the first quarter of 1993 reflecting increases across all brands with Chaps net revenues up 82.9%, Hathaway and Dior dress shirts increasing 24% and neckwear up 52.2%.

Gross profit increased 11.2% from $49.2 million in the first quarter of 1992 to $54.8 million in the first quarter of 1993. The increase in gross profit is primarily a result of the increased net revenues noted above. Gross profit as a percentage of net revenues decreased from 37.7% in the first quarter of 1992 to 35.0% in the first quarter of 1993, which is equal to the full year gross margin for fiscal 1992. The decrease in gross profit as a percentage of net revenues primarily reflects start up costs of approximately $750,000 related to three new intimate apparel manufacturing plants to increase the capacity of the intimate apparel business and a higher mix of menswear and Fruit of the Loom sales which generate a lower gross margin than the basic intimate apparel business.

Selling, administrative and general expenses increased from $28.6 million (21.9% of net revenues) in the first quarter of 1992 to $32.8 million (20.9% of net revenues) in the first quarter of 1993. The decrease in selling, administrative and general expenses as a percentage of net revenues reflects the spread of fixed costs over the higher net revenues noted above.

Income before interest and income taxes increased from $20.6 million in the first quarter of 1992 to $22.0 million in the first quarter of 1993 reflecting the increased gross profit noted above.

Interest expense decreased 37% from $15.7 million in the first quarter of 1992 to $9.9 million in the first quarter of 1993. The decrease in interest expense reflects the recapitalization in March 1992 and refinancing of the Company's 12 1/2% subordinated debentures in November 1992, which reduced outstanding debt and lowered the Company's effective interest rate from 14% to 7 1/2%.

The provision for income taxes for both periods primarily reflects accruals for taxes of foreign subsidiaries.

Income from continuing operations increased 143% from $4.4 million in the first quarter of 1992 to $10.8 million in the first quarter of 1993 reflecting the increased operating income and the decreased interest expense noted above.

The first quarter of 1993 includes a one time non-cash expense of $10.5 million (without income tax benefit) for the cumulative effect of a change in the method of accounting for employee postretirement benefits, which was recorded in accordance with the provisions of Statement of Financial Accounting Standards No. 106 ("FAS No. 106"). The adoption of FAS No. 106 is not expected to have a material impact on the results of operations in any future period.

Extraordinary items of $ (46.5) million (without income tax benefit) recorded in the first quarter of 1992 relate to premium payments and the write off of deferred financing costs due to the early extinguishment of debt.

Net income for the first quarter of 1993, after the $10.5 million FAS No. 106, adjustment, was $0.3 million compared to a net loss of $ (42.0) million for the first quarter of 1992 which reflects the extraordinary items discussed above.

Capital Resources and Liquidity

The Company's liquidity requirements arise primarily from its debt service requirements and the funding of the Company's working capital needs, primarily inventory and accounts receivable. The Company's borrowing requirements are seasonal, with peak working capital needs generally arising at the end of the second quarter and the third quarter of the fiscal year. The Company typically generates nearly all of its operating cash flow in the fourth quarter of the fiscal year reflecting third and fourth quarter shipments and the sale of inventory built during the first half of the fiscal year.

Cash used by operating activities in the first quarter of 1993 was $23.5 million which compares favorably to a use of $38.2 million in the comparable 1992 period, primarily due to a lower usage of inventory. The use of cash is attributable to a seasonal increase in working capital, primarily accounts receivable and inventories. The Company met its 1993 first quarter seasonal borrowing by increasing the outstanding balances on its revolving line of credit. At April 3, 1993 the Company had approximately $35 million of additional credit available under its various revolving credit agreements.

The Company believes that funds available under its existing credit arrangements and cash flow to be generated from future operations will be sufficient to meet working capital and capital expenditure needs of the Company, including interest and principal payments on outstanding debt obligations, for the foreseeable future.

Warnaco Short-Sellers Cite Receivables, Debt, Paltry Cash Level Despite Analysts' Support

HEARD
ON THE
STREET

By JOHN R. DORFMAN AND TERI AGINS
Staff Reporters of THE WALL STREET JOURNAL

Just when Wall Street is starting to warm up to Warnaco Group, short-sellers are betting the company will stumble.

Warnaco, a leading maker of bras under the Warner and Olga brands, recently started selling bras in discount stores under the Fruit of the Loom name. It also sells menswear such as Hathaway shirts, Christian Dior ties, and casual wear from Puritan and Chaps by Ralph Lauren. The New York company rang up $615.1 million in sales last year.

With well-known, steady brands, Warnaco isn't the type of stock short-sellers normally target. The "shorts" borrow stock and sell it, in an attempt to profit from an anticipated decline. Eventually, they must buy shares to return to the lender. But if the stock falls meanwhile, they profit. As of mid-June, 562,964 shares of Warnaco stock had been sold short.

Warnaco showed an impressive 20% year-over-year gain in sales in the first quarter, with a nice earnings increase and particularity good menswear sales. But the shorts say they see hints of underlying weakness. For example:

• Receivables (money owed the company by customers) amount to more than 70 days of sales, compared with 56 in January 1992 and 51 in January 1991.

• Warnaco shows only $35,000 in cash on its balance sheet, as of early April.

• While long-term debt has been reduced, it still is $278.2 million, or more than twice stockholders' equity. Short-term debt has edged up of late. The stated net worth includes a big chunk of intangible assets; tangible net worth (reflecting hard assets like machinery and inventories, minus liabilities) is negative.

For each criticism, Warner's chief executive officer, Linda Wachner, rattles off an answer. For example, receivables—if counted by the method the company considers sound—are holding at about 60 days of sales, she says. "I'm very happy with my 60 days." Asked if Warnaco is letting stores take longer to pay, she says, "Absolutely not."

The reduction of debt, Ms. Wachner says, is proceeding on schedule. What about that puny cash level? "A company such as ours does not sit with cash on the balance sheet," she says. "Every dollar that we receive goes to pay down our debt every night." When cash is needed, a revolving bank credit line is tapped.

Not all clothing companies choose to run without a cash cushion, however. Here are the recent cash holdings at three of Warnaco's peer companies: $13.6 million at Jones Apparel Group, $22.8 million at Crystal Brands and $32.5 million at Phillips-Van Heusen.

The shorts' bet against the stock flies in the face of several brokerage-house recommendations. Smith Barney's William N. Smith and Catherine K. Blednick recently recommended Warnaco, partly because it is gaining market share in both bras (estimated 37% market share) and menswear (19.2%).

Gary Jacobson of Kidder Peabody calls Warnaco a buy, citing "the astute guidance of Chairperson Linda Wachner and her driven team," and projecting annual 15% earnings increases. Sharon Rappaport of Morgan Stanley, a longtime fan of the stock, has reaffirmed her buy recommendation. She says Warnaco, trading at 32 a share yesterday, could hit 42 within a year.

Some money managers like the stock, too. A bra "is not like a suit that you can keep in your closet for five or six years, or if you're my husband 12 years," says money manager Eileen P. Rominger of Oppenheimer Capital. "You put this thing in the dryer a few times" and before long it's time for a replacement. Ms. Romminger also likes the stock's valuation. As she calculated it, the stock sells for a mere 11 times the earnings she expects this fiscal year.

Frank Husic, a San Francisco money manager, says Warnaco management is unusually alert. For example, it was quick to get paid by troubled retailers before they went into bankruptcy proceedings. He also praises Ms. Wachner for penetrating discount stores like Wal-Mart and Kmart with its new Fruit of the Loom bra line.

Warnaco expects the new line will become a major force. But some competitors say Warnaco won't easily dominate the discount niche as it does the department-store market. Warnaco says Fruit of the Loom bras are priced at $7.94 to $9.94, which is below the usual prices for Playtex, above Hollywood Vassarette, and about even with Hanes Her Way.

Even its enemies aren't suggesting that Warnaco is in dire financial straits. But the issues raised by the shorts bear watching. There's an old stock-market saying, "Trouble starts on the balance sheet and migrates to the income statement." At the moment, Warnaco's income statement looks fine. But wise investors look carefully at both.

Imasco Limited—Financial Services Assets

Imasco Limited is a multinational conglomerate headquartered in Canada. Its operations include Imperial Tobacco, Genstar Developments, Shoppers' Drug Mart, North Carolina based Hardee's Food Systems Inc. and CT Financial Services which offers retail financial services through Canada Trust in Canada and First Federal in the United States.

Learning Objectives
• Understand non-performing financial assets and related allowances.
• Perform a basic analysis and interpretation of a loan portfolio.

Refer to the 1995 Imasco Limited balance sheets and excerpted notes to the financial statements.

Concepts

a. Why does Imasco separate its Financial Services assets from other assets on the balance sheet?

b. Note 3 provides additional information about Imasco's financial assets. Explain in your own words what non-performing investments represent.

c. Why does Imasco set up an allowance for investment losses? Note 4 discloses information about a "specific allowance" and a "general allowance." Explain what each of these items represents.

Process

d. Consider the balance sheet line item "Loans." What is the gross amount of loans at December 31, 1995?

e. Provide the journal entries (there are two) to record 1995 activity in the allowance for investment loss account. Ignore the line item "Foreign Exchange Adjustment."

Analysis

f. Consider Imasco's "Mortgages—Commercial." What percentage of these loans does Imasco consider non-performing?

g. How many cents on the dollar does Imasco anticipate recovering on the non-performing commercial mortgages?

h. Which type of mortgage—commercial or residential—is performing better? Has performance changed from 1994 to 1995?

IMASCO LIMITED

CONSOLIDATED BALANCE SHEETS

	December 31	
In millions of dollars	1995	1994

Assets

Current assets

Cash and short term investments	$ 71	$ 148
Accounts receivable and other	356	384
Inventories	838	839
	1,265	1,371

Non-current assets

Notes receivable, investments and other (Note 1)	306	247
Capital assets (Note 6)	1,246	1,255
Goodwill	87	243
	1,639	1,745
	2,904	3,116

Financial services

Investments

Cash and short term notes	3,202	3,574
Securities (Note 5)	7,399	6,892
Loans (Note 2)	39,589	37,017
Real estate investment properties (Note 7)	890	945
Capital assets and other (Note 8)	836	702
Goodwill	1,284	1,330
	53,200	50,460

Total assets	$56,104	$53,576

Liabilities and Shareholders' Equity

Current liabilities

Banks and other short-term loans	$ 54	$ 71
Accounts payable and other	693	680
Income, excise and other taxes	139	219
	886	970

Long-term debt (Note 9)	1,781	1,927
Deferred credits and other liabilities (Note 10)	145	145

Financial services

Deposits (Note 11)	44,557	42,442
Borrowings and other liabilities (Note 12)	4,956	4,099
Deferred income taxes	58	66
Preference shares of subsidiary companies (Note 15)	410	537
Non-controlling interest (Note 14)	47	53
	50,028	47,197

Shareholders' equity

Capital stock (Note 16)	937	930
Unrealized gain on foreign currency translation	37	60
Retained earnings	2,290	2,347
	3,264	3,337

Total liabilities and shareowners' equity	$56,104	$53,576

The accompanying accounting policies and notes are an integral part of the consolidated financial statements.

IMASCO LIMITED

Note 1 Summary of Significant Accounting Policies

Investments—Financial Services

Loans

Mortgages are stated at cost, including capitalized and accrued interest, less repayments and unamortized mortgage discounts. Mortgage discounts are amortized over the term of the mortgage. Consumer and collateral loans, corporate and commercial loans, and credit card receivables are stated at cost, including accrued interest, less repayments. Receivables under equipment leases are stated at gross rentals receivable, net of unearned income. Unearned income is reflected in earnings over the term of the lease. Earned income is accrued on a daily basis.

Non-performing investments

Included in each investment category are non-performing investments. They consist of securities on which interest or preferred dividend payments have been suspended, loans in arrears, credit card receivables on which interest accrual has been suspended and restructured and reduced rate loans. In addition, management of CT Financial Services may, at any time, classify a loan as non-performing if there is evidence of deterioration in the borrower's financial condition. Once loans are classified as non-performing, revenue is recognized only as collected, unless it is virtually certain that accrued interest will be collected.

Allowance for investment losses

The allowance for investment losses consists of two parts, a specific allowance and a general allowance, in accordance with the loan loss provisioning guidelines issued by the Superintendent of Financial Institutions. The two parts are calculated as; 1) a specific allowance for individual investments to reduce carrying value to estimated realizable value and 2) a general allowance based on a historical five-year net loss experience ratio for each of mortgages, consumer and collateral loans, corporate and commercial loans, and credit card receivables, and on economic conditions and other factors which, in management's judgment, deserve recognition. Each investment category has been reduced by the applicable portion of the allowance for investment losses. Allowance for derivative financial instruments, if any, is recorded in other liabilities. Write-offs are generally recorded after all reasonable restructuring or collection activities have taken place and the possibility of further recovery is considered remote.

Note 2 Loans—Financial Services

	1995	1994	1993
Mortgages—residential	$27,663	$25,929	$23,672
Mortgages—commercial	2,401	2,846	3,214
Consumer and collateral	7,520	6,209	5,332
Corporate and commercial	747	1,035	1,382
Credit card receivables	884	611	450
Receivables under equipment leases	374	387	416
	$39,589	$37,017	$34,466

Note 3 Non-Performing Investments—Financial Services

Included in each investment category are the following non-performing investments:

	1995	1994	1993
Loans			
Mortgages—residential	$100	$ 69	$145
Mortgages—commercial	94	104	130
Corporate and commercial	127	170	174
Other	20	38	43
Securities	2	13	35
Real estate acquired			
in settlement of loans	125	115	107
Non-performing investments	468	509	634
Allowance for investments			
losses (Note 4)	(375)	(372)	(350)
Net non-performing investments	$ 93	$137	$284

Note 4 Allowance for investments losses—Financial Services

	1995	1994	1993
Beginning of year	372	350	342
Provision charged to earnings	127	140	205
Foreign exchange adjustment	(2)	6	2
Investment losses and write-offs,			
net of recoveries	(122)	(124)	(199)
End of year	$375	$372	$350

The apportionment of the allowance for investment losses is summarized below:

	1995	1994	1993
Loans			
Mortgages—residential	$ 50	$ 46	$ 64
Mortgages—commercial	73	92	69
Corporate and commercial	148	136	100
Other	44	37	35
Securities	17	23	43
Real estate acquired			
in settlement of loans	43	38	39
End of year	$375	$372	$350
Specific allowance	$141	$177	$194
General allowance	234	195	156
End of year	$375	$372	$350

The Canadian Institute of Chartered Accountants has established a new standard for accounting for impaired loans. This change in generally accepted accounting principles is effective January 1, 1996.

Replacing previous standards, the new standard requires that the value of impaired loans be reduced to the present value of expected future cash flows for the loan, discounted at the interest rate inherent in the loan or, if the absence of such information, to the fair value of the underlying security or an observable market price for the loan.

Upon adoption, on January 1, 1996, the allowance for investment losses will be increased by $73 million, and consolidated retained earnings will be reduced by $40 million, net of income taxes of $32 million and non-controlling interest of $1 million.

Clearly Canadian Beverage Corporation—Inventory

The Clearly Canadian Beverage Corporation produces and markets Clearly Canadian®, a line of natural and flavored sparkling water beverage products. Through distribution agreements, the products are sold in the United States, Canada, Mexico, the Caribbean, Japan, Great Britain, Ireland, Thailand, and certain Persian Gulf States.

Learning Objectives
- Based on the description of a company determine the nature of the inventories they hold.
- Assess the risks associated with holding inventories.
- Determine the effect of new regulations on the carrying value of inventory.
- Evaluate the disclosure of an "unusual" expense.
- Relate an accounting classification decision to management's incentives.

Refer to the 1993 financial statements of the Clearly Canadian Beverage Corporation.

Concepts

a. Based on the above description of the company and what you know about its products, what sorts of inventories do you expect Clearly Canadian to hold?

b. What are the risks of holding such items?

c. What basic issues arise in accounting for Clearly Canadian's inventory?

Analysis

d. Read the article entitled, "The Labeling Lowdown: New Regulations Cost the Industry Millions and Could Spell Long-Term Changes in Buying Habits." How might this new law affect Clearly Canadian?

e. Refer to note 12, "Termination Charges."

   i. Explain how Clearly Canadian was affected by the law you read about in part *d*.

   ii. Provide the journal entry that Clearly Canadian recorded to account for this event.

   iii. Where on the income statement did Clearly Canadian disclose this cost? How does this disclosure help users of Clearly Canadian's financial statements assess the persistence of Clearly Canadian's earnings?

   iv. Do you agree with this income statement classification? What alternative treatment could have been chosen?

   v. Explain what incentives the company's management may have to choose the treatment used.

CLEARLY CANADIAN BEVERAGE CORPORATION

CONSOLIDATED BALANCE SHEETS
(Stated in thousands of dollars, except where indicated)

| | December 31, 1993 | | December 31, 1992 |
| | (note 1(c)) | | (restated-note 14) |
	US Funds	Cdn. Funds	Cdn. Funds
Assets			
Current Assets			
Cash and short-term deposits	$ 8,466	$ 11,209	$ 786
Short-term investments (note 2)	9,542	12,633	21,793
Accounts receivable (note 3)	9,145	12,108	15,280
Inventories (note 4)	12,236	16,201	42,513
Prepaid expenses and deposits	610	807	870
	39,999	52,958	81,242
Long-Term Receivables (note 5)	3,390	4,489	4,214
Property, Plant and Equipment (note 6)	3,957	5,239	5,440
	$ 47,346	$ 62,686	$ 90,896
Liabilities			
Current Liabilities			
Bank loan (note 7)	$ —	$ —	$ 1,124
Accounts payable and accrued liabilities (note 8)	7,737	10,244	32,149
Corporate income taxes payable	103	136	1,442
	7,840	10,380	34,715
Deferred Lease Inducement	361	478	548
Capital Lease Obligation	4	6	70
	8,205	10,864	35,333
Shareholders' Equity			
Share Capital (notes 9 and 10)			
Issued and outstanding -14,441,055 common shares without par value (1992-14,904,755)	39,008	51,646	55,774
Retained Earnings (deficit)	133	176	(211)
	39,141	51,822	55,563
	$ 47,346	$ 62,686	$ 90,896

Commitments and Contingencies (note 15)

The accompanying notes form an integral part of these consolidated financial statements.

CLEARLY CANADIAN BEVERAGE CORPORATION
CONSOLIDATED STATEMENTS OF OPERATIONS AND RETAINED EARNINGS
(Stated in thousands of dollars, except where indicated)

	Year ended December 31, 1993 (note 1 (c))		Year ended December 31, 1992 (restated note 14)	Six months ended December 31, 1991	Year ended June 30, 1991
	U.S. Funds	Cdn. Funds	Cdn. funds	Cdn. funds	Cdn. funds
Sales	$90,869	$120,310	$187,579	$102,254	$71,408
Cost of Sales	69,012	91,372	144,287	85,392	57,566
Gross Profit	21,857	28,938	43,292	16,862	13,842
Selling, Administrative and General Expenses	19,075	25,255	18,275	5,669	7,040
Other Income (note 11)	(451)	(597)	(2,600)	(584)	(94)
Earnings Before the Following:	3,233	4,280	27,617	11,777	6,896
Termination Charges (note 12)	2,249	2,978	23,942	–	–
Earnings Before Income Taxes	984	1,302	3,675	11,777	6,896
Income Taxes (note 13)	691	915	1,329	2,732	–
Net Earnings	$ 293	$ 387	$ 2,346	$ 9,045	$ 6,896
Retained Earnings (Deficit) Beginning of Period, as originally reported	$ 273	$ 362	$ (2,557)	$(11,602)	$(18,498)
Prior Period Adjustment (note 14)	(433)	(573)	–	–	–
Deficit-Beginning of Period, as restated	(160)	(211)	(2,557)	(11,602)	(18,498)
Retained Earnings (Deficit) End of Period	$ 133	$ 176	$ (211)	$ (2,557)	$(11,602)
Basic Earnings per Share (dollars)	$0.02	$0.02	$0.16	$0.65	$0.59
Fully Diluted Earnings per Share (dollars)	$0.02	$0.02	$0.15	$0.62	$0.57

CLEARLY CANADIAN BEVERAGE CORPORATION

(All figures in Canadian dollars)

12. TERMINATION CHARGES

(a) Pursuant to an agreement dated October 14, 1988 between the company and Camfrey Resources Ltd. (Camfrey), the company was required to pay a royalty per case on product sales in certain territories. In 1992, the company exercised its right to terminate the royalty and, in so doing, has incurred an estimated, non-recurring, royalty termination charge of $22,900,000. In 1993, the company and Camfrey entered into arbitration to determine the final settlement of the royalty contract. On February 16, 1994, a final arbitration decision determined the final settlement to be $23,900,000 plus interest. An additional charge of $573,000, net of related income tax effect, has been recorded as a prior period adjustment (see note 14).

(b) New legislation in the U.S. effective May 1, 1994, has caused a change in labelling requirements. This resulted in the company recording an allowance of approximately $180,000 for pre-labelled glass, labels and packaging materials that will be rendered unusable by the legislation.

(c) The volume requirements of the company have declined, and the company has incurred a one-time charge of $1,178,000 to cancel two bottling contracts.

The Labeling Lowdown

New regulations cost the industry millions and could spell long-term changes in buying habits

By John N. Frank

For Barq's Inc., new federal labeling regulations effective May 8 have meant more than four months of work. "Virtually every package we have had to be redesigned," notes Barq's Rick Hill.

At White Rock Products Group, roughly 65 packages have been redone, with costs running about $5,000 per flavor, notes Alan Silverstein, vice president of sales and marketing.

Sports drink giant Gatorade has new labels for 50 SKUs while soft drink behemoth Pepsi has had to address the labeling needs of roughly 1,200 SKUs.

At bottled water powerhouse Hinckley & Schmitt, the redesign task became so complex that plant-by-plant plans were formulated to ensure the right labels for the right products reached each production facility.

The labeling saga is the same throughout the beverage industry, whether in soft drinks, bottled waters or juices, all of which must comply with the new labeling requirements (see Beverage Industry, June 1993).

Industry redesign costs could easily top $4 million, applying Silverstein's $5,000 figure across the full spectrum of soft drink and bottled water brands alone. Adding in costs for iced teas, juices and other beverages could double the figure.

But the true price of the changes—namely their long-term impact on consumer buying habits—might not be known for years. Many in the industry believe the new labels, containing nutritional and calorie information, will have little to no effect on beverage buying habits. "I don't think it's going to change anybody," says Silverstein.

But other industry watchers see the new labels increasing consumer awareness of health and nutrition issues, a mind-set change that could have future impact on buying habits.

"We believe it really will be a big bonus for us," says a Gatorade spokeswoman. In the past, Gatorade has created comparison charts showing its nutritional information compared to other beverages. "Now, the labels will provide another venue" for such comparisons, the spokeswoman says.

While sports drinks might seem an obvious beneficiary of the new regs, other beverages could be impacted as well.

Marc Johnson, president of Mad River Traders Inc., thinks the greatest impact will be "where the perception (of a beverage) is different than the reality," such as new age drinks that consumers might believe are low-calorie but aren't. Johnson estimates he'll spend $25,000 to redesign labels for his 16 SKUs. His costs include design fees and new labeler parts, should he opt for a different label size than he had been using.

Richard L. Frank, whose Washington, D.C., law firm Olsson, Frank and Weeda, PC. has worked with food and beverage clients, and closely followed the labeling issue, says, "All of this will increase consumer awareness of nutrition and health. Consumers are going to have a much better idea of what they're buying."

The new labels will provide us with a more knowledgeable consumer," says Frank. "Will (they) change purchase habits? That's another question."

While consumers won't immediately change beverage buying habits because of the new labels, they might be more circumspect in trying new products that are merely copies of existing brands, forecasts Don Chilton, vice president, sales and marketing, for Alaska Glacier in Anchorage. "If you're the leader in a category, God bless you," he chides.

Whether leader or follower, beverage makers must gear up for the new label rules. The Food and Drug Administration, prodded by industry trade groups, late last year clarified some ambiguities in the new regulations with technical amendments to the Nutrition Labeling and Education Act. Chief among these:

* The new rules apply to products labeled on or after May 8 instead of the initially proposed products introduced into interstate commerce by May 8. That change means some beverage companies could have old labels on store shelves May 8 without incurring FDA's wrath, as long as product packaged from that date bears new labels, Frank notes.

* Products that make nutritional claims such as "sodium free" or that use the term "diet" in their name must carry a statement, "Not a significant source of calories from fat, saturated fat, cholesterol, dietary fiber, sugars, Vitamin A, Vitamin C, calcium or iron." After expressions of industry concern, the FDA was considering modifying this rule to allow using "not a significant source of other nutrients" to help keep labels less cluttered.

* Bottled waters that add minerals for taste to their products will not need to add nutritional panels, the FDA told the International Bottled Water Association in an August 1993 response to an IBWA inquiry.

Claims regarding sodium are triggering the most interest in the beverage business. Diet 7Up has been reformulated so that it can keep its "very low sodium" designation (see Beverage Industry, January 1994).

For bottled water, "'Sodium' is a swear word to most consumers," notes Alaska Glacier's Chilton.

"Most of the (bottled water) companies that are now saying sodium free will continue to" and so will add required nutritional panels to their labels, says Tyrone Wilson, IBWA director of technical services.

Even water products that may not require nutritional labels likely will start carrying them rather than trigger consumer questions about why some products have the new labels and some don't, says Thomas G. Condon, corporate quality control manager at Hinckley & Schmitt.

Juice makers must start listing juice percentages and detailing what types of juices are in a product, says attorney Frank. "You can't just call it "Strawberry Punch,'" Frank explains. While a beverage company can still use such a name for its offering, it must say, "in immediate proximity" to the name, "a blend of strawberry, white grape, apple" or whatever other juices are in the product.

While the beverage industry braces for May's labeling changes, one new beverage category, nutraceuticals, isn't covered by the labeling regulations because no definition exists for such products. But expect the FDA to get to nutraceuticals as soon as it sets requirements for medical foods, predicts Frank.

Stagnito Publishing Co. February 1994
"The Labeling Lowdown." Reprinted with permission.

Lands' End, Inc.—Inventory

Lands' End, Inc. is a leading direct marketer of traditionally styled apparel, domestics (primarily bedding and bath items), soft luggage and other products. The company strives to provide exceptional value to its customers by offering quality crafted merchandise at competitive prices with a commitment to excel in customer service and an unconditional guarantee. The company offers its products principally through its regular and specialty catalogs.

Learning Objectives
- Explain how cost flow assumptions affect inventory balances and cost of goods sold.
- Explain the financial statement effects of using different cost flow assumptions.
- Understand why changes in current assets do not always tie in directly to the changes reported on the statement of cash flows.
- Analyze the activity in inventory and related accounts.
- Learn how to restate a company's financial statements to reflect an alternative inventory cost flow assumption.

Refer to the 1995 financial statements of Lands' End, Inc.

Concepts

a. In general, why must companies use cost flow assumptions to cost their inventories. What cost flow assumption does Lands' End use to cost its inventories?

b. Contrast the effect on Lands' End's balance sheet, income statement, and statement of cash flows of using the last-in, first-out (LIFO) method versus the first-in, first-out (FIFO) method of inventory costing. State any assumptions you make in arriving at your answer.

c. On the 1995 statement of cash flows, one of the adjustments to net income was the change in Inventory. The cash flow statement lists the change as an increase of $16,544. However, subtracting the 1994 balance sheet amount from the 1995 amount yields a difference of $18,964. Explain why the two numbers are not the same. (*Hint*: see Note 8 to the financial statements.)

Process

d. Set up a T-account for the Lands' End inventory account. Enter the 1994 and 1995 ending balances in the T-account. Use information from the financial statements to recreate the activity that took place in the account during fiscal 1995 and answer the following questions.

   i. How much inventory did Lands' End purchase in fiscal 1995? Assume that new inventory was acquired in a single purchase. Provide the journal entry Lands' End made to record that purchase.

   ii. Assume that Accounts Payable includes only inventory-related transactions. How much did Lands' End pay its suppliers for inventory in fiscal 1995? Assume that Lands' End made a single payment to all its suppliers in fiscal 1995. Provide the journal entry Lands' End made to record that payment.

Analysis

e. You would like to compare Lands' End's operations to those of one of its competitors. The competitor uses the FIFO method of inventory costing. Use the information from the notes to the financial statements to restate Lands' End's fiscal 1995 net income assuming that Lands' End had always used the FIFO method of inventory costing.

f. Assume that the Lands' End's inventory balances for accounting and for tax purposes are the same. Estimate the cumulative tax savings (through January 27, 1995) that Lands' End has made by using the LIFO method of inventory costing instead of the FIFO method.

g. Refer to the accompanying *Wall Street Journal* (5/17/94, page C2) article, "Despite Recent Decline in Lands' End Stock ..."

   i. Explain why some analysts are concerned about the increase in inventory at Lands' End.

   ii. Why is it important that companies communicate regularly and openly with shareholders and analysts?

LANDS' END, INC.

CONSOLIDATED STATEMENTS OF OPERATIONS
(In thousands, except per share data)

| | For the period ended | | |
	Jan. 27 1995	Jan. 28 1994	Jan. 29 1993
Net sales	$992,106	$869,975	$733,623
Cost of sales	568,634	512,521	427,292
Gross profit	423,472	357,454	306,331
Selling, general and administrative expenses	360,147	287,044	250,737
Reserve for anticipated sale of subsidiary	3,500	—	—
Income from operations	59,825	70,410	55,594
Other income (expense):			
Interest expense	(1,769)	(359)	(1,330)
Interest income	307	346	266
Other	1,300	(527)	(497)
Total other expense, net	(162)	(540)	(1,561)
Income before income taxes and cumulative effect of change in accounting	59,663	69,870	54,033
Income tax provision	23,567	27,441	20,533
Net income before cumulative effect of change in accounting	36,096	42,429	33,500
Cumulative effect of change in accounting for income taxes	—	1,300	—
Net income	$ 36,096	$ 43,729	$ 33,500
Net income per share before cumulative effect of change in accounting	$1.03	$1.18	$0.92
Cumulative effect of change in accounting	—	0.04	—
Net income per share	$1.03	$1.22	$0.92

The accompanying notes to consolidated financial statements are an integral part of these consolidated statements.

LANDS' END, INC.

CONSOLIDATED BALANCE SHEETS

(In thousands)

	Jan. 27 1995	Jan. 28 1994
Assets		
Current assets:		
Cash and cash equivalents	$ 5,426	$ 21,569
Receivables	4,459	3,644
Inventory	168,652	149,688
Prepaid expenses	11,219	11,787
Deferred income tax benefit	8,412	5,588
Total current assets	198,168	192,276
Property, plant and equipment, at cost:		
Land and buildings	69,798	60,866
Fixtures and equipment	74,745	57,769
Leasehold improvements	1,862	1,346
Total property, plant and equipment,	146,405	119,981
Less-accumulated depreciation and amortization	49,414	40,290
Property, plant and equipment, net	96,991	79,691
Intangibles, net	2,453	1,863
Total assets	$297,612	$273,830
Liabilities and Shareholders' Investment		
Current liabilities:		
Lines of credit	$ 7,539	$ —
Current maturities of long-term debt	40	40
Accounts payable	52,762	54,855
Reserve for returns	5,011	3,907
Accrued liabilities	25,952	17,443
Accrued profit sharing	1,679	2,276
Income taxes payable	9,727	12,528
Total current liabilities	102,710	91,049
Long-term debt, less current maturities	—	40
Deferred income taxes	5,379	5,200
Long-term liabilities	395	256
Shareholders' investment:		
Common stock, 40,221 and 20,110 shares issued, respectively	402	201
Donated capital	8,400	8,400
Paid-in capital	25,817	24,888
Deferred compensation	(1,421)	(2,001)
Currency translation adjustments	284	246
Retained earnings	229,554	193,460
Treasury stock, 5,395 and 2,154 shares at cost, respectively	(73,908)	(47,909)
Total shareholders' investment	189,128	177,285
Total liabilities and shareholders' investment	$297,612	$273,830

The accompanying notes to consolidated financial statements are an integral part of these consolidated balance sheets.

LANDS' END, INC.

CONSOLIDATED STATEMENTS OF CASH FLOWS

(In thousands)

	For the period ended		
	Jan. 27 1995	Jan. 28 1994	Jan. 29 1993
Cash Flows (Used for) from Operating Activities:			
Net income before cumulative effect of change in accounting	$36,096	$42,429	$33,500
Adjustments to reconcile net income to net cash flows from operating activities—			
Depreciation and amortization	10,311	8,286	7,900
Deferred compensation expense	580	243	191
Deferred income taxes	(2,645)	(1,684)	(612)
Loss on sales of fixed assets	145	684	931
Changes in current assets and liabilities excluding the effects of acquisitions:			
Receivables	(264)	(3,179)	365
Inventory	(16,544)	(41,769)	16,501
Prepaid expenses	597	(5,715)	999
Accounts payable	(2,093)	16,765	8,625
Reserve for returns	1,104	(98)	552
Accrued liabilities	8,509	3,701	(260)
Accrued profit sharing	(597)	642	400
Income taxes payable	(2,801)	1,570	(1,868)
Other	177	502	—
Net cash flows from operating activities	32,575	22,377	67,224
Cash Flows (Used for) from Investing Activities:			
Cash paid for capital additions and businesses acquired	(31,365)	(17,392)	(8,591)
Proceeds from sales of fixed assets	19	71	15
Net cash flows used for investing activities	(31,346)	(17,321)	(8,576)
Cash Flows (Used for) from Financing Activities:			
Proceeds from short-term and long-term debt	7,539	80	—
Payment of short-term and long-term debt	(40)	—	(16,349)
Tax effect of exercise of stock options	1,130	31	1,075
Purchases of treasury stock	(27,979)	(2,861)	(20,972)
Issuance of treasury stock	1,978	101	2,551
Cash dividends paid to common shareholders	—	(3,592)	(3,589)
Net cash flows used for financing activities	(17,372)	(6,241)	(37,284)
Net increase (decrease) in cash and cash equivalents	(16,143)	(1,185)	21,364
Beginning cash and cash equivalents	21,569	22,754	1,390
Ending cash and cash equivalents	$ 5,426	$21,569	$22,754
Supplemental cash flow disclosures:			
Interest paid	$ 2,828	$ 364	$ 1,315
Income taxes paid	27,595	27,475	21,905

The accompanying notes to consolidated financial statements are an integral part of these consolidated statements.

LANDS' END, INC.
NOTES TO CONSOLIDATED FINANCIAL STATEMENTS

Note 1. Summary of Significant Accounting Policies

Nature of business

Lands' End, Inc., (the company) is a direct marketer of traditionally styled apparel, domestics (primarily bedding and bath items), soft luggage, and other products.

Year-end

The company's fiscal year is comprised of 52-53 weeks ending on the Friday closest to January 31. Fiscal 1995 ended on January 27, 1995, fiscal 1994 ended on January 28, 1994, and fiscal 1993 ended on January 29, 1993. Fiscal 1996 will be a 53-week year ending on February 2, 1996. The additional week will be added in the fourth quarter of fiscal 1996.

Inventory

Inventory, primarily merchandise held for sale, is stated at last-in, first-out (LIFO) cost, which is lower than market. If the first-in, first-out (FIFO) method of accounting for inventory had been used, inventory would have been approximately $18.9 million and $19.1 million higher than reported at January 27, 1995, and January 28, 1994, respectively.

Catalog costs

Prepaid expenses primarily consist of catalog production and mailing costs that have not yet been fully amortized over the expected revenue stream, which is approximately three months from the date catalogs are mailed. The company's report of such advertising costs is in conformance with the provisions of the AICPA Statement of Position No. 93-7, "Reporting on Advertising Costs," which will become effective for the company in fiscal 1996.

Reserve for losses on customer returns

At the time of sale, the company provides a reserve equal to the gross profit on projected merchandise returns, based on its prior returns experience.

Note 8. Acquisitions and Anticipated Disposition

In July 1994, the company formed a wholly-owned subsidiary that acquired the marketing rights and assets of MontBell America, Inc., which designs, develops and distributes premier technical outdoor clothing and equipment through the wholesale channel to outdoor specialty stores, primarily in the United States.

In February 1995, the company announced its intention to sell its wholly-owned subsidiary MontBell America, Inc. The financial statements reflect an after-tax charge of $2.1 million as of January 27, 1995.

In March 1993, the company purchased a majority interest in a catalog company, The Territory Ahead. Merchandise offered in the catalog consists of private label sportswear, accessories and luggage. Beginning in 2003, the minority shareholders have the option to require the company to purchase their shares, and the company will have the option to require the minority shareholders to sell their shares in The Territory Ahead. The price per share would be based on the fair market value of The Territory Ahead.

Results of operations of MontBell America, Inc., and The Territory Ahead were not material to the company, and as a result, no pro forma data is presented. The transactions were accounted for using the purchase method. The excess of the purchase price over the fair value of net assets was recorded as goodwill. The operating results of MontBell America, Inc., and The Territory Ahead are included in the consolidated financial statements of the company from their respective dates of acquisition.

Despite Recent Decline in Lands' End Stock, Some Investors See Rebound Around Corner

HEARD
ON THE
STREET

By WILLIAM POWER
Staff Reporter of THE WALL STREET JOURNAL

It sounds like a joke: If you call the mail-order clothier Lands' End Inc. and ask for the president, you get a Mr. End.

That's William T. End, and he is the president, although his last name is just a coincidence. "When they hired me, some headlines said 'Lands' End Lands End,'" Mr. End says gamely. "That's the closest anyone came to humor."

But there isn't much that's funny about Lands' End these days—especially if you're a recent investor. After soaring 61% in 1993 and holding steady for most of this year, the stock suddenly skidded 13% in three days of pummeling on the New York Stock Exchange. From Thursday through yesterday, Lands' End has plunged 5 3/4 to 40 1/8 on higher-than-normal volume.

What's the problem? Mostly, skittishness over the Dodgeville, Wis., company's fiscal first-quarter earnings report, which was a good one except for a disclosure that unsold inventory soared 46% to $168 million in the quarter from the year-earlier period. That forced Lands' End to increase borrowing. Though the company has no long-term debt, short-term debt rose to $18 million as of April 29, the company said, compared with none a year earlier.

Betting on Rebound

But Wall Street may have overreacted. While the shares could still slide a point or two more, some investors are betting they'll rebound after that. Lands' End still has a minuscule amount of debt compared with most companies, and boasts a solid customer base for its line of mail-order squall jackets, canvas pants, tops and accessories. With the declines of the past three days, the shares trade at 17 times the past year's earnings—hardly outrageous.

"I think some of the concerns were overestimated by the Street," says Elaine Rees, who follows retailing for Dreyfus Corp. She says the mutual-fund company is retaining its 100,000-share Lands' End position, held in the Strategic Investing fund. The shares are trading at only 15 times her estimates for this year's earnings. So will Dreyfus add to its stake? "We're giving it thought," Mrs. Rees says. John D. Messner of Meridian Capital Management is also thinking about buying more shares. The San Diego firm, which manages $100 million, sold most of its Lands' End position late last year. Mr. Messner says one of the reasons was that the company didn't "communicate" well enough with institutional investors. "We're convinced now that that's improving, and we're looking for a time to get in" again, Mr. Messner says.

Mr. End acknowledges that the company hasn't been as open as analysts would have liked. That's why Lands' End is coming to New York on Thursday for an analysts' chat. "The last three were in Dodgeville," Mr. End says. "So we are trying to improve."

Says Mr. Messner: "Basically, the future is quite good for Lands' End. One of our long-term investing themes is the information revolution, and they fit in. You've got 20% of people working at home now, and they supply that audience. People are going to be wearing more casual clothes."

Analyst Warms Up

One analyst who had been bearish on Lands' End is warming up to the shares. In the wake of the stocks' rout, Kevin Silverman of Kemper Securities in Chicago upgraded Lands' End to "hold" from what had been "reduce." And if the stock gets closer to 35, "I'd be a buyer," he says.

The 47-year-old Mr. End, who joined Lands' End in 1991 from rival L.L. Bean, says inventory rose in 1994 because it was too low the prior year. "We don't consider the inventory problem a major problem," Mr. End says. "We think it's real important to have merchandise in stock."

Anyone who doubts that assertion need only talk to customers like Debbie North of suburban Philadelphia. Ms. North, 42 years old, says she uses Lands' End because it's "very reliable" with deliveries. She also likes the full-cut slacks. "Not everyone is a size three or size five," Ms. North says. "They do cater to a broader spectrum, literally."

Some analysts say Lands' End could do a better job of selling its goods electronically. Lands' End has done seven tests using computer services and other electronic ways to sell. But "there are no obvious home runs so far in the electronic area," Mr. End says.

The company, which likes to run its own show, is particularly dubious about going on a home-shopping television channel. Lands' End does see growth in corporate sales (selling its attaché cases with IBM logos, for example, or squall jackets with sports teams' names). It just sent out a special catalog for that.

Callaway Golf Company—Manufacturing Inventory

Callaway Golf Company designs, develops, manufactures and markets high quality, innovative golf clubs. The Company's golf clubs are sold at premium prices to both average and skilled golfers on the basis of performance, ease of use and appearance. Callaway's primary products, most of which incorporate the Company's S2H2® design concept, currently include Big Bertha® metal woods and irons, Big Bertha® War Bird™ metal woods, and S2H2® irons, wedges and putters.

Learning Objectives
- Disaggregate the balance sheet line item for manufacturing inventory and understand its underlying components.
- Interpret the allowance for obsolete inventory.
- Trace product cost flows from raw materials to work-in-process and through to finished goods inventory.
- Infer raw material purchases and calculate cash disbursements related to inventory.
- Calculate and analyze financial statement ratios related to inventory.

Refer to the 1993 financial statements of Callaway Golf Company.

Concepts

a. Note 2 reveals that the balance sheet inventory amount consists of three types of inventory. What types of costs do you expect to be in the raw materials inventory? In the work-in-process inventory? In the finished goods inventory?

b. The balance sheet inventory line item is called "Inventories, net." What are inventories *net* of? What is the *gross* amount of inventory in 1992? 1993?

c. What portion of the allowance for obsolescence do you think is attributable to each of the three types of inventory held by Callaway?

Process

d. Recreate the journal entry Callaway prepared to record the obsolescence in 1993.

Analysis

e. Make the following simplifying assumptions. The only activity in the "accounts payable and accrued expenses" account is for raw materials purchases and payments for those purchases. During 1993, a total of $50,000,000 of manufacturing salaries and overhead was debited to the work-in-process account. All other activity in the work-in-process account is from raw materials transfers and transfers of completed products to finished goods. The allowance for obsolescence is included in the finished goods balance presented in Note 2. Determine the following amounts. (*Hint*: Set up separate T-accounts for all three inventory accounts as well as for "cost of goods sold" and "accounts payable and accrued expenses.")

   i. The cost of finished goods sold in 1993.

   ii. The cost of finished goods transferred from work-in-process in 1993 (i.e., the cost of goods manufactured).

   iii. The cost of raw materials transferred to work-in-process in 1993.

   iv. The cost of raw materials purchased during 1993.

   v. The amount of cash disbursed for raw material purchases during 1993.

f. How many times did Callaway Golf's inventory turn over in 1993 and 1992?

g. On average, how many days did it take for inventory to turn over in 1993 and 1992? That is, what is the average inventory holding period for 1993 and 1992?

h. Assume that the obsolete inventory was entirely finished goods. What percent of finished goods was estimated to be obsolete in 1993 and 1992? What might explain the difference between the two numbers?

CALLAWAY GOLF COMPANY

CONSOLIDATED BALANCE SHEET
as at December 31
(in thousands)

	1993	1992
Assets		
Current assets:		
Cash and cash equivalents	$ 48,996	$20,019
Accounts receivable, net	17,546	11,302
Inventories, net	29,029	15,285
Deferred taxes	13,859	7,315
Other current assets	2,036	1,263
Total current assets	111,466	55,184
Property, plant and equipment, net	30,661	12,757
Other assets	2,233	996
	$144,360	$68,937
Liabilities and Shareholders' Equity		
Current liabilities:		
Accounts payable and accrued expenses	$ 11,949	$ 6,915
Accrued compensation and benefits	6,014	2,344
Accrued warranty	9,730	4,617
Income taxes payable	–	1,945
Total current liabilities	27,783	15,821
Long-term debt	–	3,366
Shareholders' equity:		
Common Stock, $ .01 par value, 60,000,000 shares authorized, 16,897,608 and 14,115,360 issued and outstanding at December 31, 1993 and 1992 (Notes 5 and 11)	169	140
Paid-in-capital	57,807	31,948
Retained earnings	58,601	17,662
Total shareholders' equity	116,577	49,750
	$144,360	$68,937

See accompanying notes to consolidated financial statements.

CALLAWAY GOLF COMPANY

CONSOLIDATED STATEMENT OF INCOME
for the year ended December 31
(in thousands, except per share data)

	1993		1992		1991	
Net sales	$254,645	100%	$132,058	100%	$54,753	100%
Cost of goods sold	115,458	45%	62,970	48%	26,175	48%
Gross profit	139,187	55%	69,088	52%	28,578	52%
Selling expenses	38,485	15%	19,810	15%	11,342	21%
General and administrative expenses	28,633	11%	14,900	11%	5,622	10%
Research and development costs	3,653	1%	1,585	1%	845	2%
Income from operations	68,416	27%	32,703	25%	10,769	20%
Other income (expense)						
Interest income (expense), net	1,024		403		(163)	
Other income, net	160		69		165	
Income before income taxes and cumulative effect of accounting change	69,600	27%	33,175	25%	10,771	20%
Provision for income taxes	28,396		13,895		4,355	
Income before effect of accounting change	41,204	16%	19,280	15%	6,416	12%
Cumulative effect of accounting change	1,658		—		—	
Net income	$ 42,862	17%	$ 19,280	15%	$ 6,416	12%

See accompanying notes to consolidated financial statements.

CALLAWAY GOLF COMPANY

CONSOLIDATED STATEMENT OF CASH FLOWS
for the year ended December 31
(in thousands, except per share data)

	1993	1992	1991
Cash Flows from Operating Activities:			
Net income	$42,862	$19,280	$6,416
Adjustments to reconcile net income to net cash provided by operating activities:			
Depreciation	3,016	1,372	633
Non-cash compensation	5,486	1,501	1,075
Increase (decrease) in cash resulting from changes in:			
Accounts receivable, net	(6,271)	(5,205)	(3,989)
Inventories, net	(13,771)	(4,097)	(2,660)
Deferred taxes	(6,544)	(5,042)	(1,808)
Other assets	(2,019)	(933)	(893)
Accounts payable and accrued expenses	5,055	1,189	3,326
Accrued compensation and benefits	2,009	1,387	671
Accrued warranty	5,114	3,316	1,074
Income taxes payable	(1,945)	782	1,163
Net cash provided by operating activities	32,992	13,550	5,008
Cash Flows from Investing Activities:			
Capital expenditures	(20,939)	(11,370)	(1,540)
Sale of fixed assets	17	3	4
Net cash used in investing activities	(20,922)	(11,367)	(1,536)
Cash Flows from Financing Activities:			
Repayments on note payable	—	—	(1,000)
Issuance of long-term debt	—	—	1,416
Issuance of Common Stock	5,603	16,461	—
Retirement of Common Stock	(336)	(5,000)	—
Retirement of stock options	—	—	(32)
Tax benefit from exercise of stock options	13,261	1,197	—
Dividends paid	(1,591)	—	—
Net cash provided by financing activities	16,937	12,658	384
Effect of exchange rate changes on cash	(30)	—	—
Net increase in cash and cash equivalents	28,977	14,841	3,856
Cash and cash equivalents at beginning of year	20,019	5,178	1,322
Cash and cash equivalents at end of year	$48,996	$20,019	$5,178

See accompanying notes to consolidated financial statements.

CALLAWAY GOLF COMPANY
NOTES TO CONSOLIDATED FINANCIAL STATEMENTS

1. The Company and Significant Accounting Policies

DESCRIPTION OF BUSINESS

Callaway Golf Company (Callaway or the Company) is a California corporation formed in 1982. The Company designs, develops, manufactures and markets high-quality, innovative golf clubs. Callaway's primary products during 1993 included Big Bertha® Metal Woods, S2H2® Irons and Metal Woods and Callaway Hickory Stick® Putters. The consolidated financial statements include the accounts of the Company and its wholly owned subsidiary, Callaway Golf (UK) Limited. All significant inter-company transactions and balances have been eliminated.

REVENUE RECOGNITION

Sales are recognized at the time goods are shipped, net of allowance for sales returns.

ADVERTISING COSTS

During 1993, the Accounting Standards Executive Committee finalized its Statement of Position (SOP) on Reporting Advertising Costs, which the Company will adopt prospectively as required in 1995. The SOP requires that advertising costs be expensed when incurred, with the exception of the costs of direct-response advertising, which are capitalized and amortized over the period that benefits are received. Adoption of the new SOP is not expected to have a significant effect on the Company's financial position or results of operations.

FOREIGN CURRENCY TRANSLATION AND TRANSACTIONS

The accounts of the Company's foreign subsidiary have been translated into United States dollars at appropriate rates of exchange. Cumulative translation gains or losses are recorded as a separate component of shareholders' equity. Gains or losses resulting from foreign currency transactions (transactions denominated in a currency other than the entity's local currency) are included in the consolidated statement of income and are not material.

During 1993, the Company entered into forward foreign currency exchange rate contracts to hedge payments due on intercompany transactions from its wholly owned foreign subsidiary. Realized and unrealized gains and losses on these contracts are recorded in net income. The effect of this practice is to minimize variability in the Company's operating results arising from foreign exchange rate movements. The Company does not engage in foreign currency speculation. These foreign exchange contracts do not subject the Company to risk due to exchange rate movements because gains and losses on these contracts offset losses and gains on the intercompany transactions being hedged, and the Company does not engage in hedging contracts which exceed the amount of the intercompany transactions. At December 31, 1993, the Company had approximately $824,000 of foreign exchange contracts outstanding. The contracts mature during January and February of 1994. The net realized and unrealized gain from foreign exchange contracts for 1993 totaled approximately $8,000.

EARNINGS PER COMMON SHARE

Primary earnings per common share are calculated by dividing net income by the weighted average number of common shares outstanding during the period increased by dilutive common stock equivalents using the treasury stock method. The calculation of fully diluted earnings per common share also includes the effect of the assumed conversion of the Company's Convertible Subordinated Bonds at the beginning of the year.

For the year ended December 31, 1991, pursuant to the requirements of the Security and Exchange Commission (SEC), common shares issued and stock options granted within one year prior to the Company's initial public offering at prices below the initial public offering price have been included in the calculation of the shares used in computing both primary and fully diluted earnings per common share as if they were outstanding for all of 1991 (using the treasury stock method). In addition, the calculation of the shares used in computing primary and fully diluted earnings per common share also includes the convertible preferred shares which converted into 8,965,588 common shares immediately preceding the closing of the initial public offering of Common Stock as if they were converted to common shares on their respective original dates of issuance.

CASH EQUIVALENTS

Cash equivalents are highly liquid investments purchased with a maturity of three months or less. Cash equivalents consist of investments in money market accounts and U.S. Treasury bills.

In May 1993, the Financial Accounting Standards Board issued Statement of Financial Accounting Standards (SFAS) No. 115 "Accounting for Certain Investments in Debt and Equity Securities," which the Company will adopt prospectively in 1994. Application of the new rules will result in the inclusion of unrealized gains and losses on certain of the Company's investments in the results of operations. Application of this accounting treatment is not expected to have a significant effect on the Company's financial position or results of operations.

INVENTORIES

Inventories are valued at the lower of cost or market. Cost is determined using the first-in, first-out (FIFO) method.

PROPERTY, PLANT AND EQUIPMENT

Property, plant and equipment are stated at cost less accumulated depreciation. Depreciation is computed using the straight-line method over estimated useful lives of five to fifteen years. Repairs and maintenance costs are charged to expense as incurred.

INCOME TAXES

Current income tax expense is the amount of income taxes expected to be payable for the current year. A deferred income tax liability or asset is established for the expected future consequences resulting from the differences in the financial reporting and tax basis of assets and liabilities. Deferred income tax expense is the net change during the year in the deferred income tax liability or asset (Note 8).

RECLASSIFICATIONS

Certain prior year balances have been reclassified to conform to the current year presentation.

2. Selected Financial Statement Information

(in thousands)

	Dec 31 1993	Dec 31 1992
Cash and Cash Equivalents:		
Cash, non-interest bearing	$591	$258
Cash, interest bearing	1,615	11,726
U.S. Treasury bills	46,790	8,035
	$48,996	$20,019
Accounts Receivable, net:		
Trade accounts receivable	$20,581	$13,084
Allowance for doubtful accounts	(3,035)	(1,782)
	$17,546	$11,302
Inventories, net:		
Raw materials	$11,853	$ 5,325
Work-in-process	577	288
Finished goods	16,599	9,672
	$29,029	$15,285

Property, Plant and Equipment:

Land	$ 2,403	—
Building	8,878	—
Machinery and equipment	5,969	$ 2,991
Production molds	1,985	791
Furniture, computers and equipment	6,484	4,004
Building improvements	4,499	3,110
Construction in process	5,445	3,990
	35,663	14,886
Accumulated depreciation	(5,002)	(2,129)
	$30,661	$12,757

Accounts Payable and Accrued Expenses:

Accounts payable	$ 7,854	$ 3,434
Accrued expenses	3,801	3,033
Other accrued expenses	294	448
	$11,949	$ 6,915

Accrued Compensation and Benefits:

Accrued payroll and taxes	$4,896	$ 1,655
Accrued vocational and sick pay	916	546
Accrued commissions	292	143
	$6,104	$ 2,344

Other:

Inventory includes an allowance for obsolescence of approximately $5,155 and $5,221 at December 31, 1993 and 1992, respectively. Total rent expense was $1,119, $1,095 and $462 in 1993, 1992 and 1991, respectively.

Frederick's of Hollywood—Property & Equipment

Frederick's of Hollywood, Inc. is a specialty retailer, operating a chain of women's intimate apparel stores throughout the United States. The Company also has a national mail order apparel business selling lingerie, bras, foundations, dresses, sportswear, leisurewear, swimwear, hosiery, specialty menswear and accessories. Frederick's of Hollywood purchases its merchandise from a variety of manufacturers.

Learning Objectives
- Synthesize information from various financial statements to analyze fixed asset and depreciation transactions.
- Prepare journal entries related to fixed asset transactions.
- Compute depreciation expenses using common accounting methods.
- Calculate gains and losses on fixed asset disposals.
- Introduce the fixed asset turnover ratio.

Refer to the 1996 financial statements of Frederick's of Hollywood, Inc.

Concepts

a. Based on the above description of Frederick's of Hollywood, what sort of property and equipment do you think the company has?

b. Does Frederick's of Hollywood *own* all the property and equipment it reports on the balance sheet?

c. The 1996 balance sheet shows accumulated depreciation of $19,479,000. How much of this is attributable to the land account? (*Hint*: You should be able to answer this without looking at the statements.)

d. How does Frederick's of Hollywood depreciate property and equipment? Does this policy seem reasonable? Explain the tradeoffs management makes in choosing a depreciation policy.

Process

e. Use T-accounts to reconstruct the activity in the "Property & equipment, at cost" and "Accumulated depreciation and amortization" accounts for the period September 3, 1995 to August 31, 1996. Begin by entering the opening and ending balances in the accounts. Then, determine the appropriate increases and decreases in the account due to the following (*Hint*: what journal entry did the company record for each event?):

    i. The purchase of new property and equipment in fiscal 1996.

    ii. Depreciation for fiscal 1996.

    iii. The sale of property and equipment in fiscal 1996.

f. According to the statement of cash flows, Frederick's of Hollywood received proceeds on the sale of fixed assets amounting to $7,000 in fiscal 1996 and recorded a loss of $84,000 on this disposal. Recalculate the loss and prepare the journal entry to record the transaction.

g. Assume that the fixed assets purchased during fiscal 1996 have an expected useful life of five years and a salvage value of $573,000. Prepare a table showing the depreciation expense and net book value of this equipment over its expected life assuming that a full year of depreciation is taken in fiscal 1996 and the company uses:

    i. Straight-line depreciation.

    ii. Double declining balance depreciation.

h. Assume the equipment purchased in fiscal 1996 was sold September 1, 1996 (i.e., the first day of fiscal 1997) for proceeds of $3,200,000. Prepare the journal entry to record the transaction assuming Frederick's accounting policy states that no depreciation is taken in the year of disposal and that the company uses:

    i.   Straight-line depreciation.

    ii.   Double declining balance depreciation.

Analysis

i. A ratio analysts use to gauge the efficiency with which management is using its invested capital is the fixed asset turnover ratio. The ratio is defined as:

$$Fixed\ Asset\ Turnover = \frac{Sales}{Average\ Fixed\ Assets}.$$

Determine Frederick's of Hollywood's fixed asset turnover ratio for fiscal 1995 and 1996. Comment on the year over year change. (The balance of Net Property and Equipment at September 3, 1994 was $19,892,000.)

FREDERICK'S OF HOLLYWOOD, INC.

CONSOLIDATED STATEMENTS OF OPERATIONS

(000's omitted)

For the fiscal year ended	August 31 1996	September 3 1995	August 28 1994
Net sales	$148,090	$142,931	$132,153
Costs and expenses:			
Cost of goods sold, buying and occupancy costs	88,059	84,203	77,409
Selling, general and administrative expenses	60,871	54,957	52,530
Provision for store closing	—	(790)	3,442
	148,930	138,370	133,381
Operating profit(loss)	(840)	4,561	(1,228)
Other income (expense):			
Interest expense	(107)	(118)	(150)
Miscellaneous	283	(31)	(327)
	176	(149)	(477)
Earnings(loss) before income taxes	(664)	4,412	(1,705)
Income taxes (benefit)	(226)	1,760	(682)
Earnings (loss) before cumulative effect of a change in accounting principle	(438)	2,652	(1,023)
Cumulative effect of a change in accounting principle	—	—	120
Net earnings(loss)	$ (438)	$ 2,652	$ (903)
Earnings(loss) per share			
Primary - Classes A & B	$ (.05)	$ .31	$ (.10)
Fully diluted - Classes A & B	$ (.05)	$ .30	$ (.10)
Weighted average shares outstanding			
Primary - Classes A & B	8 745	8,693	8,876
Fully diluted - Classes A & B	8,745	8,702	8,875

See accompanying notes to consolidated financial statements.

FREDERICK'S OF HOLLYWOOD, INC.

CONSOLIDATED BALANCE SHEETS

(000's omitted)

	August 31 1996	September 2 1995
Assets		
Current assets		
Cash and cash equivalents	$ 8,379	$11,441
Short term investment	480	—
Accounts receivable	499	658
Income tax receivable	945	213
Merchandise inventories	19,553	19,862
Deferred income taxes	843	765
Prepaid expenses	2,215	2,615
Total current assets	32,914	35,554
Property and equipment, at cost		
Land	128	128
Buildings and improvements	881	698
Fixtures and equipment	14,687	13,473
Leasehold improvements	20,130	18,878
Property under capital leases	1,686	1,686
	37,512	34,863
Less accumulated depreciation and amortization	(19,479)	(16,638)
Net property and equipment	18,033	18,225
Deferred catalog costs	1,723	2,107
Other assets	39	39
	$52,709	$55,925
Liabilities and Stockholders' Equity		
Current liabilities		
Accounts payable	$10,298	$11,617
Dividends payable	221	221
Current portion of		
Capital lease obligations	212	200
ESOP loan guarantee	240	240
Accrued payroll	430	526
Accrued insurance	828	1,018
Other accrued expenses	238	469
Total current liabilities	12,467	14,291
Capital lease obligations	672	884
ESOP loan guarantee	240	480
Deferred rent	811	669
Deferred income taxes	2,994	3,002
Stockholders' equity		
Capital stock of $1 par value Authorized 15,000,000 Class A shares, 35,000,000 Class B shares; issued 2,955,000 Class A shares, 5,903,000 Class B shares in 1996 and 1995	8,858	8,858
Additional paid-in capital	732	738
Reduction for ESOP loan guarantee	(456)	(701)
Treasury stock	(6)	(5)
Retained earnings	26,397	27,709
Total stockholders' equity	35,525	36,599
	$52,709	$55,925

See accompanying notes to consolidated financial statements.

FREDERICK'S OF HOLLYWOOD, INC.

CONSOLIDATED STATEMENTS OF CASH FLOWS

For the fiscal year ended (000's omitted)	August 31 1996	Sept. 2 1995	Sept. 3 1994
Cash Flows from Operating Activities:			
Net income (loss)	$ (438)	$2,652	$ (903)
Adjustments to reconcile net income (loss) to net cash provided by operating activities:			
Provision for store closing	—	(1,852)	3,290
Depreciation and amortization	4,174	4,105	4,206
ESOP compensation	257	224	—
Loss on sale of fixed assets	84	431	358
Changes in assets and liabilities:			
Accounts receivable	159	(130)	(54)
Income tax receivable	(732)	668	(881)
Merchandise inventories	309	(1,948)	(753)
Prepaid expenses	400	(403)	(746)
Deferred catalog costs	384	(524)	183
Other assets	—	(1)	5
Accounts payable and accrued expenses	(1,836)	677	3,011
Deferred rent	142	158	215
Deferred income taxes	(86)	779	(1,062)
Income taxes payable	—	—	(258)
Net cash provided by operating activities	2,817	4,836	6,611
Cash Flows from Investing Activities:			
Proceeds from sale of fixed assets	7	205	2
Purchase of short term investments	(480)	—	—
Capital expenditures	(4,073)	(3,082)	(2,348)
Net cash used for investing activities	(4,546)	(2,877)	(2,346)
Cash Flows from Financing Activities:			
Payment of capital lease obligations	(200)	(365)	(506)
Payment of dividends	(869)	(431)	(443)
Payment of dividends on unearned ESOP shares	(17)	(11)	—
Purchase of treasury stock	(7)	(26)	—
Proceeds from exercise of stock options	—	—	108
Net increase (decrease) in ESOP loan guarantee (liability)	(240)	(240)	960
Reduction for ESOP loan guarantee (equity)	—	—	(960)
Stock split	—	(1)	(4)
Net cash used for financing activities	(1,333)	(1,074)	(845)
Net increase (decrease) in cash and cash equivalents	(3,062)	885	3,420
Cash and cash equivalents at beginning of year	11,441	10,556	7,136
Cash and cash equivalents at end of year	$ 8,379	$11,441	$10,556

Supplemental disclosure to consolidated statements of cash flows:

Cash flow information:			
Interest paid	$ 111	$ 118	$ 150
Income taxes paid	601	802	1,386
Non-cash investing and financing transactions:			
Leases capitalized	—	747	—
Dividends declared	221	221	—
Provision for store closing			
Fixed asset disposal	—	756	475
Inventory disposal	—	183	24

FREDERICK'S OF HOLLYWOOD, INC.
NOTES TO CONSOLIDATED FINANCIAL STATEMENTS
(excerpts)

One. Summary of Significant Accounting Policies

The Company and Basis of Presentation   The consolidated financial statements include the accounts of Frederick's of Hollywood, Inc. and its subsidiaries (collectively referred to as the Company). All significant intercompany balances and transactions have been eliminated in consolidation.

Depreciation and Amortization   Properties and equipment are depreciated on the straight-line method based upon useful lives which range from 10 to 25 years for buildings and improvements and four to ten years for equipment. Leasehold improvements are amortized over the remaining term of the lease or their useful lives, whichever is shorter.

Impairment of Long-Lived Assets   In the event that facts and circumstances indicate that the cost of long-lived assets or other assets may be impaired, an evaluation of recoverability would be performed. If an evaluation is required, the estimated future undiscounted cash flows associated with the asset would be compared to the asset's carrying amount to determine if a write-down to market value or discounted cash flow value is required.

Six. Leases and Commitments

The Company leases office equipment under capital leases expiring in various years through 2000. Future minimum lease payments under capital leases are as follows (000's omitted):

1997	$ 211
1998	225
1999	238
2000	210
Total minimum lease payments	$ 884
Less amount representing interest	102
Present value of minimum lease payments	$ 782

There are no executory costs of contingent rental provisions in the capital leases.

Hilton Hotels Corporation—Capitalized Costs

Hilton Hotels Corporation is primarily engaged in the ownership and management of hotels and hotel-casinos. On February 1, 1996, Hilton owned or leased and operated 23 hotels and managed 44 hotels partially or wholly-owned by others. In addition, 164 hotels were operated under the "Hilton," "Hilton Garden Inn," and "Hilton Suites" names by others pursuant to franchises granted by a subsidiary of Hilton. The Company also partially owns and manages one river casino in the United States and owns a minority interest in a company which operates one casino in Canada.

Learning Objectives
- Explain when companies are allowed to capitalize interest and other costs.
- Understand the financial statement effect of capitalizing interest and other costs.
- Restate a company's financial statements to reflect alternative capitalization policies.

Refer to the 1995 financial statements of Hilton Hotels Corporation.

Concepts

a. Under what conditions are companies allowed to capitalize interest? Do you agree with this accounting practice? Why or why not?

b. How does Hilton account for interest costs?

c. How does Hilton account for pre-opening costs? What sorts of costs would be included in the "pre-opening costs" account?

Process

d. Provide the journal entry recorded by Hilton to account for 1995 interest costs. Ignore the line item "Interest expense, net, from unconsolidated affiliates."

Analysis

e. You want to compare the operating results of Hilton Hotels to those of another hotel chain. The other company does not capitalize interest or pre-opening costs. Assume that Hilton began capitalizing interest costs in 1985. The total interest capitalized through December 31, 1992 was $20 million. Assume that when interest is capitalized it is included in depreciable assets in the same year. Also assume that hotels are depreciated straight-line over 40 years. Pre-opening costs were not capitalized until January 1, 1993. Capitalized pre-opening costs amounted to $6 million, $9 million, and $12 million in 1993, 1994, and 1995, respectively. Assume that the amortization of pre-opening costs begins the year following their capitalization.

Restate Hilton Hotels' 1993, 1994 and 1995 net income on a basis comparable with that of its competitor.

HILTON HOTELS CORPORATION AND SUBSIDIARIES

CONSOLIDATED STATEMENTS OF INCOME
(In millions, except per share amounts)

Year Ended December 31,	1995	1994	1993
Revenue			
Rooms	$ 587.2	$ 509.6	$ 440.2
Food and beverage	265.7	247.2	236.8
Casino	511.0	480.6	502.1
Management and franchise fees	100.5	94.5	85.1
Other	125.4	124.2	93.8
Operating income from unconsolidated affiliates	59.6	57.8	35.5
	1,649.4	1,513.9	1,393.5
Expenses			
Rooms	186.4	171.8	152.5
Food and beverage	229.4	216.4	202.4
Casino	234.9	216.3	217.5
Other costs and expenses	613.2	596.5	554.4
Corporate expense	31.9	28.3	26.8
	1,295.8	1,229.3	1,153.6
Operating Income	353.6	284.6	239.9
Interest and dividend income	35.2	21.5	21.8
Interest expense	(93.5)	(85.7)	(80.4)
Interest expense, net, from unconsolidated affiliates	(16.5)	(12.2)	(14.6)
Property transactions, net	1.5	1.1	(4.5)
Foreign currency losses	—	(.7)	(1.3)
Income Before Income Taxes and Minority Interest	280.3	208.6	160.9
Provision for income taxes	102.6	85.3	58.2
Minority interest, net	4.9	1.6	—
Income Before Cumulative Effect of Accounting Changes	172.8	121.7	102.7
Cumulative effect of accounting changes, net	—	—	3.4
Net Income	$ 172.8	$ 121.7	$ 106.1
Income Per Share			
Before cumulative effect of accounting changes	$ 3.56	$ 2.52	$ 2.14
Cumulative effect of accounting changes, net	—	—	.07
Net Income Per Share	$ 3.56	$ 2.52	$ 2.21

See notes to consolidated financial statements.

HILTON HOTELS CORPORATION AND SUBSIDIARIES

CONSOLIDATED BALANCE SHEETS

(In millions)

December 31,	1995	1994
Assets		
Current Assets		
Cash and equivalents	$ 338.0	$ 184.4
Temporary investments	70.7	208.8
Deferred income taxes	24.1	26.0
Other current assets	284.5	254.5
Total current assets	717.3	673.7
Investments, Property and Other Assets		
Investments in and notes from unconsolidated affiliates	576.2	518.0
Other investments	19.1	18.7
Property and equipment, net	1,695.9	1,664.8
Other assets	51.8	50.7
Total investments, property and other assets	2,343.0	2,252.2
Total Assets	$3,060.3	$2,925.9
Liabilities and Stockholders' Equity		
Liabilities		
Current liabilities	$ 534.9	$ 328.3
Long-term debt	1,069.7	1,251.9
Deferred income taxes	123.7	124.3
Insurance reserves and other	78.3	93.6
Total liabilities	1,806.6	1,798.1
Stockholders' Equity		
Preferred stock, none outstanding	—	—
Common stock, 48.3 million and 48.1 million shares outstanding, respectively	127.6	127.6
Cumulative translation adjustment	(1.4)	(.7)
Unrealized loss on marketable securities	(4.6)	(5.3)
Retained earnings	1,274.6	1,160.7
	1,396.2	1,282.3
Less treasury shares, at cost	142.5	154.5
Total Stockholders' equity	1,253.7	1,127.8
Total Liabilities and Stockholders' Equity	$3,060.3	$2,925.9

See notes to consolidated financial statements.

HILTON HOTELS CORPORATION AND SUBSIDIARIES
CONSOLIDATED STATEMENTS OF CASH FLOWS
(In millions)

Year Ended December 31,	1995	1994	1993
Operating Activities			
Net Income	$172.8	$121.7	$106.1
Adjustments to reconcile net income to net cash provided by operating activities:			
Depreciation and amortization	141.9	133.3	118.9
Change in working capital components:			
Inventories	(.7)	.7	.7
Accounts receivable	(20.6)	(54.7)	(17.9)
Other current assets	(7.2)	(5.5)	(19.9)
Accounts payable and accrued expenses	24.1	35.9	(8.2)
Income taxes payable	4.0	(1.2)	(9.2)
Change in deferred income taxes	1.0	(20.8)	(6.6)
Change in other liabilities	(13.7)	7.8	29.4
Unconsolidated affiliates' distributions in excess of earnings	29.4	5.9	20.1
(Gain) loss from property transactions	(1.5)	(1.1)	4.5
Other	1.2	8.9	9.0
Net cash provided by operating activities	330.7	230.9	226.9
Investing Activities			
Capital expenditures	(187.1)	(254.4)	(156.8)
Additional investments	(98.3)	(156.7)	(104.7)
Decrease in long-term marketable securities	1.0	62.6	91.2
Change in temporary investments	139.1	(118.8)	64.3
Payments on notes and other	17.5	60.9	5.9
Net cash used in investing activities	(127.8)	(406.4)	(100.1)
Financing Activities			
Change in commercial paper borrowings and revolving loans	189.2	(112.9)	.8
Long-term borrowings	1.0	170.0	1.0
Reduction of long-term debt	(192.6)	(31.5)	(46.3)
Issuance of common stock	11.0	11.5	6.9
Cash dividends	(57.9)	(57.6)	(57.3)
Net cash used in financing activities	(49.3)	(20.5)	(94.9)
Increase (Decrease) in Cash and Equivalents	153.6	(196.0)	31.9
Cash and Equivalents at Beginning of Year	184.4	380.4	348.5
Cash and Equivalents at End of Year	$338.0	$184.4	$380.4

See notes to consolidated financial statements.

HILTON HOTELS CORPORATION AND SUBSIDIARIES
NOTES TO CONSOLIDATED FINANCIAL STATEMENTS

Summary of Significant Accounting Policies

Property, Equipment and Depreciation

Property and equipment are stated at cost. Interest incurred during construction of facilities is capitalized and amortized over the life of the asset.

Costs of improvements are capitalized. Costs of normal repairs and maintenance are charged to expense as incurred. Upon the sale or retirement of property and equipment, the cost and related accumulated depreciation are removed from the respective accounts, and the resulting gain or loss, if any, is included in income.

Depreciation is provided on a straight line basis over the estimated useful life of the assets. Leasehold improvements are amortized over the shorter of the asset life or lease term. The service lives of assets are generally 40 years for buildings, 30 years for riverboats and 8 years for building improvements and furniture and equipment.

Pre-Opening Costs

Costs associated with the opening of new properties or major additions to properties placed in service through December 31, 1994 were deferred and charged to income over a three year period after the opening date. For projects placed in service after December 31, 1994, pre-opening costs are deferred and amortized over the shorter of the period benefited or one year.

Property and Equipment

Property and equipment at December 31, 1995 and 1994 are as follows:

(In millions)	1995	1994
Land	$ 158.1	$ 158.1
Buildings and leasehold improvements	1,749.6	1,617.1
Furniture and equipment	517.5	490.7
Property held for sale or development	36.8	57.2
Construction in progress	28.2	85.6
	2,490.2	2,408.7
Less accumulated depreciation	794.3	743.9
Total	$1,695.9	$1,664.8

Purchases of property and equipment financed with construction payables totaled $12.8 million, $14.4 million and $2.9 million at December 31, 1995, 1994 and 1993, respectively.

Long Term Debt (excerpt)

Interest paid, net of amounts capitalized, was $95.3 million, $88.3 million and $79.8 million in 1995, 1994 and 1993, respectively. Capitalized interest amounted to $3.3 million, $7.0 million and $2.0 million, respectively.

Chambers Development Co. Inc.—Capitalizing Costs

Chambers Development Company, Inc. is one the largest providers of integrated solid waste management services in the United States, with operations in 17 states in the east and southwest. Major elements of this business include the operation, management, construction and engineering of solid waste sanitary landfills, transfer stations, recycling facilities and related operations. The company also provides services for the collection, hauling and recycling of solid waste for municipal, commercial, industrial and residential customers.

Learning Objectives
- Distinguish between costs and expenses.
- Explain the relationship between matching and conservatism.
- Distinguish between costs that should be capitalized and costs that should be expensed.
- Explain how to assess the quality of a firm's earnings.
- Understand management's incentives to engage in "aggressive accounting."

Refer to the 1990 financial statements and notes for Chambers Development.

Concepts

a. Find the "Summary of Significant Accounting Policies" (excerpts) note in the financial statements. This note discusses three areas in which Chambers delays recognition of costs in the income statement by including (i.e., capitalizing) the amounts on the balance sheet.

   i. Explain what is meant by the term "cost."

   ii. Explain what is meant by the term "expense." Are costs and expenses the same thing?

   iii. In general, when should costs be recognized as expenses and when should they be capitalized?

   iv. What becomes of costs after their initial capitalization?

b. Based only on the information provided in the financial statements, what kind of costs are included in the "Land, primarily landfill sites" account. Provide specific examples.

c. Read the *Forbes* article entitled, "Fuzzy Accounting." The article implies that matching and conservatism are mutually exclusive concepts in accounting. In your own words, explain what is meant by "matching." Next, explain what is meant by "conservatism." How are these two concepts related?

Process

d. In the months following their March 17, 1992 announcement, Chambers disclosed a number of costs that were originally capitalized by the company. For the following items, discuss whether (or under what circumstances) *you* think the company should have capitalized or expensed the cost.

   i. "Executive salaries and travel expenses."

   ii. "Public relations expense and legal fees."

   iii. "Interest expense" for purchase and development of landfills.

   iv. "Cost of disposing of waste ... in landfills owned by other waste companies during periods when [Chambers] closed its own landfills for reissuing of permits."

   v. "Internal costs relating to the acquisition of companies."

e. Based on the precipitous decline in stock price upon announcement of Chambers' "aggressive" accounting ($30.50 per share on March 17, 1992, the day before the announcement; $11.50 per share on March 18, 1992, the day after the announcement; $6.25 per share on October 20, 1992, the day after Chambers announced it was expensing $363 million of costs previously capitalized), it appears that the financial markets were fooled by the annual reports published by the company. Surely, *you* wouldn't have been fooled. Explain how you would have "seen through" the creative accounting used by the company and explain how you could have assessed that Chambers' earnings were of poor quality. Your answer should not be limited to information published by Chambers.

f. "Former employees [of Chambers] say ... a relentless push for corporate growth led to an environment in which manipulating numbers was tolerated, if not encouraged" (*Wall Street Journal*, October 21, 1992, p. A1). Why would Chambers' management engage in such "creative" accounting (i.e., deferring costs that are normally immediately expensed). That is, what incentives does management have to defer costs?

CHAMBERS DEVELOPMENT COMPANY, INC.
CONSOLIDATED STATEMENTS OF EARNINGS

(Dollars in thousands, except per share amounts) Year Ended December 31	1990	1989	1988
Net Sales	$258,201	$181,898	$137,040
Costs and Expenses			
Operating	152,747	106,757	82,835
Selling General and Administrative	31,807	21,191	17,927
Depreciation and Amortization	18,189	15,680	10,985
Earnings from Operations	55,458	38,270	25,293
Other income (Expense)			
Other income, primarily interest	6,643	7,830	5,607
Interest expense	(5,312)	(1,344)	(723)
Earnings before income taxes and effect of a change in accounting principle	56,789	44,576	30,177
Provision for income taxes	22,432	17,671	10,713
Earnings before effect of a change in accounting principle	34,357	27,085	19,464
Cumulative effect on prior years of a change in accounting principle	—	—	1,272
Net Earnings	$ 34,357	$ 27,085	$ 20,736
Earnings per common equivalent share			
Earnings before effect of a change in accounting principle	$ .63	$ .53	$ .42
Cumulative effect adjustment	—	—	.03
Net Earnings	$ .63	$ .53	$ .45
Earnings per common share assuming full dilution			
Earnings before effect of a change in accounting principle	$ .63	$ .51	$ .40
Cumulative effect of adjustment	—	—	.03
Net Earnings	$ .63	$ .51	$ .43

The accompanying notes are an integral part of these statements.

CHAMBERS DEVELOPMENT COMPANY, INC.

CONSOLIDATED BALANCE SHEETS

(Dollars in Thousands) December 31	1990	1989
Assets		
Current Assets		
Cash and cash equivalents	$156,106	$ 84,642
Marketable securities, at cost which approximates market	13,049	16,736
Accounts receivable		
Trade less allowances of $2,930 and $1,406, respectively	32,238	22,943
Other	2,867	3,470
Inventories	3,021	3,140
Prepaid expenses	3,691	3,417
Total current assets	210,972	134,348
Property and Equipment		
Land, primarily landfill sites	383,601	223,842
Vehicles and equipment	80,715	73,075
Other	44,802	32,277
	509,118	329,194
Less accumulated depreciation and amortization	71,450	52,725
Total property and equipment	437,668	276,469
Other Assets		
Funds held for escrow requirements	25,391	33,321
Deferred costs	27,573	18,303
Costs in excess of fair market value of net tangible assets of acquired businesses	74,902	51,609
Other	2,387	3,081
Total other assets	130,253	106,314
	$778,893	$517,131

CHAMBERS DEVELOPMENT COMPANY, INC.
CONSOLIDATED BALANCE SHEETS

(Dollars in Thousands)

	1990	1989
Liabilities and Stockholders' Equity		
Current Liabilities		
Notes payable to bank	$ 8,365	$ —
Current maturities of long-term obligations	15,913	13,088
Trade accounts payable	9,494	7,584
Income taxes	2,077	3,065
Accrued liabilities	33,392	24,997
Deferred revenue	5,706	5,577
Total current liabilities	74,947	54,311
Long-Term Obligations, less current maturities	279,864	77,758
Deferred Income Taxes	22,180	15,954
Deferred Revenue	23,561	32,480
Other Non-Current Liabilities	14,371	6,922
Commitments and Contingencies	—	—
6 3/4% Convertible Subordinated Notes Due September 15, 2004	110,000	110,000
Stockholders' Equity		
Preferred Stock-authorized 10,000,000 shares; no par value; no shares issued or outstanding	—	—
Class A Common Stock-authorized 100,000,000 shares: par value $.50 per share; issued 38,345,363 and 19,154,151 shares respectively	19,173	9,577
Common Stock-authorized 50,000,000 shares: par value $.50 per share; convertible into Class A Common Stock; issued 16,672,800 and 8,345,640 shares respectively	8,336	4,173
Additional paid-in capital	126,478	139,947
Retained earnings	104,133	70,159
	258,120	223,856
Less treasury stock at cost—Class A Common Stock, 400 and 200 shares respectively: Common Stock 369,200 and 184,600 shares, respectively	4,150	4,150
Total stockholders' equity	253,970	219,706
	$778,893	$717,131

The accompanying notes are an integral part of these statements

CHAMBERS DEVELOPMENT COMPANY, INC.

NOTES TO CONSOLIDATED FINANCIAL STATEMENTS

NOTE A—Summary of Significant Accounting Policies (excerpts)

Property and Equipment

Landfill disposal sites, including land and related landfill preparation and improvement costs, are stated at cost. Landfill preparation and improvement costs are amortized as consumed during the useful lives of the sites.

Deferred Costs

Deferred costs include debt issuance costs and development costs for waste collection and security guard service contracts. Debt issuance costs are amortized over the terms of the related debt. Development costs are amortized over periods which range from three to ten years.

Capitalized Interest

During the years ended December 31, 1990, 1989, and 1988, the company incurred interest costs of $17,466,000, $11,548,000, and $10,489,000 of which $12,154,000, $10,204,000, and $9,766,000 were capitalized on landfills under development.

Wall Street punished Chambers Development for its aggressive accounting. But drawing the line between expensing and capitalizing costs isn't easy.

Fuzzy accounting

Copyright 1992 Forbes, Inc.
Forbes
June 22, 1992

SECTION: LAW AND ISSUES; Numbers Game; Pg. 96
By Roula Khalaf

A FEW MONTHS AGO Chambers Development, Inc. (FORBES, Oct. 21, 1991) was the darling of Wall Street. Then, on Mar. 17, the developer of landfills dropped a bombshell. Chambers said it would start expensing indirect costs related to developing landfill sites. The company had been capitalizing these costs, which include public relations and legal costs to obtain permits for landfills.

The change resulted in a $27 million charge to earnings, wiping out more than half the company's 1991 net income—and more than $1.4 billion of Chambers' market valuation.

The debate whether to expense or defer costs is one of the biggest in accounting. And it's heating up in the wake of the Chambers writeoff. The general rule is that companies can capitalize costs only when the costs provide benefits beyond the year in which they are incurred. But it's often difficult to determine if work done today will bring future revenue, and when.

Robert Willens, an accounting expert at Shearson Lehman Brothers, thinks Chambers' capitalization was perfectly valid. Why? Because, he argues, Chambers was simply matching the cost of obtaining permits against future landfill revenues. "There's a belief that conservative accounting is accurate accounting," says Willens, "but there's a larger principle you have to adhere to, and that's to match revenues with expenses."

But in filing with the SEC, Chambers' accounting firm, Grant Thornton—it has since been fired—says it couldn't determine how much of the legal and public relations costs were attributable to the future development of the landfills. So the accountants wrote off everything. Chambers is undergoing a new audit, so the final chapter of the Chambers story won't be written until the summer.

Because the capitalization rules often aren't well defined, analysts and investors get nervous when companies seem to be aggressively capitalizing costs. For example: Short-sellers have been betting credit card issuer Advanta Corp. will eventually take a big writeoff. Why? Partly because Advanta capitalizes the costs of issuing the cards and amortizes them over five years. In 1991 Advanta deferred $24 million of such costs. Its net income last year was just $25 million. Yet its competitor MBNA Corp. expenses much of the costs within a year of when they're incurred.

Even when accountants have written specific rules on capitalization of costs, the rules are followed in a variety of ways. Take software development. The rules say a company can start capitalizing the cost of developing a product when it has reached the point of "technological feasibility." When is that? Microsoft doesn't capitalize any development costs. Most other software companies typically capitalize 10% to 20% of their total R&D budget.

But tiny ($18 million in revenues) Greensburg, Pa.-based Sulcus Computer capitalized over 60% of its $2.8 million R&D budget last year. "Maybe other companies' R&D departments haven't been as successful," says Robert Colleran, Sulcus chief financial officer. Maybe.

How can investors be protected against unexpected writeoffs that can send stocks plunging? Look for footnotes that describe a company's capitalization policy. Advanta, for instance, spells out its policies clearly. Chambers didn't. Also, look closely at what companies include in their "other assets" category on the balance sheet. That's where they tend to dump a lot of deferred costs that could come back to bite shareholders if they have to be written off.

Loren Kellogg, publisher of Financial Statement Alert, which scrutinizes accounting practices, cites Continental Medical Systems, an operator of rehabilitation hospitals, as one company where he has seen red flags. The company capitalizes costs it incurs to obtain government approval for its facilities as well as to develop the hospitals. For the fiscal year ended June 30, 1991, Continental reported $29 million in such deferred costs for some 30 facilities under development. Operating earnings: just $35 million.

Ultimately the answer lies in more detailed disclosure requirements. Had Chambers spelled out how much of its costs it was booking as assets, the writeoff wouldn't have been such a nasty surprise. Unfortunately, the market is full of Chambers Developments, waiting to happen.

Merck & Co., Inc.—Research & Development

> *Merck & Co., Inc. is a worldwide research-intensive health products company that discovers, develops, produces and markets human and animal health products and services. The Company's dominant industry segment is the Human and Animal Health Products and Services segment, which includes Medco Containment Services, Inc., acquired in November 1993.*

Learning Objectives
- Read management's discussion and analysis and use the information to infer accounting events.
- Consider the cost components that underlie the income statement line item research and development.
- Understand how U.S. GAAP differs from that of other jurisdictions on the treatment of research and development costs.
- Understand how the balance sheet, the income statement, and the statement of cash flows are affected by a decision to capitalize costs rather than expense them.
- Adjust net income and balance sheet amounts and quantify the accounting effect of capitalizing previously expensed development costs.

Refer to the 1994 financial statements of Merck & Co., Inc. and to the excerpt from the Management Discussion and Analysis which contains information about Merck's R&D program. Merck follows SFAS 2 which requires R&D costs be expensed as they are incurred.

Concepts

a. The 1994 income statement shows Research and Development Expense of (in millions) $1,230.6 in 1994, $1,172.8 in 1993 and $1,111.6 in 1992. What types of costs are likely included in these amounts?

b. If Merck was a Canadian corporation its R&D accounting would be different. Accounting principles in Canada are set by the Canadian Institute of Chartered Accountants (CICA) and promulgated through the CICA Handbook. An excerpt from the CICA Handbook, pertaining to R&D accounting, is provided following the Merck financial statements.

   Which accounting principles provide a better matching of costs and benefits, those of FASB's SFAS No. 2 or the CICA's Handbook section 3450? Explain with particular reference to Merck's research program.

Process

c. Merck's 1991 Statement of Income showed R&D expenses of $987.8 million for 1991 and $854.0 million for 1990.

   i. Calculate Merck's R&D expense for the period 1980 to 1989 inclusive.

   ii. Provide the journal entry made by Merck to record 1994 R&D expense. Consider your answer to part *a* in determining which accounts are affected.

Analysis

d. Assume that you are a financial analyst. You would like to compare Merck to a Canadian corporation. As such, you decide to prepare pro-forma information for Merck assuming they follow Canadian GAAP.

   Assume that Merck incurred no R&D expenses prior to 1980 and that each year 25% of the expenditures could be considered development costs as defined by the CICA. Assume further that

Merck amortizes development costs beginning in the year after they are incurred, and over two years.

i. What would Merck have reported as Net Income in 1994, 1993 and 1992 under Canadian R&D accounting principles?

ii. What gross asset amount would be shown on the balance sheet at the end of each of the three years under Canadian R&D accounting? What would the accumulated amortization be in each of the three years.

iii. How would cash be affected for fiscal 1994 if Merck followed Canadian GAAP? Would the cash flow statement be different?

MERCK & CO., INC. AND SUBSIDIARIES

MANAGEMENT DISCUSSION & ANALYSIS
Year Ended December 31, 1994

Research and Development

The Company's business is characterized by the introduction of new products or new uses for existing products through a strong research and development program. Approximately 6,300 people are employed in the Company's research activities. Expenditures for the Company's research and development programs were $1,230.6 million in 1994, $1,172.8 million in 1993 and $1,111.6 million in 1992 and will be close to $1.3 billion in 1995. The Company maintains its ongoing commitment to research over a broad range of therapeutic areas and clinical development in support of new products. Total expenditures for the period 1980 through 1994 exceeded $9.8 billion with a compound annual growth rate of 13 percent. Costs incurred by the joint ventures in which the Company participates, totaling $319.4 million in 1994, are not included in the Company's consolidated research and development expenses.

The Company maintains a number of long-term exploratory and fundamental research programs in biology and chemistry as well as research programs directed toward product development. Projects related to human and animal health are being carried on in various fields such as bacterial and viral infections, cardiovascular functions, cancer, diabetes, inflammation, ulcer therapy, kidney function, mental health, the nervous system, ophthalmic research, prostate therapy, the respiratory system, bone diseases, animal nutrition and production improvement, endoparasitic and ectoparasitic diseases and poultry genetics. In the development of human and animal health products, industry practice and government regulations in the United States and most foreign countries provide for the determination of effectiveness and safety of new chemical compounds through pre-clinical tests and controlled clinical evaluation. Before a new drug may be marketed in the United States, recorded data on the experience so gained are included in the NDA, the biological Product License Application or the New Animal Drug Application to the FDA for the approval required. The development of certain other products, such as insecticides, is also subject to government regulations covering safety and efficacy in the United States and many foreign countries. There can be no assurance that a compound that is the result of any particular program will obtain the regulatory approvals necessary for it to be marketed.

A new product for the Human and Animal Health segment resulting from this research and development program for which a Product License Application was submitted to the FDA in 1992 is Varivax, a vaccine for the prevention of chickenpox. On March 17, 1995, the FDA licensed Varivax for use against chickenpox. In 1993, the Company submitted an NDA for Pepcid AC, an over-the-counter form of the Company's ulcer medication Pepcid, to be marketed by the Johnson & Johnson Consumer Pharmaceuticals Co.

MERCK & CO., INC. AND SUBSIDIARIES

CONSOLIDATED STATEMENT OF INCOME
Years Ended December 31

($ in millions except per share amounts)

	1994	1993	1992
Sales	$14,969.8	$10,498.2	$9,662.5
Costs, Expenses and			
Other Materials and production	5,962.7	2,497.6	2,096.1
Marketing and administrative	3,177.5	2,913.9	2,963.3
Research and development	1,230.6	1,172.8	1,111.6
Gain on joint venture formation	(492.0)	—	—
Provision for joint venture obligation	499.6	—	—
Restructuring charge	—	775.0	—
Other (income) expense, net	176.2	36.2	(72.1)
	10,554.6	7,395.5	6,098.9
Income Before Taxes and Cumulative Effect of Accounting Changes	4,415.2	3,102.7	3,563.6
Taxes on Income	1,418.2	936.5	1,117.0
Income Before Cumulative Effect of Accounting Changes	2,997.0	2,166.2	2,446.6
Cumulative Effect of Accounting Changes:			
Postretirement benefits other than pensions	—	—	(370.2)
Income taxes	—	—	(62.6)
Postemployment benefits	—	—	(29.6)
Net Income	$ 2,997.0	$ 2,166.2	$1,984.2
Earnings Per Share of Common Stock:			
Before Cumulative Effect of Accounting Changes	$2.38	$1.87	$2.12
Cumulative Effect of Accounting Changes:			
Postretirement benefits other than pensions	—	—	(.32)
Income taxes	—	—	(.05)
Postemployment benefits	—	—	(.03)
Net Income	$2.38	$1.87	$1.72

MERCK & CO., INC. AND SUBSIDIARIES

CONSOLIDATED BALANCE SHEET
December 31

($ in millions)	1994	1993
Assets		
Current Assets		
Cash and cash equivalents	$ 1,604.0	$ 829.4
Short-term investments	665.7	712.9
Accounts receivable	2,351.5	2,094.3
Inventories	1,660.9	1,641.7
Prepaid expenses and taxes	639.6	456.3
Total current assets	6,921.7	5,734.6
Investments	1,416.9	1,779.9
Property, Plant and Equipment, at cost		
Land	212.6	212.5
Buildings	2,604.5	2,386.1
Machinery, equipment and office furnishings	4,029.4	3,769.0
Construction in progress	826.4	805.2
	7,672.9	7,172.8
Less allowance for depreciation	2,376.6	2,278.2
	5,296.3	4,894.6
Goodwill and Other Intangibles (net of accumulated amortization $291.1 million in 1994 and $97.2 million in 1993)	7,212.3	6,645.5
Other Assets	1,009.4	872.9
	$21,856.6	$19,927.5

MERCK & CO., INC. AND SUBSIDIARIES

CONSOLIDATED BALANCE SHEET

December 31

($ in millions)	1994	1993
Liabilities and Stockholders' Equity		
Current Liabilities		
Accounts payable and accrued liabilities	$ 2,715.4	$ 2,378.3
Loans payable	146.7	1,736.0
Income taxes payable	2,206.5	1,430.4
Dividends payable	380.0	351.0
Total current liabilities	5,448.6	5,895.7
Long-Term Debt	1,145.9	1,120.8
Deferred Income Taxes and Noncurrent Liabilities	2,914.3	1,744.9
Minority Interests	1,208.8	1,144.4
Stockholders' Equity		
Common stock		
Authorized—2,700,000,000 shares		
Issued—1,483,167,594 shares—1994		
—1,480,611,247 shares—1993	4,667.8	4,576.5
Retained earnings	10,942.0	9,393.2
	15,609.8	13,969.7
Less treasury stock, at cost		
235,341,571 shares—1994		
226,676,597 shares—1993	4,470.8	3,948.0
Total stockholders' equity	11,139.0	10,021.7
	$21,856.6	$19,927.5

The accompanying notes are an integral part of this financial statement.

The following passage was excerpted from the Canadian Institute of Chartered Accountants Handbook, Section 3450.

Research

.15 Expenditures incurred on research can be regarded as part of a continuing activity required to maintain an enterprise's business and its competitive position. In most cases, research activities will not produce identifiable benefits in future periods; the amount of future benefits and the period over which they will be received are usually uncertain. In general, one particular period rather than another will not be expected to benefit from an expenditure on research and, therefore, it is appropriate that such expenditures be charged to expenses as they are incurred.

.16 *Research costs should be charged as an expense of the period in which they are incurred.*

Development

.17 Development activities are normally undertaken with a reasonable expectation of commercial success and of future benefits arising from the work, either from increased revenue or from reduced costs. On these grounds, it may be argued that expenditures on development should be deferred to be matched against future revenue.

.18 The degree of certainty as to future benefits of particular development projects varies, and, in many cases, the expected future benefits may be too uncertain to justify carrying the expenditure forward.

.19 *Development costs should be charged as an expense of the period in which they are incurred except in the circumstances set out in paragraph 3450.21.*

.20 If it can be demonstrated that the product or process is technically and commercially feasible, the enterprise has shown an intention to sell or use the product or process and the enterprise has or could obtain adequate resources to complete the project, the future benefits could be regarded as being reasonably certain. Deferral of costs incurred for any project is considered to be appropriate when all the criteria set out in paragraph 3450.21 are satisfied.

.21 *Development costs would be deferred to future periods if all of the following criteria are satisfied:*

    (a) the product or process is clearly defined and the costs attributable thereto can be identified;

    (b) the technical feasibility of the product or process has been established;

    (c) the management of the enterprise has indicated its intention to produce and market, or use, the product or process;

    (d) the future market for the product or process is clearly defined or, if it is to be used internally rather than sold, its usefulness to the enterprise has been established; and

    (e) adequate resources exist, or are expected to be available, to complete the project.

.22 A development project may meet the criteria for deferment but the costs incurred may exceed the expected related revenues less estimated production, selling and administrative costs and additional development costs. In such circumstances, it would not be appropriate for the excess development costs to be carried forward to future periods. The excess would be written off as an expense of the period, with the amount expected to be recovered being deferred.

.23 *When a development project meets the criteria for deferment, as set out in paragraph 3450.21, the development costs should be deferred to the extent that their recovery can reasonably be regarded as assured.*

.24 The deferral of development costs on a particular project would commence in the fiscal year in which the criteria for deferment have been met. Development costs written off in prior years would not be reinstated because they were incurred at time when the technical and commercial feasibility of the project was too uncertain to establish a relationship with future benefits and they were, therefore, proper charges in those past periods.

.25 *Development costs charged as expense in prior years should not be reinstated even though the uncertainties which had led to their being written off no longer apply.*

.26 As with other deferred costs, deferred development costs will be amortized over future periods. The objective of the amortization should be to provide a systematic and rational matching of such costs with related benefits. To achieve this objective, the amortization would commence with commercial production or use and the basis would be established by reference to the benefits expected to arise from the sale or use of the product or process.

.27 Because of technological change and competition, it may be difficult to determine the future period over which the deferred development costs are to be amortized. However, while the uncertainties caused by technological and economic obsolescence may make it necessary to restrict any planned amortization period to a relatively short one, the selection of appropriate time period would be a matter of judgment in each case. An appropriate basis for amortizing deferred development costs would frequently be determined by reference to the estimates of future sale or use applied in satisfying the criteria for deferment.

.28 *Amortization of development costs deferred to future periods should commence with commercial production or use of the product or process and should be charged as an expense on a systematic and rational basis by reference, where possible, to the sale or use of the product or process.*

.29 At the end of each accounting period, it would be normal practice to review the unamortized balance of deferred development costs in the light of the current situation with respect to the projects to which such costs relate.

    ...

CIS Technologies, Inc.—Software Development

CIS Technologies, Inc. develops and markets computer-based healthcare reimbursement management programs and offers professional consulting and reimbursement assistance services to over 900 healthcare clients (primarily acute-care 100+ bed hospitals and physician practices) across the country. The Company's services are designed to improve the cash flows and reduce the administrative costs of its healthcare clients.

Learning Objectives
- Understand how software development costs are accounted for.
- Analyze software development activity based on footnote disclosures.
- Restate earnings based on an alternative accounting method for software development costs.
- Understand the role of management's incentives in software development cost accounting judgments.

Refer to the 1994 financial statements of CIS Technologies, Inc.

Concepts

a. How does CIS account for its software development costs?

Process

b. Refer to note 2: Property and Equipment. For each item in the reconciliation of unamortized software development costs, provide the journal entry recorded by CIS in 1994.

Analysis

c. Suppose that in 1994 CIS adopted a new policy of expensing all software development costs. What would its reported "Income before income taxes and cumulative effect of change in accounting principle" have been for 1994 had this always been the policy?

d. Explain how managers could "manage" earnings using software development costs. How can careful readers of financial statements see through such earnings management?

CIS TECHNOLOGIES, INC. AND SUBSIDIARIES

CONSOLIDATED STATEMENTS OF OPERATIONS
Years ended December 31,

	1994	1993	1992
Revenue:			
Service revenue	$30,203,268	$33,284,893	$30,523,284
Hardware and software sales	1,485,936	—	—
Total revenue	31,689,204	33,284,893	30,523,284
Operating expenses:			
Development and field operations	18,382,113	22,272,139	18,780,026
General and administrative	7,559,732	7,446,406	7,002,564
Depreciation and amortization	2,701,671	2,292,071	1,642,486
Cost of hardware and software sales	708,917	—	—
Contract termination	—	1,500,000	—
Total operating expenses	29,352,433	33,510,616	27,425,076
Operating income (loss)	2,336,771	(225,723)	3,098,208
Other income (expense)	(125,805)	(9,661)	79,166
Income (loss) before income taxes and cumulative effect of change of accounting principle	2,210,966	(235,384)	3,177,374
(Provision) benefit for income taxes (Note 8)	(13,964)	556,391	(81,919)
Income (loss) before cumulative effect of change in accounting principle	2,197,002	321,007	3,095,455
Cumulative effect of change in accounting principle (Note 8)	—	900,000	—
Net income	$ 2,197,002	$ 1,221,007	$ 3,095,455
Weighted average common and common equivalent shares outstanding	27,617,091	27,053,698	26,864,844
Earnings per common share, primary and fully-diluted:			
Income before cumulative effect of change in accounting principle	$ 0.08	$ 0.02	$ 0.12
Cumulative effect of change in accounting principle	—	0.03	—
Net income	$ 0.08	$ 0.05	$ 0.12

See notes to the consolidated financial statements.

CIS TECHNOLOGIES, INC. AND SUBSIDIARIES
NOTES TO CONSOLIDATED FINANCIAL STATEMENTS

1. Summary of Significant Accounting Policies

Software Development Costs

Software development costs are capitalized in accordance with Financial Accounting Standards Board Statement No. 86, "Accounting for the Cost of Computer Software to be Sold, Leased, or Otherwise Marketed." Costs incurred during the initial design phase of software development are expensed. Once the software has been clearly defined and technological feasibility has been established, software development costs are capitalized and amortized on a straight-line basis over an estimated useful life of five years. Software development costs are carried at their net realizable value and, as such, an annual review of software development costs is conducted and the costs of obsolete software are written off.

2. Property and Equipment

	1994	1993
Computer hardware and purchased software	$ 3,000,955	$ 3,464,777
Computer hardware under capital lease	454,708	454,708
Software development costs	10,525,606	6,677,667
Furniture and fixtures	741,160	662,553
Furniture and fixtures under capital lease	423,807	423,807
Leasehold improvements	715,013	502,433
Equipment	146,731	—
Vehicles	93,367	—
	16,101,347	12,185,945
Accumulated depreciation and amortization	(6,286,585)	(5,438,341)
Property and equipment, net	$ 9,814,762	$ 6,747,604

The following table details software development cost information for the years ended December 31, 1994, 1993 and 1992:

	1994	1993	1992
Unamortized software development costs, beginning balance	$ 4,896,443	$ 2,581,203	$ 693,290
Capitalized software development costs	3,759,784	3,676,971	2,127,828
Software acquired in acquisition	113,700	—	—
Amortization of software development costs	(1,282,096)	(741,198)	(239,915)
Write-off of software development costs	(113,004)	(620,533)	—
Unamortized software development costs, ending balance	$ 7,374,827	$ 4,896,443	$ 2,581,203

America Online, Inc.—Deferred Costs

America Online, Inc. was incorporated in the State of Delaware in May 1985 and is based in Dulles, Virginia. AOL is the leading provider of online services, including electronic mail, conferencing, entertainment, software, computing support, interactive magazines and newspapers, and online classes, as well as easy and affordable access to services of the Internet. In addition, the Company is a provider of data network services and multimedia and CD-ROM production services.

Learning Objectives
- Understand how software development costs are accounted for.
- Analyze software development activity based on footnote disclosures.
- Restate earnings based on an alternative accounting method for software development costs.
- Understand the role of management's incentives in software development cost accounting judgments.

Refer to the 1996 financial statements of America Online, Inc.

Concepts

a. What do AOL's "Product development costs, net" represent? How does AOL account for these costs?

b. What do AOL's "Deferred subscriber acquisition costs, net" represent? How does AOL account for these costs?

c. Provide arguments in support of AOL's accounting policies for these costs.

d. Provide arguments against AOL's accounting policies for these costs.

e. Is conservative accounting good accounting? Explain how conservative accounting can provide managers with opportunities to smooth or manage reported earnings.

Process

f. Consider the "Product development costs, net." Using information contained in the financial statements and Note 2, recreate and reconcile the fiscal 1995 and 1996 activity in the gross Product development costs account and the associated Accumulated amortization account. You may find a T-account analysis helpful. Provide journal entries for the fiscal 1996 transactions.

g. Consider the "Deferred subscriber acquisition costs, net." Using information contained in the financial statements and Note 2, recreate and reconcile the fiscal 1995 and 1996 activity in the Deferred subscriber acquisition costs, net account. You may find a T-account analysis helpful. Provide journal entries for the fiscal 1996 transactions.

Analysis

h. Consider the "Product development costs, net."

   i. How much Product development cost, if any, did AOL write off as obsolete in fiscal 1996?

   ii. What portion of Gross product development cost was amortized in fiscal 1996? In fiscal 1995? Comment on the trend in amortization.

i. Consider the "Deferred subscriber acquisition costs, net."

   i. According to Note 2, in fiscal 1996 AOL changed the amortization period over which these costs are charged. Had they not made this change, what would AOL have reported as Net income for fiscal 1996?

ii. Estimate the 1996 pretax effect of the change in amortization period.

iii. Evaluate the quality of AOL's 1996 earnings in light of this change.

iv. AOL provided users of its financial statements with the effect of the change in accounting estimate. In general, analysts are not always provided with this information. Make the following assumptions and arrive at your own independent estimate of the effect of the change in accounting estimate:

- AOL's Deferred subscriber acquisition costs are incurred evenly over each fiscal year. Thus, for analysis purposes, you can assume that the costs were incurred in a lump, halfway through the year.

- Prior to July 1, 1995, AOL amortized Deferred subscriber acquisition costs over a 15 month period (i.e., halfway between the 12 and 18 month period referred to in the note).

j. Refer to the accompanying article that appeared in the October 30, 1996 issue of *The Wall Street Journal Interactive Edition*.

i Restate fiscal 1996 Net income assuming that AOL had always used the new accounting policy for Deferred subscriber acquisition costs.

ii Although the company announced an accounting change that wiped out more than five times the previous five years' earnings, the stock price rose $1 per share. Speculate why the share price rose on the day bad news was announced.

AMERICA ONLINE, INC.

CONSOLIDATED STATEMENTS OF OPERATIONS

(Amounts in thousands, except per share data)

	Year ended June 30,		
	1996	1995	1994
Revenues:			
Online service revenues	$ 991,656	$ 344,309	$ 98,497
Other revenues	102,198	49,981	17,225
Total revenues	1,093,854	394,290	115,722
Costs and expenses:			
Cost of revenues	627,372	229,724	69,043
Marketing	212,710	77,064	23,548
Product development	53,817	14,263	5,288
General and administrative	110,653	42,700	13,667
Acquired research and development	16,981	50,335	—
Amortization of goodwill	7,078	1,653	—
Total costs and expenses	1,028,611	415,739	111,546
Income (loss) from operations	65,243	(21,449)	4,176
Other income (expense), net	(2,056)	3,074	1,810
Merger expenses	(848)	(2,207)	—
Income (loss) before provision for income taxes	62,339	(20,582)	5,986
Provision for income taxes	(32,523)	(15,169)	(3,832)
Net income (loss)	$ 29,816	$ (35,751)	$ 2,154
Earnings (loss) per share:			
Net income (loss)	$ 0.28	$ (0.51)	$ 0.03
Weighted average shares outstanding	108,097	69,550	69,035

See accompanying notes.

AMERICA ONLINE, INC.

CONSOLIDATED BALANCE SHEETS

(Amounts in thousands, except share data)

	June 30, 1996	1995
Assets		
Current assets:		
Cash and cash equivalents	$ 118,421	$ 45,877
Short-term investments	10,712	18,672
Trade accounts receivable	42,939	32,176
Other receivables	29,674	11,381
Prepaid expenses and other current assets	68,832	25,527
Total current assets	270,578	133,633
Property and equipment at cost, net	101,277	70,919
Other assets:		
Product development costs, net	44,330	18,949
Deferred subscriber acquisition costs, net	314,181	77,229
License rights, net	4,947	5,579
Other assets	35,878	9,121
Deferred income taxes	135,872	35,627
Goodwill, net	51,691	54,356
	$ 958,754	$405,413
Liabilities and Stockholders' Equity		
Current liabilities:		
Trade accounts payable	$ 105,904	$ 84,640
Other accrued expenses and liabilities	127,898	23,509
Deferred revenue	37,950	20,021
Accrued personnel costs	15,719	2,863
Current portion of long-term debt	2,435	2,329
Total current liabilities	289,906	133,362
Long-term liabilities:		
Notes payable	19,306	17,369
Deferred income taxes	135,872	35,627
Other liabilities	1,168	2,243
Total liabilities	446,252	188,601
Stockholders' equity:		
Preferred stock, $.01 par value; 5,000,000 shares authorized, 1,000 shares issued and outstanding at June 30, 1996	1	—
Common stock, $.01 par value; 300,000,000 and 100,000,000 shares authorized, 92,626,000 and 76,728,268 shares issued and outstanding at June 30, 1996 and 1995, respectively	926	767
Additional paid-in capital	519,342	252,668
Accumulated deficit	(7,767)	(36,623)
Total stockholders' equity	512,502	216,812
	$ 958,754	$405,413

See accompanying notes.

AMERICA ONLINE, INC.

CONSOLIDATED STATEMENTS OF CASH FLOWS
(Amounts in thousands)

	Year ended June 30,		
	1996	1995	1994
Cash flows from operating activities:			
Net income (loss)	$ 29,816	$(35,751)	$ 2,154
Adjustments to reconcile net income to net cash (used in) provided by operating activities:			
Depreciation and amortization	33,366	12,266	2,822
Amortization of subscriber acquisition costs	126,072	60,924	17,922
Loss on sale of property and equipment	44	37	5
Charge for acquired research and development	16,981	50,335	—
Changes in assets and liabilities:			
Trade accounts receivable	(10,435)	(14,373)	(4,266)
Other receivables	(18,293)	(9,086)	(626)
Prepaid expenses and other current assets	(43,305)	(19,635)	(2,873)
Deferred subscriber acquisition costs	(363,024)	(111,761)	(37,424)
Other assets	(26,938)	(6,051)	(2,542)
Trade accounts payable	21,150	60,805	10,224
Accrued personnel costs	12,856	1,850	397
Other accrued expenses and liabilities	104,531	5,747	9,474
Deferred revenue	17,929	7,190	2,322
Deferred income taxes	32,523	14,763	3,832
Total adjustments	(96,543)	53,011	(733)
Net cash (used in) provided by operating activities	(66,727)	17,260	1,421
Cash flows from investing activities:			
Short-term investments	7,960	5,380	(18,947)
Purchase of property and equipment	(50,262)	(59,255)	(18,010)
Product development costs	(32,631)	(13,054)	(5,131)
Sale of property and equipment	—	180	95
Purchase costs of acquired businesses	(4,133)	(20,523)	—
Net cash used in investing activities	(79,066)	(87,272)	(41,993)
Cash flows from financing activities:			
Proceeds from issuance of common stock, net	189,359	61,721	68,120
Proceeds from issuance of preferred stock, net	28,315	—	—
Principal and accrued interest payments on line of credit and long-term debt	(935)	(3,045)	(7,795)
Proceeds from line of credit and issuance of long-term debt	3,000	13,488	14,260
Principal payments under capital lease obligations	(1,402)	(368)	(83)
Net cash provided by financing activities	218,337	71,796	74,502
Net increase in cash and cash equivalents	72,544	1,784	33,930
Cash and cash equivalents at beginning of period	45,877	44,093	10,163
Cash and cash equivalents at end of period	$ 118,421	$ 45,877	$ 44,093

See accompanying notes.

AMERICA ONLINE, INC.

Notes to Consolidated Financial Statements

2 Summary of Significant Accounting Policies

Principles of Consolidation The consolidated financial statements include the accounts of the Company and its subsidiaries. All significant intercompany accounts and transactions have been eliminated.

Business Combinations Business combinations which have been accounted for under the purchase method of accounting include the results of operations of the acquired business from the date of acquisition. Net assets of the companies acquired are recorded at their fair value to the Company at the date of acquisition.

Other business combinations have been accounted for under the pooling of interests method of accounting. In such cases, the assets, liabilities, and stockholders' equity of the acquired entities were combined with the Company's respective accounts at recorded values. Prior period financial statements have been restated to give effect to the merger unless the effect of the business combination is not material to the financial statements of the Company.

Revenue Recognition Online service revenues are recognized over the period services are provided. Other revenues, consisting principally of the sale of merchandise, data network services, online advertising and transactions, production services and development and licensing fees are recognized as services are rendered. Deferred revenue consists primarily of monthly subscription fees billed in advance, and prepaid network and advertising fees.

Property and Equipment Property and equipment are depreciated or amortized using the straight-line method over the estimated useful life of the asset, which ranges from 5 to 40 years, or over the life of the lease.

Deferred Subscriber Acquisition Costs The Company expenses the costs of advertising as incurred, except direct response advertising, which is classified as deferred subscriber acquisition costs. Direct response advertising consists solely of the costs of marketing programs which result in subscriber registrations without further effort required by the Company. These costs, which relate directly to subscriber solicitations, principally include the printing, production and shipping of starter kits and the costs of obtaining qualified prospects by various targeted direct marketing programs and from third parties. To date all deferred subscriber acquisition costs have been incurred for the solicitation of specifically identifiable prospects. No indirect costs are included in deferred subscriber acquisition costs.

The deferred costs are amortized, beginning the month after such costs are incurred, over a period determined by calculating the ratio of current revenues related to direct response advertising versus the total expected revenues related to this advertising, or twenty-four months, whichever is shorter. All other costs related to the acquisition of subscribers, as well as general marketing costs, are expensed as incurred.

On a quarterly basis, management reviews the estimated future operating results of the Company's subscriber base in order to evaluate the recoverability of deferred subscriber acquisition costs and the related amortization period. It is possible that management's future assessments of the recoverability and amortization period of deferred subscriber acquisition costs may change based upon actual results and other factors.

Effective July 1, 1995, the Company modified the components of subscriber acquisition costs deferred, and changed the period over which it amortizes subscriber acquisition costs. The period over which the Company amortizes subscriber acquisition costs was changed from twelve and eighteen months to the period described previously in order to more appropriately match subscriber acquisition costs with associated online service revenues. The effect of this change in accounting estimate for the year ended June 30, 1996, was to increase net income by $48,106,000 ($.45 per share).

Product Development Costs The Company capitalizes costs incurred for the production of computer software used in the sale of its services. Costs capitalized include direct labor and related overhead for software produced by the Company and the costs of software purchased from third parties. All costs in the software development process which are classified as research and development are expensed as incurred until technological feasibility has been established. Once technological feasibility has been established, such costs are capitalized until the software is commercially available. To the extent the Company retains the rights to software development funded by third parties, such costs are capitalized in accordance with the Company's normal accounting policies. Amortization is provided on a product-by-product basis, using the greater of the straight-line method or current year revenue as a percent of total revenue estimates for the related software product, not to exceed five years, commencing the month after the date of product release.

Product development costs consist of the following:

(in thousands)	Year ended June 30,	
	1996	1995
Balance, beginning of year	$ 18,949	$ 7,912
Costs capitalized	32,631	13,054
Costs amortized	(7,250)	(2,017)
Balance, end of year	$ 44,330	$ 18,949

The accumulated amortization of product development costs related to the production of computer software totaled $15,152,000 and $7,902,000 at June 30, 1996 and 1995, respectively.

Included in product development costs are research and development costs totaling $16,449,000, $5,277,000, and $2,453,000 and other product development costs totaling $30,118,000, $6,969,000, and $1,050,000 in the years ended June 30, 1996, 1995 and 1994, respectively.

AOL Plans $385 Million Charge
Related To Accounting Change

By JARED SANDBERG
Staff Reporter of THE WALL STREET JOURNAL

NEW YORK—America Online Inc. disclosed plans to take a pretax charge of $385 million to reverse a much-criticized accounting approach that had let the company post quarterly profits by forgoing the immediate write-off of massive marketing expenses.

The big charge will be taken against the fiscal first quarter ended Sept. 30, and a separate charge of up to $75 million is set for the current quarter to cover restructuring expenses. The charges are part of the on-line service company's new counterpunch to growing competition from Internet access providers. America Online Tuesday reorganized into three new divisions, named a star media executive to run one of them, and unveiled its first-ever discount plan for unlimited access. AOL had resisted that pricing move, which could hurt revenues.

The accounting charge is more than five times as large as the total pretax earnings that AOL had reported for the past five fiscal years combined. It underscores just how massive the company's marketing efforts have been—and how illusory its profits may have been. The change raises the question of whether AOL will be able to report much profit at all in future quarters.

"The earnings numbers were meaningless—they were a house of cards," said Neeraj Vohra, an analyst at Wheat First Butcher Singer Inc. Mr. Vohra noted that AOL had reported fiscal 1996 earnings of 47 cents a share before charges, but had run up "deferred subscriber acquisition costs" of $1.37 a share, more than wiping out full-year earnings.

The effort also quickly raised speculation that AOL might be setting itself up for a sale. "A potential acquirer would be a large, conservative company. They wouldn't want to acquire a company that has aggressive accounting but, instead, a company more in line with their own," Mr. Vohra said.

Denied by CEO

But AOL Chairman and Chief Executive Steve Case denied that the company is preparing for a sale. He said it has had "no discussions and no interest in pursuing them."

AOL had staunchly defended the accounting method it will now abandon. As AOL spent huge sums on advertising and free trials to lure newcomers, it spread each quarter's expenses over up to two years rather than deduct the costs immediately. Backed by its outside accountants, the company had argued that spreading the costs over two years was a justifiable way to match expenses against revenue flows that would emerge later.

Mr. Case said scrapping this controversial method is aimed at stemming Wall Street concerns that had dogged the company for years. "In one fell swoop we're addressing the needs of Main Street and the concerns of Wall Street," he said of the accounting change and new pricing. "We've decided it's best not to spend all our time in this debate over accounting practices. There will be no argument over the quality of earnings."

News of the accounting change sent Wall Street analysts scrambling for their red pens. Mary Meeker of Morgan Stanley & Co., who had been projecting profit of $1 a share for fiscal 1997, now expects a per-share loss of three cents and a $130 million reduction in revenue. "AOL indicated that it would bite the bullet" on subscriber acquisition costs, Ms. Meeker, one of the company's biggest boosters, said in a report issued Tuesday. "We hope that the worst is over," she wrote, referring to the slide in AOL's stock price this year.

Stock Climbs $1

AOL shares rose on the news of the accounting change. They closed at $25.625, up $1, in composite trading on the New York Stock Exchange.

AOL has been struggling with annual customer-churn rates of 30% to 40% by some estimates, as some users quit the on-line service to use cheaper Internet access providers. Now it hopes to stem such defections by offering users unlimited access for $19.95 each month; previously, AOL had charged $19.95 for 20 hours and $2.95 for each additional hour.

"We've spent large amounts of cash to market a product that arguably wasn't responsive to market needs," said Lennert Leader, AOL's chief financial officer. AOL hopes its average cost of acquiring a subscriber can decline somewhat if the flat-rate plan can curb defections. Mr. Leader said he expects to see a 10% decrease in subscriber acquisition costs because of the new discount plan.

AOL said the one-time charge of as much as $75 million in the current quarter is to reorganize and shut down Global Network

Navigator, the Internet-only service it started just over a year ago.

Pricing Details

In addition to the unlimited pricing plan, AOL offered a new monthly rate of $9.95 for users who already subscribe to a rival but want to tap into AOL's exclusive content. Hoping to boost short-term cash flow, the company further offered an even steeper discount to subscribers who pay up-front for two full years of service: $14.95 a month for unlimited usage. Those who sign up for a year and pay in advance will be charged $17.95 a month.

That will help AOL's cash flow, which was at a negative $66.7 million before a stock offering in fiscal 1996. Though the company said it will have roughly $70 million in positive cash flow after the fiscal first half, Mr. Leader said the new up-front offers could let AOL collect as much as an additional $100 million in revenues.

He added that the company hopes to gain more revenues from advertising and on-line sale of goods. Such alternative revenues accounted for as much as $40 million in the September quarter—a number he expects will grow by 50% to $60 million for the December quarter.

News of the charge was buried in a flurry of other announcements. AOL said it reorganized into three groups and appointed former MTV executive Robert W. Pittman, who was elected to AOL's board earlier this year, to head one of them. That group, AOL Networks, will be responsible for the consumer Internet service. A second division, AOL Studios, will develop new on-line content and the third, ANS Communications, will continue to deploy high-speed networking for AOL and for business customers.

The restructuring will eliminate the need for a president and chief operating officer, a post left vacant after former Federal Express Corp. executive William Razzouk left just four months after taking the job. Instead, much of the responsibilities for the consumer on-line service division will fall on Mr. Pittman's shoulders. "He's going to fit into the culture a lot more seamlessly than Razzouk could," said Jamie Kiggen, analyst at Cowen & Co., adding that Mr. Pittman has "a real understanding of how these new media companies have evolved."

Still, AOL's evolution is uncertain, despite the widespread support for the company's moves. "On an operating basis, what the company did better reflects the realities of the market and on an accounting basis, it better reflects the true cost of acquiring subscribers," said Jonathan Cohen, managing director at Smith Barney Inc. Are the moves adequate in the fast-paced industry? "The jury is still out on that," he said.

E.I. du Pont de Nemours—Environmental Matters

E.I. DuPont de Nemours is the largest chemical producer in the world. The Company conducts fully integrated petroleum operations primarily through its wholly owned subsidiary, Conoco Inc. Conoco and other subsidiaries and affiliates of DuPont conduct exploration, production, mining, manufacturing or selling activities, and some are distributors of products manufactured by the Company. The Company is organized for financial reporting purposes into six industry segments—Chemicals, Fibers, Life Sciences, Polymers, Petroleum, and Diversified Businesses.

Learning Objectives
- Gain familiarity with environmental matters.
- Read and interpret footnotes and management's discussion and analysis pertaining to environmental matters.
- Analyze environmental liability accounts and evaluate compliance with generally accepted accounting principles for contingencies.

Refer to DuPont's 1996 financial statements, footnotes, and management's discussion and analysis (MD&A).

Concepts

a. In your own words, define "contingent liability."

b. What is DuPont's accounting policy for recording contingent environmental liabilities? Does this policy comply with generally accepted accounting principles? Why or why not?

c. What is the total environmental expense DuPont recorded on its income statement for the year ended December 31, 1996? In which account(s) does this amount most likely appear?

d. What environmental liability has DuPont recorded on its balance sheet as at December 31, 1996? As at December 31, 1995? Where on the balance sheet do these amounts most likely appear?

Process

e. Consider DuPont's remediation accruals. Provide the journal entry that DuPont made to accrue additional amounts during 1996.

f. Consider DuPont's remediation expenditures. Provide the journal entry that DuPont made to record expenditures related to the following during 1996. Ignore tax effects for both parts.

    i. CERCLA (Superfund) remediation activities.

    ii. RCRA remediation activities.

g. DuPont is actively pursuing claims against its insurers.

    i. How does DuPont account for these potential recoveries?

    ii. Is this in compliance with generally accepted accounting principles? Explain.

    iii. What insurance proceeds did DuPont receive during 1996? Provide the journal entry DuPont made to record the insurance settlements.

Analysis

h. Using a T-account and your answers to parts *e*, *f*, and *g* above, explain the change in the environmental contingent liability account during 1996.

i. The MD&A goes into detail about the costs, accruals, programs, and estimation techniques relating to DuPont's environmental responsibilities. The footnotes to the financial statements are, by comparison, less forthcoming. Speculate on this difference.

E. I. DU PONT DE NEMOURS AND CONSOLIDATED SUBSIDIARIES

CONSOLIDATED INCOME STATEMENT

For the years ended December 31,

(Dollars in millions, except per share)

	1996	1995	1994
Sales*	$43,810	$42,163	$39,333
Other Income (Note 2)	1,340	1,059	888
Total	45,150	43,222	40,221
Cost of Goods Sold and Other Operating Charges	25,144	23,363	21,810
Selling, General and Administrative Expenses	2,856	2,995	2,875
Depreciation, Depletion and Amortization	2,621	2,722	2,976
Exploration Expenses, Including Dry Hole Costs and Impairment of Unproved Properties	404	331	357
Research and Development Expense	1,032	1,067	1,047
Interest and Debt Expense (Note 3)	713	758	559
Taxes Other Than on Income* (Note 4)	6,399	6,596	6,215
Total	39,169	37,832	35,839
Earnings Before Income Taxes	5,981	5,390	4,382
Provision for Income Taxes (Note 5)	2,345	2,097	1,655
Net Income	$ 3,636	$ 3,293	$ 2,727
Earnings Per Share of Common Stock (Note 6)	$ 6.47	$ 5.61	$ 4.00

* Includes petroleum excise taxes of $5,461, $5,655, and $5,291 in 1996, 1995 and 1994, respectively.

See pages 33-50 for Notes to Financial Statements.

E. I. DU PONT DE NEMOURS AND CONSOLIDATED SUBSIDIARIES

CONSOLIDATED BALANCE SHEET

(dollars in millions, except per share)

	December 31 1996	1995
Assets		
Current Assets		
Cash and Cash Equivalents (Note 7)	$ 1,066	$ 1,408
Marketable Securities (Note 7)	253	47
Accounts and Notes Receivable (Note 8)	5,193	4,912
Inventories (Note 9)	3,706	3,737
Prepaid Expenses	297	276
Deferred Income Taxes (Note 5)	588	575
Total Current Assets	11,103	10,955
Property, Plant and Equipment (Note 10)	50,549	50,385
Less: Accumulated Depreciation, Depletion and Amortization	29,336	29,044
	21,213	21,341
Investment in Affiliates (Note 11)	2,278	1,846
Other Assets (Notes 5 and 12)	3,393	3,170
Total	$37,987	$37,312
Liabilities and Stockholders' Equity		
Current Liabilities		
Accounts Payable (Note 13)	$ 2,757	$ 2,636
Short-Term Borrowings and Capital Lease Obligations (Note 14)	3,910	6,157
Income Taxes (Note 5)	526	470
Other Accrued Liabilities (Note 15)	3,794	3,468
Total Current Liabilities	10,987	12,731
Long-Term Borrowings and Capital Lease Obligations (Note 16)	5,087	5,678
Other Liabilities (Note 17)	8,451	8,454
Deferred Income Taxes (Note 5)	2,133	1,783
Total Liabilities	26,658	28,646
Minority Interests (Note 18)	620	230
Stockholders' Equity		
Preferred Stock	237	237
Common Stock, $.60 par value; 900,000,000 shares authorized; Issued at December 31, 1996—579,042,725; 1995—735,042,724	347	441
Additional Paid-In Capital	6,676	8,689
Reinvested Earnings	4,931	9,503
Cumulative Translation Adjustments	(23)	—
Common Stock Held in Trust for Unearned Employee Compensation and Benefits (Flexitrust), at Market (Shares: December 31, 1996—15,495,795; December 31, 1995—23,546,176)	(1,459)	(1,645)
Common Stock Held in Treasury, at Cost (Shares: December 31, 1995—156,000,000)	—	(8,789)
Total Stockholders' Equity	10,709	8,436
Total	$37,987	$37,312

See accompanying notes to financial statements.

E. I. DU PONT DE NEMOURS AND CONSOLIDATED SUBSIDIARIES

NOTES TO FINANCIAL STATEMENTS (EXCERPTS)

(Dollars in millions, except per share)

1. Summary of Significant Accounting Policies (excerpts)

Environmental Liabilities and Expenditures

Accruals for environmental matters are recorded in operating expenses when it is probable that a liability has been incurred and the amount of the liability can be reasonably estimated. Accrued liabilities are exclusive of claims against third parties and are not discounted.

Costs related to environmental remediation are charged to expense. Other environmental costs are also charged to expense unless they increase the value of the property and/or mitigate or prevent contamination from future operations, in which event they are capitalized.

25. Commitments and Contingent Liabilities (excerpts)

The company is also subject to contingencies pursuant to environmental laws and regulations that in the future may require the company to take further action to correct the effects on the environment of prior disposal practices or releases of chemical or petroleum substances by the company or other parties. The company has accrued for certain environmental remediation activities consistent with the policy set forth in Note 1. At December 31, 1996, such accrual amounted to $586 and, in management's opinion, was appropriate based on existing facts and circumstances. Under adverse changes in circumstances, potential liability may exceed amounts accrued. In the event that future remediation expenditures are in excess of amounts accrued, management does not anticipate that they will have a material adverse effect on the consolidated financial position of the company.

E. I. DU PONT DE NEMOURS AND CONSOLIDATED SUBSIDIARIES

MANAGEMENT'S DISCUSSION AND ANALYSIS (EXCERPTS)

Environmental Matters

DuPont operates manufacturing facilities, petroleum refineries, natural gas processing plants and product-handling and distribution facilities around the world. Each facility is significantly affected by a broad array of environmental laws and regulations. It is company policy to fully meet or exceed legal and regulatory requirements wherever it operates. DuPont facilities worldwide are run in accordance with the highest standards of safe operation, even where those standards exceed the requirements of local law. DuPont has also implemented voluntary programs to reduce air emissions, curtail the generation of hazardous waste, decrease the volume of wastewater discharges and improve the efficiency of energy use. The costs of complying with complex environmental laws and regulations, as well as internal voluntary programs, are significant and will continue to be so for the foreseeable future. These costs may increase in the future, but are not expected to have a material impact on the company's competitive or financial position.

In 1996 DuPont spent about $300 million for environmental capital projects either required by the law or necessary to meet the company's internal waste elimination and pollution prevention goals. The company currently estimates expenditures for environmental-related capital projects will total $400 million in 1997. Significant capital expenditures may be required over the next decade for treatment, storage and disposal facilities for solid and hazardous waste and for compliance with the Clean Air Act (CAA) and its 1990 Amendments. Until all new CAA regulatory requirements are known, considerable uncertainty will remain regarding future estimates of capital expenditures. Total CAA capital costs over the next two years are currently estimated to range from $15-30 million.

Estimated pretax environmental expenses charged to current operations totaled about $800 million, before insurance recoveries, in 1996 as compared to about $800 million in 1995 and

$950 million in 1994. These expenses include the remediation accruals discussed below, operating, maintenance and depreciation costs for solid waste, air and water pollution control facilities and the costs of environmental research activities. The largest of these expenses resulted from the operation of wastewater treatment facilities and solid waste management facilities, each of which accounted for about $180 million. About two-thirds of total annual expenses resulted from the operations of the company's Chemicals, Fibers, Polymers, Life Sciences and Diversified Businesses segments in the United States.

REMEDIATION ACCRUALS

DuPont accrues for remediation activities when it is probable that a liability has been incurred and reasonable estimates of the liability can be made. These accrued liabilities exclude claims against third parties and are not discounted. Much of this liability results from the Comprehensive Environmental Response, Compensation and Liability Act (CERCLA, often referred to as Superfund), the Resource Conservation and Recovery Act (RCRA) and similar state laws that require the company to undertake certain investigative and remedial activities at sites where the company conducts or once conducted operations or at sites where company-generated waste was disposed. The accrual also includes a number of sites identified by the company that may require environmental remediation but which are not currently the subject of CERCLA, RCRA or state enforcement activities. Over the next one to two decades the company may incur significant costs under both CERCLA and RCRA. Considerable uncertainty exists with respect to these costs and under adverse changes in circumstances, potential liability may exceed amounts accrued as of December 31, 1996.

Remediation activities vary substantially in duration and cost from site to site depending on the mix of unique site characteristics, evolving remediation technologies, diverse regulatory agencies and enforcement policies and the presence or absence of potentially liable third parties. Therefore, it is difficult to develop reasonable estimates of future site remediation costs. Nevertheless, the company's assessment of such costs is a continuous process that takes into account the relevant factors affecting each specific site. At December 31, 1996, the company's balance sheet included an accrued liability of $586 million as compared to $602 million and $616 million at year-end 1995 and 1994, respectively. The moderate decline in the accrued liability reflects the completion of remediation programs at several sites. Approximately 78 percent of the company's environmental reserve at December 31, 1996 was attributable to RCRA and similar remediation liabilities and 22 percent to CERCLA liabilities. During 1996, remediation accruals of $91 million, offset by $100 million in insurance proceeds, resulted in a credit to income of $9 million, compared to a credit of $79 million in 1995, also resulting from insurance recoveries, and an accrual of $185 million in 1994.

REMEDIATION EXPENDITURES

RCRA extensively regulates the treatment, storage and disposal of hazardous waste and requires a permit to conduct such activities. The law requires that permitted facilities undertake an assessment of environmental conditions at the facility. If conditions warrant, the company may be required to remediate contamination caused by prior operations. As contrasted by CERCLA, the RCRA corrective action program results in the cost of corrective action activities being typically borne solely by the company. The company anticipates that significant ongoing expenditures for RCRA remediation activities may be required over the next two decades, although annual expenditures for the near term are not expected to vary significantly from the range of such expenditures over the past few years. Longer term, expenditures are subject to considerable uncertainty and may fluctuate significantly. The company's expenditures associated with RCRA and similar remediation activities were approximately $79 million in 1996, $94 million in 1995 and $70 million in 1994.

The company from time to time receives requests for information or notices of potential liability from the Environmental Protection Agency (EPA) and state environmental agencies alleging that the company is a "potentially responsible party" (PRP) under CERCLA or an equivalent state statute. The company has also on occasion been made a party to cost recovery litigation by those agencies or by private parties. These requests, notices and lawsuits assert potential liability for remediation costs at various sites that typically are not company owned but allegedly contain wastes attributable to the company's past operations. As of December 31, 1996, the company had been notified of potential liability under CERCLA or state law at about 335 sites around the United States, with active remediation under way at 152 of those sites. In addition, the company has resolved its liability at 80 sites, either by completing remedial actions with other PRPs or by participating in "de minimis buyouts" with other PRPs whose waste, like the company's, represented only a small fraction of the total waste present at a site. The company received notice of potential liability at 7 new sites during 1996 compared with 16 similar notices in 1995 and 17 in 1994. The company's expenditures associated with CERCLA and similar state remediation activities were approximately $28 million in 1996, $25 million in 1995 and $21 million in 1994.

For most Superfund sites, the company's potential liability will be significantly less than the total site remediation costs because the percentage of waste attributable to the company versus that attributable to all other PRPs is relatively low. Other PRPs at sites where the company is a party typically have the financial strength to meet their obligations and, where they do not, or where certain PRPs cannot be located, the company's own share of liability has not materially increased. There are relatively few sites where the company is a major participant, and neither the cost to the company of remediation at those sites, nor at all CERCLA sites in the aggregate, is expected to have a material impact on the competitive or financial position of the company.

Total expenditures for previously accrued remediation activities under CERCLA, RCRA and similar state laws were $107 million in 1996, $119 million in 1995 and $91 million in 1994. Although future remediation expenditures in excess of current reserves is possible, the effect on future financial results is not subject to reasonable estimation because of the considerable uncertainty regarding the cost and timing of expenditures. The company is actively pursuing claims against various parties with respect to remediation liabilities.

Maytag Corporation—Warranties & Deferred Taxes

Maytag Corporation is a leading appliance enterprise headquartered in Newton, Iowa. The company is focused on five principal areas of home management: laundry, cooking, dishwashing, refrigeration and floor care. Vending equipment is an additional corporate business. Maytag's appliance brands include Maytag, Hoover, Jenn-Air, Magic Chef, Dixie-Narco, Admiral, and RSD.

Learning Objectives
* Understand the role of judgment in assessing warranty costs for accounting purposes.
* Understand the accounting implications of providing multiperiod warranties on products sold.
* Understand how differences in the accounting and income tax treatment of warranty costs leads to deferred income tax balances.

For many years Maytag has been associated with the lonely repairman, waiting in his shop for a Maytag product to break and need servicing. Inspection of the notes to Maytag's financial statements shows that there must be some work for this lonely soul. Indeed, Maytag has accrued about $31 million of warranty costs at the end of 1995.

Concepts

a. From the perspective of a Maytag customer, what is a product warranty?

b. From an accrual accounting perspective, what is a warranty?

c. What judgments does management need to make to account for warranty costs?

d. In general, for income tax purposes, warranty costs are deductible only when paid. Under this general assumption, do accrued warranty costs give rise to a deferred tax asset or liability? Why?

Process

For parts *e* and *f*, do not use information in the accompanying notes to Maytag's financial statements.

e. Assume that in 1996 Maytag began selling a new washing machine on which it provided a three year warranty. A total of 500,000 units were sold in 1996. Each machine sold for $350 and cost Maytag $200 to manufacture. Maytag's engineers estimate that 5% of the machines will require service over the warranty period. The average cost of servicing a unit is (correctly) projected to be $100.

   i.   Prepare all journal entries related to the new washers sold in 1996.

   ii. In 1996, 12,000 units were serviced under the warranty plan. Prepare the journal entry related to the warranty claims on washers sold and serviced in 1996.

   iii. 6,000 and 7,500 units were serviced under the warranty plan in 1997 and 1998, respectively. Prepare the 1997 and 1998 journal entries related to the warranty claims on washers sold in 1996.

f. Assume that for income tax purposes, Maytag deducts warranty costs as they are paid. Assuming an income tax rate of 36%, provide the journal entry to record deferred taxes with respect to the warranties in each of 1996, 1997, and 1998.

g. Refer to the accompanying notes to Maytag's 1995 financial statements.

   i. Assume that Maytag spent $40 million on warranty claims in 1995. What was the total warranty expense recorded by Maytag in 1995? (*Hint*: Use a T-account to analyze the transactions in the account for the year.)

   ii. Prepare the journal entries to record Maytag's warranty payments and warranty expense for 1995.

h. The Accrued Liability note reveals that Maytag's warranty accrual decreased by $11,942,000 in 1995. Based on this, determine whether Maytag reported greater warranty expense for tax or for accounting purposes in 1995. Would you predict an increase or decrease in the related deferred tax asset?

i. According to the Income Tax note, the "Product warranty / liability accruals" component of Maytag's deferred tax assets increased by $3,586,000 in 1995. What might explain the increase during 1995 in light of your response to part *h* above?

MAYTAG CORPORATION
NOTES TO THE CONSOLIDATED FINANCIAL STATEMENTS

Accrued Liabilities

In thousands	December 31 1995	1994
Warranties	$ 31,035	$ 42,977
Advertising/sales promotion	28,297	27,315
Other	96,709	75,794
	$ 156,041	$ 146,086

Income Taxes (excerpts)

Deferred income taxes reflect the net tax effects of temporary differences between the carrying amount of assets and liabilities for financial reporting purposes and the amounts used for income tax purposes.

Significant components of the Company's deferred tax assets and liabilities are as follows:

In thousands	December 31 1995	1994
Deferred tax assets (liabilities):		
Tax over book depreciation	$ (93,173)	$(107,662)
Postretirement benefit obligation	167,783	160,291
Product warranty/liability accruals	22,473	18,887
Pensions and other employee benefits	11,112	(37,284)
Capital loss carryforward	37,876	—
Net operating loss carryforwards	4,456	67,562
Foreign tax credit carryforward	—	6,277
Other	9,037	(6,664)
	159,564	101,407
Less valuation allowance for deferred tax assets	(40,492)	(21,799)
Net deferred tax assets	$ 119,072	$ 79,608

Recognized in statements of consolidated financial condition:		
Deferred tax assets—current	$ 42,785	$ 45,589
Deferred tax liabilities—current	(956)	—
Deferred tax assets—noncurrent	91,610	72,394
Deferred tax liabilities—noncurrent	(14,367)	(38,375)
Net deferred tax assets	$ 119,072	$ 79,608

Eastman Kodak and Polaroid—Contingencies

Eastman Kodak is an international conglomerate based in Rochester, New York. It is the world's largest producer of photographic products, specializing in amateur, professional, commercial and medical imaging equipment and supplies. Kodak manufactures and markets various components of imaging systems including films, photographic papers, processing services, photographic chemicals, cameras and projectors. Recent imaging products developed by Kodak include new generations of films, cameras, photographic papers and single-use cameras.

Polaroid Corporation manufactures instant photographic equipment (cameras and film). It also sells other chemicals, optical, and electronic equipment related to imaging. Three "imaging business units" comprise Polaroid—Family, Technical/Industrial, and Business—each contribute about one-third to total sales. Foreign sales comprise almost half of worldwide sales.

Learning Objectives
- Understand the accounting implications and treatments of contingent losses and gains related to legal proceedings.
- Witness the asymmetric treatment of gains and losses and see evidence of conservatism in accrual accounting.
- Discover the strategic element involved with financial statement footnote presentation of contingent losses and gains.

Refer to the financial statements of Eastman Kodak (1990) and Polaroid Corporation (1991). Both companies refer to their mutual lawsuit in the financial statements and footnotes.

Process

a. Use the Legal Note (Eastman Kodak) and footnote 14: Contingencies (Polaroid) to prepare a summary of the important dates related to the litigation.

b. Kodak did not make an accounting entry in 1976 when the suit was filed. Why might Kodak have been reluctant to do so?

c. Recreate the entry Kodak made in 1990 to account for the decision.

d. Why did Kodak make this entry even though the suit was still on appeal at the end of the 1990 fiscal year? Why did Kodak record a loss of only $888 million when the damage award of October 1990 amounted to $909.5 million?

e. Polaroid did not make an accounting entry in 1976 when the suit was filed. Why not?

f. Reconstruct the entry Polaroid made in 1991 when the litigation was settled.

g. What prevented Polaroid from making an entry similar to this in 1990 (i.e., at the same time as Kodak made its entry)?

Analysis

h. What did Polaroid do with the settlement proceeds? (*Hint*: Refer to the statement of cash flows.)

i. What adjustments, if any, would you make to the accompanying financial statements of Eastman Kodak and Polaroid if you wanted to value the companies using a capitalized earnings valuation approach? That is, to what extent are Kodak's (1990) and Polaroid's (1991) earnings persistent?

EASTMAN KODAK COMPANY AND SUBSIDIARY COMPANIES

CONSOLIDATED STATEMENT OF FINANCIAL POSITION
(in millions)

December 31	1990	1989
Assets		
Current Assets		
Cash and cash equivalents	$ 735	$ 1,095
Marketable securities	181	184
Receivables	4,333	4,245
Inventories	2,425	2,507
Deferred income tax charges	653	306
Prepaid charges applicable to future operations	281	254
Total current assets	8,608	8,591
Properties		
Land, buildings, machinery, and equipment at cost	17,648	16,774
Less: Accumulated depreciation	8,670	8,146
Net properties	8,978	8,628
Other Assets		
Unamortized goodwill	4,448	4,579
Long-term receivables and other noncurrent assets	2,091	1,854
Total Assets	$24,125	$23,652
Liabilities And Shareowners' Equity		
Current Liabilities		
Payables	$ 6,413	$ 6,073
Taxes-income and other	588	338
Dividends payable	162	162
Total current liabilities	7,163	6,573
Other Liabilities and Deferred Credits		
Long-term borrowings	6,989	7,376
Other long-term liabilities	1,406	1,371
Deferred income tax credits	1,830	1,690
Total liabilities and deferred credits	17,388	17,010
Shareowners' Equity		
Common stock, par value $ 2.50 per share	934	934
950,000,000 shares authorized; issued		
at December 31, 1990—373,638,981		
at December 31, 1989—373,581,604		
Additional capital paid in or transferred		
from retained earnings	7	6
Retained earnings	7,859	7,802
Accumulated translation adjustment	7	(41)
Pension liability adjustment	(11)	—
	8,796	8,701
Less: Treasury stock at cost	2,059	2,059
at December 31, 1990—49,001,140 shares		
at December 31, 1989—49,004,563 shares		
Total shareowners' equity	6,737	6,642
Total Liabilities and Shareowners' Equity	$24,125	$23,652

EASTMAN KODAK COMPANY AND SUBSIDIARY COMPANIES

CONSOLIDATED STATEMENT OF EARNINGS
(in millions, except per share data)

	1990	1989	1988
Sales to: Customers in the U.S.	$10,118	$10,302	$9,554
Customers outside the U.S.	8,790	8,096	7,480
Total Sales	18,908	18,398	17,034
Costs			
Cost of goods sold	10,966	11,075	9,727
Sales, advertising, distribution, and administrative expenses	5,098	4,857	4,495
Restructuring costs	—	875	—
Total costs and expenses	16,064	16,807	14,222
Earnings from Operations	2,844	1,591	2,812
Investment income	167	148	132
Interest expense	812	895	697
Litigation judgment	888	—	—
Other income (charges)	(54)	81	(11)
Earnings before income taxes	1,257	925	2,236
Provision for income taxes	554	396	839
Net Earnings	$ 703	$ 529	$ 1,397

EASTMAN KODAK COMPANY AND SUBSIDIARY COMPANIES

CONSOLIDATED STATEMENT OF CASH FLOWS

(in millions)

	1990	1989	1988
Cash Flows from Operating Activities:			
Net earnings	$ 703	$ 529	$ 1,397
Adjustments to reconcile net earnings			
to net cash provided by operating activities:			
Depreciation and amortization	1,309	1,326	1,183
Provision for (benefit from) deferred taxes	(165)	—	160
Retirement of properties	320	322	265
Increase in receivables	(88)	(174)	(503)
Decrease (increase) in inventories	82	518	(507)
Increase in liabilities excluding borrowings	414	334	10
Other items, net	(65)	(236)	(694)
Total adjustments	1,807	2,090	(86)
Net cash provided by operating activities	2,510	2,619	1,311
Cash Flows from Investing Activities:			
Additions to properties	(2,037)	(2,118)	(1,914)
Acquisition of Sterling Drug,			
net of cash acquired	—	—	(4,781)
Marketable securities — purchases	(128)	(356)	(329)
Marketable securities — sales	126	406	684
Other items	90	10	16
Net cash used in investing activities	(1,949)	(2,058)	(6,324)
Cash Flows from Financing Activities:			
Net increase in commercial paper borrowings	114	652	768
Proceeds from other borrowings	1,691	1,085	5,505
Repayment of other borrowings	(2,102)	(1,371)	(499)
Dividends to shareowners	(649)	(649)	(600)
Other items	1	5	2
Net cash provided by (used in)			
financing activities	(945)	(278)	5,176
Effect of exchange rate changes on cash	24	(36)	(17)
Net (decrease) increase in			
cash and cash equivalents	(360)	247	146
Cash and cash equivalents,			
beginning of year	1,095	848	702
Cash and cash equivalents, end of year	$ 735	$ 1,095	$ 848

(See notes on pages 39 through 47)

EASTMAN KODAK COMPANY AND SUBSIDIARY COMPANIES
LEGAL NOTE

The action filed by Polaroid Corporation in 1976 in the United States District Court in Boston resulted in (a) a decision on October 11, 1985, holding that the Company's PR-10 instant film and EK4 and EK6 instant cameras infringed seven Polaroid patents and (b) an injunction, effective January 9, 1986, prohibiting further manufacture or sale of such products in the United States. The United States Court of Appeals for the Federal Circuit affirmed the decision on April 25, 1986, and the United States Supreme Court denied the Company's petition for certiorari on October 6, 1986. The case was returned to the District Court in Boston for trial to determine damages. On October 12, 1990, the District Court entered judgment against the Company in the amount of $ 909,457,567. Subsequently, on January 25, 1991, the District Court entered an Amended Opinion and Amended Order of Judgment reducing the award by $ 36,298,596 to a total of $ 873,158,971. The Company has accrued $888,000,000 for the amended judgment and for post-judgment interest through December 31, 1990.

Polaroid filed a notice of appeal to the Court of Appeals for the Federal Circuit on February 22, 1991, and the Company filed a notice of cross appeal to the same Court on March 8, 1991. Pursuant to an order entered by the District Court, the Company has deposited $960,475,368 (110% of the amended judgment plus $500) in escrow to secure payment of the amended judgment and execution upon the amended judgment by Polaroid has been stayed until after conclusion of the appeals. The amended judgment will accrue interest until paid, as will the funds in escrow. The cash and related amended judgment liability have been offset in the Consolidated Statement of Financial Position. Based upon the advice of counsel engaged to represent it in the case, the Company does not believe that it is likely that additional damages, if any, awarded against the Company as a result of the appeals will have a material adverse effect on the financial position of the Company.

The Company was involved in various other routine legal matters during 1990, including other litigation and investigations, which are being handled and defended in the ordinary course of business.

POLAROID CORPORATION AND SUBSIDIARY COMPANIES
CONSOLIDATED BALANCE SHEET

(in millions)	December 31, 1991	1990
Assets		
Current assets		
Cash and cash equivalents (Note 5)	$ 162.9	$ 83.8
Short-term investments	82.3	114.2
Receivables, less allowances of $ 17.4 in 1991 and $ 14.5 in 1990	476.1	441.6
Inventories (Note 4)	524.3	519.0
Prepaid expenses and other assets (Note 3)	94.3	81.7
Total current assets	1,339.9	1,240.3
Property, plant and equipment		
Land	32.1	23.4
Buildings	261.1	251.7
Machinery and equipment	1,137.2	1,069.2
Construction in process	168.5	95.7
Total property, plant and equipment	1,598.9	1,440.0
Less accumulated depreciation	1,049.5	979.0
Net property, plant and equipment	549.4	461.0
Total assets	$1,889.3	$1,701.3
Liabilities and Stockholders' Equity		
Current liabilities		
Short-term debt (Note 5)	$ 145.9	$ 168.6
Current portion of long-term debt (Note 7)	26.7	79.4
Payables and accruals (Note 6)	237.4	218.4
Compensation and benefits (Notes 10 and 11)	131.8	123.8
Federal, state and foreign income taxes	102.8	41.0
Total current liabilities	644.6	631.2
Long-term debt (Note 7)	471.8	513.8
Redeemable preferred stock equity, Series B and C, $ 1 par value (Note 8)	—	348.6
Preferred stock, Series A, $ 1 par value, 20,000,000 shares authorized and unissued	—	—
Common stockholders' equity (Note 9)		
Common stock, $ 1 par value, authorized 150,000,000 shares	75.4	75.4
Additional paid-in capital	379.5	379.5
Retained earnings	1,609.9	1,038.3
Less: Treasury stock, at cost	1,083.7	1,053.1
Deferred compensation—ESOP	208.2	232.4
Total common stockholders' equity	772.9	207.7
Total liabilities and stockholders' equity	$1,889.3	$1,701.3

See accompanying notes to consolidated financial statements.

POLAROID CORPORATION AND SUBSIDIARY COMPANIES

CONSOLIDATED STATEMENT OF EARNINGS

(In millions, except per share data)	Years ended December 31,		
	1991	1990	1989
Net sales			
United States	$1,113.6	$1,058.3	$1,091.8
International	957.0	913.4	812.9
Total net sales	2,070.6	1,191.7	1,904.7
Cost of good sold	1,082.5	1,011.8	966.0
Marketing, research, engineering and administrative expenses (Note 2)	741.5	675.6	634.5
Restructuring and other expense (Note 2)	—	—	40.5
Total costs	1,824.0	1,687.4	1,641.0
Profit from operations	246.6	284.3	263.7
Other income (expense)			
Litigation settlement, net of employee incentives (Note 14)	871.6	—	—
Interest income	25.6	19.7	37.2
Other	(2.2)	(4.7)	(2.1)
Total other income	895.0	15.0	35.1
Interest expense	58.4	81.3	86.2
Earnings before income taxes	1,083.2	218.0	212.6
Federal, state and foreign income taxes (Note 3)	399.5	67.0	67.6
Net earnings	$ 683.7	$ 151.0	$ 145.0

See accompanying notes to consolidated financial statements.

POLAROID CORPORATION AND SUBSIDIARY COMPANIES
CONSOLIDATED STATEMENT OF CASH FLOWS

(In millions)	Years ended December 31,		
	1991	1990	1989
Cash Flows from Operating Activities			
Net earnings	$683.7	$151.0	$145.0
Depreciation of property, plant and equipment	85.5	87.2	87.4
Net (increase) decrease in			
receivables, inventories and prepaid expenses	(53.3)	46.6	(72.6)
Net increase (decrease) in payables and accruals,			
compensation and benefits, and			
federal, state and foreign income taxes	83.2	(27.0)	(6.7)
Other non-cash items	23.0	30.1	14.3
Net cash provided from operating activities	822.1	287.9	167.4
Cash Flows from Investing Activities			
(Increase) decrease in			
short-term investments	32.5	35.0	135.6
Additions to property, plant and equipment	(175.8)	(120.9)	(94.5)
Proceeds from sale of fixed assets	—	—	6.1
Net cash provided from (used by)			
investing activities	(143.3)	(85.9)	47.2
Cash Flows from Financing Activities			
Net increase (decrease) in			
short-term debt	(21.8)	(70.6)	105.6
Proceeds from issuances of			
long-term debt (Note 2)	—	—	275.0
Repayments of long-term debt	(228.8)	(70.1)	(23.6)
Cash dividends paid	(38.9)	(52.2)	(34.2)
Purchase of treasury stock	(26.5)	(57.0)	(949.2)
Repurchase of preferred stock (Note 2)	(281.6)	—	—
Proceeds from issuance of preferred stock	—	—	300.0
Net cash used by financing activities	(597.6)	(249.9)	(326.4)
Effect of exchange rate changes on cash	(2.1)	.5	(2.4)
Net increase (decrease)			
in cash and cash equivalents	79.1	(47.4)	(114.2)
Cash and cash equivalents at beginning of year	83.8	131.2	245.4
Cash and cash equivalents at end of year	$162.9	$ 83.8	$131.2

See accompanying notes to consolidated financial statements.

POLAROID CORPORATION AND SUBSIDIARY COMPANIES

NOTES TO CONSOLIDATED FINANCIAL STATEMENTS

14. Contingencies

In April 1976, the Company commenced an action against Eastman Kodak Company in the United States District Court for the District of Massachusetts charging that the manufacture, use and sale by Kodak of instant cameras and instant print film infringed a number of United States patents owned by Polaroid. The suit sought injunctive relief and treble damages plus costs and other relief. After trial of the patent and infringement issues the Court, on October 11, 1985, directed entry of judgment, subsequently affirmed on appeal, that seven Polaroid film and camera patents were valid and were infringed by Kodak. Two of the patents had expired before entry of the judgment. The judgment contained an injunction, which went into effect on January 9, 1986, barring Kodak from infringing the remaining five patents.

Damage issues were presented in a trial which took place from May 1 to November 20, 1989. Those issues included: the amount of damages adequate to compensate the Company for Kodak's infringement; interest on those damages; court costs; whether Kodak's infringement was willful and deliberate, in which case the Court could increase damages up to threefold in its discretion; and whether the action was exceptional, in which case the Court could award the Company its attorneys' fees. During the trial, the Company presented evidence which it believes supported claims for damages in the amount of approximately $3.9 billion. Interest on that amount calculated at the prime rate, compounded annually, totaled approximately $2.2 billion through 1989. Kodak vigorously contested all the Company's claims, and also contended that any damages should be limited to a royalty of approximately $187 million including interest.

On October 12, 1990, the Court entered judgment for the Company in the amount of $909.5 million, consisting of $454.2 million in lost profits and royalties and $455.3 million in interest to that date. The court found that Kodak's infringement was not willful and deliberate and declined to award the Company court costs or attorney's fees.

On October 26, 1990, the Company moved for reconsideration and amendment of the judgment in several respects. Kodak also made a motion addressed to the judgment. On January 25, 1991, the Court entered an amended judgment awarding the Company $873.2 million in damages and interest. The Company appealed from the judgment on February 22, 1991. Kodak filed a cross appeal.

On July 15, 1991, the Company announced a settlement of the litigation. Under the terms of the agreement, Kodak paid the Company $924.5 million in cash and short-term instruments. Both parties agreed to dismiss their appeals pending before the Court of Appeals for the Federal Circuit as well as companion cases in the United States and in other countries of the world. The Company allocated to employees $50.0 million of pretax incentive awards attributable to the litigation settlement. The employee incentive awards and related payroll taxes of $2.9 million have been recorded as a reduction of the settlement proceeds. The settlement proceeds net of the employee incentive awards and related payroll taxes are subject to corporate income taxes.

On October 18, 1991, a former employee, as the purported representative of a class of former Polaroid employees similarly situated, caused a complaint to be entered against the Company in the Superior Court for the County of Suffolk in the Commonwealth of Massachusetts.

The complaint alleges that the Company received approximately $925 million in the July 15, 1991 settlement of its action against Eastman Kodak Company for patent infringement, and that interest on such recovery since the time of the settlement brings the total recovery to approximately $990 million. The complaint further alleges that members of the purported plaintiff class (former employees during the period from April 1976 to January 9, 1986) were deprived, as part of their compensation, of certain benefits that were to be based upon the Company's annual profits from April 1976 to January 1986, constituting the time period during which Kodak infringed the Company's patents. The benefits are alleged to have included: (a) a bonus which was to be calculated, in part, on the Company's profits in any given year and (b) contributions from the Company to the Polaroid Profit Sharing Retirement Plan, based upon a calculation of the Company's profit for each year of an individual's employment. The suit contends that the Company should restate its profits for the time period between April 1976 and January 1986, to account for the proceeds it received from its settlement with Kodak, and compensate the plaintiff class for the benefits and bonuses its members would otherwise have received during such period.

After removing the matter to the United States District Court for the District of Massachusetts, the Company answered the complaint on November 27, 1991. The Company believes that the former employee's claims are without merit, and intends to defend the action vigorously, and expects that its adjudication will not have a material effect on the Company's financial condition.

The Company, together with other parties, is currently designated a Potentially Responsible Party (PRP) by the United States Environmental Protection Agency (EPA) and certain state agencies with respect to the costs of investigation and remediation of pollution at several Superfund sites enumerated below. Due to a wide range of estimates with regard to investigation and remediation costs, the Company cannot establish with certainty its ultimate liability concerning these sites. However, the Company has accrued the minimum of the range of estimated costs for those sites where liability may exist and the amount of exposure or the minimum exposure can be reasonably estimated. Charges against income for environmental remediation projects amounted to approximately $3 million in 1991, $2 million in 1990 and $6 million in 1989.

Exxon—Tiger in Your Tank *vs.* Tony the Tiger

Exxon Corporation was incorporated in the State of New Jersey in 1882. Divisions and affiliated companies of Exxon operate in the United States and over 80 other countries. Their principal business is energy, involving exploration for, and production of crude oil and natural gas, manufacturing of petroleum products and transportation and sale of crude oil, natural gas, and petroleum products.

Learning Objective
* Understand the accounting implications and treatments of contingent losses.

A 1993, *Maclean's* magazine article reports that Kellogg Co., the makers of Frosted Flakes breakfast cereal, has filed a trademark lawsuit against Exxon Corporation for Exxon's revival of their 1960's mascot, the Esso (Exxon) Tiger. Kellogg Co. is particularly concerned that consumers might be confused by the similarity between the Exxon Tiger and Kellogg's own "Tony the Tiger." Exxon officials downplayed the claim by noting that the Exxon Tiger differs substantially from Tony the Tiger. The article is provided below for your reference.

Concepts

a. Describe three possible accounting treatments that could be applied to this lawsuit in Exxon's 1993 financial statements. Conclude, with reasons, as to which of the three you feel is appropriate.

b. How would the lawsuit likely be disclosed in Kellogg's 1993 financial statements?

MACLEAN'S APRIL 12, 1993 p. 9

A CORPORATE CATFIGHT

After a 25-year absence, the Esso tiger roared back into Canada last September on television commercials to promote Imperial Oil Ltd.'s products. But at the home of Tony the Tiger—the topcat for Frosted Flakes cereal—Kellogg Co. executives clearly thought that the revival of Imperial's 1960's mascot as less than gr-r-r-eat, as Tony might say. A month later, Kellogg complained to Imperial. "We're concerned about possible consumer confusion between the Esso tiger and Tony the Tiger," said Neil Nyberg, director of public affairs for Kellogg. Since then, trademark lawyers for the two companies have been attempting to address those concerns with a minimum of public caterwauling. Lorne Wedge, Imperial's merchandising manager for oil products, said that it would be hard for anyone to mistake his company's distinguished-looking tiger for Tony. Said Wedge: "Tony has a blue nose, wears a red scarf that says 'Tony' on it and his head looks kind of square if you see it from the side." Meow.

Maclean's Magazine-*April 12, 1993, p.9 "A Corporate Catfight." Reprinted with permission.*

Bally Entertainment Corporation—Long-Term Debt

Bally Entertainment Corporation and its subsidiaries are engaged in the operation of casinos, some with supporting hotel operations. Principal operations of the Company include: Bally's Park Place casino hotel resort in Atlantic City, The Grand casino hotel resort in Atlantic City, Bally's Las Vegas casino hotel resort, Bally's Saloon * Gambling Hall * Hotel, the Company's dockside casino and hotel in Robinsonville, Mississippi, and Bally's Casino * Lakeshore Resort, the Company's riverboat casino in New Orleans.

Learning Objectives
- Read and understand long-term debt footnote terminology.
- Infer implicit interest rates from footnote disclosure.
- Understand discounts and premiums associated with long-term debt and account for both.
- Prepare long-term debt related journal entries.

Refer to the 1995 Bally Entertainment Corporation financial statements.

Concepts

a. Consider the 10% Convertible Subordinated Debentures due in 2006.

   i.   What is meant by the terms "Convertible," "Subordinated," and "Debenture"?

   ii. What is a "Sinking Fund"?

Process

b. Consider The Grand's 10 5/8% First Mortgage Notes due in 2003. Assume no new notes were issued during the year.

   i.   What is the face value (or principal) of these notes?

   ii. How much interest was paid on the The Grand notes during 1995?

   iii. Prepare the journal entry to record interest expense on these notes for 1995. Consider both the cash and discount portions of the interest expense.

   iv. At what effective interest rate were these notes issued?

c. Consider the 10% Convertible Subordinated Debentures due in 2006.

   i.   Prepare the journal entry required to record the purchase of these debentures to satisfy the sinking fund requirement.

   ii. Why did Bally not have to pay $5,000 to purchase these debentures on the open market?

d. Consider the 6% and 8% Convertible Debentures.

   i.   Prepare the journal entry to record the exchange of these debentures in July 1995.

   ii. Assume that on January 1, 1996 the remaining 6% convertible debentures were converted. Prepare the journal entry required to record this transaction. Bally's balance sheet reveals that common stock has a par value of $0.66 2/3.

e. Consider the Park Place 9 1/4% First Mortgage Notes due 2004. Assume that interest is paid on these notes semi-annually.

   i.   At what effective annual rate of interest were these notes issued? How do you know?

   ii. Assume that interest is paid on these notes semi-annually on the last day of January and July. Prepare the interest journal entries that Bally must have recorded December 31, 1995 and January 31, 1996.

BALLY ENTERTAINMENT CORPORATION

FOOTNOTES TO CONSOLIDATED STATEMENTS

(in thousands)

LONG-TERM DEBT (Excerpts)

The carrying amounts of the Company's long-term debt at December 31, 1995 and 1994 are as follows:

	1995	1994
Bally:		
8% Convertible Senior Subordinated Debentures due 2000	$ 13,586	$ —
10% Convertible Subordinates Debentures due 2006	75,000	80,000
6% Convertible Subordinated Debentures due 1998	1,804	15,715
Casino Holdings:		
Senior Discount Notes due 1998, less unamortized discount of $42,805 and $63,319	149,755	149,281
Bally's Park Place:		
9 1/4% First Mortgage Notes due 2004	425,000	425,000
The Grand:		
10 5/8% First Mortgage Notes due 2003, less unamortized discount of $1,678 and $1,824	273,322	273,176
Bally's Las Vegas:		
10 3/8% First Mortgage Notes due 2003	315,000	315,000
Bally's Casino*Lakeshore Resort:		
Term loan	21,681	—
Construction loan		4,358
Other secured and unsecured obligations	14,453	3,660
Total long-term debt	1,289,601	1,266,190
Current maturities of long-term debt	(11,160)	(7,200)
Long-term debt, less current maturities	$1,278,441	$1,258,990

In July 1995, Bally completed an exchange offer pursuant to which Bally exchanged $13,586 of 8% Convertible Senior Subordinated Debentures due 2000 (the "8% Debentures") for $13,586 of 6% Convertible Subordinated Debentures due 1998 (the "6% Debentures"). The exchange eliminated all cash sinking fund requirements for the 6% Debentures and restrictive dividend covenants, enabling Bally to proceed with the spin-off of its fitness centers segment.

The Bally 10% Convertible Subordinated Debentures due 2006 (the "10% Debentures") require annual sinking fund payments of $5,000 through 2005. The Company purchased $5,000 principal amount of these debentures in 1995 to satisfy the annual sinking fund requirement, which resulted in a pre-tax gain of $303 (included in "Other revenues").

The 6% Debentures may be redeemed by the Company at any time, in whole or in part, without premium. At any time prior to maturity or redemption, these debentures are convertible into shares of Common Stock at a current conversion price of $26.10 per share (as adjusted for the spin-off of BFIT), subject to adjustment for certain subsequent changes in the Company's capitalization.

The Home Depot—Long Term Debt

The Home Depot is the world's largest home improvement retailer and ranks among the twenty largest retailers in the United States. Stores serve primarily do-it-yourselfers, although home improvement contractors, building maintenance professionals, interior designers and other professionals have become increasingly important customers. At the close of fiscal 1995, Home Depot operated 340 full-service, warehouse style stores; 328 in twenty-eight states and 12 in three Canadian provinces.

Learning Objectives
- Read and understand long-term debt footnotes.
- Relate debt disclosures to financial statement data.
- Prepare long-term debt-related journal entries.
- Consider the effect of different debt-related transactions.
- Explain the nature of solvency ratios.

Refer to the 1995 Home Depot financial statements and Note Two—Long Term Debt.

Concepts

a. How much long-term debt does Home Depot have at January 29, 1995?

b. Consider Home Depot's Commercial Paper at January 29, 1995.

   i. What is Commercial Paper?

   ii. The Commercial Paper has a maturity date of less than one year from January 29, 1995. Why does Home Depot classify the debt as long-term?

c. Consider the 4 1/2% Convertible Subordinated Notes due in 1997.

   i. What is meant by the term "convertible"?

   ii. What is meant by the term "subordinated"?

   iii. What is meant by the term "redeemable"?

Process

d. According to Note Two, Home Depot announced on February 28, 1995 (after the fiscal 1995 year end) that the 4 1/2% Convertible Subordinated Notes would be redeemed March 31, 1995 for a redemption price of $1,016.75 per $1,000 note. The note explains that the price includes a redemption premium and accrued interest.

   i. Explain, in your own words, what decision the noteholders face given Home Depot's announcement.

   ii. Calculate the interest that would accrue on each note to March 31, 1995 if interest was paid in full on the notes' latest anniversary date. Calculate the redemption premium per $1,000 note.

   iii. Calculate the number of shares that Home Depot would issue if all the notes were converted.

e. Assume that Home Depot's stock was trading at $36 on March 21, 1995.

   i. What decision would noteholders likely make under these circumstances.

   ii. What journal entry would Home Depot prepare to record this transaction?

f. In fact, Home Depot's stock was trading at $44 on March 21, 1995.

    i.   Predict the decision noteholders would likely make under these circumstances.

    ii.   What journal entry would Home Depot prepare to record this transaction? (*Hint*: According to the balance sheet, Home Depot's common stock has a par value of $0.05.)

Analysis

g. On February 28, 1995 (the redemption announcement date), Home Depot's stock was trading at $46 3/8, higher than the conversion price of $38.75. The conversion option was "in the money" yet bondholders did not immediately convert their notes. Why not?

h. Calculate Home Depot's debt/equity ratio both before and after the conversion of the notes. Is Home Depot more or less risky after the conversion? Explain.

i. In general, how will future Home Depot income statements be affected by this conversion?

THE HOME DEPOT, INC. AND SUBSIDIARIES

CONSOLIDATED STATEMENTS OF EARNINGS
(in thousands)

Fiscal Year Ended

	January 29, 1995	January 30, 1994	January 31, 1993
Net Sales	$12,476,697	$9,238,763	$7,148,436
Cost of Merchandise Sold	8,991,204	6,685,384	5,179,368
Gross Profit	3,485,493	2,553,379	1,969,068
Operating Expenses:			
Selling and Store Operating	2,216,540	1,624,920	1,245,608
Pre-Opening	51,307	36,816	26,959
General and Administrative	230,456	184,954	147,080
Total Operating Expenses	2,498,303	1,846,690	1,419,647
Operating Income	987,190	706,689	549,421
Interest Income (Expense):			
Interest and Investment Income	28,510	60,896	67,562
Interest Expense (note 2)	(35,949)	(30,714)	(41,010)
Interest, Net	(7,439)	30,182	26,552
Earnings Before Income Taxes	979,751	736,871	575,973
Income Taxes (note 3)	375,250	279,470	213,110
Net Earnings	$ 604,501	$ 457,401	$ 362,863
Earnings Per Common and Common Equivalent Share	$ 1.32	$ 1.01	$ .82
Weighted Average Number of Common and Common Equivalent Shares	475,947	453,037	444,989

See accompanying notes to consolidated financial statements.

THE HOME DEPOT, INC. AND SUBSIDIARIES

CONSOLIDATED BALANCE SHEET

(in thousands)

	January 29, 1995	January 30, 1994
Assets		
Current Assets:		
Cash and Cash Equivalents	$ 1,154	$ 99,997
Short-Term Investments, including current maturities of long-term investments (note 7)	56,712	330,976
Receivables, Net	272,225	198,431
Merchandise Inventories	1,749,312	1,293,477
Other Current Assets	53,560	43,720
Total Current Assets	2,132,963	1,966,601
Property and Equipment, at cost:		
Land	1,167,063	814,440
Buildings	1,311,806	891,755
Furniture, Fixtures and Equipment	634,173	451,789
Leasehold Improvements	273,015	224,933
Construction in Progress	289,157	194,482
Capital Leases (notes 2 and 5)	72,054	41,029
	3,747,268	2,618,428
Less Accumulated Depreciation and Amortization	350,031	247,524
Net Property and Equipment	3,397,237	2,370,904
Long-Term Investments (note 7)	98,022	281,623
Notes Receivable	32,528	35,470
Cost in Excess of the Fair Value of Net Assets Acquired, net of accumulated amortization of $8,636 at January 29, 1995 and $5,788 at January 30, 1994	88,513	19,503
Other	28,778	26,788
	$5,778,041	$4,700,889

THE HOME DEPOT, INC. AND SUBSIDIARIES

CONSOLIDATED BALANCE SHEET

(in thousands)

	January 29, 1995	January 30, 1994
Liabilities and Stockholders' Equity		
Current Liabilities:		
Accounts Payable	$ 681,291	$ 521,246
Accrued Salaries and Related Expenses	192,151	167,489
Sales Taxes Payable	101,011	57,590
Other Accrued Expenses	208,377	183,933
Income Taxes Payable	8,717	40,303
Current Installments of Long-Term Debt (notes 2, 5 and 6)	22,692	2,077
Total Current Liabilities	1,214,239	972,638
Long-Term Debt, excluding current installments (notes 2, 5 and 6)	983,369	874,048
Other Long-Term Liabilities	67,953	12,276
Deferred Income Taxes (note 3)	19,258	27,827
Minority Interest (note 9)	50,999	—
Stockholders' Equity (notes 2 and 4):		
Common Stock, par value $.05. Authorized: 1,000,000,000 shares; issued and outstanding — 453,365,000 shares at January 29, 1995 and 449,364,000 shares at January 30, 1994	22,668	22,468
Paid-in Capital	1,526,463	1,436,029
Retained Earnings	1,937,284	1,400,575
Cumulative Translation Adjustments	(10,887)	(121)
Unrealized Loss on Investments, Net	(1,495)	—
	3,474,033	2,858,951
Less Notes Receivable From ESOP (note 6)	31,810	44,851
Total Stockholders' Equity	3,442,223	2,814,100
Commitments and Contingencies (notes 5, 8 and 9)		
	$5,778,041	$4,700,889

See accompanying notes to consolidated financial statements.

THE HOME DEPOT, INC. AND SUBSIDIARIES
NOTES TO CONSOLIDATED FINANCIAL STATEMENTS

NOTE TWO LONG-TERM DEBT

The Company's long-term debt consists of the following (in thousands):

	January 29, 1995	January 30, 1994
4-1/2% Convertible Subordinated Notes, due February 15, 1997, convertible into shares of common stock of the Company at a conversion price of $38.75 per share. The Notes are redeemable by the Company at a premium, plus accrued interest, beginning March 3, 1995.	$ 804,985	$804,990
Commercial Paper, with a weighted average interest rate of 5.9%.	100,000	—
Capital Lease obligations payable in varying installments through January 31, 2015 (see note 5).	63,225	32,585
7.95% Unsecured Note, payable on September 1, 1995, incurred in connection with the establishment of a leveraged Employee Stock Ownership Plan and Trust (see Note 6); interest is payable semi-annually.	20,000	20,000
Variable Rate Industrial Revenue Bonds, secured by letters of credit or land, interest rates averaging 2.7% during fiscal 1994, payable in varying installments through 1999, $3,000 payable on December 1, 2010 and $5,200 payable on September 1, 2011.	9,966	10,500
Installment Notes Payable, interest imputed at rates between 9.5% and 11.5%, payable in varying installments through 2014.	7,419	7,592
Other	466	458
Total long-term debt	1,006,061	876,125
Less current installments	22,692	2,077
Long-term debt, excluding current installments	$ 983,369	$ 874,048

On February 3, 1992, the Company issued, through a public offering, $805,000,000 of its 4-1/2% Convertible Subordinated Notes at par, maturing February 15, 1997. The Notes are convertible into shares of common stock at any time prior to maturity, unless previously redeemed, at a conversion price of $38.75 per share, subject to adjustment under certain conditions. The Notes are not subject to sinking fund provisions.

On February 28, 1995, the Company announced that its outstanding 4-1/2% Convertible Subordinated Notes which had a face value of $804,985,000 would be redeemed on March 31, 1995, at a redemption price of $1,016.75 (which includes premium and accrued interest) per $1,000 principal amount of Notes. Noteholders have the right through March 21, 1995 to convert their Notes into approximately 25.81 shares of common stock of The Home Depot, Inc. for each $1,000 principal amount of Notes at the conversion price of $38.75 per share.

Conversion of all the Notes would result in the issuance of approximately 20,774,000 shares of the Company's common stock.

In January, 1995, the Company established a $300,000,000 Commercial Paper program supported by a back-up credit facility with a maximum aggregate principal amount outstanding of $300,000,000. The program expires November 1, 1997. The Commercial Paper borrowings are classified as long-term debt as it is the Company's intention to refinance them on a long-term basis. As of January 29, 1995, the Company was in compliance with all restrictive covenants.

The 7.95% Unsecured Note related to the ESOP requires, among other things, that debt shall not exceed 66-2/3% of consolidated assets, net of goodwill and current liabilities. The Company was in compliance with all restrictive covenants as of January 29, 1995. The restrictive covenants related to letter of credit agreements securing the industrial revenue bonds are no more restrictive than those referenced or described above.

Interest expense in the accompanying consolidated statements of earnings is net of interest capitalized of $17,559,000 in fiscal 1994, $13,912,000 in fiscal 1993 and $7,549,000 in fiscal 1992.

Maturities of long-term debt (excluding the 4-1/2% Convertible Subordinated Notes) are $22,692,000 for fiscal 1995, $3,197,000 for fiscal 1996, $102,706,000 for fiscal 1997, $2,594,000 for fiscal 1998, and $2,805,000 for fiscal 1999.

Based on discounted cash flows of future payment streams, assuming rates equivalent to the Company's current incremental borrowing rate on similar liabilities, the fair value of the 7.95% unsecured ESOP Note, the Variable Rate Industrial Revenue Bonds, the Installment Notes, the Capital Leases, the Commercial Paper, and other notes payable as of January 29, 1995 is $231,649,000. The fair value of the 4-1/2% Convertible Subordinated Notes as of January 29, 1995, based on the quoted market price on the last business day of the year, is $986,107,000.

American Airlines, Inc.—Leases

American Airlines Inc.'s operations fall within two major lines of business: the Air Transportation Group and the Information Services Group. The Company's Passenger Division is one of the largest scheduled passenger airlines in the world servicing more than 170 destinations. American's Cargo Division provides a full range of freight and mail services to shippers throughout the airline's system. The Information Services Group consists of three divisions including SABRE, one of the largest privately owned, real-time computer systems in the world, providing travel distribution and information services to more than 28,000 travel agencies in 74 countries on six continents.

Learning Objectives
- Understand the economic incentives of leasing versus buying assets.
- Interpret lease footnotes and MD&A discussion of commitments and contingencies.
- Relate lease footnote disclosures to balance sheet data.
- Understand the balance sheet and income statement effects of lease accounting.
- Perform present value calculations relating to lease obligations.
- Create pro forma financial statements to capitalize leases previously treated as operating.
- Understand the economic consequences and quality of earnings issues related to lease accounting.

Refer to the 1995 financial statements of American Airlines Inc.

Concepts

a. Why do companies lease assets rather than buy them?

b. What is an operating lease? What is a capital lease? What is a direct financing lease? What is a sales-type lease?

c. Why do accountants distinguish between different types of leases?

Process

d. Consider the payments made under American's operating leases outlined in Note 4, Leases. Provide the journal entry to record the anticipated lease payment for the year ended December 31, 1996.

e. The 1995 balance sheet shows "Flight Equipment, at Cost" totaling $12,442 million and "Flight Equipment" of $1,958. What do these amounts represent? How many jet aircraft does each comprise?

f. Prepare the journal entry to record aircraft depreciation and/or amortization for 1995. Assume that aircraft have a 5% residual value and a useful life of 20 years.

g. Note 4, Leases, indicates that the present value of capital lease obligations is $1,880. Explain where this figure is found on American's balance sheet.

Analysis

h. Consider the future minimum lease payments made under the capital leases disclosed in Note 4, Leases. Assume that all lease payments are made on December 31 of the respective years. Also assume that the "2001 and subsequent" payments are made evenly over 5 years. That is, lease payments of $340 million will be made on December 31, 2001 through 2005, inclusive.

   i. Estimate the average interest rate for these leases. (*Hint*: Use the internal rate of return—IRR—function on a financial calculator or spreadsheet.)

ii. Based on your calculation of the average interest rate, approximate the interest expense related to these leases for the year that will end December 31, 1996. Use the effective interest rate method.

iii. How much cash will be paid for these leases in fiscal 1996?

iv. Provide the journal entry to record the lease payment of December 31, 1996 based on your calculations in part *h ii*.

v. Based on your journal entry in part *h iv.*, what portion of the "Obligations under capital leases" is current as of December 31, 1995? Why does this differ from "Current obligations under capital leases" on the balance sheet?

i. Consider how the financial statements would look had the flight equipment under operating leases been capitalized. Make the following assumptions: the operating leases discussed in Note 4 relate only to flight equipment, they were entered into December 31, 1995, the implicit interest rate in these leases is 9%, the final payment is made December 31, 2001, and the entire $6.2 billion in guarantees pertain to that final payment (that is, the lease payment made December 31, 2001 is only $8,153).

i. Calculate the present value of the future minimum lease payments.

ii. Prepare the journal entry to capitalize these leases at December 31, 1995.

iii. What would American Airlines have reported as the cost of "Flight equipment under capital leases" at December 31, 1995? As "Total assets"?

iv. What would American Airlines have reported as "Total liabilities" at December 31, 1995? As "Total current liabilities"? As "Obligation under capital leases, less current portion"?

v. What incentives does American Airlines Inc.'s management have to report its aircraft leases as operating leases? Comment on the effect of leasing on the quality of American's earnings.

j. Refer to your solution to part *i*. Had American Airlines treated their operating leases as capital leases, key financial ratios would have been affected for 1995. Discuss how the current ratio, return on assets, return on equity, and debt to equity ratio would have been impacted. State any assumptions you make. Is it true that the decision to capitalize will always yield weaker ratios?

k. Part (1) of Note 1 to the financial statements indicates that in 1991, American changed the estimated useful lives of its Boeing 727-200 aircraft. Assume that American has not purchased or disposed of any of these aircraft since 1991.

i. By how many years did American increase the aircrafts' expected lives?

ii. Estimate the effect that this change in accounting estimate had on annual depreciation expense in 1995. Assume that each of the aircraft in question originally cost $35 million.

AMERICAN AIRLINES, INC.

CONSOLIDATED STATEMENT OF OPERATIONS

(in millions)

Year Ended December 31,	1995	1994	1993
Revenues:			
Airline Group:			
Passenger	$13,335	$12,826	$12,900
Cargo	668	648	637
Other	732	634	527
	14,735	14,108	14,064
Information Services Group	1,439	1,268	1,167
Less: Intergroup revenues	(564)	(539)	(494)
Total operating revenues	15,610	14,837	14,737
Expenses:			
Wages, salaries and benefits	5,183	5,038	4,927
Aircraft fuel	1,565	1,556	1,818
Commissions to agents	1,236	1,273	1,393
Depreciation and amortization	1,138	1,138	1,115
Other rentals and landing fees	802	780	787
Food service	675	663	693
Aircraft rentals	604	620	639
Maintenance materials and repairs	494	438	542
Other operating expenses	2,460	2,143	2,259
Restructuring costs	485	276	—
Total operating expenses	14,642	13,925	14,173
Operating Income	968	912	564
Other Income (Expense):			
Interest income	23	13	5
Interest expense	(557)	(457)	(408)
Interest capitalized	14	21	49
Miscellaneous - net	(55)	(47)	(136)
	(575)	(470)	(490)
Earnings before income taxes and extraordinary loss	393	442	74
Income tax provision	172	174	51
Earnings before extraordinary loss	221	268	23
Extraordinary loss, net of tax benefit	(13)	—	—
Net earnings	$ 208	$ 268	$ 23

The accompanying notes are an integral part of these financial statements.

AMERICAN AIRLINES, INC.
CONSOLIDATED BALANCE SHEET
(in millions)

	December 31, 1995	1994
Assets		
Current assets:		
Cash	$ 70	$ 13
Short-term investments	816	744
Receivables, less allowance for uncollectible accounts (1995—$13; 1994—$14)	1,013	877
Inventories, less allowance for obsolescence (1995—$228; 1994—$171)	516	590
Deferred income taxes	310	270
Other current assets	128	115
Total current assets	2,853	2,609
Equipment and Property:		
Flight equipment, at cost	12,442	12,522
Less accumulated depreciation	3,346	3,285
	9,096	9,237
Other equipment and property, at cost	3,911	3,765
Less accumulated depreciation	2,091	1,899
	1,820	1,866
	10,916	11,103
Equipment and Property Under Capital Leases:		
Flight equipment	1,958	2,098
Other equipment and property	254	267
	2,212	2,365
Less accumulated amortization	778	823
	1,434	1,542
Other Assets:		
Route acquisition costs, less accumulated amortization (1995—$153; 1994—$124)	1,003	1,032
Airport operating and gate lease rights, less accumulated amortization (1995—$89; 1994—$72)	323	337
Prepaid pension cost	268	99
Other	832	601
	2,426	2,069
Total Assets	$17,629	$17,323

AMERICAN AIRLINES, INC.

CONSOLIDATED BALANCE SHEET

(in millions)

| | December 31, | |
	1995	1994
Liabilities and Stockholder's Equity		
Current Liabilities:		
Accounts payable	$ 742	$ 831
Payables to affiliates	907	266
Accrued salaries and wages	686	581
Accrued liabilities	1,138	853
Air traffic liability	1,467	1,473
Current maturities of long-term debt	49	49
Current maturities of long-term debt due to parent	193	—
Current obligations under capital leases	101	110
Total current liabilities	5,283	4,163
Long-term debt less current maturities	1,318	1,518
Long-term debt due to parent	1,676	3,196
Obligations under capital leases, less current obligations	1,777	1,964
Other liabilities and credits:		
Deferred income taxes	480	268
Deferred gains	696	732
Postretirement benefits	1,431	1,247
Other liabilities and deferred credits	1,322	1,002
	3,929	3,249
Commitments, leases, and contingencies		
Stockholder's Equity:		
Common stock—$1 par value; 1,000 shares authorized, issued and outstanding	—	—
Additional paid-in capital	1,699	1,699
Minimum pension liability adjustment	(1)	(199)
Retained earnings	1,948	1,733
	3,646	3,233
Total Liabilities and Stockholder's Equity	$17,629	$17,323

The accompanying notes are an integral part of these financial statements.

AMERICAN AIRLINES, INC.
10-K EXCERPT (DECEMBER 31, 1995)

FLIGHT EQUIPMENT

Owned and leased aircraft operated by American at December 31, 1995, included:

Equipment Type	Current Seating Capacity	Owned	Capital Leased	Operating Leased	Total	Weighted Average Age Years
JET AIRCRAFT						
Airbus A300-600R	266/267	10	—	25	35	6
Boeing 727-200	150	53	14	—	67	19
Boeing 757-200	188	46	9	31	86	4
Boeing 767-200	172	8	—	—	8	13
Boeing 767-200 Extended Range	172	9	13	—	22	10
Boeing 767-300 Extended Range	215	16	3	22	41	5
Fokker 100	97	66	5	4	75	3
McDonnell Douglas DC-10-10	237/290	13	4	—	17	19
McDonnell Douglas DC-10-30	273	4	1	—	5	21
McDonnell Douglas MD-11	251/271	19	—	—	19	4
McDonnell Douglas MD-80	139	119	25	116	260	8
Total		363	74	198	635	8

Lease expirations for American's leased aircraft included in the above table as of December 31, 1995, were:

Equipment Type	1996	1997	1998	1999	2000	2001 and Thereafter
JET AIRCRAFT						
Airbus A300-600R	—	—	—	—	—	25
Boeing 727-200	—	—	—	2	4	8
Boeing 757-200	—	—	—	—	2	38
Boeing 767-200 Extended Range	—	—	—	—	—	13
Boeing 767-300 Extended Range	—	—	—	—	—	10
Fokker 100	—	—	—	—	—	9
McDonnell Douglas DC-10-10	3	1	—	—	—	—
McDonnell Douglas DC-10-30	—	—	1	—	—	—
McDonnell Douglas MD-80	—	—	—	—	3	138
	3	1	1	2	9	241

The table excludes leases for 15 Boeing 767-300 Extended Range aircraft which can be canceled with 30 days' notice during the initial 10-year lease term. At the end of that term in 1998, the leases can be renewed for periods ranging from 10 to 12 years.

Substantially all of American's aircraft leases include an option to purchase the aircraft or to extend the lease term, or both, with the purchase price or renewal rental to be based essentially on the market value of the aircraft at the end of the term of the lease or at a predetermined fixed rate.

AMERICAN AIRLINES, INC.
NOTES TO CONSOLIDATED FINANCIAL STATEMENTS

1. Significant Accounting Policies

EQUIPMENT AND PROPERTY   The provision for depreciation of operating equipment and property is computed on the straight-line method applied to each unit of property, except that spare assemblies are depreciated on a group basis. The depreciable lives and residual values used for the principal depreciable asset classifications are:

	Depreciable Life	Residual Value
Boeing 727-200	21 years(1)	5%
DC-10-10	December 31, 1998(2)	0%
DC-10-30	December 31, 1999(2)	5%
Other aircraft	20 years	5%
Major rotable parts, avionics & assemblies	Life of equipment to which applicable	10%
Improvements to leased flight equipment	Term of lease	None
Buildings and improvements	Principally on 10-30 years or term of lease	None
Other equipment	3-20 years	None

(1) In 1991, American changed the estimated useful lives of its Boeing 727-200 aircraft and engines from a common retirement date of December 31, 1994, to projected retirement dates by aircraft, which results in an average depreciable life of approximately 21 years.

(2) Approximate common retirement date.

Equipment and property under capital leases are amortized over the term of the leases and such amortization is included in depreciation and amortization. Lease terms vary but are generally 10 to 25 years for aircraft and 7 to 40 years for other leased equipment and property.

3. Commitments and Contingencies

The Company has on order four Boeing 757-200 jet aircraft scheduled for delivery in 1996. Remaining payments for these aircraft and related equipment will be approximately $100 million in 1996. In addition to these commitments for aircraft, the Company has authorized expenditures of approximately $850 million for aircraft modifications, renovations of, and additions to, airport and office facilities and various other equipment and assets. American expects to spend approximately $350 million of this amount in 1996.

In April 1995, American announced an agreement to sell 12 of its McDonnell Douglas MD-11 aircraft to Federal Express Corporation (FedEx), with delivery of the aircraft between 1996 and 1999. In addition, American has the option to sell its remaining seven MD-11 aircraft to FedEx with deliveries between 2000 and 2002. The carrying value of the 12 aircraft American has committed to sell was approximately $837 million as of December 31, 1995. Included in depreciation expense are charges related to these aircraft which totaled approximately $23 million for the year ended December 31, 1995.

American has included an event risk covenant in approximately $2.9 billion of lease agreements. The covenant permits the holders of such instruments to receive a higher rate of return (between 50 and 700 basis points above the stated rate) if a designated event, as defined, should occur and the credit rating of the debentures or the debt obligations underlying the lease agreements is downgraded below certain levels.

4. Leases

American leases various types of equipment and property, including aircraft, passenger terminals, equipment and various other facilities. The future minimum lease payments required under capital leases, together with the present value of net minimum lease payments, and future minimum lease payments required under operating leases that have initial or remaining non-cancelable lease terms in excess of one year as of December 31, 1995, were (in millions):

Year Ending December 31,	Capital Leases	Operating Leases
1996	$ 203	$ 843
1997	228	892
1998	224	905
1999	219	898
2000	285	860
2001 and subsequent	1,704	14,353
	2,863 (1)	$18,751 (2)
Less amount representing interest	983	
Present value of net minimum lease payments	$ 1,880	

(1)   Future minimum payments required under capital leases include $205 million and $203 million guaranteed by AMR and American, respectively, relating to special facility revenue bonds issued by municipalities.

(2)   Future minimum payments required under operating leases include $6.2 billion guaranteed by AMR relating to special facility revenue bonds issued by municipalities.

At December 31, 1995, the Company had 198 jet aircraft under operating leases and 74 jet aircraft under capital leases.

The aircraft leases can generally be renewed at rates based on fair market value at the end of the lease term for one to five years. Most aircraft leases have purchase options at or near the end of the lease term at fair market value, but generally not to exceed a stated percentage of the defined lessor's cost of the aircraft. Of the aircraft American has under operating leases, 15 Boeing 767-300 Extended Range aircraft are cancelable upon 30 days' notice during the initial 10-year lease term. At the end of that term in 1998, the leases can be renewed for periods ranging from 10 to 12 years.

Rent expense, excluding landing fees, was $1.2 billion for 1995, 1994 and 1993.

The Robert Mondavi Corporation—Deferred Taxes

The Robert Mondavi Winery was founded in 1966. The Company went public in 1993. Its goal is to produce California wines that belong in the company of the great wines of the world by naturally cultivating the state's outstanding soils and optimizing its ideal climate and growing conditions. Mondavi wines include Robert Mondavi, Woodbridge, Vichon, Byron, and Opus One.

Learning Objectives
- Understand the concepts underlying deferred income tax accounting.
- Interpret the income tax note to the financial statements.
- Use deferred tax asset and liability information to infer balances for tax purposes.
- Consider the tax consequences of a revenue recognition policy that is different for accounting and tax purposes.

Refer to the 1996 Consolidated Financial Statements of The Robert Mondavi Corporation.

Concepts

a. Explain in general terms why The Robert Mondavi Corporation reports deferred income taxes as part of their total income tax expense. Why don't companies simply report their current tax bill as their income tax expense?

b. Explain in general terms what deferred tax assets and deferred tax liabilities represent.

Process

c. According to Note 8—Income Taxes, Mondavi had a net deferred tax liability balance of $8,374 at June 30, 1996. Explain where that balance is found on the balance sheet.

d. What journal entry did Mondavi record for income tax expense in fiscal 1996?

Analysis

e. The largest component of the deferred tax liability relates to "Property, plant and equipment."

    i. Explain how this deferred tax liability component arose.

    ii. Using information from Note 3—Property, Plant and Equipment and Note 8—Income Taxes, estimate the company's balance for tax purposes for property, plant and equipment. Assume that the deferred tax liability was calculated using the company's effective tax rate for 1996.

f. According to Note 1—Organization and Summary of Significant Accounting Policies, Mondavi operates a wine futures program.

    i. Explain what a wine futures program is and explain how cash received under such a program is accounted for.

    ii. Assume that for tax purposes cash received under the wine futures program is considered current period taxable revenue. How would receiving cash under a wine futures program affect Mondavi's deferred tax assets and liabilities?

    iii. Under the assumption of part *f ii.*, did the deferred tax asset related to the wine futures program increase or decrease during fiscal 1996? Be sure to consider both the current and the long-term portion of the deferred revenues.

THE ROBERT MONDAVI CORPORATION

CONSOLIDATED BALANCE SHEETS

(IN THOUSANDS, EXCEPT SHARE DATA)

	JUNE 30,	
	1996	1995
Assets		
Current assets:		
Cash	$ —	$ 900
Accounts receivable—trade, net	39,495	32,601
Advances to joint ventures	118	116
Inventories	142,565	113,375
Prepaid income taxes	2,370	—
Deferred income taxes	570	—
Prepaid expenses and other current assets	722	770
Total current assets	185,840	147,762
Property, plant and equipment, net	156,754	120,934
Investments in joint ventures	17,100	11,792
Other assets	1,501	1,826
Total assets	$361,195	$282,314
Liabilities and Shareholders' Equity		
Current liabilities:		
Book overdraft	$ 403	$ —
Accounts payable—trade	13,733	9,411
Accrued payroll, bonuses and benefits	10,322	9,247
Other accrued expenses	2,828	1,986
Current portion of long-term debt	4,115	6,071
Income taxes payable	—	1,160
Deferred revenue	1,682	1,493
Deferred income taxes	—	1,495
Total current liabilities	33,083	30,863
Long-term debt, less current portion	123,713	113,017
Deferred income taxes	8,944	7,368
Deferred executive compensation	6,098	5,839
Other liabilities	1,102	665
Total liabilities	172,940	157,752
Commitments and contingencies (Note 12)		
Shareholders' equity:		
Preferred Stock: Authorized—5,000,000 shares		
Issued and outstanding—no shares	—	—
Class A Common Stock, without par value:		
Authorized—25,000,000 shares		
Issued and outstanding—7,281,529 and 4,448,853 shares	73,402	34,441
Class B Common Stock, without par value:		
Authorized—12,000,000 shares		
Issued and outstanding—7,676,012 and 8,325,781 shares	12,324	13,364
Paid-in capital	1,334	—
Retained earnings	101,195	76,757
	188,255	124,562
Total liabilities and shareholders' equity	$361,195	$282,314

See Notes to Consolidated Financial Statements.

THE ROBERT MONDAVI CORPORATION

CONSOLIDATED STATEMENTS OF INCOME
(IN THOUSANDS, EXCEPT PER SHARE DATA)

	YEAR ENDED JUNE 30,		
	1996	1995	1994
Gross revenues	$253,540	$210,361	$176,236
Less excise taxes	12,710	10,892	9,209
Net revenues	240,830	199,469	167,027
Cost of goods sold	122,385	97,254	88,102
Gross profit	118,445	102,215	78,925
Selling, general and administrative expenses	70,707	64,160	56,198
Operating income	47,738	38,055	22,727
Other income (expense):			
Interest	(8,814)	(8,675)	(6,698)
Equity in net income of joint ventures	1,751	1,547	973
Other	(208)	(1,332)	(1,278)
Income before income taxes	40,467	29,595	15,724
Provision for income taxes	16,029	11,775	6,212
Net income	$ 24,438	$ 17,820	$ 9,512
Earnings per share:	$ 1.61	$ 1.39	$ .75
Weighted average number of common shares and equivalents outstanding	15,203	12,787	12,731

See Notes to Consolidated Financial Statements.

THE ROBERT MONDAVI CORPORATION
NOTES TO CONSOLIDATED FINANCIAL STATEMENTS

NOTE 1—ORGANIZATION AND SUMMARY OF SIGNIFICANT ACCOUNTING POLICIES (excepts)

Property, plant and equipment

Property, plant and equipment is stated at cost. Vineyards infested with phylloxera are stated at the lower of cost or adjusted cost as determined by the estimated future net cash flows (Note 3). Maintenance and repairs are expensed as incurred. Costs incurred in developing vineyards, including related interest costs, are capitalized until the vineyards become commercially productive.

Depreciation and amortization is computed using the straight-line method, with the exception of barrels which are depreciated using an accelerated method, over the estimated useful lives of the assets amounting to 20 years for vineyards, 45 years for buildings and 3 to 12 years for machinery and equipment. Estimated useful lives of vineyards infested with phylloxera are adjusted to the Company's estimate of the remaining productive life of the vineyards ranging from 1 to 6 years. Leasehold improvements are amortized over the estimated useful lives of the improvements or the terms of the related lease, whichever is shorter.

Income taxes

Deferred income taxes are computed using the liability method. Under the liability method, taxes are recorded based on the future tax effects of the difference between the tax and financial reporting bases of the Company's assets and liabilities. In estimating future tax consequences, all expected future events are considered, except for potential income tax law or rate changes.

Wine futures program

The Company has a wine futures program whereby contracts to buy cased wine are sold to distributors prior to the time the wine is available for shipment. The agreement to deliver the wine in the future is recorded when the Company receives the distributor's deposit representing the total purchase price. Revenue relating to this program is deferred and recognized when the wine is shipped. Deferred revenue relating to wine scheduled for shipment during the next fiscal year is included as a current liability while the remainder of the deferred revenue is included in other liabilities in the consolidated balance sheet. Deferred revenue included in other liabilities at June 30, 1996 and 1995 totaled $23,000 and $14,000, respectively.

NOTE 3—PROPERTY, PLANT AND EQUIPMENT

The cost and accumulated depreciation of property, plant and equipment consist of the following (in thousands):

	JUNE 30,	
	1996	1995
Land	$ 38,235	$ 28,742
Vineyards	29,716	26,514
Machinery and equipment	99,211	81,096
Buildings	31,739	29,581
Vineyards under development	7,461	4,126
Construction in progress	21,429	12,928
	227,791	182,987
Less—accumulated depreciation	(71,037)	(62,053)
	$156,754	$120,934

NOTE 8—INCOME TAXES

The provision for income taxes consists of the following (in thousands):

| | YEAR ENDED JUNE 30, | | |
	1996	1995	1994
Current:			
Federal	$14,760	$ 9,182	$4,435
State	1,758	1,883	651
	16,518	11,065	5,086
Deferred:			
Federal	(824)	874	1,178
State	335	(164)	(52)
	(489)	710	1,126
	$16,029	$11,775	$6,212

Income tax expense differs from the amount computed by multiplying the statutory federal income tax rate times income before taxes, due to the following:

| | YEAR ENDED JUNE 30, | | |
	1996	1995	1994
Federal statutory rate	35.0%	35.0%	35.0%
State income taxes, net of federal benefit	3.4	4.6	3.0
Permanent differences	0.5	0.7	1.1
Other	0.7	(0.5)	0.4
	39.6%	39.8%	39.5%

The approximate effect of temporary differences and carryforwards that give rise to deferred tax balances at June 30, 1996 and 1995 are as follows (in thousands):

| | JUNE 30, | |
	1996	1995
GROSS DEFERRED TAX ASSETS		
Liabilities and accruals	$(1,388)	$(1,442)
Deferred compensation	(3,797)	(3,211)
Tax credits	(45)	(350)
Gross deferred tax assets	(5,230)	(5,003)
GROSS DEFERRED TAX LIABILITIES		
Property, plant and equipment	11,431	9,315
Retirement plans	583	485
Inventories	340	2,691
Investments in joint ventures	1,144	1,113
State taxes	106	262
Gross deferred tax liabilities	13,604	13,866
Net deferred tax liability	$ 8,374	$ 8,863

The Company has foreign tax credits at June 30, 1996, that can be carried forward five years. The state investment tax credits were fully utilized during the year ended June 30, 1996.

During the year ended June 30, 1996, the Company recognized certain tax benefits related to stock option plans in the amount of $1,334,000. These benefits were recorded as an increase in prepaid income taxes and paid-in capital.

Dell Computer Corporation—Income Taxes

Dell Computer Corporation designs, develops, manufactures, markets, services and supports a wide range of computer systems, including desktops, notebooks and network servers, and also markets software, peripherals and service and support programs. The Company markets its computer products and services under the Dell® brand name directly to its customers. These customers include major corporate, government, medical and education accounts, as well as small-to-medium businesses and individuals. The Company supplements its direct marketing strategy by marketing through value-added resellers. Based in Austin, Texas, the Company conducts operations worldwide through wholly owned subsidiaries; such operations are primarily concentrated in the United States and Europe.

Learning Objectives
- Understand the concepts underlying deferred income tax accounting.
- Interpret the income tax note to the financial statements.
- Use deferred tax asset and liability information to infer account balances.

Refer to the 1996 financial statements of Dell Computer Corporation.

Concepts

a. Explain in general terms why Dell Computer Corporation reports deferred income taxes as part of their total income tax expense. Why don't companies simply report their current tax bill as their income tax expense?

b. Explain in general terms what deferred tax assets and deferred tax liabilities represent.

Process

c. According to Note 5—Income Taxes, Dell had a net deferred tax asset balance of $67 at January 28, 1996. The balance is not shown separately on the balance sheet, it is included with some other items. Explain where the balance is found on the balance sheet.

d. What journal entry did Dell record for income tax expense in fiscal 1996?

Analysis

e. One component of the net deferred tax asset relates to "Depreciation."

   i.   Does Dell have a deferred tax asset or liability with respect to Depreciation?

   ii. Explain how this deferred tax component arose.

   iii. In light of this component of the net deferred tax asset, comment on the quality of Dell's reported 1996 earnings. Focus on the depreciation expense component of earnings.

f. Another component of the net deferred tax asset relates to "Provisions for doubtful accounts and returns."

   i.   Does Dell have a deferred tax asset or liability with respect to "Provisions for doubtful accounts and returns"?

   ii. Explain how this deferred tax component arose.

   iii. Assume that for income tax purposes Dell is not allowed to deduct bad debts or sales returns until the accounts are written off or the merchandise is returned. Dell reported that the allowance for doubtful accounts at the end of fiscal 1996 was $29 million and at the end of fiscal 1995 was $26 million. Use that information to estimate Dell's provision for sales returns at the end of fiscal 1996 and 1995.

iv. What is the trend in year end sales returns? Why would a financial analyst be interested in such a trend?

g. In Note 5, Dell indicates that the company has not recorded all the potential deferred income tax assets and liabilities that have arisen.

   i. What deferred tax item has not been recorded?

   ii. Why has Dell not recorded it? Does this treatment seem reasonable?

   iii. What is the impact of this accounting choice on Dell's total debt to equity ratio at January 28, 1996?

   iv. What is the impact of this choice on Dell's fiscal 1996 Net income available to common shareholders? (The unrecorded deferred tax liability at January 29, 1995 was $22.5 million.)

h. Dell reports that one of the reasons that its effective tax rate is less than the U.S. statutory rate of 35% is that it faces lower tax rates in foreign countries.

   i. Use information from Note 5 to estimate the average foreign income tax rate faced by Dell in fiscal 1996 and fiscal 1995.

   ii. Explain why a financial analyst would be interested in the effect of foreign tax rates on Dell's effective rate.

   iii. What questions with respect to foreign tax rates would an equity security analyst have for Dell's management?

DELL COMPUTER CORPORATION
CONSOLIDATED STATEMENT OF FINANCIAL POSITION
(IN MILLIONS, EXCEPT SHARE DATA)

	JANUARY 28, 1996	JANUARY 29, 1995
Assets		
Current assets:		
Cash	$ 55	$ 43
Marketable securities	591	484
Accounts receivable, net	726	538
Inventories	429	293
Other current assets	156	112
Total current assets	1,957	1,470
Property, plant and equipment, net	179	117
Other assets	12	7
	$2,148	$1,594
Liabilities and Stockholders' Equity		
Current liabilities:		
Accounts payable	$ 466	$ 403
Accrued and other liabilities	473	349
Total current liabilities	939	752
Long-term debt	113	113
Deferred profit on warranty contracts	116	68
Other liabilities	7	9
Commitments and contingencies	—	—
Stockholders' equity:		
Preferred stock and capital in excess of $.01 par value; shares authorized: 5,000,000; shares issued and outstanding: 60,000 and 1,250,000, respectively	6	120
Common Stock and capital in excess of $.01 par value; shares authorized: 300,000,000 and 100,000,000, respectively; shares issued and outstanding: 93,446,607 and 79,359,276, respectively	430	242
Retained earnings	570	311
Other	(33)	(21)
Total stockholders' equity	973	652
	$2,148	$1,594

The accompanying notes are an integral part of these consolidated financial statements.

DELL COMPUTER CORPORATION
CONSOLIDATED STATEMENT OF OPERATIONS
(IN MILLIONS, EXCEPT PER SHARE DATA)

	FISCAL YEAR ENDED		
	JANUARY 28, 1996	JANUARY 29, 1995	JANUARY 30, 1994
Net sales	$5,296	$3,475	$2,873
Cost of sales	4,229	2,737	2,440
Gross margin	1,067	738	433
Operating expenses:			
Selling, general and administrative	595	424	423
Research, development and engineering	95	65	49
Total operating expenses	690	489	472
Operating income (loss)	377	249	(39)
Financing and other income (expense), net	6	(36)	—
Income (loss) before income taxes	383	213	(39)
Provision for income taxes (benefit)	111	64	(3)
Net income (loss)	272	149	(36)
Preferred stock dividends	(12)	(9)	(4)
Net income (loss) available to common stockholders	$260	$140	$(40)
Earnings (loss) per common share:			
Primary	$ 2.67	$ 1.69	$ (.53)
Fully diluted	$ 2.65	$ 1.58	$ —

The accompanying notes are an integral part of these consolidated financial statements.

DELL COMPUTER CORPORATION
NOTES TO CONSOLIDATED FINANCIAL STATEMENTS

NOTE 5—INCOME TAXES

The provision for income taxes consists of the following:

	FISCAL YEAR ENDED		
	JANUARY 28, 1996	JANUARY 29, 1995	JANUARY 30, 1994
	(IN MILLIONS)		
Current:			
Domestic	$102	$52	$ 29
Foreign	25	16	8
Prepaid	(16)	(4)	(40)
Provision for income taxes (benefit)	$111	$64	$ (3)

Income (loss) before income taxes included approximately $176 million, $126 million and ($32) million related to foreign operations in the fiscal years ended January 28, 1996, January 29, 1995 and January 30, 1994, respectively.

The Company has not recorded a deferred income tax liability of approximately $70 million for additional U.S. federal income taxes that would result from the distribution of earnings of its foreign subsidiaries, if they were repatriated. The Company currently intends to reinvest indefinitely the undistributed earnings of its foreign subsidiaries.

The deferred tax asset is comprised of the following principal temporary differences:

	JANUARY 28, 1996	JANUARY 29, 1995	JANUARY 30, 1994
	(IN MILLIONS)		
Depreciation	$ 5	$(5)	$ —
Provisions for doubtful accounts and returns	25	23	20
Inventory and warranty provisions	18	26	28
Deferred service contract revenue	53	25	9
Import promotion reserve	(5)	—	—
Other	(29)	9	7
Deferred tax asset	$ 67	$78	$64

The difference between the income tax provisions in the Consolidated Financial Statements and the tax expense computed at the U.S. federal statutory rate of 35% for each of the last three fiscal years is as follows:

	FISCAL YEAR ENDED		
	JANUARY 28, 1996	JANUARY 29, 1995	JANUARY 30, 1994
	(IN MILLIONS)		
Tax provision (benefit) at the U.S. federal statutory rate	$ 134	$ 75	$(14)
Research and development credit	(1)	(1)	(1)
Foreign income taxed at different rate	(23)	(16)	10
Net operating loss carryovers	1	2	4
Other	—	4	(2)
Provision (benefit) for income taxes	$ 111	$ 64	$ (3)
Effective tax rates	29.0%	30.0%	7.6%

Enron Corp.—Pension Obligations

Enron Corp. is an integrated natural gas company with headquarters in Houston, Texas. Enron's operations, conducted through its subsidiaries and affiliates comprise the gathering, transportation and wholesale marketing of natural gas to markets throughout the world; the exploration for and production of natural gas and crude oil, natural gas liquids and refined petroleum products; the independent (i.e., non-utility) development, promotion, construction and operation of power plants, natural gas liquids facilities and pipelines; and the non-price regulated purchasing and marketing of energy-related commitments.

Learning Objectives
- Read and understand pension footnote terminology.
- Understand and account for the difference between expensing and funding pension obligations.
- Prepare pension-related journal entries.
- Evaluate the impact of actuarial assumptions on pension expense and obligations.

Refer to the 1995 Enron Corp. financial statements.

Concepts

a. There are two general types of pension plans. What are they and how do they differ? Which of the two types does Enron have?

b. Explain the terms vested and non-vested pension benefits. Find these amounts in Enron's pension footnote. What is the balance of each benefit at December 31, 1995?

c. In general, what is the difference between accumulated pension benefits and projected pension benefits? Which is larger? Why? Find these amounts in Enron's pension footnote. What is the balance of each at December 31, 1995?

d. Explain how the matching principle applies to pension accounting.

e. List some of the assumptions that are made in order to account for pensions.

Process

f. Consider Enron's pension expense.

   i. What amount was recorded in the income statement for 1995? For 1994?

   ii. What rate of return was earned on the plan assets during 1995? (*Hint*: use the average fair value of the plan assets.) How does this compare with the expected long-term return?

g. Consider Enron's pension obligation.

   i. Where on the balance sheet is Enron's pension obligation at December 31, 1995?

   ii. Is the Enron pension under or over-funded for 1995? For 1994?

   iii. Briefly explain the line item "unrecognized net loss." When, if ever, will these gains and losses appear on Enron's income statement?

   iv. Prior service costs pertain to benefits for employee services rendered in prior periods. GAAP permits these costs to be included in the calculation of pension expense prospectively rather than retroactively. Speculate on why "unrecognized prior service cost" increased during 1995 for the Enron pension plan.

   v. Briefly explain the line item "unrecognized net asset at transition." Why did it decrease during 1995?

h. During 1995, Enron changed the discount rate used to calculate its pension obligation from 8.0% to 7.5%. Which footnote numbers are affected by this rate change?

i. Enron projects wage increases of 4%. How would the footnote have been different had a larger rate been projected?

ENRON CORPORATION
FOOTNOTES TO CONSOLIDATED STATEMENTS
(in thousands)

11 Retirement Benefits Plan and ESOP

Enron maintains a retirement plan (the Enron Plan) which is a noncontributory defined benefit plan covering substantially all employees in the United States and certain employees in foreign countries. Through December 31, 1994, participants in the Enron Plan with five years or more of service were entitled to retirement benefits based on a formula that uses a percentage of final average pay and years of service. In connection with a change to the retirement benefit formula, Enron amended the Enron Plan providing, among other things, that all employees became fully vested in retirement benefits earned through December 31, 1994. The formula in place prior to January 1, 1995 was suspended and replaced with a benefit accrual of 5% of annual base pay beginning January 1, 1996.

Enron also maintains a noncontributory employee stock ownership plan (ESOP) which covers all eligible employees. Allocations to individual employees' retirement accounts within the ESOP offset a portion of benefits earned under the Enron Plan. At December 31, 1995, all shares included in the ESOP had been allocated to the employee accounts.

The components of pension expense are as follows:

(In Thousands)	1995	1994	1993
Service cost—benefits earned during the year	$ 1,654	$ 16,192	$ 11,709
Interest cost on projected benefit obligation	21,172	25,996	25,230
Actual return on plan assets	(32,299)	(22,235)	(37,507)
Amortization and deferrals	8,810	(12,225)	11,184
Pension expense (income)	$ (663)	$ 7,728	$ 10,616

The valuation date of the Enron Plan and the ESOP is September 30. The funded status as of the valuation date of the Enron Plan and the ESOP reconciles with the amount detailed below which is included in "Other Assets" on the Consolidated Balance Sheet.

(In Thousands)	1995	1994
Actuarial present value of accumulated benefit obligation		
Vested	$(275,668)	$(253,881)
Nonvested	(26,875)	(25,546)
Additional amounts related to projected wage increases	(11,536)	(54,260)
Projected benefit obligation	(314,079)	(333,687)
Plan assets at fair value (a)	294,763	352,608
Plan assets in excess of (less than) projected benefit obligation	(19,316)	18,921
Unrecognized net loss	53,524	35,563
Unrecognized prior service cost	44,476	12,416
Unrecognized net asset at transition	(36,205)	(42,238)
Contributions	553	548
Prepaid pension cost at December 31	$ 43,032	$ 25,210
Discount rate	7.5%	8.0%
Long-term rate of return on assets	10.5%	10.5%
Rate of increase in wages	4.0%	4.0%

(a) Includes plan assets of the ESOP of $152,202 and $235,540 for the years 1995 and 1994, respectively.

Assets of the Enron Plan are comprised primarily of equity securities, fixed income securities and temporary cash investments. It is Enron's policy to fund all pension costs accrued to the extent required by Federal tax regulations.

Black Clawson—Other Post-Employment Benefits

Since 1853, the Black Clawson Company has served the pulp and paper industry. Today, Black Clawson encompasses sixteen engineering/ manufacturing/ service facilities around the world. With worldwide headquarters in New York City, the multinational company serves the pulp, paper and paperboard industries; the paper, board, and plastic converting industries; and a wide range of other heavy industries.

Learning Objectives
- Gain familiarity with SFAS 106.
- Record other post-employment benefit liability and expenses.
- Evaluate the economic consequences of this standard.

Statement of Accounting Standard 106—*Employers' Accounting for Postretirement Benefits Other Than Pensions*, is in effect for fiscal years beginning after December 15, 1992. The standard reads, in part:

The Board views a postretirement benefit plan as a deferred compensation arrangement whereby an employer promises to exchange future benefits for employees' current services. Because the obligation to provide benefits arises as employees render the services necessary to earn the benefits pursuant to the terms of the plan, the Board believes that the cost of providing the benefits should be recognized over those employee service periods.

This Statement addresses, for the first time, the accounting issues related to measuring and recognizing the exchange that takes place between an employer that provides postretirement benefits and the employees who render services in exchange for those benefits. The Board believes the accounting recognition required by this Statement should result in more useful and representationally faithful financial statements. However, this Statement is not likely to be the final step in the evolution of more useful accounting for postretirement benefit arrangements.

The Board's objectives in issuing this Statement are to improve employers' financial reporting for postretirement benefits in the following manner:

a. *To enhance the relevance and representational faithfulness of the employer's reported results of operations by recognizing net periodic postretirement benefit cost as employees render the services necessary to earn their postretirement benefits.*

b. *To enhance the relevance and representational faithfulness of the employer's statement of financial position by including a measure of the obligation to provide postretirement benefits based on a mutual understanding between the employer and its employees of the terms of the underlying plan.*

c. *To enhance the ability of users of the employer's financial statements to understand the extent and effects of the employer's undertaking to provide postretirement benefits to its employees by disclosing relevant information about the obligation and cost of the postretirement benefit plan and how those amounts are measured.*

d. *To improve the understandability and comparability of amounts reported by requiring employers with similar plans to use the same method to measure their accumulated postretirement benefit obligations and the related costs of the postretirement benefits.*

Concepts

a. Explain, in general terms, what the FASB accounting standard on other post-employment benefits (OPEB) requires.

b. Contrast this with the common alternative method previously used by most corporations.

c. In a December 19, 1989 *Wall Street Journal* article, Carl C. Landegger—Chairman of Black Clawson Co.—was quoted as saying,

"My company, which makes heavy machinery for the paper, plastics and pipe industry, has about 2,000 employees at our four U.S. plants. By 1997, the FASB proposal on medical benefits [post-retirement benefits] could reduce the net worth of Black Clawson by half and force us to cut our credit lines substantially. It could also hinder any expansions and reduce our usually heavy research and development outlays."

As a result, Mr. Landegger says Black Clawson will have to sharply reduce health care benefits for new retirees. "The FASB should reconsider this rule. The new information it may provide users of financial statements isn't worth all the pain and suffering it will impose."

Assume that the actuarial estimate of Black Clawson's OPEB liability at the end of 1992 was $200 million. Prepare the journal entry that would be required under SFAS 106. Assume that Black Clawson's income tax rate is 34% and that OPEB expenses are tax deductible only when paid.

d. How would cash have been affected in 1992 had Black Clawson recorded the OPEB liability? When is there a cash effect from this liability? How might the recording of the liability in 1992 affect future cash outflows?

e. Critically evaluate Mr. Landegger's comments. Explain why you agree or disagree with him.

Gannett Company, Inc.—Treasury Stock

Gannett Company, Inc. (Gannett) is a diversified news and information company that publishes newspapers (e.g. USA TODAY), operates broadcasting stations and outdoor advertising businesses, and is engaged in research, marketing, commercial printing, a newswire service, data services and programming. The company has facilities in 41 states and 8 countries. Corporate headquarters are located at Arlington, Virginia.

Learning Objectives
- Explain how companies account for treasury stock transactions.
- Explain why treasury stock is treated as a contra-equity account and not as an asset.
- Consider the effect of treasury stock transactions on the effective ownership of the company.

Refer to the Consolidated balance sheets and Note 8—Capital stock, stock options, incentive plans (excerpt) from Gannett's 1994 consolidated financial statements.

Concepts

a. Common stock is classified as authorized, issued, and outstanding.

   i. How many shares of common stock is Gannett authorized to issue?

   ii. How many shares of common stock has Gannett actually issued at December 25, 1994?

   iii. How many shares of Gannett common stock are outstanding at December 25, 1994?

   iv. Why do companies repurchase shares of their own company?

Process

b. During the year ended December 25, 1994, Gannett repurchased a number of its own common shares on the open market. The company reissued some of these "treasury shares" in fiscal 1994.

   i. How many shares of its own common stock did Gannett repurchase on the open market during the fiscal-year ended December 25, 1994?

   ii. What was the total amount and average cost per share paid by Gannett for its stock during fiscal 1994?

   iii. How many shares of treasury stock did Gannett reissue in connection with the purchase of a television station during fiscal 1994?

   iv. For what other reason did Gannett reissue treasury stock during 1994? Approximately how many shares of stock did Gannett reissue in conjunction with this transaction?

c. Describe the method used by Gannett to account for its treasury stock transactions. Prepare a single journal entry that summarizes Gannett's treasury stock *purchase* activity in 1994.

d. Provide definitions of the financial statement elements "asset" and "shareholders' equity." Where are the treasury shares classified in Gannett's consolidated balance sheet? Based on how Gannett uses these shares, the treasury shares appear to embody an expected future economic benefit. Why didn't Gannett disclose its treasury stock as an asset?

Analysis

e. According to the Proxy Statement filed with the SEC on March 15, 1995, "the only person or group known to the Company to be the beneficial owner of more than 5% of the outstanding shares of Gannett Common Stock was The Capital Group Companies, Inc., ["Capital"] ... As of December 31, 1994, The Capital Group Companies, Inc. ... held 7,867,600 shares of Gannett

Common Stock, which then constituted 5.63% of the total outstanding shares." Assume that on January 1, 1995 Capital wishes to own 10% of Gannett's outstanding common stock.

i   How many shares would Capital have to purchase on the open market to acquire a 10% interest in the company? What journal entry would Gannett prepare to record the purchase of stock by Capital? (Assume the average stock price for this transaction was $52.57.)

ii. Now assume that Gannett's Board of Directors supports Capital's bid to become a 10% shareholder. How many shares of its own common stock would Gannett have to repurchase on the open market to result in a 10% stake for Capital? What journal entry would Gannett prepare in this case? (Again, assume that the average stock price for this transaction was $52.57 per share.)

GANNETT COMPANY, INC.

CONSOLIDATED BALANCE SHEETS

(In thousands of dollars)

Assets	Dec. 25, 1994	Dec. 26, 1993
Current assets		
Cash	$ 44,229	$ 32,461
Marketable securities, at cost, which approximates market	23	43,034
Trade receivables (less allowance for doubtful receivables of $15,846 and $13,915, respectively)	487,615	449,063
Other receivables	29,745	135,036
Inventories	53,047	53,094
Prepaid expenses	36,178	45269
Total current assets	650,837	757,957
Property, plant and equipment:		
Land	130,166	131,676
Buildings and improvements	690,589	689,103
Advertising display structures	259,532	262,145
Machinery, equipment and fixtures	1,669,192	1,673,237
Construction in progress	64,977	38,449
Total	2,814,456	2,794,610
Less accumulated depreciation	(1,386,312)	(1,316,341)
Net property, plant and equipment	1,428,144	1,478,269
Intangible and other assets		
Excess of acquisition cost over the value of assets acquired (less amortization of $361,204 and $320,934, respectively)	1,472,002	1,501,102
Investments and other assets (Notes 2 and 5)	156,069	86,470
Total intangible and other assets	1,628,071	1,587,572
Total assets	$3,707,052	$3,823,798

GANNETT COMPANY, INC.

CONSOLIDATED BALANCE SHEETS

(In thousands of dollars)

Liabilities and Shareholders' Equity	Dec. 25, 1994	Dec. 26, 1993
Current liabilities		
Current maturities of long-term debt (Note 4)	$ 1,026	$ 164
Accounts payable		
Trade	202,550	169,425
Other	13,335	17,783
Accrued liabilities		
Compensation	60,574	53,922
Interest	11,658	11,774
Other	76,274	74,761
Dividend payable	47,739	48,399
Income taxes (Note 7)	37,618	5,760
Deferred income	76,280	73,151
Total current liabilities	527,054	455,139
Deferred income taxes (Note 7)	164,691	205,314
Long-term debt (Note 4)	767,270	850,686
Postretirement medical and life insurance		
liabilities (Note 6)	306,863	308,024
Other long-term liabilities	118,936	96,715
Total liabilities	1,884,814	1,915,878
Shareholders' equity (Notes 4 and 8)		
Preferred stock, par value $ 1: Authorized, 2,000,000		
shares: Issued, none		
Common stock, par value $ 1:		
Authorized, 400,000,000 shares:		
Issued, 162,211,590 shares	162,212	162,212
Additional paid-in capital	76,604	70,938
Retained earnings	2,639,440	2,366,246
Foreign currency translation adjustment	(12,894)	(9,442)
	2,865,362	2,589,954
Less Treasury stock, 22,444,480 shares		
and 15,244,733 shares, respectively, at cost	(1,008,199)	(643,787)
Deferred compensation related to ESOP (Note 8)	(34,925)	(38,247)
Total shareholders' equity	1,822,238	1,907,920
Commitments and contingent liabilities (Note 9)		
Total liabilities and shareholders' equity	$3,707,052	$3,823,798

Note 8—Capital stock, stock options, incentive plans (excerpt)

During 1988, the Company's Board of Directors authorized the repurchase of up to 7.5 million shares of its outstanding common stock. During the period 1988-1991, the Company purchased 4.5 million shares of its common stock under this program at a cost of $158 million. In 1994, the Company purchased the remaining 3 million shares, and the program was expanded by an additional 5 million shares, which were also purchased. The total cost of the share repurchase program in 1994 was $399 million.

In December 1994, the Company issued 506,000 shares of its common stock from treasury as consideration for the purchase of KTHV-TV in Little Rock. In January 1993, the Company issued 1,980,000 shares of its common stock from treasury as partial consideration for the purchase of the Honolulu Advertiser.

Certain of the shares acquired by the Company have been reissued in settlement of employee stock awards or were sold to an Employee Stock Ownership Plan which was established in 1990. The remaining shares are held as treasury stock.

The weighted average number of common shares outstanding used in the computation of earnings per share was 144,276,000 in 1994, 146,474,000 in 1993 and 144,148,000 in 1992.

L.A. Gear, Inc.—Mandatorily Redeemable Preferred Stock

> L.A. Gear designs, develops, and markets fashionable, high-quality athletic and leisure footwear and apparel. Products are typically sold through retail department and sporting goods stores. The company manufactures its shoe-related products in South Korea and Taiwan and its apparel in the U.S. Distributions are made to approximately 10 different countries.

Learning Objectives
- Understand the debt and equity characteristics of mandatorily redeemable preferred stock.
- Determine the economic consequences of balance sheet classification of mandatorily redeemable preferred stock.

Refer to the Consolidated balance sheet and footnote excerpts of L.A. Gear, Inc.

Concepts

a. How much total shareholders' equity does L.A. Gear have at November 30, 1992? How much long-term debt does L.A. Gear have at November 30, 1992?

b. What is Mandatorily Redeemable Preferred Stock? How has L.A. Gear classified this item on its balance sheet?

c. Support the statement "The mandatorily redeemable preferred stock should be classified as long-term debt on L.A. Gear's balance sheet."

d. Support the statement "The mandatorily redeemable preferred stock should be classified as shareholders' equity on L.A. Gear's balance sheet."

Analysis

e. Calculate L.A. Gear's debt to equity ratio at November 30, 1992 with Mandatorily Redeemable Preferred Stock classified as debt vs. equity. Explain how the balance sheet classification of these shares might affect L.A. Gear's bond covenants.

L.A. GEAR, INC. AND SUBSIDIARIES

CONSOLIDATED BALANCE SHEETS

(in thousands)

November 30,	1992	1991
Assets		
Current assets:		
Cash and cash equivalents	$ 55,027	$ 1,422
Collateralized cash	28,955	—
Accounts receivable, net	56,369	111,470
Inventories	61,923	141,115
Prepaid expenses and other current assets	2,557	8,506
Refundable income taxes	25,269	22,795
Deferred income taxes	—	11,763
Total current assets	230,100	297,071
Property and equipment, net	17,667	26,869
Other assets	1,735	1,631
	$249,502	$325,571

Liabilities, Mandatorily Redeemable Preferred Stock and Shareholders' Equity

	1992	1991
Current liabilities:		
Borrowings under line of credit	$ —	$ 20,000
Accounts payable and accrued liabilities	49,753	55,856
Dividends payable on mandatorily redeemable preferred stock	7,746	—
Costs related to discontinued operations	4,552	18,000
Total current liabilities	62,051	93,856
Mandatorily redeemable preferred stock:		
7.5% Series A Cumulative Convertible Preferred Stock, $100 stated value; 1,000,000 shares authorized, issued and outstanding; redemption value of $100 per share	100,000	100,000
Shareholders' equity:		
Common stock, no par value; 80,000,000 shares authorized; 22,898,182 shares issued and outstanding at November 30, 1992; (19,542,513 shares issued and outstanding at Nov. 30, 1991)	127,714	92,331
Preferred stock, no stated value; 9,000,000 shares authorized; no shares issued	—	—
Retained earnings (accumulated deficit)	(40,263)	39,384
Total shareholders' equity	87,451	131,715
Commitments and contingencies	—	—
	$249,502	$325,571

See accompanying Notes to Consolidated Financial Statements.

Note 8. Series A Cumulative Convertible Preferred Stock

In September 1991, the Company consummated the sale of one million shares of Series A Cumulative Convertible Preferred Stock (the "Series A Preferred Stock") to Trefoil Capital Investors, L.P. ("Trefoil") for an aggregate purchase price of $ 100 million. With respect to dividend rights and rights on liquidation, dissolution and winding up, Series A Preferred Stock ranks senior to the Company's Common Stock and senior to any other series or class of Preferred Stock which may be issued by the Company (collectively, "Junior Securities").

In the event of any liquidation, dissolution or winding up of the Company, holders of Series A Preferred Stock will be entitled to receive in preference to holders of Junior Securities an amount equal to $ 100 per share plus all accrued but unpaid dividends. As long as shares of Series A Preferred Stock remain outstanding, the holders of such shares are entitled to receive, when, as and if declared by the Board of Directors out of assets of the Company legally available therefor, cumulative cash dividends at an annual rate of 7.5% (if in arrears, compounded quarterly at a rate of 8.625% per annum with respect to dividends in arrears, through the date of payment of such arrearages), payable quarterly in arrears on the last business day of February, May, August and November.

Each of the shares of Series A Preferred Stock is convertible at the option of the holder into ten shares of Common Stock (the "Conversion Ratio"), subject to certain antidilution adjustments. The "Conversion Price" is $ 10.00, subject to certain antidilution adjustments.

The Series A Preferred Stock may be redeemed by the Company any time after the second anniversary of the Issue Date (in integral multiples having an aggregate Stated Value of at least $ 15 million) if (i) all quarterly dividends on the Series A Preferred Stock have been paid in full and (ii) the market price of the Common Stock is equal to at least 175% of the Conversion Price for thirty consecutive trading days preceding the notice of redemption. In any such event, the redemption price per share will be equal to $ 100, plus accrued and unpaid dividends to the redemption date (the "Redemption Price"). Prior to the second anniversary of the issuance of the Series A Preferred Stock, the Company may redeem all (but not less than all) of the Series A Preferred Stock in the event of a merger of the Company with or into another corporation which is approved by the Board of Directors and in which the per share consideration to be received by the holders of Common Stock upon the consummation thereof is payable only in cash in an amount equal to at least 175% of the Conversion Price. In any such event, the redemption price per share will be equal to the per share merger consideration times the Conversion Ratio.

The Company is required to redeem 350,000 shares of the original issue on August 31, 1996, and 162,500 shares on each August 31 thereafter until all remaining shares of Series A Preferred Stock have been redeemed. The number of shares to be redeemed by the Company on any mandatory redemption date shall be reduced by the number of shares optionally redeemed by the Company prior to such date, to the extent such shares have not previously been credited against the Company's mandatory redemption obligations. If the Company shall fail to redeem shares of Series A Preferred Stock when required, the annual dividend rate on the outstanding shares of Series A Preferred Stock will be increased to 10.125% (compounded quarterly with respect to dividends in arrears at a rate of 11.644% per annum) on an amount equal to $ 100 per share plus accrued and unpaid dividends from the date of failure to redeem through the date of redemption. If less than all of the outstanding shares of Series A Preferred Stock are to be redeemed, the shares of Series A Preferred Stock to be redeemed shall be selected pro rata.

Pursuant to restrictions contained in the bank credit agreement terminated by the Company on November 30, 1992, the Company was prohibited from paying required quarterly dividends on the Series A Preferred Stock during fiscal 1992. Consequently, on August 31, 1992, the date on which three full quarterly dividends became in arrears, Trefoil (as the holder of all of the issued and outstanding shares of Series A Preferred Stock) became entitled to elect four additional directors to the Company's Board of Directors. On September 1, 1992, Trefoil elected two additional directors and reserved its right to appoint an additional two members of the Board.

The failure of the Company to pay an amount equal to three full quarterly dividends also caused the termination of the standstill and other related provisions (including, among other things, limitations on Trefoil's right to acquire additional shares of Common Stock) contained in the Stock Purchase Agreement, dated as of May 27, 1991 and amended as of July 25, 1991, between the Company and Trefoil.

On February 17, 1993, the Company declared a dividend payment of $ 9.79 million (payable on February 26, 1993). The payment represents all accrued and unpaid dividends on, as well as the quarterly dividend scheduled to be paid on February 26, 1993 with respect to, the Series A Preferred Stock. Consequently, the terms of the two directors appointed by Trefoil in September 1992, as well as Trefoil's right to elect an additional two directors, expired on February 26, 1993.

Deere & Company—Marketable Securities

Deere & Company and its subsidiaries (collectively, John Deere) have operations in six business segments. The worldwide agricultural equipment segment manufactures and distributes equipment used in commercial farming. The industrial equipment segment manufactures and distributes machines used in construction, earthmoving and forestry. The lawn and grounds care equipment segment manufactures and distributes equipment for commercial and residential uses. The credit segment finances and services retail notes related to sales by John Deere dealers and non-Deere dealers, leases of John Deere equipment to retail customers, unsecured revolving charge accounts acquired from merchants, and wholesale notes from certain dealers of the foregoing equipment. The Company also has an insurance segment and a health care segment.

Learning Objectives
- Understand SFAS No. 115 requirements for accounting for marketable securities.
- Read and interpret marketable securities footnotes.
- Prepare mark-to-market journal entries for certain classes of marketable securities.

Refer to the 1995 Deere & Company financial statements.

Concepts

a. In general, how are each of the following categories of Marketable Securities reported on the balance sheet? How are realized and unrealized gains and losses accounted for?

 i. Marketable debt and equity securities classified as "Trading."

 ii. Marketable debt and equity securities classified as "Available-for-Sale."

 iii. Marketable debt securities classified as "Held-to-Maturity." Why are equity securities never classified as "Held-to-Maturity"?

 iv. SFAS No. 115, *Accounting for Certain Investments in Debt and Equity Securities*, sets very stringent criteria that need to be met to classify debt securities as Held-to-Maturity. What kinds of behavior on the part of managers was the FASB seeking to prevent by setting these strict criteria?

b. What balance did Deere & Company report on its balance sheet for each of the following categories of Marketable Securities at October 31, 1995?

 i. Marketable debt and equity securities classified as "Trading."

 ii. Marketable debt and equity securities classified as "Available-for-Sale."

 iii. Marketable debt securities classified as "Held-to-Maturity."

Process

c. Assume that Deere & Company uses two accounts for each category of marketable securities: one to keep track of original costs and one to keep track of fair value adjustments.

 i. Assume that Deere & Co marked their securities portfolio to market for their quarterly financial statements in July 1995. Provide the adjusting journal entries required to arrive at the year-end reported balance sheet amounts if the following balances were found on Deere & Company's unadjusted trial balance at October 31, 1995. Ignore deferred taxes.

 Held to Maturity, at cost or amortized cost   490 Dr.
 Available-for-Sale, at cost   326 Dr.
 Available-for-Sale, fair value adjustment   1 Dr.

 ii. Provide the journal entry that Deere & Company would have recorded had the Available-for-Sale securities been classified as Trading securities.

d. According to the Notes to Deere & Company's 1995 financial statements, certain Available-for-Sale securities were sold in 1995. Assume that these securities were sold in October, had last been marked to market for financial statement purposes on July 31, 1995, and had gross unrealized gains of $2 million.

   i.   Provide the journal entry to record the sale of Available-for-Sale securities in fiscal 1995. Assume that these securities had gross unrealized gains of $1 million. Ignore the disposal of the Available-for-Sale securities associated with the sale of the John Deere Life Insurance Company. Ignore deferred taxes.

   ii. Provide the journal entry that Deere & Company would have recorded with respect to the sale in part *d i.* if the company had classified the securities as Trading securities. Assume that the securities had all been purchased in fiscal 1995. Ignore deferred taxes.

Analysis

e. According to the Notes to Deere & Company's 1995 financial statements, in November 1995 Deere & Company reclassified its Held-to-Maturity debt securities to Available-for-Sale.

   i.   Assume that no purchases of Held-to-Maturity securities occurred between the end of fiscal 1995 and the date of the reclassification. Assume further that the market price of the securities did not change during that period. If, during the period between year end and the date of the reclassification, Deere & Company sold only Held-to-Maturity securities that had unrealized losses associated with them, what was the amortized cost of those securities?

   ii. What would Deere & Company have reported as 1995 Net Income had the reclassification occurred in fiscal 1995? As Total Assets at October 31, 1995?

DEERE & COMPANY
STATEMENT OF CONSOLIDATED INCOME

(IN MILLIONS OF DOLLARS EXCEPT PER SHARE AMOUNTS)

	CONSOLIDATED (DEERE & COMPANY AND CONSOLIDATED SUBSIDIARIES) YEAR ENDED OCTOBER 31			EQUIPMENT OPERATIONS (DEERE & COMPANY WITH FINANCIAL SERVICES ON THE EQUITY BASIS) YEAR ENDED OCTOBER 31			FINANCIAL SERVICES YEAR ENDED OCTOBER 31		
	1995	1994	1993	1995	1994	1993	1995	1994	1993
NET SALES AND REVENUES									
Net sales of equipment	$8,830.2	$7,663.1	$6,479.3	$8,830.2	$7,663.1	$6,479.3	—	—	—
Finance and interest income	660.4	547.8	562.8	105.3	81.3	84.0	561.2	471.9	482.4
Insurance and health care premiums	627.6	609.4	496.7	—	—	—	674.6	648.3	540.4
Investment income	95.4	93.9	97.5	—	—	—	95.4	93.9	97.6
Other income	76.9	62.9	59.7	28.4	24.0	23.3	52.0	43.7	42.0
Total	10,290.5	8,977.1	7,696.0	8,963.9	7,768.4	6,586.6	1,383.2	1,257.8	1,162.4
COSTS AND EXPENSES									
Cost of goods sold	6,922.1	6,019.6	5,368.9	6,943.8	6,032.6	5,381.1	—	—	—
Research and development expenses	327.4	275.7	269.8	327.4	275.7	269.8	—	—	—
Selling, administrative and general expenses	1,001.4	907.6	844.1	707.7	638.3	602.8	305.9	282.9	255.5
Interest expense	392.4	303.0	369.1	126.7	117.1	180.3	271.7	191.3	192.5
Insurance and health care claims and benefits	499.2	512.5	427.5	—	—	—	515.6	529.6	450.3
Other operating expenses	55.3	37.8	37.1	25.5	17.0	18.0	30.0	20.8	19.2
Restructuring costs	—	—	107.2	—	—	107.2	—	—	—
Total	9,197.8	8,056.2	7,423.7	8,131.1	7,080.7	6,559.2	1,123.2	1,024.6	917.5
INCOME OF CONSOLIDATED GROUP BEFORE INCOME TAXES AND CHANGES IN ACCOUNTING	1,092.7	920.9	272.3	832.8	687.7	27.4	260.0	233.2	244.9
Provision for income taxes	397.8	332.2	97.2	303.8	254.7	14.4	94.1	77.5	82.8
INCOME OF CONSOLIDATED GROUP BEFORE CHANGES IN ACCOUNTING	694.9	588.7	175.1	529.0	433.0	13.0	165.9	155.7	162.1
EQUITY IN INCOME OF UNCONSOLIDATED SUBSIDIARIES AND AFFILIATES BEFORE CHANGES IN ACCOUNTING									
Credit	.7	—	—	120.9	113.7	122.2	—	—	—
Insurance	—	4.9	2.2	29.4	31.2	31.1	.7	4.9	2.2
Health care	—	—	—	16.3	15.7	11.0	—	—	—
Other	10.5	10.0	7.1	10.5	10.0	7.1	—	—	—
Total	11.2	14.9	9.3	177.1	170.6	171.4	.7	4.9	2.2
INCOME BEFORE CHANGES IN ACCOUNTING	706.1	603.6	184.4	706.1	603.6	184.4	166.6	160.6	164.3
Changes in accounting	—	—	(1,105.3)	—	—	(1,105.3)	—	—	(6.9)
NET INCOME (LOSS)	$706.1	$603.6	$(920.9)	$706.1	$603.6	$(920.9)	$166.6	$160.6	$157.4

PER SHARE DATA*

	1995	1994	1993
Primary and fully diluted:			
Income before changes in accounting	$2.71	$2.34	$.80
Changes in accounting	—	—	(4.77)
Net income (loss)	$2.71	$2.34	$(3.97)
Dividends declared	$.75	$.68 1/3	$.66 2/3

DEERE & COMPANY
CONSOLIDATED BALANCE SHEET

(IN MILLIONS OF DOLLARS EXCEPT PER SHARE AMOUNTS)

	CONSOLIDATED (DEERE & COMPANY AND CONSOLIDATED SUBSIDIARIES) OCTOBER 1		EQUIPMENT OPERATIONS (DEERE & COMPANY WITH FINANCIAL SERVICES ON THE EQUITY BASIS) OCTOBER 31		FINANCIAL SERVICES OCTOBER 31	
	1995	1994	1995	1994	1995	1994
Assets						
Cash and short-term investments	$ 363.7	$ 245.4	$ 71.0	$ 104.0	$ 292.7	$ 141.4
Cash deposited with unconsolidated subsidiaries	—	—	460.1	—	—	—
Cash and cash equivalents	363.7	245.4	531.1	104.0	292.7	141.4
Marketable securities	829.7	1,126.3	—	—	829.7	1,126.3
Receivables from unconsolidated subsidiaries and affiliates	2.3	8.9	55.5	196.9	—	—
Dealer accounts and notes receivable - net	3,259.7	2,939.4	3,259.7	2,939.4	—	—
Credit receivables - net	5,345.2	4,501.7	118.3	115.8	5,226.9	4,385.9
Other receivables	492.4	429.7	3.2	15.2	490.2	415.5
Equipment on operating leases - net	258.8	219.5	119.3	94.3	139.5	125.2
Inventories	720.8	698.0	720.8	698.0	—	—
Property and equipment - net	1,335.6	1,314.1	1,295.0	1,281.8	40.6	32.3
Investments in unconsolidated subsidiaries and affiliates	115.2	154.3	1,378.4	1,285.9	—	55.1
Intangible assets - net	305.0	283.7	295.4	266.4	9.6	16.9
Other assets	61.6	61.8	29.4	31.1	32.1	30.7
Deferred income taxes	639.8	679.8	578.9	620.5	61.0	59.2
Deferred charges	117.6	118.6	79.1	60.7	38.5	57.9
Total	$13,847.4	$12,781.2	$8,464.1	$7,710.4	$7,160.8	$6,446.4

Liabilities and Stockholders' Equity

	1995	1994	1995	1994	1995	1994
LIABILITIES						
Short-term borrowings	$ 3,139.8	$ 2,637.4	$ 395.7	$ 53.8	$2,744.1	$2,583.5
Payables to unconsolidated subsidiaries and affiliates	27.5	34.0	27.5	34.0	513.3	187.9
Accounts payable and accrued expenses	2,533.0	2,285.2	1,859.9	1,617.3	674.1	668.9
Insurance and health care claims and reserves	470.3	761.3	—	—	470.3	761.3
Accrued taxes	72.8	80.2	72.4	79.7	.3	.5
Deferred income taxes	15.6	13.5	15.6	13.5	—	—
Long-term borrowings	2,175.8	2,053.9	702.9	1,019.4	1,472.9	1,034.5
Retirement benefit accruals and other liabilities	2,327.2	2,357.8	2,304.7	2,334.8	22.6	23.0
Total liabilities	10,762.0	10,223.3	5,378.7	5,152.5	5,897.6	5,259.6
STOCKHOLDERS' EQUITY						
Common stock, $1 par value (authorized – 600,000,000* shares; issued – 262,524,084* shares in 1995 and 259,915,584* shares in 1994) at stated value	1,728.7	1,491.4	1,728.7	1,491.4	209.4	209.5
Retained earnings	1,690.3	1,353.9	1,690.3	1,353.9	1,054.3	980.3
Minimum pension liability adjustment	(300.4)	(248.4)	(300.4)	(248.4)	—	—
Cumulative translation adjustment	(11.6)	(17.9)	(11.6)	(17.9)	(4.1)	(3.0)
Unrealized gain on marketable securities available for sale	3.6	—	3.6	—	3.6	—
Unamortized restricted stock compensation	(12.1)	(8.8)	(12.1)	(8.8)	—	—
Common stock in treasury, 549,387* shares in 1995 and 652,803* shares in 1994, at cost	(13.1)	(12.3)	(13.1)	(12.3)	—	—
Total stockholders' equity	3,085.4	2,557.9	3,085.4	2,557.9	1,263.2	1,186.8
Total	$13,847.4	$12,781.2	$8,464.1	$7,710.4	$7,160.8	$6,446.4

MARKETABLE SECURITIES

Marketable securities are held by the insurance and health care subsidiaries. The company adopted FASB Statement No. 115, Accounting for Certain Investments in Debt and Equity Securities, in the first quarter of 1995. Held-to-maturity debt securities are carried at amortized cost. Available-for-sale debt securities and equity securities are carried at fair value with unrealized gains and losses shown as a separate component of stockholders' equity. Previously, the company valued all its debt securities on an amortized cost basis and its equity securities on a cost basis. Realized gains or losses from the sales of marketable securities are based on the specific identification method.

The amortized cost and fair value of marketable securities in millions of dollars follow:

	Amortized Cost or Cost	Gross Unrealized Gains	Gross Unrealized Losses	Fair Value
OCTOBER 31, 1995				
Held-to-Maturity:				
U.S. Government and agencies	$ 79	$ 5	$ —	$ 84
States and municipalities	170	11	1	180
Corporate	126	7	—	133
Mortgage-backed securities	124	6	1	129
Total	499	29	2	526
Available-for-Sale:				
Equity securities	6	—	—	6
U.S. government and agencies	111	2	1	112
States and municipalities	24	1	—	25
Corporate	151	3	1	153
Mortgage-backed securities	30	1	—	31
Other	4	—	—	4
Total	326	7	2	331
MARKETABLE SECURITIES	$ 825	$ 36	$ 4	$ 857
OCTOBER 31, 1994				
Equity securities	$34	$5	$1	$38
U.S. government and agencies	21	4	11	209
States and municipalities	214	9	5	218
Corporate	416	8	20	404
Mortgage-backed securities	236	3	20	219
Other	10	—	—	10
MARKETABLE SECURITIES	$1,126	$ 29	$ 57	$1,098

The contractual maturities of debt securities at October 31, 1995 in millions of dollars follow:

	Held-to-Maturity		Available-for-Sale	
	Amortized Cost	Fair Value	Amortized Cost	Fair Value
Due in one year or less	$ 7	$ 7	$ 28	$ 28
Due after one through five years	107	109	184	185
Due after five through 10 years	107	114	50	52
Due after 10 years	278	296	54	56
DEBT SECURITIES	$499	$526	$316	$321

Actual maturities may differ from contractual maturities because some borrowers have the right to call or prepay obligations. Proceeds from the sales of available-for-sale securities were $79 million in 1995, and gross realized gains and losses on those sales were $9 million and $2 million, respectively. The increase in the net unrealized holding gain on available-for-sale securities was $5 million ($3 million after income taxes) during 1995. In 1995, the John Deere Life Insurance Company was sold, including its held-to-maturity marketable securities of $229 million and available-for-sale securities of $100 million.

During November 1995, in concurrence with the adoption of "A Guide to Implementation of Statement 115 on Accounting for Certain Investments in Debt and Equity Securities—Questions and Answers," the company transferred all its held-to-maturity debt securities to the available-for-sale category. The amortized cost of these securities at the time of transfer was $484 million and the unrealized gain was $29 million ($19 million after income taxes). Although the company's intention to hold a majority of its debt securities to maturity has not changed, the transfer was made to increase flexibility in responding to future changes.

J.P. Morgan is a global banking firm that has built its business, over 150 years, on a commitment to excel in serving clients with complex financial needs. Drawing on commercial, investment, and merchant banking traditions, J.P. Morgan is an international leader in capability and character, and channels capital to productive uses to earn superior returns over time for its stockholders.

Learning Objectives
- Interpret footnote disclosures of investment securities.
- Distinguish between securities classified as trading, available-for-sale, and held-to-maturity.
- Understand the accounting treatment for each type of investment security under SFAS No. 115.
- Analyze investment security accounts.
- Infer and prepare mark-to-market journal entries.

Refer to the 1994 Financial Statements and notes for J.P. Morgan & Co. Incorporated.

Process

a. Consider the balance sheet accounts "Trading account assets" and "Trading account liabilities."

   i. What are these assets? What are these liabilities? How does J.P. Morgan account for trading account assets and liabilities? (*Hint*: See Notes 1 and 7 to the financial statements.)

   ii. Assume that the 1994 unadjusted trial balance for trading account assets was $57 billion. Prepare the adjusting journal entry that would have been required to mark this portfolio to market. Ignore any deferred tax considerations for this part.

b. Consider the balance sheet account "Debt investment securities available-for-sale."

   i. When does J.P. Morgan classify a debt security as "available-for-sale?"

   ii. What is the 1994 year end balance in this account?

   iii. What is the market value of these securities? What is the original cost of these securities? What does the difference represent?

   iv. How are unrealized gains and losses in these securities accounted for?

c. According to Notes 1 and 6, J.P. Morgan's wholly-owned non-bank subsidiary, J.P. Morgan Capital Corporation, owns equity securities classified as available-for-sale.

   i. What is the total amount of these securities and where do they appear on the balance sheet?

   ii. What is the market value of these securities? What is the original cost of these securities? What does the difference represent?

   iii. How are unrealized gains and losses in these securities accounted for?

   iv. Speculate as to why the non-banking subsidiary holds these securities.

d. Consider the stockholders' equity account "Net unrealized gains on investment securities, net."

   i. In general, what are these "Net unrealized gains?"

   ii. What are "Net unrealized gains, net" net of? That is, what does the second net refer to?

iii. Use the information in Notes 2 and 6 to the financial statements and your answers to parts *b* and *c* to reconcile the 1994 year end balance in the "Net unrealized gains on investment securities, net" account. You may wish to use the table below in your reconciliation.

	1994	1993	Difference (1994 − 1993)
Debt Investment Securities:			
Net unrealized gains (i.e. fair market value less cost)	?	?	?
Equity Investment Securities:			
Net unrealized gains (i.e. fair market value less cost)	?	?	?
Deferred taxes (plug)	?	(724)	?
Total net unrealized gains per balance sheet	456	1,165	709

iv. Prepare the reconciling journal entry for the account "Net unrealized gains on investment securities, net." (*Hint*: Use the difference column from the table.)

v. What would J.P. Morgan have reported as 1994 Net income had they classified these securities as "Trading account assets?"

e. Early versions of SFAS No. 115 would have required all marketable securities to be marked to market at the end of the reporting period. What are the arguments against this method of accounting? What are some of the arguments in support of this market value accounting?

J.P. MORGAN & CO. INCORPORATED

CONSOLIDATED STATEMENT OF INCOME

In millions, except per share data

	1994	1993	1992
Net interest revenue			
Interest revenue	$8,379	$7,442	$7,281
Interest expense	6,398	5,670	5,573
Net interest revenue	1,981	1,772	1,708
Provision for credit losses	–	–	55
Net interest revenue after provision for credit losses	1,981	1,772	1,653
Noninterest revenue			
Trading revenue	1,019	2,059	959
Corporate finance revenue	434	532	439
Credit related fees	204	224	214
Investment management fees	517	464	377
Operational service fees	546	491	409
Net investment securities gains	122	323	388
Other revenue	694	406	164
Total noninterest revenue	3,536	4,499	2,950
Operating expenses			
Employee compensation and benefits	2,217	2,221	1,738
Net occupancy	275	391	293
Technology and communications	645	512	409
Other expenses	555	456	414
Total operating expenses	3,692	3,580	2,854
Income before income taxes and cumulative effects of accounting changes	1,825	2,691	1,749
Income taxes	610	968	619
Income before cumulative effects of accounting changes	1,215	1,723	1,130
Cumulative effect of change in method of accounting for postretirement benefits, net of related income taxes	–	–	(137)
Cumulative effect of change in method of accounting for income taxes	–	–	452
Net income	$1,215	$1,586	$1,582
Per common share			
Income before cumulative effects of accounting changes	$6.02	$8.48	$5.66
Cumulative effect of change in method of accounting for postretirement benefits, net of related income taxes	–	–	(0.68)
Cumulative effect of change in method of accounting for income taxes	–	–	2.29
Net income	$6.02	$7.80	$7.95
Dividends declared	2.79	2.48	2.23

Earnings per share amounts for 1994 and 1993 represent both primary and fully diluted earnings per share. Earnings per share amounts for 1992 represent primary earnings per share. For 1992 fully diluted earnings per share before and after the cumulative effect of the change in accounting for income taxes were $5.63 and $7.92 respectively.

The accompanying notes are an integral part of these financial statements.

J.P. MORGAN & CO. INCORPORATED

CONSOLIDATED BALANCE SHEET (IN MILLIONS)

December 31	1994	1993
Assets		
Cash and due from banks	$ 2,210	$ 1,008
Interest earning deposits with banks	1,362	1,221
Debt investment securities available for sale carried at fair value	22,657	19,547
Trading account assets	57,065	41,349
Securities purchased under agreements to resell ($21,170 in 1994 and $22,645 in 1993) and federal funds sold	21,350	22,706
Securities borrowed	12,127	10,818
Loans	22,080	24,380
Less: allowance for credit losses	1,131	1,157
Net loans	20,949	23,223
Customers' acceptance liability	586	406
Accrued interest and accounts receivable	5,028	4,938
Premises and equipment, net	2,016	1,853
Other assets	9,567	6,819
Total assets	$154,917	$133,888
Liabilities		
Noninterest bearing deposits:		
In offices in the U.S.	3,693	4,681
In offices outside the U.S.	767	839
Interest bearing deposits:		
In offices in the U.S.	1,826	2,401
In offices outside the U.S.	36,799	32,481
Total deposits	43,085	40,402
Trading account liabilities	36,407	18,216
Securities sold under agreements to repurchase ($30,179 in 1994 and $36,306 in 1993) and federal funds purchased	35,768	39,412
Commercial paper	3,507	2,573
Other liabilities for borrowed money	10,900	10,127
Accounts payable and accrued expenses	6,231	6,416
Liability on acceptances	586	413
Long term debt not qualifying as risk based capital	3,605	2,817
Other liabilities	2,063	1,194
	142,152	121,570
Long term debt qualifying as risk based capital	3,197	2,459
Total liabilities	145,349	124,029
Commitments and contingencies (Notes 8, 16, 17, 18, and 20)		
Stockholders' equity		
Preferred stock	494	494
Common stock, $2.50 par value (authorized shares: 500,000,000; issued: 200,668,373 in 1994 and 199,531,757 in 1993)	502	499
Capital surplus	1,452	1,393
Retained earnings	7,044	6,386
Net unrealized gains on investment securities, net	456	1,165
Other	367	250
	10,315	10,187
Less: treasury stock (12,966,917 shares in 1994 and 6,445,226 shares in 1993) at cost	747	328
Total stockholders' equity	9,568	9,859
Total liabilities and stockholders' equity	$154,917	$133,888

J.P. MORGAN & CO. INCORPORATED
NOTES TO CONSOLIDATED FINANCIAL STATEMENTS

1. Accounting Policies (excerpts)

J.P. Morgan is the holding company for subsidiaries engaged globally in providing a wide range of financial services. The accounting and reporting policies and practices of J.P. Morgan and subsidiaries, including Morgan Guaranty Trust Company of New York and subsidiaries (Morgan Guaranty), conform with generally accepted accounting principles. The following is a description of significant accounting policies and practices.

DEBT INVESTMENT SECURITIES

Debt investment securities are held to maximize total return over the longer term. Beginning December 31, 1993, investment securities that may be sold in response to or in anticipation of changes in interest rates and prepayment risk, liquidity considerations, and other factors are considered available for sale. Such securities are carried at fair value with unrealized gains and losses, including the effect of hedges, reported as a net amount within the stockholders' equity account, Net unrealized gains on investment securities, net of taxes, until realized.

Realized gains and losses on investment securities, which are generally computed by the specific identification method, and other-than-temporary impairments in value are included in Net investment securities gains. Debt investment securities transactions are recorded on their trade dates. Carrying values of individual debt investment securities are reduced through write-downs to reflect other-than-temporary impairments in value.

In instances where J.P. Morgan has the positive intent and ability to hold to maturity, investment securities will be carried at cost, adjusted for amortization of premiums and accretion of discounts.

Prior to December 31, 1993, but subsequent to June 30, 1992, debt investment securities were carried at the lower of aggregate amortized cost or market value with aggregate unrealized net valuation adjustments, if any, included in Net investment securities gains. Prior to June 30, 1992, investment securities were carried at cost, adjusted for amortization of premiums and accretion of discounts.

EQUITY INVESTMENT SECURITIES

Equity investment securities of companies in which the percentage of investment in voting stock is less than 20% are held for long-term appreciation and are included in Other assets. Beginning December 31, 1993, equity investment securities with available market quotations are carried at fair value with unrealized gains and losses reported as a net amount within the stockholders' equity account, Net unrealized gains on investment securities, net of taxes, until realized. Prior to December 31, 1993, marketable equity securities were carried at the lower of aggregate cost or market value. Equity investment securities without available market quotations are carried at cost. Carrying values of individual marketable and nonmarketable equity investment securities are reduced through write-downs to reflect other-than-temporary impairments in value. Realized gains and losses, which are generally computed by the specific identification method, and other-than-temporary impairments in value are included in Other revenue.

TRADING ACCOUNT ASSETS AND LIABILITIES

Trading account assets and liabilities (short trading positions) are carried at market value and are recorded as of their trade dates. Short trading positions are classified as liabilities. Gains and losses on trading positions are recognized currently.

2. Accounting Changes (excerpts)

ACCOUNTING FOR CERTAIN INVESTMENTS IN DEBT AND EQUITY SECURITIES

Effective December 31, 1993, J.P. Morgan adopted SFAS No. 115, Accounting for Certain Investments in Debt and Equity Securities, which resulted in a change in the accounting for debt and marketable equity investment securities held for investment purposes. Those securities, which J.P. Morgan previously carried at the lower of aggregate cost or market value, are considered available for sale and carried at fair value. Unrealized gains and losses are excluded from earnings and reported net of taxes as a separate component of stockholders' equity until realized. Upon adoption of this standard, J.P. Morgan recorded increases in Debt investment securities of $859 million and Other assets of $1,030 million for marketable equity investment securities, and a deferred tax liability of $724 million related to the appreciation of the affected securities, resulting in an increase of $1,165 million in stockholders' equity, net of tax.

6. Investment Securities (excerpts)

DEBT INVESTMENT SECURITIES

At December 31, 1994 and 1993, the debt investment securities portfolio was classified as available for sale and measured at fair value with unrealized gains (losses) excluded from earnings and reported as a net amount within the stockholders' equity account Net unrealized gains on investment securities, net of taxes, until realized. Prior to the adoption of this accounting standard, the debt investment securities portfolio was carried at LOCOM.

Gross unrealized gains and losses as well as a comparison of the cost, fair value, and carrying value of debt investment securities at December 31, 1994, 1993, and 1992, are presented in the table below.

	Cost	Gross unrealized gains	Gross unrealized losses	Fair and carrying value
1994 (carried at fair value)				
U.S. Treasury	$ 1,651	$ 14	$ 42	$ 1,623
U.S. government agency, principally mortgage backed	13,531	210	88	13,653
U.S. state and political subdivision	2,396	157	58	2,495
U.S. corporate and bank debt	265	17	—	282
Foreign government	3,758	20	65	3,713
Foreign corporate and bank debt	802	7	19	790
Other	100	1	—	101
Total debt investment securities	$22,503	$426	$272	$22,657

	Cost	Gross unrealized gains	Gross unrealized losses	Fair and carrying value
1993 (carried at fair value)				
U.S. Treasury	$ 2,461	$115	$ 3	$ 2,573
U.S. government agency, principally mortgage backed	7,645	233	53	7,825
U.S. state and political subdivision	2,229	302	—	2,531
U.S. corporate and bank debt	280	18	—	298
Foreign government	4,279	178	5	4,452
Foreign corporate and bank debt	1,665	74	—	1,739
Other	129	1	1	129
Total debt investment securities	$18,688	$921	$62	$19,547

At December 31, 1994, there were no securities of a single issuer whose fair value exceeded 10% of stockholders' equity.

EQUITY INVESTMENT SECURITIES

Equity investment securities are held for long-term appreciation and are included in Other assets. These securities, which are acquired primarily through private placements, recapitalizations, and corporate restructurings and consist of both marketable and nonmarketable securities, are generally owned by J.P. Morgan Capital Corporation, a wholly-owned nonbank subsidiary of J.P. Morgan. Quoted or estimated values of equity investment securities do not necessarily represent net realizable amounts, as the timing or size of transactions and the liquidity of the markets may not support realization of these values. Most of our equity investment securities are subject to legal, regulatory, and contractual restrictions that limit our ability to dispose of them freely.

At December 31, 1994 and 1993 marketable equity investment securities were classified as available for sale and carried at fair value. Net realized gains on equity investment securities during 1994 of $606 million are reflected in Other revenue. Gross unrealized gains and losses as well as a comparison of the cost, fair value, and carrying value of marketable equity investment securities at December 31, 1994 and 1993, follows.

In millions: December 31	1994	1993
Cost	$183	$ 241
Gross unrealized gains	579	1,030
Gross unrealized losses	(3)	—
Fair and carrying value	$759	$1,271

Nonmarketable equity investment securities are outside the scope of SFAS No. 115 and continue to be carried at a cost of $432 million at December 31, 1994, compared with a cost of $283 million at December 31, 1993. The estimated fair value of securities without available market quotations was $528 million and $464 million at December 31, 1994 and 1993, respectively.

7. Trading Account Assets and Liabilities (excerpts)

Trading account assets and liabilities, including derivative instruments used for trading purposes, are carried at fair value. The following tables present the carrying value of trading account assets and liabilities at December 31, 1994 and the average balance for the year then ended.

1994 In millions	Carrying value	Average balance
Trading account assets		
U.S. Treasury	$ 6,668	$ 7,675
U.S. government agency	3,332	4,579
Foreign government	17,073	17,569
Corporate debt and equity	7,409	7,915
Other securities	3,088	2,885
Interest rate and currency swaps	10,914	11,036
Foreign exchange contracts	3,573	5,032
Interest rate futures and forwards	152	1,510
Commodity and equity contracts	1,146	1,219
Purchased option contracts	3,710	3,959
	$57,065	$62,020
Trading account liabilities		
U.S. Treasury	$ 7,187	$ 9,015
Foreign government	8,481	8,640
Corporate debt and equity	2,519	2,445
Other securities	1,165	888
Interest rate and currency swaps	8,283	8,455
Foreign exchange contracts	2,605	4,178
Interest rate futures and forwards	182	132
Commodity and equity contracts	1,300	815
Written option contracts	4,685	3,984
	$36,407	$38,552

BCE Inc.—Investments in Other Companies

BCE (Bell Canada Enterprises) is a management holding corporation whose core businesses are the provision of telecommunications services and the manufacture of telecommunications equipment. BCE has the largest number of registered shareholders of any Canadian corporation and its common shares are listed on exchanges in Canada, the United States, Europe, and Japan.

Learning Objectives
- Understand the accounting for investments in the shares of other companies.
- Trace transactions affecting the investment account through the financial statements.
- Explain how a change in effective ownership affects the accounting for the investment.

Refer to the 1990 financial statements of BCE Inc. The annual report of BCE Inc. indicates that the company has investments in the equity securities of Bell Canada, Northern Telecom, Bell-Northern Research, Montreal Trust, TransCanada PipeLines, Maritime Telegraph and Telephone Company, and many others.

Concepts

a. Why does BCE own shares in so many other companies?

b. When BCE owns between 20 and 50% of the voting shares of other companies, it refers to the companies as "associated companies."

   i.   What accounting method does BCE use to account for its investments in associated companies?

   ii. Explain in general terms how this method works.

c. Indicate where associated company earnings and dividends are reflected on each of BCE's financial statements.

Process

d. Provide the journal entries BCE made in 1990 to record the earnings of and the dividends received from its associated companies.

e. Refer to note 4(b) and explain how a change in BCE's effective interest (i.e., percentage ownership) in Encor Inc. led them to change their method of accounting for this investment. How does BCE now account for its shares in Encor?

f. Is this considered a "change in accounting principle"? Should the new method be applied retroactively or prospectively?

BCE INC.

CONSOLIDATED INCOME STATEMENT

For the Year Ended December 31
($ Millions)

	1990	1989	1988
Telecommunications services			
Operating revenues	$8,468	$8,011	$7,092
Operating expenses	6,284	5,976	5,254
Net revenues—telecommunications services	2,184	2,035	1,838
Telecommunications equipment manufacturing			
Revenues (note 1)	7,851	7,161	6,598
Cost of revenues	4,707	4,340	3,903
Selling, general, administrative and other expenses	2,357	2,198	2,203
Restructuring costs (note 2)	—	—	242
	7,064	6,538	6,348
Net revenues—telecommunications equipment manufacturing	787	623	250
Financial services			
Revenues—Investment and loan income	1,387	851	—
Revenues—Fees and commissions	188	134	—
	1,575	985	—
Less: Interest expense	1,208	730	—
Operating expenses	306	197	—
	1,514	927	—
Net revenues—financial services	61	58	—
Other operations			
Operating revenues	479	524	755
Operating expenses	452	506	715
Net revenues—other operations	27	18	40
Total revenues	3,059	2,734	2,128
Other income (expense)			
Equity in net income of associated companies (note 4)	155	173	38
Allowance for funds used during construction	41	39	41
Interest—long-term debt	(730)	(661)	(573)
Interest—other debt	(222)	(208)	(138)
Unrealized foreign currency gains (losses) (notes 1 and 24)	(3)	2	2
Miscellaneous—net (note 8)	(176)	156	152
	(935)	(499)	(478)
Income before income taxes and minority interest	2,124	2,235	1,650
Income taxes (note 7)	628	733	634
Income before minority interest	1,496	1,502	1,016
Minority interest	349	301	163
Income from continuing operations	1,147	1,201	853
Loss from discontinued real estate operations (note 3)	—	(440)	(7)
Net income (note 24)	1,147	761	846
Dividends on preferred shares	85	37	5
Net income applicable to common shares	$1,062	$ 724	$ 841

The important differences between Canadian and United States generally accepted accounting principles affecting the consolidated income statement are described and reconciled in note 24.

BCE INC.

CONSOLIDATED BALANCE SHEET

At December 31

	1990	1989
Assets		
Current assets		
Cash and temporary cash investments	$ 308	$ 141
Accounts receivable (note 11)	3,930	3,611
Inventories (note 13)	1,043	1,100
Other (principally prepaid expenses)	480	463
	5,761	5,315
Financial services		
Short-term securities	1,028	936
Loans receivable (note 14-a)	9,442	8,349
Bonds, stocks and other investments (note 14-b)	1,493	1,457
	11,963	10,742
Investments		
Associated companies (at equity) (notes 1 and 4)	2,338	2,904
Other investments (notes 4 and 5)	948	736
	3,286	3,640
Property, plant, and equipment		
At cost (note 15)	29,087	26,946
Less: Accumulated depreciation	10,513	9,655
	18,574	17,291
Other assets		
Long-term notes and receivables	1,333	1,304
Deferred charges—unrealized foreign currency losses, less amortization	15	—
Other deferred charges	373	283
Cost of shares in subsidiaries in excess of underlying net assets, less amortization (note 1)	682	686
	2,403	2,273
Total assets	$41,987	$39,261

On behalf of the Board of Directors:

Marcel Belanger
Director

R.M. Barford
Director

Donald R. Newman
Vice-President and Comptroller

BCE INC.

CONSOLIDATED BALANCE SHEET
At December 31

	1990	1989
Liabilities and Shareholders' Equity		
Current liabilities		
Accounts payable	$ 2,659	$ 2,501
Advance billing and payments	183	162
Dividends payable	217	215
Taxes accrued	180	169
Interest accrued	297	291
Debt due within one year (note 16)	1,878	2,342
	5,414	5,680
Financial services		
Demand deposits (note 14-c)	1,071	1,041
Investment certificates and borrowing (note 14-c)	10,655	9,359
	11,726	10,400
Long-term debt		
Long-term debt (note 17)	7,431	7,005
Deferred credits		
Income taxes	2,425	2,430
Other	389	448
	2,814	2,878
Minority interest in subsidiary companies		
Preferred shares	1,309	1,262
Common shares	1,968	1,630
	3,277	2,892
Preferred shares		
Preferred shares (note 18) (Includes $579 million redeemable at option of holders, not before 1995 (1989—$200 million))	1,235	858
Common shareholders' equity		
Common shares (note 19)	5,407	5,276
Common shares purchase warrants (note 20)	39	—
Contributed surplus	1,034	1,034
Retained earnings	3,727	3,448
Foreign exchange adjustment (note 21)	(117)	(210)
	10,090	9,548
Commitments and contingent liabilities (note 12)		
Total liabilities and shareholders' equity	$41,987	$39,261

BCE INC.

CONSOLIDATED STATEMENT OF CHANGES IN FINANCIAL POSITION
For the years ended December 31
($ millions)

	1990	1989	1988
Cash and temporary cash investments were provided from (used for)			
Operations	$ 3,481	$ 2,774	$ 2,578
Investments	(4,173)	(5,059)	(3,946)
Financing	1,870	3,332	2,022
Dividends declared	(1,011)	(919)	(811)
Increase (decrease) in cash and temporary cash investments	167	128	(157)
Cash and temporary cash investments at beginning of year	141	13	170
Cash and temporary cash investments at end of year	$ 308	$ 141	$ 13

Cash Provided from (Used for) Operations

	1990	1989	1988
Income from continuing operations	$ 1,147	$ 1,201	$ 853
Items not affecting cash			
Depreciation	2,018	1,813	1,598
Minority interest	349	301	163
Deferred income taxes	70	88	188
Equity in net income of associated companies lower than (in excess of) dividends received	(49)	(69)	56
Allowances for funds used during construction	(41)	(39)	(41)
Other items	68	(74)	(94)
Changes in working capital other than cash and debt			
(Increase) decrease in current assets:			
Accounts receivable	(319)	(463)	(256)
Inventories	57	(29)	(31)
Other current assets	(17)	(123)	(161)
Income and other taxes receivable	—	103	(31)
Increase (decrease) in current liabilities:			
Accounts payable	158	83	270
Advance billing and payments	21	(269)	69
Dividends payable	2	6	27
Taxes accrued	11	166	(79)
Interest accrued	6	79	47
Net cash provided from operations	$ 3,481	$ 2,774	$ 2,578

Cash Provided from (Used for) Investments

	1990	1989	1988
Capital expenditures (net)	(3,312)	(3,191)	(3,052)
Investments—Acquisition of Montreal Trustco Inc.	—	(874)	—
—Other	(372)	(526)	(1,064)
Sales of investments in TCPL and Encor (notes 4-a and 4-b)	710	—	—
Long-term notes and receivables	(29)	6	(98)
Net securities and loans—Financial services			
Short-term securities	(92)	313	—
Loans receivable	(1,093)	(661)	—
Bonds, stocks and other investments	(36)	(275)	—
Other items	51	149	268
Net cash used for investments	$(4,173)	$(5,059)	$(3,946)

BCE INC.

CONSOLIDATED STATEMENT OF CHANGES IN FINANCIAL POSITION (CONTINUED)

For the years ended December 31 ($ millions)	1990	1989	1988
Cash Provided from (Used for) Financing			
Proceeds from long-term debt	656	1,233	1,179
Reduction of long-term debt	(372)	(239)	(443)
Issue of preferred shares	371	847	—
Issue of common shares			
Common shareholder purchase plans	126	132	159
Acquisition of Montreal Trustco Inc.	—	336	—
Issues of preferred and common shares by subsidiaries to minority shareholders	236	463	190
Redemption of preferred shares by subsidiaries	(79)	(51)	(11)
Notes payable and bank advances	(358)	61	1,127
Net deposits and borrowings—Financial services			
Demand deposits	30	80	—
Investment certificates and borrowings	1,296	560	—
Other items	(36)	(90)	(179)
Net cash provided from financing	$ 1,870	$ 3,332	$ 2,022
Dividends Declared			
By BCE Inc.			
Preferred shares	(85)	(37)	(5)
Common shares	(769)	(743)	(705)
By subsidiaries to minority shareholders	(157)	(139)	(101)
Total dividends declared	$(1,011)	$ (919)	$ (811)

BCE INC.

CONSOLIDATED STATEMENT OF RETAINED EARNINGS

For the years ended December 31 ($ millions)	1990	1989	1988
Balance at beginning of year	$ 3,448	$ 3,477	$ 3,345
Net income	1,147	761	846
	4,595	4,238	4,191
Deduct:			
Dividends			
Preferred shares	85	37	5
Common shares	769	743	705
	854	780	710
Costs related to issuance and redemption of share capital of BCE Inc. and of subsidiaries	14	10	4
	868	790	714
Balance at end of year	$ 3,727	$ 3,448	$ 3,477

BCE INC.
NOTES TO CONSOLIDATED FINANCIAL STATEMENTS

1. Accounting Policies

The financial statements have been prepared in accordance with Canadian generally accepted accounting principles and all figures are in Canadian dollars. These statements conform in all material respects with International Accounting Standards. Certain previously reported figures have been reclassified to conform with the current presentation.

With respect to the consolidated financial statements of BCE, the important differences between Canadian and United States generally accepted accounting principles are described and reconciled in note 24.

Consolidation

The consolidated financial statements include the accounts of all majority-owned subsidiaries, either direct or indirect, with the exception of BCE Development Corporation (BCED) (see note 3). The financial subsidiaries of Northern Telecom Limited (Northern Telecom) are also fully consolidated. The investments in associated companies (20% to 50% owned) are accounted for by the equity method.

At December 31, 1990, the direct and indirect subsidiaries of BCE (100% owned, unless otherwise indicated) included Bell Canada, Tele-Direct (Publications) Inc., Northern Telecom Limited (53.1%), Montreal Trustco Inc., BCE Telecom International Inc. (formerly BCE Information Services Inc.), NewTel Enterprises Limited (55.7%), Telebec Ltée, Northern Telephone Limited (99.9%), Northwestern Inc., Bell Canada International Inc. and BCE Mobile Communications Inc. (69.7%).

The excess of cost of shares over acquired equity (goodwill) of subsidiary and associated companies is being amortized to earnings on a straight-line basis over its estimated life. The amortization, over periods up to 40 years, amounted to $68 million in 1990 (1989-$59 million, 1988-$45 million).

Telecommunications equipment purchased by Bell Canada and the other telecommunications subsidiaries of BCE, from Northern Telecom and its subsidiaries, is reflected in BCE's consolidated balance sheets at the cost to the purchasing companies, and is included in telecommunications equipment manufacturing revenues in the consolidated income statement. To the extent that any income related to these revenues, and those from associated companies, has not been offset by depreciation or other operating expenses, it remains in consolidated retained earnings and consolidated income. This practice is generally followed with respect to activities of regulated industries. All other significant intercompany transactions have been eliminated in the consolidated financial statements.

Telecommunications equipment manufacturing revenues comprise:

($ millions)	1990	1989	1988
Revenues from			
Bell Canada	$1,477	$1,495	$1,416
Other telecommunications subsidiary and associated companies of BCE	266	238	181
Revenues from others	6,108	5,428	5,001
Total	$7,851	$7,161	$6,598

4. Investments in Associated Companies

BCE uses the equity method of accounting for investments in companies where ownership by BCE, or a subsidiary, ranges from 20% to 50%. Under this accounting method, BCE's proportional share of income of such companies, from the dates of their acquisition, net of amortization of excess purchase price over net assets acquired, is taken into income and added to the cost of investments. Income received from these companies reduces the carrying amounts of the investments.

Three-Year Summary of Investments in Associated Companies:

($ millions)	TCPL* (a)	STC PLC (c)	MT&T and Bruncor Inc. (d)	Memotec Data Inc. (e)	Quebecor Inc. (f)	Other companies	Total
1988							
Balance-January 1, 1988	$ 998	$1,247	$176	$209	$ —	$119	$2,749
Cost of investments	134	40	9	20	80	13	296
Equity income (loss)	(65)	63	23	6	2	9	38
Income received	(50)	(26)	(15)	(1)	(1)	(1)	(94)
Currency translation	(17)	(163)	—	(2)	—	—	(182)
Sale of investments	—	—	—	—	—	(57)	(57)
Balance-December 31, 1988	$1,000	$1,161	$193	$232	$81	$ 83	$2,750
1989							
Cost of investments	237	—	10	4	—	12	263
Equity income	62	78	21	3	3	6	173
Income received	(51)	(29)	(16)	(5)	(1)	(2)	(104)
Currency translation and other adjustments	(12)	(152)	—	—	(1)	(13)	(178)
Balance-December 31, 1989	$1,236	$1,058	$208	$234	$82	$ 86	$2,904
1990							
Cost of investments	8	—	7	5	1	14	35
Equity income	52	60	21	—	16	6	155
Income received	(45)	(35)	(17)	(6)	(1)	(2)	(106)
Currency translation and other adjustments	1	186	—	(2)	(1)	(16)	168
Sale of investments	(498)	—	—	—	—	—	(498)
Transfer of Encor (b)	(320)	—	—	—	—	—	(320)
Balance-December 31, 1990	$ 434	$1,269	$219	$231	$97	$ 88	$2,338

* Includes Encor Inc. to July 1990; see (b) on the following page.

4. Investments in Associated Companies (continued)

(a) TCPL (excerpt)

At December 31, 1990, BCE owned approximately 24.4% of common shares (37,647,081 shares) of TransCanada PipeLines Limited (TCPL) (1989-48.9% (74,611,977 shares), 1988-49.1% (73,896,249 shares)), while at the same date warrants to purchase 37,500,000 TCPL common shares from BCE were also outstanding.

The reduction in ownership in 1990 reflects the sale of 37,500,000 TCPL common shares, as part of units, by BCE to a group of underwriters pursuant to an underwriting agreement entered into in September 1990. The units offered by BCE consisted of 37,500,000 TCPL common shares sold on an installment basis and warrants to purchase a further 37,500,000 TCPL common shares from BCE at $17.50 per share for a total exercise price of $656 million. The purchase price for the TCPL common shares is payable in two installments for a total consideration of $618.8 million (excluding underwriters' fee and expenses of issue). The warrants were sold for an aggregate consideration of $18.7 million (excluding underwriters' fee and expenses of issue) and expire on December 15, 1992. The first installment of $309.4 million for the common shares and $18.7 million for the warrants was received on October 1, 1990, and the remaining $309.4 million is due by October 1, 1991. BCE realized a gain of $149 million ($120 million after tax) on the 37,500,000 TCPL common shares and the warrants sold as part of the units.

Equity income of TCPL was based on 24.4% ownership from October 1, 1990.

(b) Encor

As a result of a restructuring of TCPL, which became effective on May 2, 1989, TCPL distributed to its common shareholders one common share of a recapitalized Encor Inc. (Encor) for each common share of TCPL they owned. As a result of that distribution, BCE received 48.9% of the outstanding Encor common shares.

At December 31, 1990, BCE owned approximately 19.3% of common shares (29,702,130 shares) of Encor, compared with 48.9% (74,253,930 shares) at December 31, 1989, and 100% of the redeemable convertible preferred shares of Encor convertible into 74,618,433 common shares which were acquired on May 2, 1989. At December 31, 1990, warrants to purchase from BCE 29,701,200 Encor common shares were also outstanding. The reduction in ownership reflects the sale by BCE, in July 1990, of units consisting of 44,551,800 Encor common shares and warrants to purchase 29,701,200 Encor common shares from BCE at $2.65 per share for a total exercise price of $79 million. BCE's common shareholding was reduced to 29,702,130 common shares of Encor prior to exercise of the warrants. The net proceeds received in July 1990 amounted to $99 million. The warrants expire on January 21, 1992.

Commencing with the third quarter of 1990, BCE no longer accounts for its common share investment in Encor by the equity method. Therefore, the carrying value of the remaining investments in common shares after the above-mentioned sale ($79 million) and preferred shares of Encor have been transferred to Other investments.

Abitibi-Price Inc.—Joint Ventures

Canada-based Abitibi-Price manufactures and markets newsprint and value-added uncoated groundwood paper products. The company sells newsprint to newspaper publishers in North America and throughout the world. Major customers include the New York Times and Washington Post newspapers. Its office products division supplies information processing products to customers in North America and western Europe. Products include printer toner, ribbons, tapes, disks, optical discs, fax machines, printers, and modems. Abitibi-Price also purchases and resells lumber and waferboard for 3rd-party manufacturers. In 1997, the company announced that it is merging with Stone-Consolidated, a move that will create the world's biggest newsprint maker.

Learning Objectives
- Understand what joint ventures are and why companies use them.
- Understand the two most common methods of accounting for joint ventures.
- Conduct and interpret ROE analyses of a company that has joint ventures.
- Compare the results of the ROE analyses under different accounting methods for joint ventures.

Refer to the 1995 financial statements of Abitibi-Price Inc.

Concepts

a. What is a joint venture?

b. Why do companies enter into joint ventures?

c. How are investments in joint ventures accounted for in the United States?

d. What common alternative method of accounting for joint ventures is used by Abitibi-Price, a Canadian company?

e. Which method do you believe better reflects the economic reality of the investment?

Process

f. Provide the journal entry made by Abitibi-Price to record its share of 1995 earnings of its joint ventures. *Note*: this journal entry is made before Abitibi-Price consolidates the joint ventures.

g. Provide the journal entry made by Abitibi-Price to consolidate its investments in joint ventures. *Note*: the information provided in Note 2 precludes you from providing the *detailed* journal entry. Use the summary data in Note 2.

h. How does the use of the equity method to account for joint ventures affect:

   i. The income statement?

   ii. The balance sheet?

   iii. The statement of cash flows?

Analysis

i. Conduct and interpret analyses of decomposed return on equity for 1994 and 1995 under each of the following assumptions:

   i. Abitibi-Price uses the equity method to account for its investments in joint ventures.

   ii. Abitibi-Price uses the proportionate consolidation method to account for its investments in joint ventures.

Use the following model to decompose return on equity:

$$ROE = \frac{NI}{EBT} \times \frac{EBT}{EBIT} \times \frac{EBIT}{Sales} \times \frac{Sales}{Total\ Assets} \times \frac{Total\ Assets}{Common\ Equity}$$

where NI is net income, EBT is earnings before tax, and EBIT is earnings before interest and tax. The first subcomponent measures the proportion of earnings before tax that are kept by the company. The second subcomponent measures the effect of debt; it indicates the proportion of earnings before interest and tax that are retained after paying interest. The third subcomponent measures the company's operating return on sales; it can be broken down into further subcomponents such as the gross margin percent. The fourth subcomponent measures asset utilization; it can be broken down into further subcomponents such as account receivable turnover, inventory turnover, and plant asset turnover. The final subcomponent measures the effect of leverage on ROE.

ABITIBI PRICE INC.

CONSOLIDATED EARNINGS

Year ended December 31
(millions of Canadian dollars, except per share amounts)

	1995	1994
Net sales	$2,782	$2,110
Cost of sales	2,063	1,879
Selling and administrative expenses	120	94
Depreciation and depletion	113	111
Restructuring costs (note 4)	6	8
	2,302	2,092
Operating profit from continuing operations	480	18
Interest expense on long-term debt (note 5)	(61)	(74)
Unusual items (note 6)	4	(21)
Other income and expense, net (note 7)	(4)	(3)
Earnings (loss) from continuing operations before income taxes	419	(80)
Recovery of (provision for) income taxes (note 8)	(146)	29
Earnings (loss) from continuing operations	273	(51)
Loss on disposal of discontinued operations, net of income tax recoveries of $2 (note 9)	–	(4)
Net earnings (loss) for the year	273	(55)
Provision for dividends on preferred shares	(1)	(1)
Net earnings (loss) attributable to common shareholders	$ 272	$ (56)
Per common share:		
Earnings (loss) from continuing operations	$3.24	$(0.62)
Earnings (loss) for the year		
Basic	3.24	(0.66)
Fully diluted	2.90	(0.66)
Dividends declared	0.30	–
Dividends payable	0.10	–
Weighted average number of common shares outstanding (millions)		
Basic	84.0	84.4
Fully diluted	95.4	96.6
Fully diluted number of common shares outstanding	91.4	99.6

CONSOLIDATED RETAINED EARNINGS

Year ended December 31 (millions of Canadian dollars)

	1995	1994
Retained earnings, beginning of year	$298	$359
Net earnings (loss) for the year	273	(55)
	571	304
Purchase of common shares in excess of average stated capital (note 10)	(140)	–
Unamortized convertible subordinated debenture issue costs, net of income tax recoveries of $1 (note 11)	(3)	–
Dividends declared		
Preferred shares	(1)	(1)
Common shares	(25)	–
Expenses of common share issue, net of income tax recoveries of $2 in 1994	–	(5)
Retained earnings, end of year	$402	$298

ABITIBI PRICE INC.
CONSOLIDATED BALANCE SHEET
December 31 (millions of Canadian dollars)

	1995	1994
Assets		
Current assets		
Cash and deposits	$178	$272
Accounts receivable (note 12)	214	183
Inventories (note 13)	234	180
Prepaid expenses	11	11
	637	646
Fixed assets (note 14)	1,526	1,316
Investments and other assets (note 15)	90	104
Deferred pension cost	92	95
Goodwill	25	28
	207	227
	$2,370	$2,189
Liabilities		
Current liabilities		
Dividend payable	$ 9	$ —
Bank loan (note 16)	17	32
Income taxes payable	20	1
Current portion of long-term debt		
Recourse (note 5(a))	24	12
Non-recourse—joint ventures (note 5(b))	52	15
Accounts payable and Accrued liabilities	397	352
	519	412
Long Term Debt		
Recourse(note 5 (a)	294	329
Non-recourse—joint ventures (note 5(b))	255	337
Deferred income taxes	253	112
CONVERTIBLE SUBORDINATED DEBENTURES AND SHAREHOLDERS' EQUITY		
Convertible subordinated debentures (note 11)	24	150
Shareholders' equity		
Capital stock (note 10)		
Preferred shares	10	11
Common shares	613	540
Retained earnings	402	298
	1,025	849
	$2,370	$2,189

ABITIBI PRICE INC.

CHANGES IN CONSOLIDATED CASH POSITION
Year ended December 31 (millions of Canadian dollars)

	1995	1994
Continuing operating activities		
Earnings (loss) for the year from continuing operations	$273	$(51)
Depreciation and depletion	113	111
Unusual items	(4)	21
Provision for (recovery of) deferred income taxes	150	(32)
Other non-cash items	23	(3)
	555	46
Changes in the non-cash working capital components of continuing operations (note 17)	(31)	(25)
Cash generated by continuing operating activities	524	21
Financing activities of continuing operations		
Purchase of common shares for cancellation	(194)	—
Increase in (repayment of) long-term debt and bank loan, net	(66)	6
Retirement of preferred shares	(1)	(6)
Issue of common shares, net of expenses	—	169
Cash generated by (used in) financing activities of continuing operations	(261)	169
Investing activities of continuing operations		
Additions to fixed assets, net of $8 (1994—$2) of investment tax credits	(327)	(82)
Increase in investments and other assets	(5)	(9)
Proceeds from sales of discontinued operations and operating divisions, net of $40 debentures received from purchasers in 1994	—	33
Acquisition of Gaspesia Pulp & Paper Company Limited (note 3)	—	(2)
Cash used in investing activities of continuing operations	(332)	(60)
Dividends paid		
Preferred shareholders	(1)	(1)
Common shareholders	(16)	—
Cash used to pay dividends	(17)	(1)
Cash generated by (used in) continuing operations	(86)	129
Cash used in discontinued operations	(8)	(7)
Increase (decrease) in cash during the year	(94)	122
Cash and deposits, beginning of year	272	150
Cash and deposits, end of year	$178	$272

Notes to Consolidated Financial Statements

December 31, 1995 and 1994 (tabular amounts in millions of Canadian dollars)

1. SUMMARY OF SIGNIFICANT ACCOUNTING POLICIES

These financial statements are expressed in Canadian dollars and are prepared in accordance with accounting principles generally accepted in Canada (Canadian GAAP).

(A) Basis of presentation: The financial statements consolidate the accounts of Abitibi-Price Inc., its subsidiary companies, the Company's proportionate interest in its U.S. joint venture partnerships comprising Augusta Newsprint Company (Augusta)—50%, Alabama River Newsprint Company (Alabama)—50% and Alabama River Recycling Company (Alabama Recycling)—50%, and its ownership interest in Gaspesia Pulp & Paper Company Limited (Gaspesia)—51% to December 15, 1994 and 100% after that date (see note 3).

(B) Translation of foreign currencies: Assets and liabilities denominated in foreign currencies are translated at year-end exchange rates. Revenues and expenses are translated at prevailing market rates.

The net U.S. dollar assets of self-sustaining joint ventures and subsidiaries hedge a portion of the Company's U.S. dollar debt. Any remaining U.S. dollar debt is hedged by future U.S. dollar revenues. Exchange gains or losses on U.S. dollar debt hedged by future revenue are deferred and included in earnings in the period that the revenue is recognized.

(C) Financial instruments: Realized gains and losses on option and forward exchange rate contracts that hedge anticipated revenues are included in earnings when that revenue is recognized.

(D) Inventories: Inventories are valued at the lower of average cost and net recoverable amount.

(E) Fixed assets and depreciation: Fixed assets are recorded at cost, which includes capitalized interest and preproduction costs. Investment tax credits and government capital grants received reduce the cost of the related fixed assets.

Depreciation is provided at rates which amortize the fixed asset cost over the productive life of the asset. The principal fixed asset category is production equipment which is generally depreciated over 20 years on a straight-line-basis.

(F) Environmental costs: Environmental expenditures that continue to benefit the Company are recorded at cost and capitalized as part of fixed assets. Depreciation is charged to income over the estimated future benefit period of the asset. Environmental expenditures that do not provide benefits to the Company in future periods are expensed as incurred.

(G) Investments: Long-term investments are recorded at the lower of cost and net recoverable amount.

(H) Pension costs: Earnings are charged with the cost of pension benefits earned by employees as services are rendered. Pension expense is determined using management's best estimates of expected investment yields, wage and salary escalation, mortality rates, terminations and retirement ages. Adjustments arising from pension plan amendments, experience gains and losses, and assumption changes are amortized to earnings over the average remaining service lives of the members. Any difference between pension expense (determined on an accounting basis) and funding (as required by regulatory authorities) gives rise to deferred pension costs.

(I) Goodwill: Goodwill is recorded at the lower of book value and net recoverable amount and is amortized over its estimated period of future benefit-currently 20 years.

Any impairment in value is recorded in earnings when it is identified.

(J) Income taxes: Deferred income taxes result from differences in the timing of income and expense recognition for accounting and tax purposes.

(K) Research and development costs: Research costs are expensed as incurred. Development costs for technically and commercially feasible products or processes which management intends to produce and market and/or use are deferred until commercial use begins. At that time, these costs are charged to earnings over the estimated commercial life of the product or process.

2. CHANGE IN ACCOUNTING FOR NEWSPRINT JOINT VENTURES

As required by changes in Canadian GAAP, in 1995, the Company adopted the proportionate consolidation method of accounting for its newsprint joint ventures. Previously, the Company's investments in joint ventures were accounted for using the equity method. The financial statements for the year ended December 31, 1994 have been restated to reflect this change in accounting policy.

Shareholders' equity and net earnings are unaffected by this change in accounting policy. However, the consolidated balance sheet, earnings and cash position statements were impacted as follows:

	1995 Equity Accounting for Joint Ventures	Increase (Decrease)	1995 Proportionate Accounting for Joint Ventures as Reported	1994 Equity Accounting for Joint Ventures as Reported	Increase (Decrease)	1994 Proportionate Accounting for Joint Ventures as Restated
Consolidated Balance Sheet						
Current Assets	$590	$47	$637	$605	$41	$646
Fixed assets	1,140	386	1,526	906	410	1,316
Investments in newsprint joint ventures	138	(138)	—	95	(95)	—
Deferred pension cost	97	(5)	92	100	(5)	95
Other assets	102	13	115	115	17	132
Total assets	$2,067	$303	$2,370	$1,821	$368	$2,189
Current liabilities	$471	$48	$519	$381	$31	$412
Long-term debt:						
Recourse	294	—	294	329	—	329
Non-recourse - joint ventures	—	255	255	—	337	337
Deferred income taxes	253	—	253	112	—	112
Convertible subordinated debentures	24	—	24	150	—	150
Shareholders' equity	1,025	—	1,025	849	—	849
Total liabilities and equity	$2,067	$303	$2,370	1,821	$368	$2,189
Consolidated Earnings Statement						
Net sales	$2,782	—	$2,782	$2,110	$ —	$2,110
Operating Profit	404	76	480	16	2	18
Income (loss) from joint ventures	45	(45)	—	(33)	33	—
Interest expense	(29)	(32)	(61)	(40)	(34)	(74)
Unusual items & other income and expense, net	(1)	1	—	(23)	(1)	(24)
Earnings (loss) from continuing operations before income taxes	419	—	419	(80)	—	(80)
Net earnings (loss)	$273	$ —	$273	$(55)	$ —	$(55)
Changes in Consolidated Cash Position						
Cash generated by (used in) continuing operations						
Operating activities	$459	$65	$524	$22	$(1)	$21
Financing activities	(222)	(39)	(261)	147	22	169
Investing activities	(322)	(10)	(332)	(49)	(11)	(60)
Dividends paid	(17)	—	(17)	(1)	—	(1)
	$(102)	$16	$(86)	$119	$10	$129

The Seagram Company Ltd. is a leading worldwide producer and marketer of distilled spirits, wines, fruit juices, coolers, and mixers with affiliates in 30 countries. Among the company's major assets are significant investments in the common stock of E. I. DuPont de Nemours and Company and Time Warner, Inc. In April 1995, Seagram announced that it was selling its shares in DuPont back to the company. It also announced its intention to purchase a majority interest in MCA, Inc.

Learning Objectives
- Understand the difference between alternate methods of accounting for investments: cost, market value, equity method, and consolidation.
- Learn to prepare pro-forma financial statements based on information in the financial press.

Refer to the 1995 financial statements of The Seagram Company.

Concepts

a. Find Seagram's investment in DuPont on the Consolidated balance sheet. What was the January 31, 1995 balance in the account? What was the 1994 balance?

b. Find Seagram's investment in Time Warner on the Consolidated balance sheet. What was the January 31, 1995 balance in the account? What was the 1994 balance?

c. Refer to Note 1 of Seagram's financial statements. How does Seagram account for its investment in DuPont? In general, when do companies use this method of accounting?

Process

d. Describe how $1 of DuPont's net income would be reflected in Seagram's financial statements. What journal entry would Seagram prepare for this hypothetical event? Explain why the FASB requires Seagram to account for its investment in DuPont in this way.

e. Describe how $1 of dividends declared and paid by DuPont would be reflected in Seagram's financial statements. What journal entry would Seagram prepare for this hypothetical event? Explain why the FASB requires Seagram to account for its investment in DuPont in this way.

f. Assume that DuPont's stock price increased by $1 per share during the 12-month period ending January 31, 1995. What journal entry would Seagram prepare for this hypothetical event? Explain why the FASB requires Seagram to account for its investment in DuPont in this way.

g. Does the DuPont financial information in Note 1 tie into the Seagram financial statements? Explain how it does or why it does not.

h. Describe how $1 of Time Warner's net income would be reflected in Seagram's financial statements. What journal entry would Seagram prepare for this hypothetical event? Explain why the FASB requires Seagram to account for its investment in Time Warner in this way.

i. Describe how $1 of dividends declared and paid by Time Warner would be reflected in Seagram's financial statements. What journal entry would Seagram prepare for this hypothetical event? Explain why the FASB requires Seagram to account for its investment in Time Warner in this way.

j. Assume that Time Warner's stock price increased by $1 per share during the 12-month period ending January 31, 1995. What journal entry would Seagram prepare for this hypothetical event? Ignore any deferred income tax effects. Explain why the FASB requires Seagram to account for its investment in Time Warner in this way.

k. Refer to the *Business Week* article entitled "The Mogul." How much cash will Seagram receive for selling its DuPont common stock back to DuPont? Assuming the sale occurred on January 31,

1995, what journal entry would Seagram book for this transaction? Ignore any income tax effects.

l. Use the following table to complete the remaining parts of this case. In column 1, summarize Seagram's balance sheet information from the published financial statements. In column 2, enter the effects of the journal entry proposed for the sale of DuPont's common stock. Compute the pro-forma balances in column 3 by adding columns 1 and 2.

	(Column 1) Information from Seagram's 1995 balance sheet	(Column 2) Proposed Sale of DuPont Common Stock	(Column 3) Pro-forma balance sheet (after DuPont Sale)	(Column 4) Purchase of 80% of MCA Common Stock	(Column 5) Pro-forma balance sheet (after DuPont Sale and MCA purchase)	(Column 6) Consolidating (ledger) journal entry	(Column 7) Pro-forma Consolidated balance sheet (after DuPont Sale and MCA purchase)
Current assets							
Excess of cost over fair value of assets acquired							
Other noncurrent assets							
Current liabilities							
Noncurrent liabilities							
Shareholders' equity							

m. Again refer to the *Business Week* article. How much did Seagram propose to pay for 80% of the outstanding common stock of MCA, Inc.? Based on the amount Seagram is willing to pay for MCA's common stock, what is the estimated total fair market value of MCA?

n. Assume that MCA has the following book values and market values for its individual assets and liabilities at January 31, 1995.

(in millions)	January 31, 1995 Book Values	January 31, 1995 Market Values
Current assets	$ 2,000	$ 2,500
Noncurrent assets	8,000	9,000
Current liabilities	2,000	2,000
Noncurrent liabilities	3,000	3,000

Assume that the purchase occurred on January 31, 1995. What journal entry would Seagram book to record its purchase of 80% of MCA's outstanding common stock? What "method" would Seagram use to account for its investment in MCA? What "basis of presentation" would Seagram use in its financial statements for its investment in MCA?

o. In column 4 of the worksheet, enter the effects of the journal entry proposed in part *n*. Calculate the pro-forma balances in column 5.

p. Based on the market values presented in part *n*, prepare a consolidating entry to eliminate the "Investment in common stock of MCA, Inc." account. Post this entry in column 6. Calculate the pro-forma balances in column 7.

THE SEAGRAM COMPANY LTD. AND SUBSIDIARY COMPANIES

CONSOLIDATED BALANCE SHEET

U.S. dollars in millions	January 31 1995	1994
Assets		
Current Assets		
Cash and short-term investments at cost, which approximates market	$ 157	$ 131
Receivables	1,328	1,170
Inventories	2,519	2,350
Prepaid expenses	172	143
Total Current Assets	4,176	3,794
Common Stock of E.I. DuPont de Nemours and Company, at equity	3,670	3,154
Common stock of Time Warner, Inc., at market (cost at January 31, 1995—$2,170)	2,043	1,769
Property, plant and equipment, net	1,267	1,220
Excess of cost over fair value of assets acquired	1,547	1,520
Sundry assets	253	261
	$12,956	$11,718
Liabilities And Shareholders' Equity		
Current Liabilities		
Short-term borrowings and indebtedness payable within one year	$ 2,475	$ 1,844
Payables and accrued liabilities	1,423	1,011
Income and other taxes	193	141
Total Current Liabilities	4,091	2,996
Long-Term indebtedness	2,841	3,053
Deferred income taxes and other credits	515	668
Shareholders' Equity		
Shares without par value	638	617
Cumulative currency translation adjustments	(359)	(479)
Cumulative (loss) gain on equity securities, net of tax	(85)	46
Retained earnings	5,315	4,817
Total Shareholders' Equity	5,509	5,001
	$12,956	$11,718

THE SEAGRAM COMPANY LTD. AND SUBSIDIARY COMPANIES

CONSOLIDATED STATEMENT OF INCOME

U.S. dollars in millions, except per share amounts

	Fiscal Years Ended January 31		
	1995	1994	1993
Sales and other income	$6,399	$6,038	$6,101
Cost of sales	3,654	3,451	3,535
	2,745	2,587	2,566
Selling, general and administrative expenses	2,020	1,833	1,804
Operating Income	725	754	762
Dividend income	318	295	286
	1,043	1,049	1,048
Interest expense	396	339	326
Income before income taxes and unremitted DuPont earnings	647	710	722
Provision for income taxes— current year	124	171	176
1981 transaction	65	—	—
Income Before Unremitted DuPont Earnings	458	539	546
Equity in unremitted DuPont earnings (loss)	353	(160)	(72)
Net Income	811	379	474
Cumulative effect of accounting changes for United States Generally Accepted Accounting Principles (GAAP)	(75)	—	(1,374)
Net Income (Loss) under United States GAAP	$ 736	$ 379	$ (900)
Earnings per share			
Income before unremitted DuPont earnings	$ 1.23	$1.45	$ 1.45
Equity in unremitted DuPont earnings (loss)	.95	(.43)	(.19)
Net Income	2.18	1.02	1.26
Cumulative effect of accounting changes for United States GAAP	(.20)	—	(3.64)
Net Income (Loss) under United States GAAP	$ 1.98	$ 1.02	$(2.38)

Sales and cost of sales include excise taxes of $836, $811, and $887 for the fiscal years ended January 31, 1995, 1994, and 1993, respectively.

THE SEAGRAM COMPANY LTD. AND SUBSIDIARY COMPANIES

CONSOLIDATED STATEMENT OF CASH FLOWS

U.S. dollars in millions

Fiscal Years Ended January 31

	1995	1994	1993
Operating Activities			
Income before unremitted DuPont earnings	$ 458	$ 539	$ 546
Adjustments to Reconcile Income before unremitted DuPont earnings to Net cash Provided			
Depreciation	138	125	122
Amortization of excess of cost over fair value of assets acquired	46	41	42
Decrease in restructuring accrual	(5)	(31)	(69)
Sundry	28	26	39
Changes in assets and liabilities			
Receivables	(157)	(73)	34
Inventories	(23)	24	8
Prepaid expenses	(36)	(7)	(6)
Payables and accrued liabilities	363	35	(92)
Income and other taxes	38	14	(64)
Deferred income taxes	(114)	17	3
	278	171	17
Net cash provided by operations and dividends	736	710	563
Investing Activities			
Capital expenditures	(172)	(163)	(168)
Purchase of Time Warner common stock	(474)	(1,695)	—
Increase in DuPont investment related to 1981 transaction	(162)	—	—
Sundry	(46)	(112)	(69)
Net cash used for investing activities	(854)	(1,970)	(237)
Financing Activities			
Dividends paid	(216)	(209)	(205)
Issuance of shares upon exercise of stock options and conversion of LYONs	22	26	23
Purchase of shares for retirement	(23)	(61)	(189)
Increase in long-term indebtedness	3	605	237
Decrease in long-term indebtedness	(252)	(104)	(638)
Increase in short-term borrowings and indebtedness payable within one year	610	1,018	296
Net cash (used for) provided by financing activities	144	1,275	(476)
Net Increase (Decrease) In Cash And Short-Term Investments	$ 26	$ 15	$ 150

THE SEAGRAM COMPANY LTD. AND SUBSIDIARY COMPANIES

NOTES TO CONSOLIDATED FINANCIAL STATEMENTS

Note 1 Equity in DuPont

At January 31, 1995 the Company owned 164.2 million shares, or 24.1 percent of the outstanding common stock of DuPont. The Company and DuPont have entered into an agreement which provides that the Company will be entitled to representation on the DuPont board of directors proportional to its stock ownership. The Company will not as a general matter exceed a 25 percent holding of DuPont common stock unless another party acquires or offers to acquire a substantial stock position, and DuPont will have a right of first refusal if the Company offers its DuPont shares for sale or transfer during the term of the agreement subject to certain exceptions. The agreement may be terminated on notice of two years given at any time on or after April 2, 1997, but is subject to earlier termination upon the occurrence of specified events, including dilution of the Company's ownership position.

The Company accounts for its interest in DuPont using the equity method, whereby its proportionate share of DuPont earnings is included in income. Cumulative unremitted DuPont earnings of $668 million are included in consolidated retained earnings at January 31, 1995. The balance sheet reflects costs related to the DuPont investment and cumulative unremitted earnings. Summarized financial information for DuPont, based upon its publicly reported financial statements, follows:

DUPONT FINANCIAL INFORMATION
In millions

Years ended December 31,	1994	1993	1992
Sales and other income	$40,259	$37,841	$38,352
Cost of goods sold and all other expenses	35,877	36,883	36,541
Provision for income taxes	1,655	392	836
Income before extraordinary item and cumulative effect of accounting changes	2,727	566	975
Extraordinary charge from early extinguishment of debt	—	(11)	(69)
Cumulative effect of accounting changes	—	—	(4,833)
Net income (loss)	$ 2,727	$ 555	$ (3,927)

	December 31, 1994	1993
Current assets	$11,108	$10,899
Noncurrent assets	25,784	26,154
	$36,892	$37,053
Current liabilities	$ 7,565	$ 9,439
Noncurrent liabilities	16,505	16,384
Stockholders' equity	12,822	11,230
	$36,892	$37,053

Note 2 Investment in Time Warner

At January 31, 1995, the Company owned 56.8 million shares or 14.9 percent of the outstanding common stock of Time Warner; 12.6 million shares were acquired in the fiscal year ended January 31, 1995. The total cost of this investment was $2.17 billion.

THE MOGUL

Just how risky is Edgar Bronfman Jr.'s Hollywood gamble?

Much has been made of Edgar Bronfman Jr.'s early and unspectacular career as a theater and film producer. Most telling, perhaps, is that it began at an age when most kids are learning to drive. A pudgy-faced rich kid in Levis and sneakers, Bronfman latched on to a 30-year-old Broadway producer named Bruce Stark while still in high school. Bronfman Sr. was funding Stark's efforts, so entree was easy.

The surprising part is that Stark was happy to have him. What he remembers most is Bronfman's chutzpah. In meetings with powerful agents and assorted glitterati of the entertainment world, young Bronfman did all the talking. No doubt the teenager's money and family ties got him through the door, but his charm and wit made people take him seriously. "He was an amazing kid," says Stark. "He has a language facility that's really quite amazing. He often made me feel like I was kind of incompetent." For the past two weeks, such praise has been hard to come by for the 39-year-old chief executive of $6.4 billion Seagram Co. More common have been the cries of dismay over what is probably the ultimate expression of Bronfman's moxie: His two-step deal to transform Seagram from a liquor company with a 24% stake in DuPont Co. to a broad-based entertainment company focused squarely on the Information Highway. The news drove Seagram stock down 18%, to a low of 263/8, from which it has yet to recover significantly. Wall Street came alive with protest. "I think the Bronfman kid is making a terrible error," said Scott Black of Boston's Delphi Management Inc., which holds 206,000 Seagram shares.

NEXT STOP, A NETWORK? Right or wrong, the complex set of transactions will surely rank among the flashiest and most controversial deals of the 1990s. First of all is the irresistible urge to paint the event in made-for-Hollywood terms. To many, this was the tale of a rich, young scion risking the family fortune to pursue his star-struck fantasies. No one really knows what motivates a person, but it is worth pointing out that Bronfman has been rich all his life and already knows plenty of celebrities. Says film producer David Puttnam, whom Edgar Jr. lived with for a period in high school: "He got his illusions out of his system by the age of 24 or 25. He could have been a producer like Steve Tisch. He

had the money. But he didn't think it was something serious people did."

The more serious aspect of these deals, of course, is what will make them endure as symbols. Like the failed $35 billion merger of Bell Atlantic Corp. and Tele-Communications Inc., Bronfman's big bet makes the business world focus anxiously on the real value inherent in the mythical I-way. By selling Seagram's DuPont stake back to the company for $8.8 billion so he could buy 80% of MCA Inc. for $5.7 billion, Bronfman raised a fundamental question: What's more valuable, a steady, old-line industrial business like chemicals or a glitzy, high-promise technology play like entertainment? Wall Street, for now at least, has voted with its feet.

But was this budding mogul's bet so misplaced? Experts in the entertainment industry say that depends entirely on how well he plays out his hand. It is easy (and scary) to see what Bronfman gave up: unencumbered cash flow from DuPont dividends, which should top $300 million this year (page 128). Determining MCA's true value is far more difficult. A wager on Seagram stock right now is a bet on both the future and Edgar Jr.'s ability to manage it. Says one Wall Street executive close to Seagram: "This will require a good deal of luck and skill, which Edgar may or may not have."

One thing is clear: Even priced at a rich 15 times 1994 cash flow (a peak year), MCA and its Universal Studios unit provide a ripe opportunity. Bronfman has the advantage of little debt, plenty of excess capital to play with, and a board of directors that isn't likely to cross the Bronfman family, given its 36% stake in the parent company. After paying down some debt, Bronfman will have at least $1 billion left over from the DuPont deal. And a 14.9% stake in Time Warner Inc. is worth about $2 billion. MCA's cash flow, meanwhile, can probably finance $3 billion to $4 billion in leverage, if need be.

Bronfman's big disadvantage, however, is that, besides cash, Seagram brings nothing to the entertainment party in terms of management or assets. Viacom Inc. may have paid a similar multiple for Paramount Communications Inc. in 1993, but the owner of MTV, Showtime, and Nickelodeon had loads of Hollywood experience.

Moreover, making MCA a true player against giants such as Time Warner and Disney may take all of Bronfman's resources—and more. At going rates, just finding a top-notch executive to run MCA for him could cost hundreds of millions in stock and salary. That's especially true if he hires Hollywood superagent Michael Ovitz, as people close to Bronfman say he would like to do. Filling out a new management team could cost millions more.

Then there are the investments required to take MCA into the future. To guarantee distribution for the studio's TV shows, most experts think MCA will go after one of the networks. Bronfman and Barry Diller are rumored to be mulling a run at Laurence A. Tisch's CBS Inc. But Tisch is asking a stiff $5 billion. MCA, meanwhile, has already committed to spending $3 billion for theme-park upgrades, including a new Jurassic Park ride at its 50%-owned property near Orlando. Says one entertainment executive: "It's the kind of deal where you buy it and then start spending money."

DIPLOMATIC SKILLS. From what little he has said publicly about the deal, Bronfman's view is this: DuPont was a passive investment in a cyclical business. With MCA, Seagram will control its own destiny and reap the rewards. So finding new management is Bronfman's first priority. He badly needs someone who can decipher the kaleidoscopic future of the entertainment business. And more immediately, he needs to find ways to squeeze more cash out of MCA as it exists today.

Chief Executive Lew R. Wasserman, 82, and President Sidney J. Sheinberg, 60, have managed MCA well over the years. But they've complained that MCA's former owner, Japan's Matsushita Electric Industrial Co., wouldn't let them spend enough money. Rivals say privately that the company also suffered because Wasserman and Sheinberg are themselves conservative. Contends one competitor: "MCA needs an injection of leadership and pizzazz to go along with the same fiscal constraint."

Here's what's likely to happen, according to sources close to Sheinberg: Wasserman will be given an emeritus title with a big salary at MCA and a seat on Seagram's board. Bronfman, meantime, will set up Sheinberg with a well-funded but separate production company where he can make movies with his two sons, Jonathan and Billy. Bronfman then would be free to bring in Ovitz and let him decide the fate of the existing studio hierarchy.

Ovitz denies he has any part in this scenario. He says he has turned down similar offers to manage studios in the past and would rather keep running Creative Artists Agency (CAA), his powerful talent shop. Still, most close observers believe his long ties to Bronfman as a friend and confidant make him candidate No.1. Sources also say that while Ovitz has distanced himself from the process while Bronfman deals with Wasserman and Sheinberg, he has dispatched two trusted CAA officials to help Edgar Jr. sort through personnel issues.

If Bronfman has demonstrated he is good at anything over the years, it is making people comfortable with

his agenda. In 1988, he spent long hours coaxing the Martell family of France to sell the Bronfmans its lucrative cognac brand. Sources close to the deal say his gentle cajoling during two trips to Osaka persuaded Matsushita's managers to give Seagram exclusive rights for two weeks to negotiate for MCA. Even the wooing of his current wife, Venezuelan Clarissa Alcock, took three years of work. He had to convince her Catholic parents to bless her marriage to a Jew. "This is not a capricious man," says producer Puttnam.

Bronfman will need all of his diplomatic skills to make this management transition a smooth one. Because Hollywood is a business built on relationships, moving Wasserman and Sheinberg aside is a delicate proposition. The foremost consideration is MCA's biggest moneymaker, director Steven Spielberg, who began his career at Universal and feels strong loyalty to its two top executives. Bronfman has toured Universal's 428 acres with Sheinberg and spent long hours listening to the executive's views on MCA's future. And in a lengthy meeting on Apr. 11 at Spielberg's Amblin Entertainment, which sits on Universal's lot, he did his best to lend comfort to Spielberg.

Solving the management issue is crucial. But it is only a first step toward unlocking MCA's values. Boosting performance will be tricky. When Michael D. Eisner brought his team to Walt Disney Co. in 1984, there were obvious ways to increase value. He ratcheted up theme-park ticket prices and began a vigorous strategy to spin characters such as Snow White and Mickey Mouse into video rereleases and merchandise sales. Similarly, when Viacom bought Paramount in 1993, the studio's income was depressed, a situation that quickly reversed itself thanks to such films under way as Forrest Gump and Clear and Present Danger.

ANEMIC SYNDICATION. MCA has no such quick fix. In fact, its pipeline is clogged with an enormous liability called Waterworld. This infamous Kevin Costner epic could end up costing $175 million. And though some who have seen it say it is O.K., it will likely lose money even if it scores big. Rumor has it that the company has already taken an extra $50 million reserve against earnings. It has been disruptive in other ways as well. Because it was late, the studio apparently urged director Ron Howard to push up the release of Apollo 13 from November to June 30 to take over Waterworld's early summer slot. Studio sources say the rush to finish hiked the price tag by about $5 million.

Waterworld-type fiascos are rare at MCA. But ironically, that's the reason it will be hard for Bronfman to get a Disney-like bounce in cash flow just by fixing obvious problems. Bronfman told analysts MCA had $475 million in 1994 cash flow, a number generally thought to represent a peak. Squeezing out more will mean reenergizing every part of the business, with the possible exception of MCA Music and Geffen Records, which contributed 40% of cash flow last year and are going great guns.

Most experts believe revamping the TV production business is crucial. After making a killing in the mid-1980s by syndicating hour-long shows such as

Magnum P.I., MCA was slow to see the trend toward half-hour sitcoms such as Cosby and Roseanne. Today, its only half-hour hits are Coach and Major Dad. Without more, an anemic syndication business will remain so. In cable, MCA's only entry is the USA Network, a 50-50 joint venture with Viacom. It is widely thought to be unfocused and sluggish.

Theme parks are probably MCA's fastest-growing unit. But adding attractions like the Jurassic Park ride due to open in Florida will cost billions. And it is often forgotten that MCA only owns 50% of the park in Florida, which means that it only gets half of every dollar of profit.

Finally, there's the film unit and its dependence on Spielberg. Blockbusters such as Jurassic Park and Schindler's List have carried Universal for the past two years. The Jurassic Park video alone supplied one-third of MCA's operating profit in 1994, says a source close to the company.

THE HOUSE OF STEVEN. It may just be that in weaning itself from Spielberg, MCA would, in the long run, be better off. While much has been made of the director's relationship with Wasserman and Sheinberg, the tie has had its downside as well. Most damaging is that MCA has become known as The House of Steven. Spielberg's typical deal—he takes 15% off the top of every film he makes—leaves little money to pay other big picture directors, such as James Cameron and John Hughes. All this argues against depending on him for too much volume.

Bronfman's next steps are still unclear. There's plenty of speculation that he's itching to do a network deal with Diller. That would boost MCA's syndication business right away and add $460 million in cash flow, says Furman Selz Inc. analyst John Tinker. Sources within Universal say Bronfman also hopes to quickly create a cable channel out of MCA's library of 4,700 films, something like Ted Turner's TNT network. "The library is the one asset you can't overvalue," says Alan Horn, the chairman of Turner's Castle Rock studio. "Just ask the folks who thought Ted overpaid for the MGM library." Bronfman's likely partner in such a venture: TCI's John C. Malone, whose Encore pay channel has a multibillion-dollar, nine-year deal to air Universal's first-run movies.

The opportunity is indeed ripe. But questions still outnumber answers. Could Bronfman, whose creative urge dates back to his childhood, resist undue interference with his new manager? And if he snares Ovitz, can Hollywood's ultimate power player make the transition from agent to studio head? Given declining worldwide liquor consumption and sluggishness at Tropicana, Bronfman's performance at Seagram hasn't silenced critics who say he was born to his position and didn't earn it. "He'll be dogged by that the rest of his life," says old friend Bruce Stark. Edgar Jr. has used his position to create the chance of a lifetime. Making the bet pay off, however, will take a lot more than chutzpah.

By Michael Oneal in New York and Ronald Grover in Los Angeles, with William C. Symonds in Toronto

Edgar Jr.'s Brave New World

1994 REVENUES	MCA
UNIVERSAL PICTURES $2.3 BILLION*	Producer of Jurassic Park, E.T., Jaws, Back to the Future, Psycho. Library of 4,700 films.
MCA MUSIC ENTERTAINMENT GROUP $1.4 BILLION*	Fine Young Cannibals, Meat Loaf, Reba McEntire. Geffen Records label handles Aerosmith, Nirvana, Counting Crows.
MCA TELEVISION GROUP $600 MILLION*	Owns 50% of USA Network. Produces TV shows Coach, Murder She Wrote, and Northern Exposure.
THEME PARKS $350 MILLION*	Owns Universal Studios tour in Hollywood and 50% of Florida theme park.
MCA BOOK PUBLISHING $240 MILLION*	Owns Putnam Berkeley Group and Price Stern Sloan. Authors include Tom Clancy, Alice Hoffman, Dean Koontz.
CINEPLEX ODEON $150 MILLION*	Owns 42% of this 2,800-screen, $359 million movie theater operator.
	SEAGRAM
SPIRITS AND WINE $4.9 BILLION	Brands include Chivas Regal, Martell Cognac, and Sterling Vineyards wines.
TROPICANA $1.5 BILLION	Fruit juices, coolers, mixers.

* Estimate   DATA: BUSINESS WEEK, SEAGRAM CO.

Universal's Pipeline: Hardly a Gusher

FILM	CHANCES	RELEASE
CASPER Spielberg uses Jurassic Park-type technology to bring ghosts to life. But a good ghost won't scare up enough merchandise business to make this a blockbuster.	B	MAY 26
APOLLO 13 With two-time Oscar winner Tom Hanks in this NASA disaster flick, word of mouth will be strong.	B+	JUNE 30
WATERWORLD With a $175 million price tag and Costner's bad vibes abounding, this Titanic in the making could be a blockbuster and still lose buckets of money.	D	JULY
BABE, THE GALLANT PIG Small budget and small premise: A bighearted pet pig that thinks it's a sheepdog. Huh?	C-	SUMMER
TO WONG FOO, THANKS FOR EVERYTHING, JULIE NEWMAR No pigs, but Wesley Snipes and Patrick Swayze as drag queens?	C	FALL
CLOCKERS Spike Lee takes on the drug scene. Spike is the champion of hype, but his flicks rarely fill seats.	C+	FALL
SUDDEN DEATH Jean-Claude Van Damme is likely to kickbox his way to a small fortune in this one.	A	FALL
CASINO Scorsese's tale of '70s Vegas. With Sharon Stone, Robert DeNiro, and Joe Pesci, could be the best-looking mobster flick this side of Goodfellas.	B	FALL
BALTO Spielberg animation. This tale of a heroic Alaskan sled dog should have more bite than his We're Back miscue. Still, even Spielberg ain't Disney.	C-	FALL

DATA: BUSINESS WEEK

General Electric Company—Consolidations

General Electric is one of the largest and most diversified industrial companies in the world. Revenues in 1995 were over 70 billion dollars. GE's businesses fall into three categories: Technology, which includes aircraft engines, plastics, medical systems and factory automation; Services, which includes financial, broadcasting (e.g. NBC) and communications; and Core Manufacturing, which includes appliances, lighting, industrial power systems, electrical equipment (e.g. RCA), electric motors and transportation equipment.

Learning Objectives
- Read footnotes and understand consolidation disclosures.
- Infer and recreate the adjusting journal entries made by the parent company in preparation of the consolidated financial statements.
- Understand the journal entries required to eliminate inter-company transactions.

Refer to General Electric's 1995 financial statements.

Concepts

a. GE's annual report comprises three complete sets of financial statements. There are balance sheets, income statements, and statements of cash flow for "General Electric Company and consolidated affiliates," "GE," and for "GECS" (General Electric Capital Services). How are these reporting entities related? Why are so many statements presented?

Process

b. Set up a spreadsheet to accommodate GE's income statement and balance sheet data (see example, below). In the first column, enter the 1995 amounts for "GE." In the second column, enter the 1995 amounts for "GECS." In the third column, add together the amounts from columns 1 and 2. In the fourth column, enter the 1995 income statement and balance sheet data presented under the heading "General Electric Company and Consolidated Affiliates." Finally, in the fifth column, calculate the difference between the third and fourth columns.

	GE data (1)	GECS data (2)	GE + GECS (3)	Consolidated data (4)	Difference (3 – 4)
1995 Income					
Statement					
Items					
1995 Balance					
Sheet					
Items					

c. Note 1 indicates that the consolidated data "represent the adding together of all affiliates; companies that General Electric directly or indirectly controls, either through majority ownership or otherwise." Based on your spreadsheet analysis, is this true? In general, what explains the income statement and balance sheet account differences? (*Hint*: refer to Note 1.)

d. Refer to your income statement spreadsheet data.

   i. What is the biggest difference? What explains this difference?

   ii. Apart from the difference in part *i*, add together the rest of the differences under "Revenues." Compare this amount to the total difference for "Costs and Expenses." What types of transactions caused these discrepancies?

e. Refer to your balance sheet spreadsheet data.

    i.   The "Investment in GECS" account is the biggest difference. What explains this difference? What does "Investment in GECS" (from column 1) relate to in column 2? Is this coincidental? Why or why not?

    ii.   Apart from the "Investment in GECS" account, what is the total difference in "Assets?" "Liabilities?" Speculate on how these differences arose.

GENERAL ELECTRIC COMPANY AND CONSOLIDATED AFFILIATES
STATEMENT OF EARNINGS

For the years ended December 31 (In millions)	General Electric Company and Consolidated Affiliates		
	1995	1994	1993
Revenues			
Sales of goods	$33,157	$30,740	$29,509
Sales of services	9,733	8,803	8,268
Other income (note 3)	752	793	735
Earnings of GECS before accounting change	—	—	—
GECS revenues from operations (note 4)	26,386	19,773	17,189
Total revenues	70,028	60,109	55,701
Costs and expenses (Note 5)			
Cost of goods sold	24,288	22,748	22,606
Cost of services sold	6,682	6,214	6,308
Interest and other financial charges (note 7)	7,286	4,949	4,054
Insurance losses and policy holder and annuity benefits	5,285	3,507	3,172
Provision for losses on financing receivables (note 8)	1,117	873	987
Other costs and expenses	15,429	12,987	12,287
Minority interest in net earnings of consolidated affiliates	204	170	151
Total costs and expenses	60,291	51,448	49,565
Earnings from continuing operations before income taxes and accounting change	9,737	8,661	6,136
Provision for income taxes (note 9)	3,164	2,746	1,952
Earnings from continuing operations before accounting change	6,573	5,915	4,184
Earnings from discontinued operations (note 2)	—	(1,193)	993
Earnings before accounting change	6,573	4,726	5,177
Cumulative effect of accounting change (note 6)	—	—	(862)
Net Earnings	$ 6,573	$ 4,726	$ 4,315

GENERAL ELECTRIC COMPANY AND CONSOLIDATED AFFILIATES

STATEMENT OF EARNINGS

For the years ended December 31

(In millions)	GE 1995	GE 1994	GE 1993	GECS 1995	GECS 1994	GECS 1993
Revenues						
Sales of goods	$33,177	$30,767	$29,533	$ —	$ —	$ —
Sales of services	9,836	8,863	8,289	—	—	—
Other income (note 3)	753	783	730	—	—	—
Earnings of GECS before accounting change	2,415	2,085	1,567	—	—	—
GECS revenues from operations (note 4)	—	—	—	26,492	19,875	17,276
Total revenues	46,181	42,498	40,119	26,492	19,875	17,276
Costs and expenses (note 5)						
Cost of goods sold	24,308	22,775	22,630	—	—	—
Cost of services sold	6,785	6,274	6,329	—	—	—
Interest and other financial charges (note 7)	649	410	525	6,661	4,545	3,538
Insurance losses and policy holder and annuity benefits	—	—	—	5,285	3,507	3,172
Provision for losses on financing receivables (note 8)	—	—	—	1,117	873	987
Other costs and expenses	5,743	5,211	5,124	9,769	7,862	7,236
Minority interest in net earnings of consolidated affiliates	64	31	17	140	139	134
Total costs and expenses	37,549	34,701	34,625	22,972	16,926	15,067
Earnings from continuing operations before income taxes and accounting change	8,632	7,797	5,494	3,520	2,949	2,209
Provision for income taxes (note 9)	2,059	1,882	1,310	1,105	864	642
Earnings from continuing operations before accounting change	6,573	4,726	5,177	2,415	2,085	1,567
Earnings (loss) from discontinued operations (note 2)	—	(1,189)	993	—	(1,189)	240
Earnings before accounting change	6,573	4,726	5,177	2,415	896	1,807
Cumulative effect of accounting change (note 20)	—	—	(862)	—	—	—
Net Earnings	$ 6,573	$ 4,726	$ 4,315	$ 2,415	$ 896	$ 1,807

GENERAL ELECTRIC COMPANY AND CONSOLIDATED AFFILIATES
STATEMENT OF FINANCIAL POSITION

At December 31 (In millions)	General Electric Co. and Consolidated Affiliates	
	1995	1994
Assets		
Cash and equivalents	$ 2,823	$ 2,591
Investment securities (note 10)	41,067	30,965
Current receivables (note 11)	8,735	7,527
Inventories (note 12)	4,395	3,880
GECS financing receivables (investment in time sales, loans and financing leases) - net (notes 8 and 13)	93,272	76,357
Other GECS receivables	12,417	5,763
Property, plant and equipment (including equipment leased to others) - net (note 14)	25,679	23,465
Investment in GECS	—	—
Intangible assets (note 15)	13,342	11,373
All other assets (note 16)	26,305	23,950
Total Assets	$228,035	$185,871
Liabilities and Equity		
Short-term borrowings (note 18)	$ 64,463	$ 57,781
Accounts payable, principally trade accounts	9,061	6,766
Progress collections and price adjustments accrued	1,812	2,065
Dividends payable	767	699
All other GE current costs and expenses accrued (note 17)	5,898	5,543
Long-term borrowings (note 18)	51,027	36,979
Insurance liabilities, reserves and annuity benefits (note 19)	39,699	29,438
All other liabilities (note 20)	15,363	13,161
Deferred income taxes (note 22)	7,380	5,205
Total liabilities	195,470	157,637
Minority interest in equity of consolidated affiliates (note 23)	2,956	1,847
Common stock (1,857,013,000 shares issued)	594	594
Unrealized gains (losses) on investment securities	1,000	(810)
Other capital	1,663	1,112
Retained earnings	34,528	30,793
Less common stock held in treasury	8,176	5,312
Total share owners' equity (notes 24 and 25)	29,609	26,387
Total Liabilities and Equity	$228,035	$185,871

GENERAL ELECTRIC COMPANY AND CONSOLIDATED AFFILIATES

STATEMENT OF FINANCIAL POSITION

At December 31 (In millions)	GE 1995	GE 1994	GECS 1995	GECS 1994
Assets				
Cash and equivalents	$ 874	$ 1,373	$ 1,949	$ 1,218
Investment securities (note 10)	4	93	41,063	30,872
Current receivables (note 11)	8,891	7,807	—	—
Inventories (note 12)	4,395	3,880	—	—
GECS financing receivables (investment in time sales, loans and financing leases) - net (notes 18 and 13)	—	—	93,272	76,357
Other GECS receivables	—	—	12,897	6,012
Property, plant and equipment (including equipment leased to others) - net (note 14)	10,234	9,525	15,445	13,940
Investment in GECS	12,774	9,380	—	—
Intangible assets (note 15)	6,643	6,336	6,699	5,037
All other assets (note 16)	11,901	12,419	14,404	11,531
Total Assets	$55,716	$50,813	$185,729	$144,967
Liabilities and Equity				
Short-term borrowings (note 18)	$ 1,666	$ 906	$ 62,808	$ 57,087
Accounts payable, principally trade accounts	3,968	3,141	5,952	3,777
Progress collections and price adjustments accrued	1,812	2,065	—	—
Dividends payable	767	699	—	—
All other GE current costs and expenses accrued (note 17)	5,747	5,798	—	—
Long-term borrowings (note 18)	2,277	2,699	48,790	34,312
Insurance liabilities, reserves and annuity benefits (note 19)	—	—	39,699	29,438
All other liabilities (note 20)	8,928	8,468	6,312	4,571
Deferred income taxes (note 22)	508	268	6,872	4,937
Total liabilities	25,673	24,044	170,433	134,122
Minority interest in equity of consolidated affiliates (note 23)	434	382	2,522	1,465
Common stock (1,857,013,000 shares issued)	594	594	1	1
Unrealized gains (losses) on investment securities	1,000	(810)	989	(821)
Other capital	1,663	1,122	2,266	2,006
Retained earnings	34,528	30,793	9,518	8,194
Less common stock held in treasury	8,176	5,312	—	—
Total share owners' equity (notes 24 and 25)	29,609	26,387	12,774	9,380
Total Liabilities and Equity	$55,716	$50,813	$185,729	$144,967

GENERAL ELECTRIC COMPANY AND CONSOLIDATED AFFILIATES

NOTES TO CONSOLIDATED FINANCIAL STATEMENTS

Note 1 Summary of Significant Accounting Policies

CONSOLIDATION. The consolidated financial statements represent the adding together of all affiliates—companies that General Electric directly or indirectly controls, either through majority ownership or otherwise. Results of associated companies—generally companies that are 20% to 50% owned and over which GE, directly or indirectly, has significant influence—are included in the financial statements on a "one-line" basis.

FINANCIAL STATEMENT PRESENTATION. Financial data and related measurements are presented in the following categories.

- GE. This represents the adding together of all affiliates other than General Electric Capital Services, Inc. ("GECS"), whose continuing operations are presented on a one-line basis.

- GECS. This affiliate owns all of the common stock of General Electric Capital Corporation (GE Capital) and GE Global Insurance Holding Corporation (GE Global Insurance). GE Capital, GE Global Insurance and their respective affiliates are consolidated in the GECS columns and constitute its business.

- CONSOLIDATED. These data represent the adding together of GE and GECS. The effects of transactions among related companies within and between each of the above-mentioned groups are eliminated. Transactions between GE and GECS are not material.

Ford Motor Co.—Accounting for Investment in Jaguar

Ford Motor Company is the second-largest United States automobile manufacturer, accounting for one in every five cars or trucks sold in the U.S. Other industry segments include tractor and farm implements, electronic equipment and financial services.

Learning Objectives
- Understand the difference between the equity method and full consolidation.
- Understand the effects of accounting decisions on financial statements and ratios.

Refer to Note 17 from the 1990 Ford Motor Company Annual Report.

Concepts

a. Explain the difference between using the equity method and consolidation for Ford's acquisition of Jaguar.

Analysis

b. Explain why Ford accounted for Jaguar using the equity method in 1989 despite the fact that the company had acquired a majority interest. Why did Ford then consolidate the investment in 1990 even though the number of shares held in the investee remained constant since the acquisition?

Note 17

Automotive—Jaguar. In December 1989, the company, through its wholly owned subsidiary Ford Motor Company Limited ("Ford Britain"), acquired a majority interest in Jaguar, a British manufacturer of luxury cars. The acquisition was accounted for using the purchase method. Because the acquisition occurred in late 1989, Jaguar was accounted for on an equity basis at year-end 1989. After the acquisition was completed in the first quarter of 1990, Jaguar was treated as a consolidated subsidiary.

Boston Beer & Lion Brewery—Financial Statement Analysis

> *Boston Beer is the largest craft brewer by volume in the United States. In 1996, the company sold 1,213,000 barrels of beer, which it believes to be more than the next five largest craft brewers combined. The company's business strategy is to continue to lead the craft-brewed beer market by creating and offering a wide variety of the highest quality full-flavored beers, while increasing sales through new product introductions and substantial trade and consumer awareness programs, supported by a large, well trained and rapidly expanding field sales organization.*
>
> *The Lion Brewery, Inc., is a brewer and bottler of brewed beverages, including malta, specialty beers and specialty soft drinks. Malta is a non-alcoholic brewed beverage which the company produces for major Hispanic food distribution companies primarily for sale in the eastern United States. Specialty beers are brewed by the company both for sale under its own labels and on a contract basis for other marketers of craft beer brands. The company also produces specialty soft drinks, including all-natural brewed ginger beverages, on a contract basis for third parties and brews beer for sale under company-owned labels for the local market at popular prices.*

Learning Objectives
- Read and compare financial statements for two companies in the same industry.
- Consider how different strategic choices lead to different financial statement relationships.
- Perform an analysis of financial information using common-size balance sheets and income statements, ratios, and other comparative techniques.
- Critically evaluate two companies based on financial information and form recommendations.

Refer to the 1996 financial statements and Form 10-K excerpts of the Boston Beer Company and the Lion Brewery Inc. *Note*: both companies received unqualified audit opinions from their auditors.

Analysis

a. Prior to reading the financial statements, review the background information about each company. This information was extracted from each company's Form 10-K. On the basis of these descriptions what differences in the financial statements of the two companies do you expect? That is, as a result of the companies' strategic operating, investing, and financing decisions, how would you expect major financial statement relationships to differ?

b. Prepare common-size balance sheets and income statements for the two companies. Recall that common-size balance sheets scale each line item by total assets and that common-size income statements scale each line item by net sales. What trends do you notice for each firm over time? What comparisons can you make between the two companies? Are the differences you expected in part *a* apparent?

c. Evaluate the profitability of each company. Calculate the return on assets, return on equity, and gross margin percentage for the two companies. Are these key ratios increasing or decreasing for each company? What does this indicate? Do the intercompany differences make sense in light of your knowledge of the companies' strategic choices?

d. Assess the cash flow of each company. Are cash flows from operations a source or a use of cash? How are operations and investments being financed? What differences do you note?

e. Measure how each company is utilizing assets. Calculate key turnover ratios. Compare and contrast the two firms by determining whether they both use their assets efficiently. Are turnovers improving or deteriorating over time? Do the intercompany differences make sense in light of your knowledge of the companies' strategic choices?

f. Evaluate debt utilization and servicing and solvency. Are the companies likely to meet debts as they come due? Is there any "off-balance sheet" financing that will constrain future cash flow?

g. Consider the future prospects of both companies and evaluate the risks they face. Which company demonstrates the most potential to increase its owners' wealth through operations? Why? Are there any unusual or non-recurring items that need to be considered in your analysis? That is, are the earnings of high quality? Are the earnings persistent?

h. As a potential investor, are either of these companies worth seeking further information about? What sort of information would you want?

THE BOSTON BEER COMPANY, INC.
Item 1. Business

General

Boston Beer is the largest craft brewer by volume in the United States. In fiscal 1996, the Company sold 1,213,000 barrels of beer, which it believes to be more than the next five largest craft brewers combined.

The Company's net sales have grown from $29.5 million in 1991 to $191.1 million in fiscal 1996, representing a compounded annual growth rate of 46%. The Company's net sales increased 26% in 1996 from 1995.

In 1996, in addition to its flagship brand, Samuel Adams Boston Lager, the Company brewed seventeen beers under the Boston Beer Company name: Boston Ale, Lightship, Cream Stout, Honey Porter, Scotch Ale, Double Bock, Triple Bock, Octoberfest, Winter Lager, Old Fezziwig, Cherry Wheat, Summer Ale, Cranberry Lambic, Golden Pilsner, and three beers brewed under the LongShot label. The Company also sells beer brewed under the Oregon Original brand name through a separate sales organization and utilizes both separate and shared brewing operations. The Company brews its beer under contract at five breweries located in Pittsburgh, Pennsylvania, Lehigh Valley, Pennsylvania, Portland, Oregon, Rochester, New York, and Cincinnati, Ohio. Effective March 1, 1997, the Company, through an affiliate, Samuel Adams Brewery Company, Ltd., acquired the equipment and other brewery-related personal property of The Schoenling Brewing Company in Cincinnati, Ohio and leased the real estate on which the brewery is located. The Company intends to purchase the real estate of the Cincinnati brewery once certain pre-conditions have been satisfied. ...

Industry Background

The Company is the largest brewer by volume in the craft-brewing/micro-brewing segment of the U.S. brewing industry. The terms craft brewer and micro-brewer are often used interchangeably by consumers and within the industry to mean a small, independent brewer whose predominant product is brewed with only traditional brewing processes and ingredients. Craft brewers include contract brewers, small regional brewers, and brewpubs. Craft beers are full-flavored beers brewed with higher quality hops, malted barley, yeast, and water, and without adjuncts such as rice, corn, or stabilizers, or with water dilution used to lighten beer for mass production and consumption. The Company estimates that in 1996 the craft brew segment accounted for approximately 4.7 million barrels. Over the five- year period ended December 31, 1996, craft beer shipments have grown at a compounded annual rate of approximately 39%, while total U.S. beer industry shipments have remained substantially level.

The primary cause for the rapid growth of craft-brewed beers is consumers' rediscovery of and demand for more traditional, full-flavored beers. Before Prohibition, the U.S. beer industry consisted of hundreds of small breweries that brewed such full-flavored beers. Since the end of Prohibition, U.S. brewers have shifted production to milder, lighter beers, which use lower cost ingredients, and can be mass-produced to take advantage of economies of scale in production and advertising. This shift toward these mass-produced beers has coincided with extreme consolidation in the beer industry. Today, three major brewers control over 75% of all U.S. beer shipments. ...

In response to increased consumer demand for more flavorful beers, the number of craft-brewed beers has increased dramatically. Currently there are more than 500 craft brewers. In addition to the many independent brewers and contract brewers, the three major brewers (Anheuser-Busch, Inc., Miller Brewing Co., and Coors Brewing Co.) have all entered this fast-growing market, either through developing their own specialty beers or by acquiring in whole or part, or forming partnerships with existing craft brewers. It should be noted that in the last four months of 1996, the growth of the craft beer market has slowed materially. This slow down in growth may be accelerating in early 1997.

Business Strategy

The Company's business strategy is to continue to lead the craft-brewed beer market by creating and offering a wide variety of the highest quality full-flavored beers, while increasing sales through new product introductions and substantial trade and consumer awareness programs, supported by a large, well trained and rapidly expanding field sales organization. This strategy is detailed below.

Quality Assurance

The Company employs nine brewmasters and retains a world recognized brewing authority as consulting brewmaster to monitor the Company's contract brewers. Over 125 test, tastings, and evaluations are typically required to ensure that each batch of Samuel Adams conforms to the Company's standards. Its brewing department is supported by a quality control lab at the Company's small brewery in Boston. In order to assure that its customers enjoy only the freshest beer, the Company requires its contract brewers to include a "freshness" date on its bottles of Samuel Adams products. Boston Beer was among the first craft brewers to follow this practice. For Samuel Adams products, the Company uses only higher quality hops grown in Europe and in England.

Product Innovations

The Company is committed to developing new products in order to introduce beer drinkers to different styles of beer and promote the Samuel Adams product line and to remain a leading innovator in the craft beer industry. These new products allow the Samuel Adams drinker to try new styles of beer while remaining loyal to the Samuel Adams brand. New products also help the Company obtain more shelf space in retail stores and increased distributor and retailer focus on Boston Beer products. In 1996, the Company launched a "Homebrew" line of beers, under the LongShot label, based on selected home brewers' recipes. Other beers were developed in 1996 under the Company's joint venture with Joseph E. Seagram & Sons, Inc. ("Seagram"). The Company continues to market its line of Oregon Originals through the Oregon Ale and Beer Company. In 1997, the Company plans to launch a hard cider line of beverage under the trademark, "HardCore".

Contract Brewing

The Company believes that its strategy of contract brewing, which utilizes the excess capacity of other breweries, gives the Company flexibility as well as quality and cost advantages over its competitors. The Company carefully selects breweries with (i) the capability of utilizing traditional brewing methods, and (ii) first rate quality control capabilities throughout brewing, fermentation, finishing, and packaging. By using the current excess capacity at other breweries, the Company has avoided potential start up problems of bringing a new brewery on line. Furthermore, by brewing in multiple locations, the Company can reduce its distribution costs and deliver fresher beer to its customers than other craft brewers with broad distribution from a single brewery. While the Company currently plans to continue its contract-brewing strategy, it has, as discussed above, acquired an existing brewery in Cincinnati and will also regularly evaluate the economic and quality issues involved with acquiring other breweries, as well as continuing with its contract brewing arrangements. It should be noted that the acquisition of the assets of the Cincinnati brewery and the subsequent ownership of the brewery assets will cause an erosion of the Company's consolidated gross profit margin and that on a line of business basis, the Cincinnati operation is expected to show a loss.

The Company currently has contracts with five brewers, one of whom is an affiliate of the Company, to produce its Samuel Adams lines of beers in the U.S., each of which is described in greater detail below. The Company believes that its current contract brewers have capacity, to which the Company has access, to brew annually approximately one and one half times as much of the Company's beer as the Company sold during 1996.

The Company continues to brew its Samuel Adams Boston Lager at each of its contract brewers but does not brew each of its other products at each contract brewer. Therefore, at any particular time, the Company may be relying on only one supplier for its products other than Samuel Adams Boston Lager. …

Strong Sales and Distribution Presence

Boston Beer sells its products through a dynamic sales force, which the Company believes is the largest of any craft brewer and one of the largest in the domestic beer industry. The Company sells its beer through wholesale distributors, which then sell to retailers such as pubs, restaurants, grocery chains, package stores, and other retail outlets. The Company's sales force has a high level of product knowledge, and is trained in the details of the brewing process. Its sales force receives selling skills training each year from outside training experts. Sales representatives typically carry hops, barley, and other samples to educate wholesale and retail buyers as to the quality and taste of its beers. The Company has developed strong relationships with its distributors and retailers, many of which have benefited from the Company's premium pricing strategy and rapid growth.

Advertising and Promotion

The Company has historically invested in advertising and promotion. The Company uses radio advertising as well as outdoor advertising and, opportunistically, print media. In the second half of 1996, the Company began testing its television advertising campaign, which is now being evaluated. The Company works closely with its distributors and customers to develop and implement innovative promotions designed to increase consumer awareness and sales. Its on-premise promotions, where legal, include beer tastings and extensive use of user-friendly menu cards. Off-premise promotions include incentive contests, periodic discounts to retailers and other programs which often combine consumer, distributor, and retailer elements.

Products

The Company's product strategy is to create and offer a world class variety of traditional beers and to promote the Samuel Adams product line. At the end of 1996, the Company marketed twelve year-round and 6 seasonal beers under the Samuel Adams and LongShot brand names. … The Company's Samuel Adams Boston Lager has historically accounted for the majority of the Company's sales. …

The Company uses its Boston brewery to develop new types of innovative and traditional beers and to supply draft beer for the local market. Product development entails researching market needs and competitive products, sample brewing, and market taste testing.

In 1994, the Company formed the Oregon Ale and Beer Company ("Oregon Ale and Beer") to develop and market Pacific Northwest style beers. Oregon Ale and Beer markets its beers under the Oregon Original brand through a sales force separate from that which sells Samuel Adams' styles. Oregon Original ales have been brewed in Oregon at two breweries, one in Lake Oswego and the other in Portland.

On March 19, 1996, the Company entered into an Agreement with Seagram, pursuant to which Seagram sells a line of beers developed jointly by it, the Company and a third party craft brewer, under the "Devil Mountain" name. As of December 28, 1996, the Company had spent approximately $1,435,000 with respect to this venture. The Company expects to spend up to an additional $750,000, principally to cover marketing expenses to aid the introduction of these new beers and will, in return, receive royalties commencing on the second anniversary following the date of the first shipment of such products by Seagram. The Company will also provide certain technical assistance. The agreement also sets forth the circumstances in which the relationship can be terminated and the terms on which rights to the product line will revert to the Company or may be acquired by the Company.

Ingredients and Packaging

The Company has been successful to date in obtaining sufficient quantities of the ingredients used in the production of its beers. These ingredients include:

Malt. The Company currently directs the purchase of the malt used in the production of its beer to three suppliers, although it enters into discussions from time to time with other vendors. The two-row varieties of barley used in the Company's malt are grown in the U.S. and Canada.

Hops. The Company currently buys principally Noble hops for its Samuel Adams beers. Noble hops are varieties from specific growing areas usually recognized for superior taste and aroma properties and include Hallertau-Hallertauer, Tettnang-Hallertauer, Tettnang-Tett-nauer, and Spolt-Spolter from Germany, and Bohemian Saaz from the Czech Republic. Noble hops are rarer and more expensive than other varieties of hops. Traditional English hops, East Kent Goldings and English Fuggles, are used in the Company's ales. The Company has yet to find alternative hops which duplicate the flavor and aroma of the Noble hops and traditional English ale hops. As a result, the Company must purchase sufficient quantities of these Noble hops to continue to increase production. The Company has been working with its Bavarian hops dealers to increase acreage of the Hallertau-Hallertauer varieties of hops. The Company stores its hops in multiple cold storage warehouses to minimize the impact of a catastrophe at a single site.

The Company purchases its hops from hops dealers, the largest of which (Joh. Barth & Son) has over the past five years accounted for between 30% and 61% of the hops purchased each year by the Company. The Company generally enters into forward contracts to ensure its supply of a portion of its requirements for up to five years.

The Company's hops contracts are denominated in German marks or English pounds, depending on the location of the supplier. Prior to late 1996, the Company has, as a practice, not hedged the foreign currency risk associated with these contracts. Through that date, the Company's gains and losses from exchange rate volatility have not been material. Beginning in late 1996, the Company began to hedge some of its currency risks.

Yeast. The Company maintains a supply of proprietary strains of yeast that it supplies to its contract brewers. Since these yeasts would be impossible to duplicate if destroyed, the Company maintains supplies in several locations. In addition, the Company's contract brewers maintain a supply of these yeasts that are reclaimed from the batches of beer brewed. The contract brewers are obligated by their brewing contracts only to use these yeasts to brew the Company's beers and the Company's yeasts cannot be used without the Company's approval to brew any other beers produced at the respective breweries.

Packaging Materials. The Company maintains multiple competitive sources of supply of packaging materials, such as bottles and shipping cases. Other packaging materials, such as labels, crowns and six-pack carriers are currently supplied by single sources, although the Company believes that alternative suppliers of these materials are available. In those instances where the Company can negotiate preferential pricing, the Company enters into limited term supply agreements with these vendors. These materials are supplied to or resold to contract brewers depending on the arrangement.

To date, the Company has not experienced material difficulties in obtaining timely delivery from its suppliers. Although the Company believes there are alternate sources available for the ingredients and packaging materials described above, there can be no assurance that the Company would be able to acquire such ingredients or packaging materials from other sources on a timely or cost effective basis in the event current suppliers were unable to supply them on a timely basis. The loss of a supplier could, in the short-term, adversely affect the Company's business until alternative supply arrangements were secured.

Sales and Marketing

The Company's products are sold to independent distributors by a large field sales. With few exceptions, the Company's products are not the primary brands in the distributor's portfolio. Thus, the Company, in addition to competing with other beers for a share of the consumer's business, competes with other beers for a share of the distributor's attention, time, and selling efforts. The Company considers its distributors its primary customers and is focused on the relationship it has with its distributors.

In addition to this distributor focus, the Company has set up its sales organization to include on-premise and retail account specialists. This is designed to develop and strengthen relations at the chain headquarter level, and to provide educational and promotional programs aimed at distributors, retailers, and consumers, in each channel of distribution.

The Company has also historically engaged in extensive media campaigns, primarily radio. In addition, its sales force complements these efforts by engaging in sponsorships of cultural and community events, local beer festivals, industry-related trade shows, and promotional events at local establishments for sampling and awareness. All of these efforts are designed to stimulate consumer demand by educating consumers, retailers, and distributors, on the qualities of beer. The Company uses a wide array of point-of-sale items (banners, neons, umbrellas, glassware, display pieces, signs, menu stands, etc.) designed to stimulate impulse sales and continued awareness. It should be noted that this rate of increase in sales versus prior periods is slowing for the Company as well as for the market.

Distribution

The Company distributes its beers in every state in the U.S., as well as the District of Columbia and Puerto Rico. The Company distributes its beer through a network of over 400 distributors. During 1996, the Company's two largest distributors each accounted for approximately 6% of the Company's net sales. No other distributors accounted for more than 3% of the Company's net sales during 1996. In some states, the terms of the Company's contracts with its distributors may be affected by laws that restrict enforceability of some contract terms, especially those related to the Company's right to terminate the services of its distributors.

The Company also distributes its beers to Canada, Sweden, Germany, Hong Kong and the United Kingdom, along with select Caribbean islands. Exports, however, represented less than 1% of 1996 revenues.

The Company typically receives orders by the tenth of a month with respect to products to be shipped the following month. Products are shipped within days of completion and, accordingly, there has historically not been any significant product order backlog.

Competition

The craft-brewed and high-end segments of the U.S. beer market are highly competitive due to continuing product proliferation from craft brewers and the recent introduction of specialty beers by national brewers. Recent growth in the sales of craft-brewed beers has increased competition and, as a result, the Company's growth rate compared to the preceding years is declining. The Company's products also compete generally with other alcoholic beverages, including other segments of the beer industry and low alcohol products. The Company competes with other beer and beverage companies not only for consumer acceptance and loyalty but also for shelf and tap space in retail establishments and for marketing focus by the Company's distributors and their customers, all of which also distribute and sell other beers and alcoholic beverage products. The principal methods of competition in the craft-brewed segment of the beer industry include product quality and taste, brand advertising, trade and consumer promotions, pricing, packaging, and the development of new products. The competitive position of the Company is enhanced by its uncompromising product quality, its development of new beer styles, innovative point of sale materials, a large motivated sales force, tactical introduction of seasonal beers and pricing strategies generating above-average profits to distributors and retailers.

The Company expects competition with craft brewers to increase as new craft brewers emerge and existing craft brewers expand their capacity and distribution. While some of the smaller micro-brewers and craft brewers have already left the marketplace due to the intense competition in the marketplace which they were unable to withstand with their oftentimes limited resources, new entrants into the market continue and competition, overall, is high. In addition, large brewers have developed or are developing niche brands and are acquiring small brewers to compete in the craft-brewed segment of the domestic beer market. These competitors may have substantially greater financial resources, marketing strength, and distribution networks than the Company.

The Company competes directly with regional specialty brewers such as Sierra Nevada Brewing Company, Pyramid Brewing Company, Anchor Brewing Company, other contract brewers such as Pete's Brewing Company, Massachusetts Bay Brewing, foreign brewers such as Heineken, Molson, Corona, Amstel, and Becks, and other regional craft brewers and brewpubs. Niche beers produced by affiliates of certain major domestic brewers such as Anheuser-Busch, Incorporated, Miller Brewing Co., and Coors Brewing Co., also compete with the Company's products.

The Company believes that with the bulk of its production of beers being produced as a contract brewer, it has competitive advantages over the regional craft brewers because of its higher quality, greater flexibility, and lower initial capital costs. Its use of contract brewing frees up capital for other uses and allows the Company to brew its beer closer to major markets around the country, providing fresher beer to customers and affording lower transportation costs. The Company's recent purchase of a brewery in Cincinnati where it previously contract-brewed its beers, will continue to provide certain logistical advantages while at the same time providing the Company with added flexibility of production through its ownership which complements its strategy of contract brewing. The Company also believes that its products enjoy competitive advantages over foreign beers, including lower transportation costs, no import charges, and superior product freshness. ...

Taxation

The federal government and each of the states levy excise taxes on alcoholic beverages, including beer. For brewers producing no more than 2,000,000 barrels of beer per calendar year, the federal excise tax is $7.00 per barrel on the first 60,000 barrels of beer removed for consumption or sale during a calendar year, and $18.00 per barrel for each barrel in excess of 60,000. For brewers producing more than 2,000,000 barrels of beer in a calendar year, the federal excise tax is $18.00 per barrel. As the brewer of record of its beers, the Company has been able to take advantage of this reduced tax on the first 60,000 barrels of its beers produced. Individual states also impose excise taxes on alcoholic beverages in varying amounts, which have also been subject to change. The state excise taxes are usually paid by the Company's distributors. ...

Trademarks

The Company has obtained U.S Trademark Registrations for the marks Samuel Adams Boston Lager (as well as for its design logo), Boston Ale, Lightship, Winter Lager, and other marks. The Samuel Adams Boston Lager mark and other Company marks are also registered or pending in various foreign countries. The Company regards its Samuel Adams Boston Lager and other trademarks as having substantial value and as being an important factor in the marketing of its products. The Company is not aware of any infringing uses that could materially affect its current business or any prior claim to the trademarks that would prevent the Company from using such trademarks in its business. The Company's policy is to pursue registration of its marks whenever possible and to oppose vigorously any infringements of its marks.

The Company occasionally makes available its trademarks to independent on-premise retailers of its products.

In 1996, the Company entered into a license arrangement with Whitbread PLC, the fourth largest brewery in the United Kingdom, pursuant to which a new hybrid brew was developed and marketed under the trademark, "Boston Beer". The recipe was developed by Whitbread Beer Company, a subsidiary of Whitbread PLC, with assistance from Boston Beer Company's brewers. The Company owns the trademarks for the new product and has granted Whitbread an exclusive license to use that trademark in Great Britain and Ireland. Boston Beer Company receives a royalty from the sale of this new beer.

On March 19, 1996, the Company entered into a Trademark License and Technical Assistance Agreement with Joseph E. Seagram & Sons, Inc. ("Seagram"), pursuant to which the Company licensed the "Devil Mountain" trademarks for use by Seagram on beers which Seagram developed, with technical assistance from the Company. The Agreement provides for stated royalties to commence on the second anniversary following the date of the first shipment of such products by Seagram.

In addition, the Company has licensed its trademark, "Samuel Adams Brew House" to certain entities for purposes of establishing Samuel Adams Brew Houses at airport locations and elsewhere. The Company does not receive a royalty pursuant to these license arrangements. ...

Employees

The Company employs approximately 350 employees. None of the Company's employees is represented by a labor union, except for 75 of those employees employed at the Company's newly-acquired brewery in Cincinnati, Ohio. The Schoenling Brewing Company, from whom the Company acquired certain brewery assets in Cincinnati, and from whom the Company hired those employees represented by labor unions, has enjoyed a good relationship with those labor unions. The Company has no reason to believe that a good working relationship with those labor unions will not continue. The Company has experienced no work stoppages and believes that its employee relations are good.

THE BOSTON BEER COMPANY, INC.
SELECTED FINANCIAL DATA

	Year Ended					
	Dec. 28 1996	Dec. 31 1995	Dec. 31 1994	Dec. 31 1993	Dec. 31 1992	Dec. 31 1991

(in thousands, except per share, per barrel and employee data)

Income Statement Data:

	Dec. 28 1996	Dec. 31 1995	Dec. 31 1994	Dec. 31 1993	Dec. 31 1992	Dec. 31 1991
Sales	$213,879	$169,362	$128,077	$85,758	$53,343	$32,302
Less excise taxes	22,763	18,049	13,244	8,607	5,165	2,845
Net sales	191,116	151,313	114,833	77,151	48,178	29,457
Cost of Sales	95,786	73,847	52,851	35,481	22,028	13,039
Gross Profit	95,330	77,466	61,982	41,670	26,150	16,418
Advertising, promotional, and selling expenses	70,131	60,461	46,503	32,669	21,075	12,105
General and administrative	12,042	7,585	6,593	4,105	3,306	2,247
Total operating expenses	82,173	68,046	53,096	36,774	24,381	14,352
Operating income	13,157	9,420	8,886	4,896	1,769	2,066
Other income (expense), net	1,714	959	199	(2)	(124)	23
Income before income taxes	14,871	10,379	9,085	4,894	1,645	2,089
Provision (benefit) for income taxes *	6,486	(2,195)	—	—	—	—
Net income	$8,385	$12,574	$9,085	$4,894	$1,645	$2,089
Income before income taxes		$10,379	$9,085	$4,894	$1,645	$2,089
Pro forma income taxes (unaudited) **	—	4,483	3,765	2,040	691	859
Pro forma net income (unaudited) **		$5,896	$5,320	$2,854	$954	$1,230
Earnings per share	$0.41					
Pro forma earnings per share (unaudited) **		$0.33	$.29			
Weighted average shares outstanding ***	20,296	17,949	18,171			
Statistical Data:						
Barrels sold	1,213	961	714	475	294	174
Net sales per barrel	$158	$158	$161	$162	$164	$169
Employees	253	196	138	110	87	69
Net sales per employee	$755	$772	$832	$701	$554	$427

Balance Sheet Data at period end:

Working capital	$47,769	$45,266	$3,996	$8,173	$6,169	$6,053
Total assets	$96,553	$76,690	$31,776	$24,054	$15,780	$11,981
Total long term debt	$1,800	$1,875	$1,950	$2,000	$2,050	$2,100
Total partners/ stockholders' equity	$64,831	$54,798	$6,600	$8,854	$6,434	$5,954
Dividends	—	—	—	—	—	—

* In 1995, the Company recorded a one-time tax benefit of $1,960,000 upon change in tax status of the entity, and a tax benefit of $235,000 for the period November 21, 1995 to December 31, 1995.
** Reflects pro forma provisions for income taxes using statutory federal and state corporate income tax rates that would have been applied had the Company been required to file income tax returns during the indicated period. See Note B of notes to the consolidated financial statements.
*** Reflects weighted average number of common and common equivalent shares of the Class A and Class B Common Stock assumed to be outstanding during the respective periods. For the years ended December 31, 1995 and December 31, 1994, shares reflect pro forma weighted average numbers. See Note B of notes to the consolidated financial statements.

THE BOSTON BEER COMPANY, INC.

CONSOLIDATED BALANCE SHEETS
(in thousands, except share data)

	December 28, 1996	December 31, 1995
Assets		
Current Assets:		
Cash & cash equivalents	$ 5,060	$ 1,877
Short term investments	35,926	34,730
Accounts receivable	18,109	16,265
Allowance for doubtful accounts	(1,930)	(175)
Inventories	13,002	9,280
Prepaid expenses	674	437
Deferred income taxes	2,968	1,011
Other current assets	3,882	1,858
Total current assets	77,691	65,283
Restricted investments	611	602
Equipment and leasehold improvements, at cost	21,043	9,690
Accumulated depreciation	(6,412)	(3,531)
Deferred income taxes	151	1,777
Other assets	3,469	2,869
Total assets	$ 96,553	$ 76,690
Liabilities and Stockholders' Equity		
Current Liabilities:		
Accounts payable	$ 17,783	$ 9,793
Accrued expenses	12,064	10,149
Current maturities of long-term debt	75	75
Total current liabilities	29,922	20,017
Long-term debt, less current maturities	1,800	1,875
Commitments and Contingencies (Note I)	—	—
Stockholders' Equity:		
Class A Common Stock, $.01 par value; 20,300,000 shares authorized; 15,972,058, and 15,643,664 issued and outstanding as of December 28, 1996 and December 31, 1995, respectively	160	156
Class B Common Stock, $.01 par value; 4,200,000 shares authorized; 4,107,355 issued and outstanding as of December 28, 1996 and December 31, 1995, respectively	41	41
Additional paid-in-capital	55,391	53,482
Unearned compensation	(363)	(509)
Unrealized loss on investments in marketable securities	(442)	—
Unrealized gain on forward exchange contract	31	—
Retained earnings	10,013	1,628
Total stockholders' equity	64,831	54,798
Total liabilities and stockholders' equity	$ 96,553	$ 76,690

The accompanying notes are an integral part of the financial statements.

THE BOSTON BEER COMPANY, INC.

CONSOLIDATED STATEMENTS OF INCOME

(in thousands, except per share data)

	For the Years Ended		
	December 28, 1996	December 31, 1995	December 31, 1994
Sales	$ 213,879	$ 169,362	$ 128,077
Less excise taxes	22,763	18,049	13,244
Net sales	191,116	151,313	114,833
Cost of sales	95,786	73,847	52,851
Gross profit	95,330	77,466	61,982
Operating expenses:			
Advertising, promotional and selling expenses	70,131	60,461	46,503
General and administrative expenses	12,042	7,585	6,593
Total operating expenses	82,173	68,046	53,096
Operating income	13,157	9,420	8,886
Other income (expense):			
Interest income	1,932	452	429
Interest expense	(236)	(250)	(233)
Other income, net	18	757	3
Total other income	1,714	959	199
Income before income taxes	14,871	10,379	9,085
Provision (benefit) for income taxes	6,486	(2,195)	—
Net income	$ 8,385	$ 12,574	$ 9,085
Pro forma data (unaudited) (Note B):			
Income before pro forma income taxes		10,379	9,085
Pro forma income tax expense		4,483	3,765
Pro forma net income		$ 5,896	$ 5,320
Net income per common and common equivalent share	$ 0.41	$ 0.33 *	$ 0.29 *
Weighted average number of common and common equivalent shares	20,352	17,949 *	18,171 *

*   Pro forma, see Note B.

The accompanying notes are an integral part of the financial statements.

THE BOSTON BEER COMPANY, INC.

CONSOLIDATED STATEMENTS OF CASH FLOWS

(in thousands)

	For the Years Ended		
	December 28, 1996	December 31, 1995	December 31, 1994
Cash flows from operating activities:			
Net income	$ 8,385	$ 12,574 *	$ 9,085 *
Adjustments to reconcile net income to net cash provided by operating activities:			
Depreciation and amortization	3,030	1,565	925
(Gain) loss on disposal of fixed asset	(4)	38	21
Bad debt expense	1,832	(557)	391
Stock option compensation expense	186	250	280
Changes in assets & liabilities:			
Accounts receivable	(1,921)	(5,473)	(2,339)
Inventory	(3,722)	(1,525)	(4,049)
Prepaids expense	(237)	64	(285)
Other current assets	(1,993)	(753)	(593)
Deferred taxes	(331)	(2,195)	—
Other assets	(743)	(2,459)	(172)
Accounts payable	7,990	(494)	6,353
Accrued expenses	3,291	1,405	3,673
Total adjustments	7,378	(10,134)	4,205
Net cash provided by operating activities:	15,763	2,440	13,290
Cash flows for investing activities:			
Purchases of fixed assets	(11,359)	(4,268)	(2,621)
Proceeds on disposal of fixed assets	4	45	—
(Purchases) maturities of government securities	2,648	(27,027)	(2,624)
Purchase of marketable securities	(4,286)	—	—
Purchase of restricted investments	(1,225)	(612)	(1,171)
Maturities of restricted investments	1,216	615	1,145
Net cash used in investing	(13,002)	(31,247)	(5,271)
Cash flows from financing activities:			
Proceeds from issuance of common stock	—	49,691	—
Proceeds from exercise of stock option plans	560	—	—
Proceeds from sale under stock purchase plan	40	—	—
Repurchase of shares under employee investment and incentive share plans	(103)	—	—
Principal payments on long-term debt	(75)	(50)	(50)
Partners' distributions	—	(19,055)	(11,619)
Net cash provided by (used for) financing activities	422	30,586	11,669
Net increase (decrease) in cash and cash equivalents	3,183	1,779	(3,650)
Cash and cash equivalents at beginning of period	1,877	98	3,748
Cash and cash equivalents at end of period	$ 5,060	$ 1,877	$ 98
Supplemental disclosure of cash flow information:			
Interest paid	$ 224	$ 252	$ 236
Taxes paid	$ 5,992	—	—

*   Net income for the fiscal year ended December 31, 1995 is before pro forma income taxes. See Note B.

The accompanying notes are an integral part of the financial statements.

THE BOSTON BEER COMPANY, INC.
NOTES TO THE CONSOLIDATED FINANCIAL STATEMENTS

A. Basis of Presentation:

The Boston Beer Company, Inc. (the "Company"), is engaged in the business of marketing and selling beer and ale products throughout the United States and in select international markets. On November 20, 1995, in connection with the initial public offering of the Company's stock effected that date, the non-corporate limited partners transferred their respective partnership interests to the Company and the owners of the general partner and corporate limited partners transferred their respective ownership interests in such entities to the Company. In exchange, the transferors received an aggregate of 16,641,740 shares of the Company's common stock on a pro rata basis, based on their then respective percentage equity interests in the Partnership. The aforementioned transactions are collectively referred to hereinafter as the "Recapitalization."

B. Summary of Significant Accounting Policies:

Fiscal Year
Effective in fiscal 1996, the Company changed its fiscal year to end on the last Saturday in December. The impact on the current year of two fewer days of operations was not material.

Principles of Consolidation
The consolidated financial statements include the accounts of the Company, its subsidiaries, and the Partnership. All intercompany accounts and transactions have been eliminated.

Revenue Recognition
Revenue is recognized when goods are shipped to customers. Accounts receivable balances are reflected net of an allowance for uncollectible accounts of approximately $1,930,000 and $175,000 at December 28, 1996 and December 31, 1995, respectively.

Cash and Cash Equivalents
Cash and cash equivalents include cash in hand and short-term, highly liquid investments with original maturities of three months or less at the time of purchase.

Short Term Investments and Restricted Investments
Short term investments consist primarily of U.S. Government securities and marketable equity securities with original maturities beyond three months and less than twelve months. All short term investments have been classified as available-for-sale and are reported at fair value with unrealized gains and losses included in stockholders' equity. Fair value is based on quoted market prices as of December 28, 1996.

Restricted investments consist solely of the unexpended proceeds from the debt as discussed in Note G. These investments, consisting of treasury notes which mature within one year, are expected to be held to maturity and accordingly are valued at amortized cost, which approximates fair value.

Inventories
Inventories, which consist principally of hops, bottles, and packaging, are stated at the lower of cost, determined on a first-in, first-out (FIFO) basis, or market.

Use of Estimates
The preparation of the financial statements in conformity with generally accepted accounting principles requires management to make estimates and assumptions that affected the reported amounts of assets and liabilities at the date of the financial statements and the reported amounts of revenue and expenses during the reporting period. Actual results could differ from those estimates.

Concentrations of Credit Risk
Financial instruments which potentially subject the Company to concentrations of credit risk consist principally of temporary cash, short-term investments, and trade receivables. The Company places its temporary cash and short-term investments with high credit quality

financial institutions. The Company sells primarily to independent beer and ale distributors across the United States. Receivables arising from these sales are not collateralized; however, credit risk is minimized as a result of the large and diverse nature of the Company's customer base. The Company establishes an allowance for doubtful accounts based upon factors surrounding the credit risk of specific customers, historical trends, and other information.

Equipment and Leasehold Improvements

Equipment and leasehold improvements are recorded at cost. Expenditures for maintenance, repairs, and renewals are charged to expense; major improvements are capitalized. Upon retirement or sale, the cost of the assets disposed of and the related accumulated depreciation are removed from the accounts and any resulting gain or loss is included in the determination of net income. Provision for depreciation is computed on the straight-line method based upon the estimated useful lives of the underlying assets as follows:

Kegs and equipment	3 to 10 years
Office equipment and furniture	3 to 5 years
Leasehold improvements	5 years, or the life of the lease, whichever is shorter

Deposits

The Company recognizes a liability for estimated refundable deposits in kegs and for unclaimed deposits on bottles which are subject to state regulations. A liability for refundable deposits (redemptions) on reusable bottles in 1995 was not recorded, nor was there an offsetting adjustment to inventory. As of December 28, 1996, the Company recorded an estimated liability of $587,000, with an offsetting adjustment to cost of goods sold for re-used glass which had not been redeemed as of the end of the year. The Company recorded this liability to recognize that the re-used glass may not be placed back into production in the future. Total redemptions associated with reusable bottles during the years ended December 28, 1996, December 31, 1995, and 1994 were $3,053,000, $1,441,000, and $1,402,000 respectively.

Fair Value of Financial Instruments

The carrying amount of the Company's long term debt, including current maturities, approximates fair value because the interest rates on these instruments change with market interest rates. The carrying amounts for accounts receivable and accounts payable approximate their fair values due to the short term maturity of these instruments.

Advertising and Sales Promotions

Advertising and sales promotional programs are charged to expense during the period in which they are incurred. Total advertising and sales promotional expense for the years ended December 28, 1996, December 31, 1995, and 1994, were $35,730,000, $35,039,000, and $27,598,000 respectively.

Purchase Commitments

The Company recognizes losses on hops purchase commitments when amounts from the sale price of the related product are expected to be less than the cost of the product. The Company has not historically experienced any losses related to hops purchase commitments.

Forward Exchange Contracts

Unrealized gains and losses on contracts designated as hedges of existing assets and liabilities are accrued as exchange rates change and are recorded as a component of Stockholders' Equity. Realized gains and losses are recognized in income as contracts expire.

Stock-Based Compensation

Statement of Financial Accounting Standards No. 123 "Accounting for Stock-Based Compensation" ("SFAS 123"), requires the Company to either elect expense recognition or the disclosure-only alternative for stock-based employee compensation. SFAS 123 has been adopted in the Company's 1996 financial statements with comparable disclosures for the prior year. The Company has reviewed the adoption and impact of SFAS 123, and has elected to adopt the disclosure-only alternative and accordingly this standard has no impact on the Company's results of operations or its financial position.

Income Taxes

The Company records income taxes under the liability method whereby deferred tax assets and liabilities are determined based on differences between financial reporting and tax bases of assets and liabilities, and are measured by applying enacted tax rates for the taxable years in which those differences are expected to reverse.

Pro Forma Income Taxes (unaudited)

The financial statements of the Company for the periods prior to the Recapitalization do not include a provision for income taxes because the taxable income of the Company, up until the effective date of the Recapitalization, is included in the income tax returns of the Partnership's partners and former Subchapter S corporation's shareholder. The statements of income include a pro forma income tax provision on taxable income for financial statement purposes using an estimated effective federal and state income tax rate which would have resulted if the Partnership and Subchapter S corporation had filed a corporate income tax return during those periods.

Earnings Per Share

Earnings per share is based on the weighted average number of shares outstanding during the period after consideration of the dilutive effect, if any, for stock options. Fully diluted net income per share has not been presented as the amount would not differ significantly from those presented.

Pro Forma Earnings Per Share (unaudited)

Pro forma earnings per share is based on the weighted average number of common and common equivalent shares outstanding during the respective periods (assuming a conversion of partnership units for the periods prior to the Recapitalization), and an additional 3,109,279 shares issued during November 1995 in connection with the Company's initial public offering. In addition, pursuant to the rules of the Securities and Exchange Commission, approximately 273,000 shares and 965,000 shares in 1995 and 1994, respectively, have been included in the share calculation representing distributions in excess of net income and, in 1994, distributions expected to be funded by debt repaid with the proceeds from the offering. The calculations include 686,000 and 564,000 common equivalent shares for the years ended December 31, 1995 and 1994, respectively, using the treasury stock method. Fully diluted earnings per share is not materially different from primary earnings per share.

New Accounting Pronouncements

In February, 1997, the Financial Accounting Standards Board issued Statement of Financial Accounting Standards No. 128, "Earnings Per Share" (SFAS 128), which is effective for fiscal years that end after December 15, 1997, including interim periods. Earlier application is not permitted. However, an entity is permitted to disclose pro forma earnings per share amounts computed using SFAS 128 in the notes to financial statements in periods prior to adoption. The Statement requires restatement of all prior-period earnings per share data presented after the effective date. SFAS 128 specifies the computation, presentation, and disclosure requirements for earnings per share and is substantially similar to the standard recently issued by the International Accounting Standards Committee entitled International Accounting Standards, "Earnings Per Share" (IAS 33). The Company plans to adopt SFAS 128 in 1997 and has not yet determined the impact.

Reclassifications

Beginning in 1996, certain expenses which were previously classified as general and administrative expenses were reclassified as advertising, promotional, and selling expenses. All financial information has been restated to conform with this year's presentation. Certain other prior year amounts have also been reclassified to conform with the current year's presentation.

C.   Short Term Investments:

Short term investments consist of marketable equity securities having a cost of $4,286,000 and a market value of $3,844,000, which resulted in an unrealized loss of $442,000 at December 28, 1996. The Company did not have any investments in marketable equity securities as of December 31, 1995. In addition, the Company has investments in U.S. Government securities having a cost of $32,082,000 and $34,730,000 at December 28, 1996 and December 31, 1995, respectively, which approximates fair value.

D.   Inventories:

	December 28, 1996	December 31, 1995
	(in thousands)	
Raw material, principally hops	$ 12,677	$ 8,543
Work in process	—	518
Finished goods	325	219
	$ 13,002	$ 9,280

E.   Equipment and Leasehold Improvements:

	December 28, 1996	December 31, 1995
	(in thousands)	
Kegs and equipment	$ 16,457	$ 7,012
Office equipment and furniture	3,527	1,623
Leasehold improvements	1,059	1,055
	$ 21,043	$ 9,690
Less accumulated depreciation	6,412	3,531
	$ 14,631	$ 6,159

The Company recorded depreciation expense related to these assets of $2,886,000, $1,565,000, and $925,000 for the years ended December 28, 1996, December 31, 1995, and December 31, 1994, respectively.

F.   Accrued Expenses:

	December 28, 1996	December 31, 1995
	(in thousands)	
Advertising	$ 4,019	$ 4,451
Keg deposits	1,813	1,276
Employee wages and reimbursements	1,906	1,586
Point of sale related accruals	1,288	1,000
Other accrued liabilities	3,038	1,836
	$ 12,064	$ 10,149

For the year ended December 28, 1996, the Company included $1,117,000 of accrued freight costs in accounts payable. For the year ended December 31, 1995, $1,189,000 of freight costs previously recognized as a component of accrued expenses were reclassified to accounts payable.

G.   Long-Term Debt and Line of Credit:

Long-Term Debt
During 1988, the Company entered into a $2,200,000 loan with the Massachusetts Industrial Finance Authority ("MIFA"), which matures July 15, 2007. As of December 28, 1996, the loan requires scheduled annual principal payments as follows:

	(in thousands)
1997	$ 75
1998	75
1999	100
2000	100
2001	100
Thereafter	1,425
	1,875
Less: current portion	75
Total long-term debt	$ 1,800

Interest accrues at 11.5 % and is paid semiannually. The proceeds from the MIFA loan were used to fund approximately $1,500,000 of engineering and design efforts, which were subsequently abandoned in 1989, and to acquire approximately $200,000 of various assets for the brewery. The unexpended proceeds referenced in Note B were restricted to the further development of the Company's Boston brewery, a leased facility. All assets acquired with the proceeds of the loan are reflected as equipment or leasehold improvements. The loan is collateralized by the related fixed assets and any unexpended proceeds which approximated, including interest, $611,000 and $602,000 at December 28, 1996 and December 31, 1995, respectively.

The loan agreement contains various covenants, the most restrictive of which is that the Company's equity may not be less than $700,000 as of the end of each fiscal year, and the debt to equity ratio of the Company may not exceed 4 to 1 at the end of any fiscal year. As of December 28, 1996, the Company's equity was $65,000,000 and the debt to equity ratio was .03 to 1.

Line of Credit

On May 2, 1995, the Company entered into an unsecured Revolving Line of Credit Agreement (the "Agreement") with a bank providing for borrowings of up to $14,000,000 at either the bank's prime rate (8.25% at December 28, 1996) or the applicable Libor Rate plus .50% for terms of 30, 60, or 90 days. The Company pays a commitment fee of .15% of the unused portion of the line. The Agreement, which expires on May 1, 1997, requires the Company to maintain certain financial ratios related to tangible net worth, interest coverage, and profits, and restricts the Company's ability to incur additional indebtedness, incur certain liens and encumbrances, make investments in other persons, engage in a new business, or enter into sale and leaseback transactions. The Agreement also contains certain events of default, including the failure of the Company's president to control and be actively engaged on a full-time basis in the business of the Company. As of December 28, 1996 and December 31, 1995, no borrowings were outstanding thereunder.

H.   Income Taxes:

Income Taxes

Effective with the Recapitalization described in Note A, the Company became subject to federal and state income taxes. The historical income tax benefit reflects the recording of a one-time tax benefit of $1,960,000 upon the change in tax status of the entity as required by SFAS 109, and a tax benefit of $235,000 for the period from November 21 to December 31, 1995.

Significant components of the Company's deferred tax assets and liabilities as of December 28, 1996 and December 31, 1995 are as follows:

| | | 1996 | | | | 1995 | |
	Current	Long-Term	Total	Current	Long-Term	Total
Deferred Tax Assets:						
Incentive/investment unit and option plans	$ 11	$ 1,052	$ 1,063	$ 21	$ 1,856	$1,877
Accrued expenses not currently deductible	943	—	943	467	—	467
Reserves	1,828	—	1,828	88	—	88
Deferred Compensation	—	90	90	—	65	65
Net operating loss	—	—	—	334	—	334
Other	250	(2)	248	101	—	101
Total deferred tax assets	3,032	1,140	4,172	1,011	1,921	2,932
Deferred tax liabilities:						
Depreciation	—	(814)	(814)	—	(144)	(144)
Tax installment sale	(64)	(175)	(239)	—	—	—
Net deferred tax assets	$2,968	$ 151	$3,119	$1,011	$ 1,777	$2,788

The deferred tax asset balance at December 31, 1995 includes a $593,000 net deferred tax asset of the corporate limited partners recorded upon the Recapitalization.

Based upon prior earnings history and expected future taxable income, the Company does not believe that a valuation allowance is required for the net deferred tax asset.

Significant components of the income tax provision (benefit) for income taxes for the years ended December 28, 1996 and December 31, 1995 are as follows:

| | (in thousands) | |
	1996	1995
Current:		
Federal	$ 5,261	—
State	1,556	—
Total current	6,817	—
Deferred:		
Federal	(251)	$ (1,667)
State	(80)	(528)
Total deferred	$ (331)	$ (2,195)
Total income tax expense (benefit)	$ 6,486	$ (2,195)

The reconciliation of income tax computed at statutory rates to actual income tax expense for the years ended December 28, 1996 and December 31, 1995, are as follows:

	1996	1995
Statutory rate	35.0%	35.0%
State income tax, net of federal benefit	6.5	(1.8)
Permanent differences	1.2	0.3
Income for the period prior to the Recapitalization not subject to tax	—	(36.9)
Deferred tax asset resulting from change in tax status	—	(15.9)
Other	0.9	(1.8)
	43.6%	(21.1%)

At December 31, 1995, the Company had a tax net operating loss carryforward of approximately $765,000, which arose during the period from November 21 to December 31, 1995, which was fully utilized in 1996.

I.   Commitments and Contingencies:

Purchase Commitments

In the normal course of business, the Company has entered into various supply agreements with brewing companies. These agreements are cancelable by the Company and by the brewing companies with advanced written notice. Title to beer products brewed under these arrangements remains with the brewing company until shipped by it and accordingly, the liquid is not reflected as inventory by the Company in the accompanying financial statements. The Company is required to reimburse the supplier for all unused material and beer products on termination of the agreements and under certain conditions to purchase excess materials. At December 28, 1996, there was approximately $4,468,000 of material and beer products in process at the brewing companies which had not yet been transferred to the Company. Purchases under these agreements for the years ended December 28, 1996, December 31, 1995, and 1994 were approximately $57,766,000, $41,199,000, and $28,808,000, respectively.

The Company has entered into contracts for the supply of a portion of its hops requirements. These purchase contracts, which expire at various dates through 2003, specify both the quantities and prices the Company is committed to. The prices are denominated in foreign currencies and the Company does not hedge these commitments in French francs, but does in German marks and English pound sterling. The amount of these commitments outstanding at December 28, 1996 in U.S. dollars, is $52,530,000. Purchases under these contracts for the years ended December 28, 1996, December 31, 1995, and 1994 were approximately $10,000,000, $5,924,000, and $6,061,000 respectively. The performance of the dealers under such contracts may be materially affected by factors such as adverse weather, the imposition of export restrictions and changes in currency exchange rates resulting in increased prices.

At December 28, 1996, the Company had outstanding purchase commitments of approximately $8,000,000 principally related to capital expenditures, including the initial payment for the purchase of the Schoenling brewery, and advertising expenditures through December 1997. There is a possibility the Company could expend additional capital investments at the brewing locations in the approximate range of $5,000,000 to $20,000,000 during 1997. It should be noted, that at this point in time, there is no commitment to expend this additional investment.

Lease Commitments

The Company has various operating lease agreements primarily involving real estate. Terms of the leases include purchase options, renewals, and maintenance costs, and vary by lease. These lease obligations expire at various dates through 2001.

Minimum annual rental payments under these agreements are as follows:
(in thousands)

1997	$ 802
1998	673
1999	668
2000	565
2001	565
Thereafter	—
	$ 3,273

Rent expense for the years ended December 28, 1996, December 31, 1995, and 1994 was approximately $512,000, $340,000, and $276,000 respectively.

Distribution

The Company's two largest distributors each accounted for approximately 6% of the Company's net sales.

License Agreement

The Company signed a contract in March, 1996, with a major beverage company with respect to a transaction in which that company will license and sell a new craft brew beer whose trademark and trade names are owned by the Company. The Company is expected to expense up to $750,000 in 1997 and 1998, principally to cover marketing expenses to aid the introduction of this new beer and will, in return, receive a royalty on sales after a certain period of time. The Company will also provide certain technical assistance. The agreement also sets forth the circumstances in which the relationship can be terminated and the terms on which rights to the product will revert to the Company or may be reacquired by the Company. There can be no assurance that any contemplated royalty will be earned by the Company.

Litigation

In early 1996, Boston Brewing Company, Inc. ("Boston Brewing"), an affiliate of both Boston Beer Company Limited Partnership and The Boston Beer Company, Inc., had an action filed against it by one of its distributors, such action having been filed in a court in England. The action contains a claim for damages of an alleged breach of a Distributorship Agreement between Boston Brewing and the plaintiff. The action is being vigorously defended by the Company and at present is in the discovery stage.

In addition, the Company is subject to legal proceedings and claims which arise in the ordinary course of business. In the opinion of management, the amount of ultimate liability with respect to these actions will not materially affect the financial position or results of operations of the Company.

J.   Common Stock:

Initial Public Offering

On November 20, 1995, the Company completed an initial public offering and sold an aggregate of 3,109,279 shares of Common Stock, of which 990,000 shares were sold for $15.00 per share in a best efforts offering and 2,119,279 shares were sold for $20.00 in an underwritten offering, resulting in net proceeds, after deducting underwriting discounts and expenses, of $49,691,000. In addition, as described in Note A, upon Recapitalization the owners of the general and corporate limited partners transferred their respective ownership interests to the Company. In exchange, the transferors received an aggregate of 16,641,740 shares of the Company's common stock on a pro rata basis based on their then respective equity interest in the Partnership. The total number of shares of Class A and Class B Common Stock outstanding after completion of the offering was 19,751,019.

Upon Recapitalization, the Company recognized no gain or loss upon receipt of the units of the Partnership from individual partners, and no gain or loss upon receipt of stock in the corporate partners from the stockholders of the corporate partners in exchange for the Company's stock based upon an opinion from the Company's legal counsel interpreting the Internal Revenue Code of 1986, as amended (the "Code"), the regulations of the Treasury Department (the "Regulations"), and judicial opinions interpreting the Code. The opinion is qualified by detailed and material limitations set forth in the opinion concerning, among other things, the possibility of Regulations being adopted with a retroactive effect. Any new legislation, changes to and clarifications of the administrative positions of the IRS, including by way of amendments to existing Regulations or adoption of new Regulations, and subsequent judicial decisions including any retroactive effects could have a material consequence to the Company.

Stock Compensation Plan

The Company's Employee Equity Incentive Plan (the "Equity Plan") was adopted effective November 20, 1995 as the successor to the Partnership's 1995 Management Option Plan, which was, in turn, the successor to a series of the Partnership's Incentive Share Plans. In connection with the Recapitalization, the grants under the Partnership's Incentive Share Plans, as adjusted for the one and one half conversion of partnerships units, became grants to acquire Class A Common Stock.

The Plan permits the grant of management options, discretionary options, and investment shares. The Plan is administered by the Compensation Committee of the Board of Directors which consists of non-employee directors. Management options are granted to selected management optionees to acquire shares of the Company's Class A Common Stock at an exercise price of $.01 per share. The number of shares subject to each option shall be determined by the Committee based on the salary of each elected management optionee, taking into consideration job performance criteria, divided by the fair market value of shares of Class A Common Stock as of January 1 of each year. Vesting shall be over a five year period.

The Committee may also grant to eligible employees discretionary options to acquire shares of Class A Common Stock upon such terms and conditions, including exercise price, as the Committee shall determine.

Information related to the options granted under the Equity Plan is as follows:

	Shares	Option Price	Weighted Average Exercise Price
Outstanding at December 31, 1994	—	—	—
Granted upon conversion of incentive plans to Class A Common Stock options	310,871	$ .01	$ .01
Granted upon conversion of Class B partnership unit options to Class A Common Stock options	682,383 *	$ 2.00-14.00	$ 6.47
Granted	10,422	$ .01	$ .01
Canceled	(999)	$ .01	$ .01
Exercised	—	—	—
Outstanding at December 31, 1995	1,002,677	$ .01-14.00	$ 4.40
Granted	403,729	$ .01-25.56	$13.15
Canceled	(10,749)	$ .01-20.00	$ 2.19
Exercised	(264,530)	$ .01-20.00	$ 2.45
Outstanding at December 28, 1996	1,131,127	$ .01-25.56	$ 8.00

*   This amount represents options to purchase partnership units which were outstanding prior to the Recapitalization of the Company in November 1995. Compensation expense on these partnership units would have been reflected in fiscal 1994 and as result, there is no pro forma compensation expense recognized in fiscal 1995 related to these shares.

As of December 28, 1996, 579,341 stock options were exercisable.

The Equity Plan also permits Company employees who have been with the Company for at least one year to invest up to ten percent of their annual earnings in Class A Common Stock ("Investment Shares"). The price at which Investment Shares are issued to participating employees is at a discount from current market value of from 0% to 40% based on the employee's tenure with the Company. These shares vest ratably over a five year period. At December 28, 1996 and December 31, 1995, there were 66,249 and 67,731 investment shares issued and outstanding, of which 55,269 and 40,134 shares were vested.

Prior to the Recapitalization, the Partnership had various other employee investment unit plans in which eligible employees could purchase the economic equivalent of partnership units at not less than 60% of the unit value. The total expense recognized for the years ended December 31, 1995 and 1994, approximated $20,000 representing all discount amortized over the related vesting period.

Upon Recapitalization, the investment units were replaced with 67,731 investment shares. Effective with the issuance of the shares, approximately $411,000 of the investment unit plan accrued liability recorded was reclassified as equity in consideration of the stock issued.

The Company has reserved 235,594 and 1,687,500 shares of Class A Common Stock for issuance pursuant to the Equity Plan as December 28, 1996 and December 31, 1995, respectively grant.

In October 1995, the FASB issued SFAS 123, "Accounting for Stock-Based Compensation " SFAS 123 is effective for periods beginning after December 15, 1995. The Company adopted the disclosure provisions of SFAS 123 in 1996 and has applied APB Opinion 25 and related Interpretations for its stock option plan. Had compensation cost for the Company's stock-based compensation plans been determined based on the fair value at the grant dates as calculated in accordance with SFAS 123, the Company's net income and earnings per share for the years ended December 28, 1996 and December 31, 1995 would have been reduced to the pro forma amounts indicated below:

(in thousands, except per share amounts)

	1996		1995	
	Net Income	Earnings Per Share	Net Income	Earnings Per Share
As Reported	$ 8,385	$ 0.41	$ 5,896 *	$ 0.33
Pro forma	$ 8,305	$ 0.41	$ 5,896	$ 0.33

* Pro forma, see Note B.

The fair value of each stock option is estimated on the date of grant using the Black-Scholes option-pricing model with the following weighted average assumptions: an expected life of from 5.5 years to 6.5 years for stock options, expected volatility of 45%, a dividend yield of 0%, and a risk-free interest rate that ranges from 5.43% to 7.79%, depending upon the term of the respective stock options. The weighted average fair value of stock options granted in 1996 and 1995 was $7.06 and $19.80, respectively.

Because some options vest over several years and additional awards may be made each year, the pro-forma amounts above may not be representative of the effects on net income for future years.

In 1996, there were 10,000 options granted with an exercise price that exceeded fair value. The weighted average of these grants was $25.56. In 1996, net of forfeitures, there were 8,729 options granted with an exercise price of less than fair value, and the weighted average exercise price of these grants was $4.82. In 1995, there were 321,293 options granted with an exercise price less than fair value, and the weighted average exercise price of these grants was $.01.

The following table summarizes information about stock options outstanding at December 28, 1996:

	Options Outstanding			Options Exercisable	
Range of Exercise Prices	Number Outstanding	Weighted-Average Remaining Contractual Life	Weighted-Average Exercise-Price	Number Exercisable	Weighted-Average Exercise Price
$ .01-$ 2.00	485,744	5 years	$ 1.01	439,043	$ .59
$ 9.00-$14.00	590,383	11 years	$ 12.41	148,472	$11.51
$18.00-$26.00	55,000	9 years	$ 21.16	16,666	$19.41
Total	1,131,127			604,181	

Under the restricted stock plan, grants were made during 1996 and 1995. The shares granted for these years were 2,577 and 34,658, respectively. The weighted average grant prices for grants made in 1996 and 1995 were $15.26 and $8.90, respectively. As of December 28, 1996 and December 31, 1995, the number of restricted shares was 16,399 and 26,584, respectively.

The Company recognized compensation expense of $186,000 and $250,000 under the described programs for the years ending December 28, 1996 and December 31, 1995, respectively.

K. Financial Instruments:

During 1996, the Company entered into a forward exchange contract to reduce exposure to currency movements affecting existing foreign currency denominated assets, liabilities, and firm commitments. The contract duration matches the duration of the currency position. The future value of the contract and the related currency position is subject to offsetting market risk resulting form foreign currency exchange rate volatility. The carrying amounts of the contract and the unrealized gain recognized as a component of Stockholders' Equity totaled $1,195,000 and $31,070, respectively, at December 28, 1996. There were no realized gains or losses on the contract as of December 28, 1996.

L. Related Party Transactions:

At December 31, 1995, borrowings of $150,000 under a recourse note due on December 31, 1997 from the Company's Chief Operating Officer were outstanding. The note bears interest based on the applicable federal rate. This note was repaid in its entirety during 1996.

The Company has a deferred compensation agreement with its Chief Operating Officer which calls for specific payments upon retirement on or after April 1, 2000 with pro-rated annual payments called for upon early retirement. The Company has expensed approximately $59,000, $56,000, and $49,000 for the three years ended December 28, 1996, December 31, 1995 and 1994, respectively.

M. 401 (k) Savings Plan:

During 1993, the Company established the Boston Beer Company 401(k) Savings Plan (the "Plan"). The Plan is a defined contribution plan which covers substantially all of the Company's employees. Participants may make voluntary contributions of their annual compensation.

The Company made contributions to the Plan in each of the three years ended December 28, 1996, December 31, 1995, and 1994 of $280,000, $175,000, and $142,000 respectively.

N. Sale of Distribution Rights:

In September 1995, the Company sold its distribution rights to a major metropolitan area and associated receivables and inventories for approximately $1,200,000 and the assumption of certain deposit liabilities and truck leases. On closing approximately $420,000 was paid in cash with the remainder in the form of a note which is payable in equal monthly installments of $13,000 plus interest at 10% per annum. This transaction resulted in a gain to the Company of approximately $807,000 and is included in other income. The sale of the distribution rights is not expected to result in any significant change in future operations of the Company when compared to historical results.

O. Subsequent Event:

Effective March 1, 1997, the Company acquired all of the equipment and other brewery-related personal property from the Schoenling Brewing Company and leased the real estate on which the brewery is situated. In addition, subject to the satisfaction of certain pre-conditions, the Company has agreed to purchase the real estate on which the brewery is located. The acquisition of the brewery assets and real estate will be accounted for under the purchase method of accounting. The purchase price allocation has not yet been determined.

P.   Valuation and Qualifying Accounts:

The information required to be included in Schedule II, Valuation and Qualifying Accounts, for the years ended December 31, 1994, 1995, and December 28, 1996 is as follows:

	Balance at Beginning of Period	Additions Charged to Costs and Expenses (in thousands)	Net Additions (Deductions)	Balance At End of Period
Allowance for Doubtful Accounts				
1994	$ 146	47	(11)	182
1995	182	107	(114)	175
1996	175	1,832	(77)	1,930
Inventory Reserves				
1994	$ 457	381	(590)	248
1995	248	782	(1,014)	16
1996	16	2,860	(386)	2,490

Deductions from allowance for doubtful accounts represent the write-off of uncollectible balances whereas deductions from inventory reserves represent inventory destroyed in the normal course of business.

THE LION BREWERY, INC.

ITEM 1. BUSINESS

GENERAL

The Lion Brewery, Inc. ("The Lion Brewery" or the "Company") is a producer and bottler of brewed beverages, including malta, specialty beers and specialty soft drinks. The Lion Brewery was incorporated in Pennsylvania on April 5, 1933. The Company is the dominant producer of malta in the continental United States. Specialty beers, generally known as craft beers, are brewed by the Company both for sale under its own label and on a contract basis. Craft beers are distinguishable from other domestically produced beers by their fuller flavor and adherence to traditional European brewing styles. In 1996, the Company produced a flavored, alcoholic, malt based brew under contract. The Company also produces specialty soft drinks, including all-natural brewed ginger beverages, on a contract basis for third parties. The Lion Brewery also brews beer for sale under traditional Company owned labels for the local market at popular prices.

The Company's growth strategy is to rapidly expand its production and marketing of specialty beers, while maintaining the growth in its non-alcoholic beverages. By owning and operating its own brewery and with its significant brewing and packaging experience, the Company believes it is well positioned to optimize the quality and consistency of its products as well as to formulate new products. The Company plans to increase sales of its specialty beer labels through increased penetration of these brands in its existing markets, expansion into contiguous regional markets, new product introductions, increased marketing efforts and additions to brewing and bottling capacity.

The Company's original specialty beers—1857 Premium Lager, Liebotschaner Cream Ale and Stegmaier Porter—are reminiscent of the Company's rich beer brewing heritage. Since the brewhouse was built at the turn of the century in Wilkes-Barre, Pennsylvania, The Lion Brewery is the beneficiary of a long brewing tradition. The Company's flagship line of distinctive full-flavored beers are marketed under the Brewery Hill name. The Company currently produces seven styles of beer under the Brewery Hill label, two of which are seasonal flavors. Brewery Hill PennCenntenial Lager was recently introduced in November 1996 along with our winter seasonal, Brewery Hill Caramel Porter.

The Company established its reputation as a quality leader in the rapidly growing craft beer market by winning three Gold Medals at the Great American Beer Festival. The Lion Brewery's 1857 Premium Lager was voted Best American Premium Lager in 1994 and Liebotschaner Cream Ale won back to back gold medals in the American Lager Cream Ale Category in 1994 and 1995. ... In addition, craft beers and specialty soft drinks brewed by the Company under contract have won several awards.

COMPANY HISTORY AND INDUSTRY BACKGROUND

The brewhouse in which the Company continues to brew its products was built at the turn of the century in Wilkes-Barre, Pennsylvania. At that time, the U.S. brewing industry comprised nearly 2,000 breweries, most of which were small operations that produced distinctive beers for local markets. The Company was incorporated as The Lion, Inc. in April 1933 to operate the brewery, which was one of the fewer than 1,000 breweries to reopen following Prohibition. Over the ensuing decades, lighter, less distinctively flavored beers appealing to broad segments of the population and supported by national advertising programs became prevalent. These beers use lower cost ingredients and are mass produced to take advantage of economies of scale. This shift toward mass produced beers coincided with extreme consolidation in the beer industry. In keeping with this consolidation trend, the Company purchased other labels including the Stegmaier brands, which had been produced on Brewery Hill in Wilkes-Barre since 1857. Of the more than 60 breweries existing in eastern Pennsylvania 50 years ago, only two, including the Lion Brewery, remain. Today, according to industry sources, approximately 90% of all domestic beer shipments come from the four largest domestic brewers.

Beginning in the mid 1980s and continuing in the 1990s, a number of domestic craft brewers began selling higher quality, more full-flavored beers, usually in local markets, as a growing number of consumers began to migrate away from less flavorful mass-marketed beers towards greater taste and broader variety, mirroring similar trends in other beverage and food categories. As an established regional specialty brewer, the Lion Brewery believes it is well-positioned to benefit from this shift in consumer preferences. In 1995, according to industry sources, the craft beer segment increased to approximately 3.8 million barrels, representing approximately 2.1% of the 180 million barrel, $50 billion retail domestic beer market. Over the five year period ended December 31, 1995, craft beer shipments increased at a compound annual rate of approximately 40%, while shipments in the total U.S. beer industry remained relatively flat. Industry analysts have attributed this flat overall beer consumption to a variety of factors, including increased concerns about the health consequences of consuming alcoholic beverages, safety consciousness and concerns about drinking and driving; a trend toward a diet including lighter, lower calorie beverages such as diet soft drinks, juices and sparkling water products; the increased activity of anti-alcohol consumer protection groups; an increase in the minimum drinking age from 18 to 21 years in all states; the general aging of the population; and increased federal and state excise taxes. Today the top three national brewers have entered into this fast growing craft segment by introducing their own specialty beers and/or by acquiring or investing in smaller regional craft brewers.

Before the emergence of the market opportunity in specialty beer, the Lion Brewery diversified into other products to sustain operations and continue to utilize its brewhouse and bottling facility. The Company's strategic entry into malta production in 1982 has resulted in the Company becoming the dominant producer of malta in the continental United States. Malta was originally developed many years ago by German brewers operating in the Caribbean area. The brewers developed malta by blending the excess molasses production from sugar with grain mash. Malta is still popular throughout the Caribbean and South America. In addition to malta, the Company also diversified into producing premium soft drinks in 1991.

BUSINESS STRATEGY

The Company intends to enhance its position as a leading producer of specialty brewed beverages by rapidly expanding production and marketing of craft beers and other malt based premium products; while maintaining the growth of its nonalcoholic brewed beverages. Key elements of the Company's business strategy are to:

Produce High Quality Brewed Beverages. The Company is committed to producing a variety of full-flavored brewed beverages. The Company employs a Head Brewmaster, an assistant brewmaster and a brewing assistant and retains a world recognized brewing authority to ensure the high quality and consistency of its products. To monitor the quality of its products, the Company maintains its own quality control laboratory staffed with two full-time quality control technicians and submits its products for analysis to the Seibel Institute of Technology, an independent laboratory, on a continuous basis. To monitor freshness, the Company dates each bottle and case with the date and time of its bottling. The Company brews its craft beers according to traditional styles and methods, selecting and using only high quality ingredients.

Brew Products in Company-Owned and Operated Facilities. The Company owns and operates its own brewing facility, which enables the Company to optimize the quality and consistency of its products, to achieve the greatest control over its production costs and to formulate new brewed products. The Company believes that its ability to engage in new product development through onsite experimentation in its brewhouse and to continuously monitor and control product quality in its own facilities are competitive advantages.

Expand Distribution of Craft Beers. The Company distributes craft beer under its own labels through a network of wholesale distributor relationships. Currently the Company distributes its products in twelve states, although the majority of its sales remain concentrated in Pennsylvania. The Company intends its penetration in existing markets and to enter new markets by increasing the size of its sales force and its marketing efforts. The Company chooses wholesaler distributors that the Company believes will best promote and sell the brands. The Company, through on site tours and presentations, actively educates its distributors in the total brewing process and the growing craft beer industry.

Introduce New Products. The Company is committed to developing and introducing new products to appeal to the strong consumer interest in full-flavored craft beers. The Company's diversified product mix and brewing expertise enhance its ability to create successful new products. The Company believes that new product introductions have helped the Company gain consumer awareness in its existing markets. Currently, the Company markets seven craft beers under the Brewery Hill label. In 1996, the Company introduced Brewery Hill Pale Ale in March, Brewery Hill Cherry Wheat; its summer seasonal, in May, Brewery Hill PennCenntenial Lager and Brewery Hill Caramel Porter; a winter seasonal, in November. The Company is also is developing new soft drink products for its contract customers.

Increase Production Capacity and Efficiency. The Company is in the process of increasing its annual production capacity from 340,000 to 400,000 barrels based upon its anticipated product mix. This expansion will modify its existing seven ounce bottling line to also accommodate 12 oz. bottles, the bottle size for most of the Company's products. In addition, The Company has increased its fermentation and lagering capacity with the relining of nine storage tanks. The Company also completed an upgrade of a boiler and is in the process of adding a malt storage and elevation system.

Provide a High Level of Customer Service. The Company, through its high quality brewing standards and timely availability of product, believes it provides a high level of customer service to its malta, contract craft beer and specialty soft drink customers. The Company believes its emphasis on customer service has enabled the Company to increase sales to these customers.

PRODUCTS

The Lion Brewery's diversified product portfolio consists of a variety of styles of malta, craft beers and specialty brewed beverages and soft drinks, including all-natural brewed ginger beverages, and popularly priced beer sold under traditional Company-owned labels. The Company distributes its products in glass bottles and kegs and its products are dated to monitor freshness. …

The Company also brews many distinctive craft beers and other specialty malt beverages under contract for other labels. Some of these customers are microbreweries and brewpubs that need additional brewing capacity to meet their production requirements and which typically provide their own recipes. In other instances, the Company formulates beer and specialty malt beverages for customers marketing their own labels. Most of these contract brewing customers provide their own packaging and labels. The Company arranges shipment to distributors F.O.B. the Company's warehouse and handles invoicing as a service to these customers. …

The Lion Brewery craft beer and specialty malt beverages produced for sale under its own labels and under contract for others accounted for approximately 14% and 10% of its annual barrel shipments and 19% and 12% of its net sales in fiscal 1996 and 1995, respectively.

SPECIALTY SOFT DRINKS. The Lion Brewery first began blending and bottling specialty soft drinks in 1987. The Company currently produces specialty soft drinks under contract for five customers including:
• Reed's. In June 1991, the Lion Brewery began producing for this customer Reed's All Natural Ginger Beer, a soft drink based on brewed ginger root. The Lion is currently the sole brewer of beverages sold under the Reed's label. Sales of this product line grew 48% and 44% in fiscal 1996 and 1995, respectively. This product was originally developed and produced in a small microbrewery in Colorado and the Company believes that Reed's is the leading brewed soft drink in health food stores. …
• Mad River. The Company produces eleven varieties of premium all natural blended soft drinks for Mad River. The product is sold to consumers primarily in resort locations and in upscale specialty food stores.
• The Company also produces specialty soft drinks for Goya Foods, Vitarroz and Virgil's. Specialty soft drinks accounted for approximately 12% and 10% of the Lion Brewery's barrel shipments and 9% and 8% of its net sales in fiscal 1996 and 1995, respectively.

POPULAR PRICED BEER. The Company brews beer for sale at popular prices in local markets under several traditional Company-owned brands. A majority of this beer is bottled in 16 oz. returnable bottles. The Company is intentionally reducing its production of popular priced beer in conjunction with a general decline in market demand for lower priced beer marketed in 16 oz. returnable bottles and in recognition of the significantly greater profitability for the Company using its production capacity for craft beer. Popular priced beer accounted for approximately 6% and 7% of barrel shipments and 4% and 5% of net sales in fiscal 1996 and 1995, respectively. …

SALES AND MARKETING

The Lion Brewery's four largest malta customers, Goya Foods, Vitarroz, Cerveceria India and 7-Up/RC Puerto Rico, accounted for 95% of the Company's total malta sales for fiscal 1996 and 1996. Mr. Lawson, the Company's Chief Executive Officer, is primarily responsible for selling and marketing these and the Company's other contract accounts. The Head Brewmaster and the Vice President of Logistics are also actively involved with these customer relationships in discussing product recipes, new product formulations, production scheduling and delivery. …

The Company's strategy is to increase its penetration into its existing markets while expanding to other markets. This strategy will be implemented by further developing the existing distributor relationships and establishing new distributors in target markets. The Company anticipates significantly increasing its sales and marketing efforts by hiring additional sales personnel and increasing public brand name exposure through print, outdoor and electronic advertising on a selective basis. …

EXCERPT FROM MANAGEMENT'S DISCUSSION AND ANALYSIS

Operating Data

| | Year Ended September 30, | | | | | |
| | Percent of Net Sales | | | Net Sales Per Barrel | | |
	1996	1995	1994	1996	1995	1994
Malta	67.8%	75.0%	78.6%	$ 80	$ 78	$ 73
Beer:						
Craft:						
Company label	6.7	4.9	1.2	127	110	83
Contract	12.4	7.4	6.7	99	84	74
	19.1	12.3	7.9			
Popular priced	3.7	5.0	6.8	55	55	54
Total beer	22.8	17.3	14.7			
Specialty soft drinks	9.4	7.7	6.7	64	62	59
	100.0%	100.0%	100.0%	$ 80	$ 76	$ 71

THE LION BREWERY, INC.

BALANCE SHEETS
SEPTEMBER 30, 1996 AND 1995

	1996	1995
Assets		
Current assets:		
Cash and cash equivalents	$1,992,000	$ 0
Accounts receivable, less allowance for doubtful accounts of $157,000 and $129,000 at September 30, 1996 and 1995, respectively	2,001,000	2,476,000
Inventories	2,128,000	2,003,000
Prepaid expenses and other assets	190,000	277,000
Total current assets	6,311,000	4,756,000
Property, plant & equipment, net of accumulated depreciation of $1,684,000 and $1,122,000 at September 30, 1996 and 1995, respectively	3,600,000	3,254,000
Goodwill, net of accumulated amortization of $475,000 and $311,000 at September 30, 1996 and 1995, respectively	6,039,000	6,203,000
Deferred financing costs and other assets, net of accumulated amortization of $144,000 at September 30, 1995	4,000	228,000
	$15,954,000	$14,441,000
Liabilities and Shareholders' Equity		
Current liabilities:		
Current portion of long-term debt	$ 0	$ 1,745,000
Accounts payable	1,663,000	1,978,000
Accrued expenses	839,000	478,000
Refundable deposits	205,000	171,000
Income taxes payable	178,000	330,000
Total current liabilities	2,885,000	4,702,000
Long-term debt, less current portion	0	6,131,000
Net pension liability	243,000	218,000
Deferred income taxes	206,000	351,000
Total liabilities	3,334,000	11,402,000
Warrants	0	722,000
Shareholders' equity:		
Common stock, $.01 par value; 10,000,000 shares authorized; 3,885,052 and 1,851,183 shares issued and outstanding at September 30, 1996 and 1995, respectively	39,000	19,000
Additional paid-in capital	10,612,000	1,304,000
Adjustment to reflect minimum pension liability, net of deferred income taxes	(42,000)	(10,000)
Retained earnings	2,011,000	1,004,000
Total shareholders' equity	12,620,000	2,317,000
Total liabilities and shareholders' equity	$ 15,954,000	$ 14,441,000

The accompanying notes to financial statements are an integral part of these balance sheets.

THE LION BREWERY, INC.

STATEMENTS OF INCOME

FOR THE YEARS ENDED SEPTEMBER 30, 1996 AND 1995

	Year ended September 30, 1996	Year ended September 30, 1995
Gross sales	$26,983,000	$25,175,000
Less excise taxes	544,000	382,000
Net sales	26,439,000	24,793,000
Cost of sales	19,939,000	18,834,000
Gross profit	6,500,000	5,959,000
Operating expenses:		
Delivery	824,000	827,000
Selling, advertising and promotional expenses	1,240,000	782,000
General and administrative	1,373,000	1,336,000
	3,437,000	2,945,000
Operating income	3,063,000	3,014,000
Interest expense and amortization of debt discount, net	520,000	1,042,000
Income before provision for income taxes and extraordinary item	2,543,000	1,972,000
Provision for income taxes	1,125,000	921,000
Income before extraordinary item	1,418,000	1,051,000
Extraordinary item, net of income tax benefit of $228,000	(322,000)	(0)
Net income	1,096,000	1,051,000
Warrant accretion	89,000	300,000
Net income available to common shareholders	$ 1,007,000	$ 751,000
Income per share before extraordinary item	$ 0.47	$ 0.40
Extraordinary item - loss per share	(0.11)	(0.00)
Net income per share	$ 0.36	$ 0.40
Shares used in per share calculation	2,835,000	1,898,000

The accompanying notes to financial statements are an integral part of these statements.

THE LION BREWERY, INC.

STATEMENTS OF CASH FLOWS
FOR THE YEARS ENDED SEPTEMBER 30, 1996 AND 1995

	1996	1995
Cash flows from operating activities:		
Net income	$1,096,000	$1,051,000
Adjustments to reconcile net income to net cash provided by operating activities		
Extraordinary item	550,000	0
Depreciation and amortization	830,000	947,000
Bad debt expense	12,000	36,000
Provision for inventory reserve	75,000	45,000
Benefit for deferred income taxes	(145,000)	(132,000)
Loss on disposal of equipment	0	2,000
Changes in assets and liabilities:		
(Increase) decrease in:		
Accounts receivable	463,000	153,000
Inventories	(200,000)	(212,000)
Prepaid expenses and other assets	87,000	23,000
Increase (decrease) in:		
Accounts payable, accrued expenses and refundable deposits	80,000	248,000
Income taxes payable	(152,000)	330,000
Pension liability	(7,000)	(16,000)
Net cash provided by operating activities	2,689,000	2,475,000
Cash flows from investing activities:		
Proceeds from sale of equipment	0	12,000
Purchase of equipment	(908,000)	(319,000)
Net cash used in investing activities	(908,000)	(307,000)
Cash flows from financing activities:		
Net proceeds from sale of common stock	9,466,000	0
Repurchase of common stock	(950,000)	0
Deferred financing costs	0	(25,000)
Issuance of long term debt	0	500,000
Net reductions in line of credit	(721,000)	(1,860,000)
Repayment of long term debt	(7,584,000)	(924,000)
Net cash provided by (used in) financing activities	211,000	(2,309,000)
Net increase (decrease) in cash and cash equivalents	1,992,000	(141,000)
Cash and cash equivalents, beginning of year	0	141,000
Cash and cash equivalents, end of year	$1,992,000	$ 0
Supplementary disclosure of cash flow information:		
Cash paid for:		
Interest	$ 516,000	$ 951,000
Income taxes	$1,183,000	$ 672,000

The accompanying notes to financial statements are an integral part of these statements.

THE LION BREWERY, INC.
NOTES TO FINANCIAL STATEMENTS

1. BASIS OF PRESENTATION AND DESCRIPTION OF THE BUSINESS

The Lion Brewery, Inc. (the Company), formerly The Lion, Inc., is a brewer and bottler of brewed beverages, including malta, specialty beers and specialty soft drinks. Malta is a non-alcoholic brewed beverage which the Company produces for major Hispanic food distribution companies primarily for sale in the eastern United States. Specialty beers, generally known as craft beers, are brewed by the Company both for sale under its own labels and on a contract basis for other marketers of craft beer brands. Craft beers are distinguishable from other domestically produced beers by their fuller flavor and adherence to traditional European brewing styles. The Company also produces specialty soft drinks, including all-natural brewed ginger beverages, on a contract basis for third parties. The Lion Brewery also brews beer for sale under traditional Company-owned labels for the local market at popular prices.

The Company was incorporated in Pennsylvania on April 5, 1933. On October 4, 1993, Lion Partners Company, L.P. (the Partnership) acquired shares of common stock of the Company for $2,100,000. Prior to this transaction, the Partnership had no affiliation with the Company. The Company then redeemed shares of common stock for $6,983,000 (of which $2,500,000 was payable in a note), including $1,008,000 of direct acquisition costs. After these transactions, the Partnership owned 81% of the common stock of the Company.

The Company accounted for these transactions as a purchase by the Partnership whereby the cost of acquiring 81% of the Company was pushed down to establish a new accounting basis which is reflected in the accompanying financial statements. The Company allocated the cost of the acquisition of 81% of the Company to the assets acquired and liabilities assumed based on their fair values and carried over 19% of the historical cost at the date of the acquisition. The purchase price was $8,677,000 and was allocated to tangible assets ($8,782,000) and liabilities ($6,619,000). The excess of the purchase price over net assets acquired of $6,514,000 was assigned to goodwill.

2. SUMMARY OF SIGNIFICANT ACCOUNTING POLICIES

Use of Estimates
The preparation of financial statements in conformity with generally accepted accounting principles requires management to make estimates and assumptions that affect the recorded amounts of assets and liabilities at the date of the financial statements and the reported amounts of revenues and expenses during the reporting period. Actual results could differ from those estimates.

Revenue Recognition
Revenue is generally recognized upon shipment. For products brewed under beer and soft drink contracts, revenue is generally recognized upon completion of production.

Cash and cash equivalents
The Company considers all highly liquid investments with maturities at the date purchase of three months or less to be cash equivalents. The carrying amount of cash equivalents approximates fair value.

Inventories
Inventories are stated at the lower of cost or market determined on a first-in, first-out method (FIFO).

Property, Plant and Equipment
Property, plant and equipment are recorded at cost and are depreciated using the straight-line method over the useful lives of the assets. All significant additions and improvements are capitalized and repairs and maintenance charges are expensed as incurred. The new accounting pronouncement on impairment of long lived assets had no impact on the Company's financial statements. Estimated useful lives for the assets are as follows:

	Years
Buildings	20
Machinery and equipment	3-10
Kegs and bottles	3-7

Income taxes

The Company recognizes deferred tax assets and liabilities for the estimated future tax effects of events based on temporary differences between financial statement and tax basis of assets and liabilities using enacted tax rates in effect in the years the differences are expected to be reversed. Valuation allowances are established when necessary to reduce deferred tax assets to the amounts expected to be realized. Income tax expense is comprised of current taxes payable and the change in deferred tax assets and liabilities during the year.

Intangible Assets

The excess of the cost of the acquired assets over their fair values is being amortized using the straight-line method over forty years. The Company continually evaluates the remaining estimated useful lives and the recoverability of its intangible assets utilizing the undiscounted cash flow method.

Product and Customer Concentrations

The sale of malta, beer and soft drinks has accounted for all of the Company's sales, with malta accounting for 68% and 75% for the years ended September 30, 1996 and 1995. The Company's top three customers accounted for 60% and 68% of sales in fiscal 1996 and 1995. Accounts receivable from these three customers totaled $1,712,000 and $1,831,000 at September 30, 1996 and 1995. The Company's largest customer accounted for 27% and 30% of sales in fiscal 1996 and 1995. The Company does maintain contracts with several of its top customers; however there are no minimum purchase requirements. The Company does not have a contract with its largest customer. The length of such contracts range from two to four years. The decision by a major customer to switch production of its contract beverages from the Company to another brewer, or to build facilities to brew its own product, could have a materially adverse effect on the Company's financial results.

Excise Taxes

The U.S. federal government currently imposes an excise tax of $18 per barrel on every barrel of beer produced for consumption in the United States. However, any brewer with production under 2 million barrels per year pays a federal excise tax of $7 per barrel on the first 60,000 barrels it produces annually. Individual states also impose excise taxes on alcoholic beverages in varying amounts. The Company records the excise tax as a reduction of gross sales in the accompanying financial statements.

Net Income Per Share

Net income per share is computed using the weighted average number of common and dilutive common equivalent shares outstanding during the period. Common equivalent shares consist of stock options and warrants (using the treasury stock method for all periods presented). Accretion relating to the Company's warrants (see Note 11) is deducted in computing income applicable to common stock.

Stock split

In January 1996, the Company's Board of Directors amended the Company's Articles of Incorporation to effect a 3,091.33 for 1 stock split. All common shares and per share amounts in the accompanying financial statements have been adjusted retroactively to give effect to the stock split.

Financial Instruments

Financial instruments that potentially subject the Company to credit risk consist principally of trade receivables. The fair value of accounts receivable approximates carrying value.

Stock Based Compensation

In October 1995, the Financial Accounting Standards Board issued Statement No. 123, "Accounting for Stock-Based Compensation," which requires companies to measure employee stock compensation plans based on the fair value method using an option pricing model or to continue to apply APB No. 25, "Accounting for Stock Issued to Employees," and provide pro forma footnote disclosures under the fair value method. The Company continues to apply APB No. 25 and will provide the pro forma footnote disclosures.

3. INVENTORIES

Inventories consist of the following:

	1996	1995
Raw materials	$163,000	$ 176,000
Finished goods	673,000	663,000
Supplies	1,292,000	1,164,000
	$2,128,000	$ 2,003,000

4. PROPERTY, PLANT AND EQUIPMENT

Property, plant and equipment consist of the following:

	1996	1995
Land and building	$ 1,024,000	$ 1,014,000
Machinery and equipment	4,038,000	3,167,000
Kegs and bottles	222,000	195,000
	5,284,000	4,376,000
Less accumulated depreciation	1,684,000	1,122,000
	$ 3,600,000	$3,254,000

5. ACCRUED EXPENSES

Accrued expenses consist of the following:

	1996	1995
Payroll and related accruals	$ 427,000	$ 346,000
Other accruals	412,000	132,000
	$ 839,000	$ 478,000

6. INCOME TAXES

The provision for income taxes is as follows:

	1996	1995
Current:		
Federal	$ 786,000	$ 755,000
State	256,000	298,000
	1,042,000	1,053,000
Deferred:		
Federal	(105,000)	(102,000)
State	(40,000)	(30,000)
	(145,000)	(132,000)
	$ 897,000	$ 921,000

The principal items accounting for the difference between income taxes computed at the statutory rate and the provision for income taxes reflected in the statements of income are as follows:

	1996	1995
United States statutory rate	35%	35%
State taxes (net of federal tax benefit)	7	9
Nondeductible expenses - goodwill amortization	3	3
	45%	47%

Components of the Company's deferred tax balances are as follows:

	1996	1995
Deferred tax assets:		
Benefit accruals	$ 235,000	$ 160,000
Accounts receivable	71,000	53,000
Inventories	96,000	46,000
Other	—	18,000
	402,000	277,000
Deferred tax liabilities:		
Property, plant and equipment	559,000	628,000
Other	49,000	—
	608,000	628,000
	$ 206,000	$ 351,000

7. DEBT

Debt at September 30, 1995 consists of the following:

	1995
Revolving credit loan	$ 721,000
Term loan	1,019,000
Senior subordinate notes	3,631,000
Junior subordinate notes	2,500,000
Other	5,000
	7,876,000
Current portion	1,745,000
	$6,131,000

On May 2, 1996, the Company completed an initial public offering of equity securities. A portion of the proceeds were used to repay indebtedness of the Company (See Note 12). The extraordinary item recorded in 1996 consists of prepayment penalties of $160,000, unamortized debt discounts of $213,000 and the write-off of unamortized deferred financing costs of $177,000 related to the early extinguishment of debt, net of an income tax benefit of $228,000.

The Company is currently negotiating a $5,000,000 revolving line of credit and a $2,500,000 revolving equipment line of credit. Both facilities would be unsecured and interest will be paid monthly based upon either the Bank's prime rate minus 1/2%, LIBOR plus 75 basis points or the Bank's offered rate. There can be no assurance that such agreement will be finalized.

8. PENSION PLANS

The Company maintains a noncontributory defined benefit pension plan covering nonunion employees. The plan provides benefits based on years of service and compensation levels. The Company's funding policy for these plans is predicted on allowable limits for federal income tax purposes.

The components of net periodic pension cost for the defined benefit plan are as follows:

	1996	1995
Service cost - benefits earned during the period	$ 30,000	$ 24,000
Interest cost on projected benefit obligation	36,000	36,000
Actual return on plan assets	(23,000)	(39,000)
Net amortization and deferral	19,000	38,000
Effect of settlement	—	15,000
Net pension expense	$ 62,000	$ 74,000

Assumptions used in the accounting for the defined benefit plan are as follows as of September 30, 1996 and 1995:

Weighted average discount rate	8.5%
Expected long-term rate of return on assets	9.0
Average salary increase	5.0

The following table sets forth the funded status and the net pension liability included in the balance sheet for the defined benefit plan:

	1996	1995
Actuarial present value of benefit obligation:		
Accumulated benefit obligation (including vested benefits of $392,000 and $327,000)	$ 403,000	$ 340,000
Projected benefit obligation	438,000	413,000
Plan assets at fair value	160,000	122,000
Projected benefit obligation in excess of plan assets	(278,000)	(291,000)
Unrecognized net loss	111,000	87,000
Adjustment required to recognize minimum liability	(76,000)	(14,000)
Net pension liability recognized in balance sheet	$ 243,000	$ 218,000

The Company also participates in a multi-employer pension plan which provides defined benefits to union employees. Contributions are based on a fixed amount per hour worked. Pension cost aggregated $162,000 and $142,000 for the years ended September 30, 1996 and 1995, respectively.

9. COMMITMENTS AND CONTINGENCIES

The Company leases warehouse facilities and equipment under noncancelable operating leases. Future minimum lease payments under these leases are:

1997	$234,000
1998	246,000
1999	187,000
2000	136,000
2001	102,000

Rent expense for all leased facilities amounted to $294,000 in 1996 and $249,000 in 1995.

The Company has entered into employment agreements with the Company's President and Chief Financial Officer at annual base salaries aggregating $235,000. Bonuses are determined at the discretion of the Board of Directors. The contracts also provide for up to 2 years severance in the case of involuntary termination.

The Company is engaged in certain legal and administrative proceedings incidental to its normal course of business activities. Management believes the outcome of these proceedings will not have a material adverse effect on the Company's financial position or results of operations.

10. RELATED PARTY TRANSACTIONS

Quincy Partners, a general partner of Lion Partners Company, L.P. had a management consulting agreement with the Company providing for an annual fee of $130,000. This agreement was terminated on May 2, 1996, the effective date of the initial public offering (see Note 12). In connection with the offering Quincy Partners received a consulting fee of $80,000. The chairman of the Board of Directors receives $50,000 annually plus stock options for his services in this capacity.

The Company obtained covenants not to compete from two selling employee/shareholders for an aggregate of $600,000 payable in annual installments of $100,000 over a six year noncompete period, one covenant ending in October, 1999 and the other ending in October, 2000.

11. STOCK OPTION PLANS AND WARRANTS

The Company's 1996 Employee Stock Option Plan (the Plan) permits the granting of options to directors and employees of the Company. The Plan is administered by the Compensation Committee of the Board of Directors, which generally has the authority to select individuals who are to receive options and to specify the terms and conditions of each option so granted, including the number of shares covered by the option, the type of option (incentive stock option or nonqualified stock option), the exercise price (which in all cases must be at least 100% of the fair market value of the common stock on the date of grant), vesting provisions, and the overall option term. Options to purchase a total of 400,000 shares of common stock were reserved for future grants of options under the Plan. In January 1996, the Company granted options for an aggregate of 238,431 shares of common stock to a director, certain officers and other key employees of the Company. All of these options vest over a period of two years and have an exercise price of $6 per share.

On March 21, 1994, the Company's Board of Directors granted options to purchase an aggregate of 57,251 shares of common stock of the Company to the President at $1.40 per share (estimated fair market value on the date of grant) expiring in 2001. The options vest over three years. Vesting accelerated at the initial public offering (see Note 12).

The senior subordinated noteholders received warrants for the purchase of 291,565 shares of the Company's common stock having a nominal exercise price. The loan agreement provides that the noteholders may put these warrants to the Company and accordingly, the warrants were accreted to the estimated redemption price. During fiscal 1996 and 1995, accretion of $89,000 and $300,000, respectively, was recorded and charged to retained earnings. The warrants were exercised in December 1995. The Company used $950,000 of the net proceeds of the initial public offering to repurchase 132,696 shares of common stock issued upon the exercise of the warrants.

12. PUBLIC OFFERING AND PREFERRED STOCK AUTHORIZATION

On May 2, 1996, the Company completed an initial public offering of 1,875,000 shares of common stock for $6.00 per share, including the partial exercise of the over-allotment option. The proceeds of the initial public offering, including the partial exercise of the over-allotment option, net of the underwriting commissions and expenses totaled $9,466,000. A portion of these proceeds were used to repay indebtedness of the Company of $7,948,000 and to retire 132,696 shares of Common Stock, in connection with the termination of a loan agreement, at a cost of $950,000.

In connection with this offering, the Company issued warrants to the underwriters to purchase up to 135,000 shares of common stock at an exercise price of $7.20, which are exercisable for a period of five years from the date of the offering. The holders have certain rights to obtain the registration of these shares under the Securities Act.